D0142181

PERSONAL PERSPECTIVES

WORLD WAR I

PERSONAL PERSPECTIVES

---◆---

WORLD WAR I

TIMOTHY C. DOWLING

Editor

GCLS/MULLICA HILL BRANCH
389 WOLFERT STATION ROAD
MULLICA HILL, NJ 08062

A B C · C L I O

Santa Barbara, California • Denver, Colorado • Oxford, England

Copyright © 2006 by Timothy C. Dowling

All rights reserved. No part of this publication may be reproduced, stored in a retrieval system, or transmitted, in any form or by any means, electronic, mechanical, photocopying, recording, or otherwise, except for the inclusion of brief quotations in a review, without prior permission in writing from the publishers.

Library of Congress Cataloging-in-Publication Data
    Personal perspectives. World War I / Timothy C. Dowling, editor.
       p. cm.
    Includes bibliographical references and index.
    ISBN 1-85109-565-9 (hardcover : alk. paper)—ISBN 1-85109-570-5 (eBook)
1. World War, 1914-1918. I. Title: World War I. II. Title: World War I.
III. Title: World War One. IV. Dowling, Timothy C.
    D521.P426 2006
    940.4'81—DC22

                                                              2005028703

09 08 07 06 10 9 8 7 6 5 4 3 2 1

This book is also available on the World Wide Web as an eBook. Visit abc-clio.com for details.

ABC-CLIO, Inc.
130 Cremona Drive, P.O. Box 1911
Santa Barbara, California 93116-1911

The acquisitions editor for this title was Jim Ciment, the project editor was Carla Roberts, the media editor was Ellen Rasmussen, the media manager was Caroline Price, the assistant production editor was Cisca Schreefel, the production manager was Don Schmidt, and the manufacturing coordinator was George Smyser.

This book is printed on acid-free paper.
Manufactured in the United States of America

CONTENTS

———————— ◆ ————————

Introduction . . . .*vii*

The African-American Experience in World War I 1

"Over the Dirty Waters":
The Experience of British Indians in World War I 29

The War on the Periphery: The Experience of Soldiers
Fighting in European Colonies, 1914–1918 51

"In a Stupid Cap and a Grey Jacket": Soldiers' Experiences
of World War I in the Neutral Netherlands 73

"Good Luck (. . .) Dig In!": The Experience of Trench Warfare
during World War I 91

Victims of a Greenish Cloud:
The Experience of a Gas Attack during World War I 115

"Like Getting into the Witch's Oven":
The Experience of Tank Combat in World War I 127

Life in a Tin Can: The Experience of Submarine
Personnel during World War I 149

"It's Only the Ones Who Might Live Who Count":
Allied Medical Personnel in World War I 161

"Service for Soldiers": The Experience of
American Social Welfare Agencies in World War I 205

Prisoners of War in World War I: British and
Allied Civilian Internees at Ruhleben Camp, Germany 259

Mothers, Wives, Workers, and More: The Experience of
American Women on the Home Front during World War I 273

Struggling Not to Fight: The Experience of
Radicals and Pacifists during World War I 297

Timeline 323

Bibliography 333

List of Contributors 337

Index 339

About the Editor 355

INTRODUCTION

—————◆—————

This is not a standard war volume—the accounts of battles, strategies, and tactics are intentionally limited. Nor is it a standard history volume, for the contextual framework has been kept to a minimum. It is designed as a resource of a different nature, a place where students can go to find out what it felt like to be in, or working with, the things they read about in the standard texts. War, after all, is more than a series of dates and places. It is more, even—much more—than numbers of men killed, wounded, and taken prisoner. Numbers are perhaps the easiest aspect of war to comprehend; they are impersonal and translate well. Beyond these items, though, war is often difficult to understand.

We can read about war in many places and in many ways. The Great War, as it was known, has a particularly rich literature. There are dozens of standard histories of the First World War, dozens more that are less comprehensive but more detailed area studies and unit histories, and thousands upon thousands of memoirs, diaries, notebooks, and sketches. The poetry and art of the war are genres unto themselves, equally vast and equally varied. Yet getting a sense of what World War I was about remains difficult because of its breadth and scope. Today we can watch wars unfold on television and computer screens, and yet there, too, it is difficult to get a sense of what wars are about. Sometimes they seem all-too-real, right in front of us, and at other times watching a war can be almost like a video game, surreal and impersonal.

Reading memoirs, in comparison, can be too narrow and too personal, drawing the reader into one viewpoint, one life, and one perspective. Wars are personal, but they are much more than that. They affect people, groups, and nations in ways we can only imagine—and sometimes in ways that we cannot imagine. Why men (and women) go to war, and what they find there, is almost incomprehensible to those who have not been in combat. Even the smallest war and the shortest battle have broad effects, and World War I, though not the largest war to date, has had perhaps the largest and most lasting effect of any war or any battles. Verdun has entered the modern lexicon along with Marathon; the Somme is as well known as Yorktown or Waterloo; the "massacre of innocents" at Ypres remains a lasting symbol of the horrors of modern warfare as much as Auschwitz or Hiroshima. Millions of people were drawn into the conflict, and hundreds of millions more felt the impact.

This volume is an attempt to capture some sense of that impact. It draws together groups of experiences, placing individual experiences in relative frameworks. The intent of *Perspectives,* if the pun can be forgiven, is to put perspectives into perspective. It is not meant to be comprehensive, but impressionistic. It is designed to give a sense of what the war *was,* as well as what the war was about, for a broad spectrum of people. It is meant to be easily accessible and enjoyable to read. If the reader wishes to explore a particular topic in greater detail, suggestions for further reading are listed at the end of each chapter. As the title suggests, *Perspectives* is intended to provide a different look at a war that, even a century later, was pivotal in shaping the present world.

Looking back on World War I in the 1930s, Winston Churchill wrote,

> It is . . . the most mournful conflict of which there is record. All three empires, both sides, victors and vanquished, were ruined. All of the Emperors or their successors were slain or deposed. The Houses of Romanov, Hapsburg and Hohenzollern woven over centuries of renown into the texture of Europe were shattered and extirpated. The structure of three mighty organisms built by generations of patience and valour and representing the traditional groupings of noble branches of the European family, was changed beyond all semblance. (Churchill 1932, 1)

The Hapsburg Empire disappeared, and in its place there arose a swath of new states based, supposedly, on the democratically expressed will of like peoples to live under a government of their own choosing: Poland, Czechoslovakia, Yugoslavia, Hungary, Austria. In Russia, the tsar meekly gave way to a "bourgeois republic" that in turn yielded to Bolshevism, revolution, and civil war. Latvia, Lithuania, Estonia, and Ukraine proclaimed their independence; Central Asia became, briefly, a jigsaw puzzle of new republics. The Romanov family met its end in Yekaterinburg, gunned down in a cellar by revolutionaries. The German Kaiser, proud but confused, fled to the Netherlands and watched as the nation he once ruled dissolved into chaos. Soviet republics rose and fell in Hamburg and Bavaria.

It was not just the eastern empires of Europe that had changed, though—a soviet republic sprang up briefly in Edinburgh, Scotland—and not just the politics. It was not even just Europe that had been altered by the war; indeed, the conflict had touched states on nearly every continent and all segments of society. The far-flung dominions of the United Kingdom—from Australia to Zanzibar, from Canada to India—contributed troops and aid, as did the empire of the French. Europeans fought in Africa, and Africans fought in Europe. African Americans counted among the U.S. armed forces in significant numbers for the first time, once the United States finally entered the war. When they came back, it was with a renewed sense that the struggle for equality must be carried on at home as well as on the fields of France. One scholar has argued that the idea of the "New Negro" stemmed largely from contact with European culture during 1917–1918 and after (Foley 2003). Others have even more clearly linked the burgeoning American civil rights movement, including the race riots of the 1920s and 1930s, to the experience of African Americans during the First World War. But what was that experience?

This is precisely the phenomenon this volume seeks to explore: *what experience the war brought to people of all ranks and races.* The chapters herein, written by scholars conversant with the literature of the topic, attempt to use the words of the participants more than those of professors and generals. They are specifically designed to complement the *Encyclopedia of the First World War,* edited by Spencer Tucker. Instead of describing the history of African Americans in the United States Army, for instance, Bob Wintermute's essay draws on official records as well as memoirs and newspaper accounts in an attempt to convey what it was like to *be* an African American in the U.S. Army during the First World War, in combat and in boot camp. Rather than telling the story of the battle or the history of the technology—which the encyclopedia does quite well—Alan Allport uses the words of the men of the early tank corps to take us inside a tank, to let us feel what it was like to fight in a tin can. As a whole, the chapters seek to relate the experience of the common person in the fighting using their own words wherever possible. Knowing about the war and knowing what the war was like are two very different things.

There was no single "experience" of the war, but there were common threads among groups. Students familiar with the poetry that emerged from the war, for instance, can find similarities in the words of the men who served along the western front, but those who look closely will also find almost infinite variation. Wilfred Owen, Sigfried Sassoon, and their compatriots who served on the western front, moreover, represent only a small portion of the whole. This book seeks to represent some small portion of the rest, and to guide readers to other sources on the many and varied experiences of World War I. This is particularly important, it seems, in a century where warfare itself is undergoing transformations not unlike those of 1914–1918 and the effects on society are likely to be as great, to examine the effects of that technology and those changes on the people who fought the war. Looking at war not from a political or strategic view but from a personal one offers a different set of perspectives (hence, again, the title of this volume) and a different set of lessons.

More than sixty million men entered the armed services in the years 1914–1918; nearly ten million gave their lives in the conflict known as the Great War, along with some twenty million others. Eight and one-half million Europeans were interned as prisoners of war, by far the largest number incarcerated to that time (Rachmoninov 2002). The soldiers of World War I fought under conditions that varied greatly, from the established trenches on both European fronts to the more mobile warfare of Africa, from the frozen marshes of eastern Galicia to the cliffs and beaches of Gallipoli. They fought using gases for the first time, using tanks for the first time, and using aircraft for the first time. It was a new type of warfare that developed between 1914 and 1918. It came to be known as "total war," and the experience of it was both unlike anything that had come before and similar to the experiences of war everywhere.

The sheer numbers of soldiers and of casualties produced their own effects. Small professional armies with an elite officer corps ceased to exist. In some instances, they were wiped out in a single campaign, if not a single battle. By the end of 1914, for example, the Russian army had suffered almost a million dead, including most of its trained officers (Wildman 1980/1987). The experienced officers in the British, French, and German armies suffered largely the same fate, and so as what was thought likely to be a small, rapid war expanded into the First World War, it became, truly, "the People's

War." The "Pals Battalions" of British field marshal H. H. Kitchener—units comprised of the men of one town, or one area, who volunteered to fight together—are perhaps the most exemplary embodiment of this new type of war. When these battalions suffered heavy casualties or, in some cases, were wiped out, entire towns and villages felt the impact. Entire generations of French, British, German, and Russian men went "missing" during the war, killed or incapacitated. They left a demographic gap rarely seen or matched in history, more specifically targeted than the Black Death of the Middle Ages and broader than the nineteenth-century famines that swept Ireland or the devastating American Civil War. It was thus the first war experienced by societies as a whole across the globe—arguments for the Seven Years' War notwithstanding.

It was the First World War also that introduced the term "home front," whereby women, children, and those not enrolled in the armed services "fought" for their country by providing armaments, food, and moral support. While the men were at the front, dying or being taken prisoner, women filled positions and did jobs previously unthinkable for them. Even as the Pals Battalions fought at the front, towns and villages came together behind the lines to supply them and to support them. Movements for female suffrage, and of women into the workforce, existed long before World War I, but the demands and perceptions of that conflict altered social relations irrevocably. It is therefore important to try to see and understand how women experienced the war, what feelings they had, and what they took forward. As Molly Wood's fine essay on women on the American home front demonstrates, the "weaker sex" not only gained a greater realization of their true strength but forced governments and institutions everywhere to acknowledge that strength and their contributions. In a different context, the role of women in the Red Cross and as army auxiliaries has been seen as shaping women's sense of capability and power. Did women sense and desire this when they volunteered, however? Kenneth Steuer's essay on the role of social service agencies in the First World War provides an answer. Did African Americans see the war as something that empowered them while it was going on, or was this a notion that came later, shaped by scholars and the course of events? Bob Wintermute provides the evidence that can lead us to an answer there as well. By compiling the recollections, accounts, and tales of the people who experienced the war firsthand, *Perspectives* offers another, different tool for examining these important questions and for exploring further.

References

Churchill, Winston S. 1932. *The Unknown War. The Eastern Front.* New York: Charles Scribner's Sons.

Foley, Barbara. 2003. *Spectres of 1919: Class and Nation in the Making of the New Negro.* Champaign: University of Illinois Press.

Rachmoninov, Alon. 2002. *POWs and the Great War: Captivity on the Eastern Front.* Legacy of the Great War series. New York: Berg.

Wildman, Allan K. 1980/1987. *The End of the Russian Imperial Army.* 2 vols. Princeton: Princeton University Press.

THE AFRICAN-AMERICAN EXPERIENCE IN WORLD WAR I

---◆---

We tried to treat the Negroes with exactly the same consideration shown the whites. We had the same speakers to address them. The Rotary Club presented them with small silk flags, as they did the whites. The band turned out to escort them to the train; and the Negroes went to camp with as cheerful a spirit as did the whites. One of them when asked if he were going to France, replied: "No sir; I'm not going 'to France.' I am going 'through France.'"

—REPORT OF OKLAHOMA DRAFT BOARD,
recounted by W. Allison Sweeney, 1918

It (The United States) insults us. It has organized a nationwide and latterly a worldwide propaganda of deliberate and continuous insult and defamation of black blood wherever found. It decrees that it shall not be possible in travel nor residence, work nor play, education nor instruction for a black man to exist without tacit or open acknowledgment of his inferiority to the dirtiest white dog. And it looks upon any attempt to question or even discuss this dogma as arrogance, unwarranted assumption and treason.

This is the country to which we Soldiers of Democracy return. This is the fatherland for which we fought! But it is our fatherland. It was right for us to fight. The faults of our country are our faults. Under similar circumstances, we would fight again. But by the God of Heaven, we are cowards and jackasses if now that that war is over, we do not martial every ounce of our brain and brawn to fight a sterner, longer, more unbending battle against the forces of hell in our own land.

We return.

We return from fighting.

We return fighting.

Make way for Democracy! We saved it in France, and by the Great Jehovah, we will save it in the United States of America, or know the reason why.

— Editorial by W. E. B. DuBois,
The Crisis, May 1919, 14

After the United States declared war on Germany on 7 April 1917, African Americans set out to make their own contributions to the war effort. The decision to do so was not taken casually. Many in the African-American community, especially those among the small literary and journalistic elite, recalled the disappointments of the Spanish-American War. Then black leaders had put aside their personal reservations about the prospect of fighting for the rights of the Cuban people while American blacks remained subject to gross inequities, all in the hope of improving their social and political standing at home. Such hopes remained unfulfilled, and the extent of racial prejudice and discrimination in the United States actually increased after 1898. The tenor of race relations grew increasingly dark, as lynchings and violent race riots plagued African Americans throughout the American South. But despite such disappointments, the prospects for improved race relations following wartime participation were too great to ignore. African-American writers, journalists, and educators from both sides of the political divide between assimilationists and activists supported the war. In the pages of his journal *The Crisis*, W. E. B. DuBois viewed the war as a tremendous opportunity to reverse the rising tide of violent racism plaguing African Americans:

Despite the unfortunate record of England, of Belgium, and of our own land in dealing with colored peoples, we earnestly believe that the greatest hope for ultimate democracy, with no adventitious barriers of race and color, lies on the side of the Allies, with whom our country has become companion in arms. In justification of this belief we point on the one hand to the splendid democracy of France, the recent freeing of our fellow-sufferers in Russia, and the slow but steady advance of principles of universal justice in the British Empire and in our own land; and on the other hand we point to the wretched record of Germany in Africa and her preachment of autocracy and race superiority.

We, therefore, earnestly urge our colored fellow citizens to join heartily in this fight for eventual world liberty; we urge them to enlist in the army; to join in the pressing work of providing food supplies; to labor in all ways by hand and thought in increasing the efficiency of our country. We urge this despite our deep sympathy with the reasonable and deep-seated feeling of revolt among Negroes at the persistent insult and discrimination to which they are subject and will be subject even when they do their patriotic duty. Let us, however, never forget that this country belongs to us even more than to those who lynch, disfranchise, and segregate. As our country it rightly demands our whole-hearted defense as well today as when with Crispus Attucks we fought for independence and with 200,000 black soldiers we helped hammer out our own freedom. . . .

Let our action, then include unfaltering loyalty to our country, unbounded effort toward realizing the larger, finer objects of this world battle of America and her allies; simultaneous with this and in further, stronger determination to realize world peace and self-government, let us insist that neither the world nor America can be happy and democratic so long as twelve million Americans are lynched, disfranchised, and insulted—so long as millions of other darker folk are exploited and killed. (*The Crisis,* June 1917, 59–60)

Educated black men and women took various opportunities to contribute to the war effort. Members of the small educated elite went to work in high-profile positions, acting as intermediaries between the Wilson administration and the African-American community. Emmett J. Scott, secretary of the Tuskegee Institute and Booker T. Washington's personal secretary, was appointed special assistant to the secretary of war for negro affairs. The head of the Tuskegee Institute, Dr. R. R. Moton, was enlisted by the White House to serve as President Woodrow Wilson's personal representative to France. Alice Dunbar Nelson was recruited by the Women's Committee of the Council of National Defense to serve as that organization's field representative to the African-American community.

Other educated African Americans joined in, making direct contributions of their own. More than sixty ministers enlisted in the military to serve as chaplains, and 350 were enrolled as YMCA secretaries. In November 1918, eighteen African-American nurses applied and were accepted into the Army Nurse Corps on an "experimental basis." They worked at six training camps—Camps Funston, Sherman, Grant, Dix, Taylor, and Dodge.

Despite their willingness to participate, however, most black Americans were denied the chance to contribute to the war effort. The overt racism of Jim Crow America intruded into the political arena, leaving the War Department with little choice but to restrict African-American military participation. The Wilson administration's control of the war effort depended heavily upon a razor-thin Democratic majority in Congress. Southern Democratic congressmen and senators were thus empowered to impose their own segregationist views on the war effort.

The immediate result was the deliberate exclusion of thousands of eligible African Americans eager to fight. W. Allison Sweeney, contributing editor to the *Chicago Defender,* described the concerns of the black community over this willful dismissal of their patriotism by the War Department:

> He [the African American] was willing; anxious to volunteer and offered himself in large numbers at every recruiting station, without avail. True, he was accepted in numerous instances, but the condition precedent, that of filling up and rounding out the few Negro Regular and National Guard organizations below war strength, was chafing and humiliating. Had the response to the call for volunteers been as ardent among all classes of our people, especially the foreign born, as it was from the American Negro, it is fair to say that the selective draft would not necessarily have been so extensive. (Sweeney 1970, 73–74)

Only with the passage of the Selective Service Act were African Americans in substantial numbers taken into the army. When the Selective Service Act was drafted, it included no specific barriers to African-American conscription into the army. Between 5 June 1917 and 12 September 1917, a total of 2,290,527 blacks were examined and signed up by draft boards. This was

9.63 percent of the American males registered. This proportionate represen-
tation in the draft prompted the army's provost marshal general responsible
for administering the draft, Major General Enoch H. Crowder, to comment
favorably on the conduct of draft boards with regard to African Americans:

> In consequence, there appears to have been no racial discrimination made
> in the determination of his claims. Indeed, the proportion of claims granted
> to claims filed by members of the Negro race compares favorably with the
> proportion of claims granted to members of the white race. (Scott 1969, 70)

The official language of the Selective Service Act did not take into account the informal actions of local draft boards, or the policies of the War
and Navy Departments. Save for a handful of individuals, African Americans
were excluded from sitting on draft boards to review prospective inductees.
Local draft boards often required black registrants to tear off the corner of
their draft card. This made it easier for local boards to either single out
blacks for conscription or to ignore them, depending upon each community's particular attitude toward the war. In the South, property-owning
blacks were readily drafted, while young day laborers and sharecroppers
working for white property owners were exempted. There was a tremendous
proportionate disparity between the numbers of whites and blacks who were
exempted. In Fulton County, Georgia, for example, 64 percent of whites—
526 out of 815 men—were exempted. Only six blacks out of a total pool of
202 (2.97 percent) were excused.

Some communities took advantage of the draft to further harass African
Americans. On occasion, postmen deliberately withheld draft registration
forms from eligible black men, then reported them as draft resisters to the
local police. The arresting officer would, in turn, be eligible for a $50 re-
ward—which was split with the informing postal worker. The army, for its
part, adapted the Selective Service Act to fit with its existing segregationist
policy. African Americans were called up in separate drafts and inducted
only as segregated line and staff units were created or needed replacements.
Despite these restrictions, the army conscripted over 367,000 African Americans, some 13 percent of the total number of draftees during World War I.

An additional 1,353 African Americans were commissioned as officers
following a public outcry from the National Association for the Advancement of Colored People (NAACP) and other prominent educated blacks.
The June 1917 issue of *The Crisis* editorialized:

Give us Negro officers for Negro troops. This is the slogan and let no specious argument turn us from it. Liars tell us that only white men can lead
black men, and they tell us this in the face of the record of Sonni Ali, Touis-
saint L'Ouverture, General Dodd, Charles Young, and Frank Dennison. Give
us Negro officers for Negro troops. (60)

Even as W. E. B. DuBois's editorial was being typeset, news arrived of a re-
versal by the War Department that, on 15 June 1917, authorized the establishment of a colored officers' reserve training camp at Fort Des Moines,
Iowa. An initial cadre of 1,250 men was selected to participate. Two hundred and fifty were noncommissioned officers from the army's four regular
regiments; the remainder were taken from the civilian population.

After reporting to the camp, the officer candidates underwent a rigorous
training regimen that eliminated nearly half of the class. The remaining 639
members graduated on 14 October 1917, and the new officers went out to
join units of the 92nd Infantry Division, one of the army's two segregated divisions, in training. Fort Des Moines was closed, and future black officer candidates were sent to other camps for training related to their military occupation
specialty: machine-gun officers at Camp Hancock, Georgia; infantry officers at
Camp Pike, Arkansas; and artillery officers at Camp Taylor, Kentucky.

Racial prejudice and discrimination were constant factors during training for black soldiers and officer candidates. From the start, African Americans were concerned about the prospect of mistreatment and persecution
by bigoted whites in uniform, as well as the inevitable clashes with the local
community. Few could have anticipated the violent reaction of white civilians and the military, especially in the South.

The chief factor behind the more extreme racist violence in southern
communities directed toward African-American soldiers were inherent fears
of violence provoked by well-armed blacks. The prospect of armed and organized blacks wreaking a bloody vengeance against their former masters
had obsessed southern whites since the Civil War. Coupled with lurid sce-
narios of sexual assault, such rumors and fabrications fueled a fierce back-
lash against black soldiers stationed in southern training camps.

Towns near the training camps frequently lobbied the War Department
directly in attempts to prevent the stationing of African-American troops
nearby. In October 1917, for example, the citizens of Spartanburg, South
Carolina, rejected plans to move the Second and Third Battalions of the
369th Infantry Regiment to nearby Camp Wadsworth for training. "The

most tragic consequences would follow the introduction of the New York Negro with his Northern ideas into the community life of Spartanburg," they claimed (Scott 1969, 199). In this case, the consequences extended no further than closing the doors of a number of businesses to black soldiers and general harassment on the streets of the town. The soldiers from New York kept their tempers, however, and ignored much of the abuse hurled upon them until they were moved to the Port of Embarkation at Hoboken, New Jersey, two weeks later.

Other units experienced similar boycotts and treatment. At Camp Funston, near Manhattan, Kansas, Major General Charles C. Ballou, commander of the 92nd Infantry Division, issued a much-debated and questioned bulletin, Bulletin No. 35, on 28 March, 1918, in response to growing tensions between the townspeople and the soldiers in his command. Ballou, who had served during the Philippine insurrection, essentially confined the men of his command to the camp, choosing to abrogate their rights instead of defending them from civilian bigotry (Scott 1969, 97–98).

HEADQUARTERS 92D DIVISION CAMP FUNSTON, KANSAS
March 28, 1918

1. It should be well known to all colored officers and men that no useful purpose is served by such acts as will cause the 'color question' to be raised. It is not a question of legal rights, but a question of policy, and any policy that tends to bring about a conflict of races, with its resulting animosities, is prejudicial to the military interest of the 92d Division, and therefore prejudicial to an important interest of the colored race.

2. To avoid such conflicts the Division Commander has repeatedly urged that all colored members of his command, and especially the officers and non-commissioned officers, should refrain from going where their presence will be resented. In spite of this injunction, one of the sergeants of the Medical Department has recently precipitated the precise trouble that should be avoided, and then called on the Division Commander to take sides in a row that should never have occurred had the sergeant placed the general good above his personal pleasure and convenience. The sergeant entered a theater, as he undoubtedly had a legal right to do, and precipitated trouble by making it possible to allege race discrimination in the seat he was given. He is strictly within his legal rights in this matter, and the theater manager is legally wrong. Nevertheless the sergeant is

guilty of the GREATER wrong in doing ANYTHING, NO MATTER HOW LEGALLY CORRECT, that will provoke race animosity.

3. The Division Commander repeats that the success of the Division with all that success implies, is dependent upon the good will of the public. That public is nine-tenths white. White men made the Division, and they can break it just as easily if it becomes a trouble maker.

4. All concerned are again enjoined to place the general interest of the Division above personal pride and gratification. Avoid every situation that can give rise to racial ill-will. Attend quietly and faithfully to your duties, and don't go where your presence is not desired.

5. This will be read to all organizations of the 92d Division.

By command of Major-General Ballou:

(Signed) Allen J. Greer, Lieutenant Colonel, General Staff, Chief of Staff.

Bulletin No. 35 prompted a firestorm of complaints and calls for General Ballou's resignation in African-American journals and newspapers. The general defended his communiqué by noting that his overriding interest was in preserving military discipline and avoiding a replay of the race riots that had recently taken place in east St. Louis and Houston. He also claimed a direct link to military readiness:

> Our enemies do not wish the United States to have its military power increased by colored soldiers, and they stand ready to add fuel to every race discord in order to embarrass our country as much as possible in this war. Is it any wonder then, in view of what the enemy has accomplished in the past and is seeking to accomplish again, that the Commander of the colored Division seeks to nip troubles in the bud, and while prosecuting white men for their offences against his soldiers, urges the soldiers to do their part to keep the peace and promote harmony. (Scott 1969, 101)

Though Ballou remained in command of the 92nd Division, after Bulletin No. 35 he was seen as a meek and ineffectual leader who caved in to the demands of junior southern white officers and refused to stand up for the rights of his men.

The army administration contributed to the climate of racial discrimination. Black military policemen frequently were unarmed, even though they were charged with performing the same enforcement duties as white MPs. This gave many white soldiers the impression that they could ignore them completely, if not openly taunt them. At camps where the two races were trained together, black soldiers were frequently assigned to the most demeaning and onerous tasks: kitchen police, latrine cleaning, and construction details. Such assignments were generally excused on the grounds that it freed up white companies for essential training—regardless of the fact that such training was equally important to black soldiers. White enlisted men and junior officers alike also tended to ignore protocols of rank when confronted with senior African-American personnel. It was not uncommon for salutes to be denied black noncommissioned officers and junior grade officers. Orders from blacks frequently were ignored by white soldiers altogether until they were restated by a white officer.

On occasion, these inherent tensions led to an explosion. The most violent racial incident took place in August 1917 in Houston, Texas. A riot between members of the Third Battalion of the 24th Infantry Regiment, city police, and National Guardsmen sparked by the beating and arrest of two black military police by white civilian officers ended with fifteen whites dead and twelve wounded. The Third Battalion was swiftly moved to Fort Columbus, New Mexico, and a court-martial was convened for 110 soldiers identified as participants. Sixteen men were hung, and an additional sixty-five were given life sentences.

The incident caused a sensation in the press. Southern newspapers, like the Shreveport, Louisiana, *Journal,* expressed a grim satisfaction with the result: "The swaggering of a Negro trooper in uniform is not a thing to be desired or to be suffered silently" (reprinted in *The Crisis,* October 1917, 302–303). African-American editorials lamented the unfair circumstances that provoked a militant response among well-disciplined troops:

It is difficult for one of Negro blood to write of Houston. Is not the ink within the very wells crimsoned with the blood of black martyrs? Do they not cry unavenged, saying:—Always WE pay; always WE die; always, whether right or wrong, it is SO MANY NEGROES killed, so many NEGROES wounded. But here, at last, at Houston is a change. Here, at last, white folk died. Innocent, adventitious strangers, perhaps, as innocent as the thousands of

Negroes done to death in the last two centuries. Our hands tremble to rise and exult, our lips strive to cry. . . .

What it was they had to stand, we learn only in tortuous driblets from sources bitterly prejudiced. These facts, at least, are clear: Contrary to all military precedent the Negro provost guard had been disarmed and was at the mercy of citizen police who insulted them until blood ran. At last, they stole their own arms and turned and fought. They were not young recruits; they were not wild and drunken wastrels; they were disciplined men who said, "This is enough; we'll stand no more." That they faced and faced fearlessly the vision of a shameful death, we do not doubt. We ask no mitigation of their punishment. They broke the law. They must suffer. But before Almighty God, if those guiltless of their black brothers' blood shot the punishing shot, there would be no dead men in that regiment. (*The Crisis*, October 1917, 284–285)

In many quarters, African Americans were stereotyped—contrary to all evidence since the Civil War—as poor soldiers, incapable of following sophisticated direction.

It had been charged that Negroes could not develop into artillerymen. A strong prejudice against inducting them into that branch of the service had always existed in the army. It was especially affirmed that the Negro did not possess the mathematical ability necessary to qualify as an expert artillery officer. (Sweeney 1970, 79)

Many people believed that African Americans would have problems responding to military discipline. Contemporary stereotypes promoting the alleged inferiority of blacks fed the arguments against training them as soldiers. If worked too hard, so-called experts claimed, black conscripts would simply desert at the first opportunity. Accounts alleging wholesale desertion by African Americans in training and in France were widespread enough to prompt Major General Enoch Crowder to testify otherwise on 20 December 1918:

These figures of reported desertions, however, lose their significance when the facts behind them are studied. . . . With striking unanimity the draft authorities replied that this was due to two causes: first, ignorance and illiteracy; especially in the rural regions, to which may be added a certain shiftlessness in ignoring civic obligations; and secondly, the tendency of the Negroes to shift from place to place. . . .

  With equal unanimity the draft executives report that the amount of willful delinquency or desertion has been almost nil. Several describe the strenuous efforts of the Negroes to comply with the regulations, when the requirements were explained to them, many registrants travelling long distances to report in person to the adjutant general of the state. (Sweeney 1970, 113)

Interestingly, in defending the intentions of African-American conscripts, Major General Crowder used traditional negative stereotypes—laziness, ignorance, and shiftlessness—rather than attempt to identify deficiencies in the system itself.

This kind of racial insensitivity and repression, even when well intended, continued after African-American soldiers in the American Expeditionary Force (AEF) arrived in France. Courts-martial were used with greater frequency against black enlisted and commissioned personnel alike, often on the most specious and absurd grounds. Bigoted officers—northern and southern alike—insulted the black soldiers under their command publicly and questioned their intelligence, courage, and morality. When the first black regiments were brigaded with the French, official circulars were sent secretly to the French army advising them of American racial preferences and warning of "dangers" inherent in racial mingling (*The Crisis*, May 1919, 16–18).

FRENCH MILITARY MISSION
Stationed with the American Army August 7, 1918
SECRET INFORMATION CONCERNING BLACK AMERICAN TROOPS

1. It is important for French officers who have been called upon to exercise command over black American troops, or to live in close contact with them, to have an exact idea of the position occupied by Negroes in the United States. The information set forth in the following communication ought to be given to these officers and it is to their interest to have these matters known and widely disseminated. It will devolve likewise on the French Military Authorities, through the medium of the Civil Authorities, to give information on this subject to the French population residing in the cantonments occupied by American colored troops.

2. The American attitude upon the Negro question may seem a matter for discussion to many French minds. But we French are not in our province if we undertake to discuss what some call "prejudice." American opinion is unanimous on the "color question" and does not admit of any discussion.

The increasing number of Negroes in the United States (about 15,000,000) would create for the white race in the Republic a menace of degeneracy were it not that an impassable gulf has been made between them.

As this danger does not exist for the French race, the French public has become accustomed to treating the Negro with familiarity and indulgence.

This indulgence and this familiarity are matters of grievous concern to the Americans. They consider them an affront to their national policy. They are afraid that contact with the French will inspire in black Americans aspirations which to them [the whites] appear intolerable. It is of the utmost importance that every effort be made to avoid profoundly estranging American opinion.

Although a citizen of the United States, the black man is regarded by the white American as an inferior being with whom relations of business or service only are possible. The black is constantly being censured for his want of intelligence and discretion, his lack of civic and professional conscience and for his tendency toward undue familiarity.

The vices of the Negro are a constant menace to the American who has to repress them sternly. For instance, the black American troops in France have, by themselves, given rise to as many complaints for attempted rape as all the rest of the army. And yet the [black American] soldiers sent us have been the choices to physique and morals, for the number disqualified at the time of mobilization was enormous.

CONCLUSION

1. We must prevent the rise of any pronounced degree of intimacy between French officers and black officers. We may be courteous and amiable with these last, but we cannot deal with them on the same plane as with the white American officers without deeply wounding the latter. We must not eat with them, must not shake hands or seek to talk or meet with them outside of the requirements of military service.

2. We must not commend too highly the black American troops, particularly in the presence of [white] Americans. It is all right to recognize their good qualities and their services, but only in moderate terms, strictly in keeping with the truth.

3. Make a point of keeping the native cantonment population from "spoiling" the Negroes. [White] Americans become greatly incensed at any public expression of intimacy between white women with black men. They have recently uttered violent protests against a picture in the *"Vie Parisienne"* entitled "The Child of the Desert" which shows a [white] woman in a *"cabinet particulier"* with a Negro. Familiarity on the part of white women with black men is furthermore a source of profound regret to our experienced colonials who see in it an over-weening menace to the prestige of the white race.

Military authority cannot intervene directly in this question, but it can through the civil authorities exercise some influence on the population.

(Signed) LINARD.

With the exception of W. E. B. DuBois, influential African Americans tended to downplay such incidents, cautious of a potential reaction by the Wilson administration or whites if too much attention were drawn to racial incidents. Though *Chicago Defender* editor W. Allison Sweeney criticized the color line in all wartime matters dealing with the African American, he kept his comments low key:

There has always been fostered a spirit in the counsels and orders of the Department of War, as in all the other great government departments, to restrain rather than encourage the patriotic and civic zeal of their faithful and qualified Negro aids and servants. That is to say, to draw before them a certain imaginary line, beyond and over which the personal ambitions of the race, smarting for honorable renown and promotion, predicated on service and achievement, they were not permitted to go. A virtual "Dead Line"; its parent and wet nurse being that strange thing as American Prejudice, unknown of anywhere else on earth, which was at once a crime against its marked and selected victims, and a burden of shame which still clings to it; upon the otherwise great nation, that it has condoned and still remains silent in its present. (Sweeney 1970, 74–75)

Another writer advised that

If properly trained and instructed, the colored man makes as good a soldier as the world has ever seen. This history of the Negro in all our wars, includ-

ing the Indian Campaigns, shows this. He is by nature of a happy disposition;
he is responsive and tractable; he is amenable to discipline; he takes pride in
his uniform; he has faith and confidence in his leader; he possesses physical
courage—all of which are valuable military assets.

Make the colored man feel you have faith in him. Be strict with him but
treat him fairly and justly making him realize that in your dealings with him
he will always be given a square deal. Commend him when he does well and
punish him when he is refractory—that is to say, let him know he will always
know that he will get what is coming to him be it reward or punishment. In
other words, treat and handle the colored man as you would any other
human being out of whom you would make a soldier, and you will have as
good a soldier as history has ever known—a man who will drill well, shoot
well, march well, obey well, fight well—in short, a man who will give a good
account of himself in battle, and who will conduct and behave himself properly in camp, in garrison and in other places. (quoted in Scott 1969, 79)

The War Department's response to the political pressures coming from
the racist white South and the African-American community was at best
halfhearted. The army's four colored regiments—some 20,000 men out of
the army's peacetime establishment of 75,000 soldiers—were retained in
the United States for garrison duty. The Ninth Cavalry Regiment was sent
to the Philippines; the Tenth Cavalry and 24th Infantry were deployed
along the Mexican border; and the 25th Infantry Regiment was assigned to
Hawaii. The overwhelming majority of African Americans entering the
army during the war were assigned to labor battalions. Over 150,000 men
were placed in stevedore companies and labor battalions in the United
States and France.

The labor battalions were the invisible actors responsible for the AEF's
rapid buildup in 1918. Black stevedores offloaded the supplies needed by
the growing army from convoys arriving in French ports. Black construction
laborers built the training camps for the new infantry divisions and laid
down the American-gauge railways that brought men and supplies from the
Atlantic coast into the French interior. Twenty-six years before the "Red Ball
Express" acquired its own fame for keeping the U.S. Army supplied as it
raced across France, black truck drivers carried men and material to the
front from supply depots and cantonments.

The soldiers in the labor battalions were directly supervised by southern
white sergeants. Ironically, the War Department reasoned that they were

best suited for the task, having ample experience in "motivating" black laborers in the rural South. Frequently this "motivation" came in the form of overwork, verbal abuse, imprisonment, and in some cases, physical assault. Nonetheless, the labor battalions continued to excel in the tasks assigned them, as reports attest:

> Everybody joins to testify to this: the white slave-drivers, the army officers, the French, the visitors—all say that the American Negro was the best laborer in France, of all the world's peoples gathered there; and if American food and materials saved France in the end from utter exhaustion, it was the Negro stevedore who made that aid effective. (*The Crisis*, June 1919, 65)

When pressured to establish combat units for service in France with the American Expeditionary Force, the army created two divisions. The first, the 92nd Infantry Division, was made up exclusively of draftees from the South. The second, the 93rd Infantry Division, was cobbled together from conscripts and the few all-black National Guard regiments, battalions, and companies organized in the Northeast and the border states. The 92nd Division's four infantry regiments, the 365th, 366th, 367th, and 368th Regiments, were made up entirely of African-American enlisted personnel and junior officers, but all regimental and divisional senior officers were white. Some of these senior officers, including its regimental commanders, had served with the United States Colored Troops during the Civil War. The majority of the division's junior officers were graduates of the army's segregated officer's training camp at Des Moines, Iowa.

Prior to its departure for France on 7 June 1918, the 92nd Division's four infantry regiments and its support arms trained at camps throughout the Northeast and Midwest. The division was still commanded by Major General Ballou, but after arriving in France it was immediately turned over to the French army for extensive field training before entering the trenches. Over the next two months the infantrymen were put through an intensive regimen by their French instructors, who labored to overcome the deficiencies in their stateside training.

Even as the 92nd trained, though, white senior officers began to voice doubts about the use of African-American officers commanding line companies and artillery batteries. On 23 January 1918, an inspector general's report of the 368th Infantry Regiment's training at Camp Meade, Maryland, stated it in the following terms:

368th Infantry: Personnel: The field and staff officers are white; the company officers are colored. These company officers are composed of young men with officer's training camp experience, and of former non-commissioned officers of the army. The former have more or less intelligence and education; the latter have experience but not much education. The enlisted men are, as a general rule, illiterate and uneducated and of a low order of intelligence—affording little material for good non-commissioned officers. The Commanding Officer is doubtful whether some of these colored officers can ever be made efficient. They do not possess the necessary education or intelligence. (U.S. Army War College 1918, 10)

General John J. Pershing, commander of the AEF, made similar observations following an inspection:

During my visit to the 92nd Division (colored) it was learned that the situation as to training, especially of colored officers, was not entirely satisfactory. . . . None of the junior officers had received more than superficial training and most of them were unaccustomed to the management of men. The general officers of the division, who had all served with colored regiments of the Regular Army, were not sanguine regarding the possibility of reaching a high standard of instruction among their troops.

It was well known that the time and attention that must be devoted to training colored troops in order to raise their level of efficiency to the average were considerably greater than for white regiments. More responsibility rested upon officers of colored regiments owing to the lower capacity and lack of education of the personnel. . . . It would have been wise to have followed the long experience of our Regular Army and provided these colored units with selected white officers. (Pershing 1931, 228–229)

Pershing's comments reflected the prejudice of many of his peers in the army officer corps that though African Americans could be effective soldiers, they were not intelligent enough to lead men or make informed combat decisions, and should remain under the command of white officers. Coincidentally, Pershing had spent several years early in his career as a young lieutenant and captain serving with the Tenth Cavalry Regiment, one of the army's four colored regiments.

After completing training on 12 August 1918, the 92nd Division was moved into the Saint Die sector in the rugged Vosges region. Soon after, the

Officers of the "Buffalos," 367th Infantry, 77th Division in France during World War I. (National Archives)

Germans attacked the division's 367th Infantry Regiment at Frapelle. Despite being subjected to heavy artillery and gas shelling, the 367th withstood the attack and held the line until it was relieved on 20 September 1918. Then it was returned to American control in time for the opening of the Meuse-Argonne offensive.

Here the division faltered, albeit under extreme conditions. Assigned to the French 38th Corps, the 368th Infantry Regiment was ordered to attack the German line in the area of Binarville on 26 September 1918. The results, the record shows, were not good:

The attack was made at 5:25 a.m., with poor artillery support. It finally developed into separate movements by three different groups. The one nearest here had worked its way by dusk into the German trenches in the valley ahead. The other two groups had penetrated the German lines for a considerable distance but later in the day retired to a position about 1/4 mile behind the line from which they had started. (American Battle Monuments Commission 1938, 367)

This brief official description of the action at Binarville, however, omitted the full accounting of the obstacles faced by the men of the 368th Infantry. During the operation, the 368th Infantry was to advance along a front of two kilometers—an area later deemed too large for the size of the unit. The regiment's commander, Colonel Fred R. Brown, recalled the tremendous obstacles facing his men as they went over the top:

> It was a terrible job getting thru that Boch wire. I have never seen anything equal to it. There were two or three kilometers of solid mass of French and German wire in "No Man's Land," and thruout the German trench system which they had been working on for four years, and the whole country, except in the bayous and trenches, was covered with this mass of barbed wire and covered with second growth brush. The new growth had grown up through this barbed wire and was absolutely impenetrable. After they got beyond the Ravine Metruese it opened out a little bit and they were able to progress other than in bayous. . . .
>
> The position had been held by both the French and the Germans for the entire war, and had been constantly improved by both sides. It consisted of a rolling country cut up by ravines and covered with the ruined debris of the Argonne Forest blasted away by four years of shell fire and interlaced by solid wire defenses of every kind. . . . It was generally considered one of the strongest parts of the Hindenburg line, especially because of the fact that this wire had not been destroyed by shell fire or tank or any similar means. (U.S. Army War College 1918, 26)

Inadequate preparation only added to the difficulty. The regiment received far too few wire-cutters and maps. When the assault commenced, it went forward without a preliminary artillery bombardment. Any anticipated benefit of surprise was quickly lost as the soldiers of the 368th Infantry ran up against the dense wire and well-positioned machine-gun nests. Pinned down by the wire, the regiment began to suffer from heavy German shelling and strafing attacks. The shock of heavy combat, combined with a general level of exhaustion—the unit arrived in the line after an all-night march—caused the attack to lose its momentum. Two more days of attacks against the German line failed to achieve any significant gains. By 6 P.M. on 29 September, the regiment's Third Battalion reached its breaking point and withdrew in confusion to the positions it had held at the start of the attack.

The 368th Infantry Regiment's performance at Binarville was later cited as evidence of the overall poor quality of African Americans as soldiers. The regimental commander's report laid blame solely on the African-American junior officers:

> A careful reading of the unsatisfactory and incomplete reports of company commanders will show how the companies and battalion utterly failed to carry out these orders, and, as I firmly believe, without justification, and due almost entirely to the inefficiency and cowardice of the company officers who repeatedly withdrew their companies and platoons, without orders and without suffering losses which could possibly justify such action. The character of the terrain and the German defense system made the advance depend entirely on the aggressiveness and leadership of the company and platoon commanders. In this they failed and whatever advance they made was usually due to the presence and energy of the battalion commanders. Owing to the extent of the front covered and the necessity for advancing by small groups, the battalion commanders could influence only a small part of their commands. (U.S. Army War College 1918, 33)

Five black officers were singled out and court-martialed on charges of cowardice, and four were sentenced to death. The commanding general of the Second Army, Major General Robert L. Bullard, previously a supporter of blacks in uniform based on his experience during the Spanish-American War commanding a volunteer colored regiment, used the experience of the 92nd Infantry to support his own postwar observations:

> The Negroes were a great disappointment. This experience did not agree with the experience of the Regular Army of the United States with Negro soldiers. I could not ascribe the failure to poor quality in their higher officers. These officers generally, as I have said, were good, in most cases excellent. The French had had like experience with their Negro troops in their front-line trenches against the enemy. The Negro, it seems, cannot stand bombardment. . . .
>
> Altogether my memories of the 92nd Negro Division are a nightmare. When all my thought, time, and effort were needed to make war against a

powerful enemy, they had for a week to be given over entirely to a danger-ous, irritating race question that had nothing to do with war-making, the paramount matter of the time. I fear that it will always be so with Negroes wherever they are in contact with whites.

This thought and my experience led me to this conclusion: If you need combat soldiers, and especially if you need them in a hurry, don't put your time upon Negroes. The task of making soldiers of them and fighting with them, if there are any white people near, will be swamped in the race ques-tion. If racial uplift or racial equality is your purpose, that is another matter. (Bullard 1925, 296–298)

The observations of Major General Bullard and General Pershing on the 92nd Infantry Division directly influenced the army's future policies on African-American soldiers. After the end of the war in 1918, the army put less stock in its four colored regiments. Constantly kept under strength dur-ing the interwar years, these units were increasingly used exclusively as labor and construction units. The Tenth Cavalry Regiment suffered the indignity of being scattered across the country, with some of its men being used as sta-ble grooms attending to the needs of cadets at the U.S. Military Academy at West Point, New York. When the United States entered World War II, the perception that blacks could not fight promoted by critics of the 92nd Divi-sion had completely replaced the legacy and memory of the U.S. Colored Troops in the Civil War and the "Buffalo Soldiers" of the western frontier, Cuba, the Philippines, and Mexico.

The experience of the 368th at Binarville, however, was the exception and not the rule. The 92nd Division's other three regiments fared better than the 368th Infantry Regiment in the remaining months of the war and took part in several attacks against German positions through 10 November 1918. As of the 11 November 1918 Armistice, the 92nd Division had suf-fered 750 soldiers killed and over 5,000 wounded. Passing the next two months in training in the event that the war would resume, the 92nd Divi-sion finally sailed for home in February 1919. On 7 March 1919, the divi-sion was formally demobilized in New York City, and its men were sent back to their homes across the country.

Though established at the same time as the 92nd Division, the 93rd In-fantry Division did not see combat as a complete division. Indeed, save for a brief period during the Meuse-Argonne offensive, the 93rd Division's four regiments were under French command for the duration of their active

Members of the 369th Infantry pause after a battle in France during World War I. The 369th served with the French 4th Army and played a major role in the defeat of Germany on the western front. Two of the men were decorated with the French Croix de Guerre. (National Archives)

service. Three of the division's four regiments—the 369th, 370th, and 372nd Regiments—were created from existing National Guard units. Two of these were the 15th New York (369th Infantry) and the 8th Illinois (370th Infantry). A host of smaller state guard units—the 9th Ohio Infantry Battalion, 1st Separate Battalion of the District of Columbia, and infantry companies from Connecticut, Maryland, Massachusetts, and Tennessee—made up the 372nd Infantry. The division's fourth regiment, the 371st Infantry, was made up entirely of draftees from Mississippi and South Carolina. As a result, all of the division's regiments trained at different locations throughout the country and had their own unique experiences with racial discrimination before they were shipped to Europe.

Even after arriving in Europe, the 93rd Division remained a fragmented outfit. Just as with the 92nd Division, American commanders were reluctant to use the all-black outfit alongside other white-only divisions. In comparison, the French army was desperate for manpower and, so many believed, had better experience dealing with black troops. After all, for three years the French had been using entire divisions of African colonial troops—Senegalese and Moroccan—to good effect. The French attitude toward colored troops was much different than white Americans imagined, however. Rather than treating them with harsh discipline, the French army and civilians exhibited little racial bias toward these men, and welcomed the "Men of Bronze" openly and warmly as friends and heroes.

Whereas the U.S. air service remained a white-only preserve during the war, one African American flew in the French Flying Corps. Eugene Jacque Bullard, a native of Columbus, South Carolina, had emigrated to France in 1912. When Germany invaded France in August 1914, he volunteered for the French Foreign Legion. Discharged from the infantry after he was seriously wounded at Verdun, Bullard joined the French air service. After learning to fly, he was assigned to the Lafayette Escadrille, the famous American volunteer unit flying for France. Even though he was trained as a combat pilot, his countrymen initially refused to allow him to fly, instead treating him like an orderly. French observers intervened, however, and Bullard made his first combat flight on 8 September 1917. Bullard flew twenty missions before he was transferred again to the infantry—the French 170th Infanterie Regiment—in January 1918. When the war ended on 11 November 1918, Bullard not only was recognized as an ace but also was awarded the Croix de Guerre and the Legion d'Honneur.

The African-American 369th Infantry Regiment was one of the first units to travel to Europe from the United States, departing with the first 100,000 troops sent to France. The regiment owed this honor to the readiness it achieved as the 15th New York Infantry Regiment. During an inspection on 8 April 1917, the outfit was recognized as fit for deployment as part of the federalized National Guard. Following training at Peekskill, New York, the regiment's infantry battalions were dispatched across the Northeast to accomplish various tasks: guarding railroads against saboteurs, guarding German internees at Ellis Island, and building new camp buildings at Camp Upton, New York, and Camp Dix, New Jersey. The regiment was scheduled to leave the United States aboard the army transport *Pocahontas* on 12 November 1917, but weather and engineering delays kept the men from arriving in France until 27 December 1917.

Soon after its arrival, the regiment was brigaded to the French 16th Infantry Division. During its refitting and training with French equipment at Givrey-En-Argonne, the regiment acquired a reputation for excellent discipline and, after entering the line on 12 April 1918, of ferocity. The regiment acquired its nickname, "Harlem Hellfighters," during the German army's fifth and final 1918 offensive, when it joined in repelling the German attacks aimed at Paris. On 26 September 1918, the regiment participated in some of the opening actions of the American Meuse-Argonne offensive, taking the town of Ripont along with several hundred prisoners and several artillery pieces. When the Armistice ended fighting on 11 November 1918, the 369th Infantry Regiment was still in the front lines.

In the following weeks, it took part in the Allied pursuit of the retreating German army and had the distinction of being the first Allied unit to reach the Rhine River, deep in German territory. The men of the 369th settled in as the military occupation force guarding towns in Germany, which put them in the unusual position of policing the white German population. When the 369th Infantry was sent home, one of its white officers, Major Arthur W. Little, summarized its record in combat:

> Recruited as fighting men under ridicule, trained and mustered into service under more ridicule, sent to France as a safe political solution for a volcanic political problem, loaned to the French Army as another easy solution . . . these black fighters lived for 191 days under heavy fire, never lost a foot of ground, and had not a single man captured by the Germans. Unappreciated and scorned when they left these shores [America], France learned to honor them. (Little 1936, 350)

By the end of the war, 170 men from the unit had been awarded the Croix de Guerre for gallantry, and fifteen had received the Distinguished Service Cross. More significantly, the 369th Infantry was awarded a regimental Croix de Guerre for its actions in the French Champagne offensive of September and October 1918.

The signal action of the 369th Infantry did not take place in a major offensive but rather involved just two men on a dark spring night. Early in the morning of 16 May 1918, Sergeant Henry Johnson and Private Needham Roberts were standing watch over a quiet section of the line when they were alerted to the quiet sound of wire-cutters in no-man's-land. Sergeant Johnson later recounted his story:

Private Henry Johnson and Needham Roberts, respectively, were decorated with the French Croix de Guerre, for putting to flight a band of German raiders in a hand-to-hand grenade fight. Both were members of the 369th Infantry. 21 May 1918. (Bettman/Corbis)

Somewhere around two o'clock I heard the Germans cutting our wire out in front and I called to Roberts. When he came I told him to pass the word to the lieutenant. He had just started off when the snippin' and clippin' of the wires sounded near, so I let go with a hand grenade. There was a yell from a lot of surprised Dutchmen [*sic*] and then they started firing. I hollered to Needham to come back.

A German grenade got Needham in the arm and through the hip. He was too badly wounded to do any fighting, so I told him to lie in the trench and hand me up the grenades. "Keep your nerve," I told him. "All the Dutchmen in the woods are at us, but keep cool and we'll lick 'em."

Roberts crawled into the dugout. Some of the shots got me, one clipped my head, another my lip, another my hand, some in my side and one smashed my left foot so bad that I have a silver plate holding it up now.

The Germans came from all sides. Roberts kept handing me the grenades and I kept throwing them and the Dutchmen kept squealing, but jes' the same they kept comin' on. When the grenades were all gone I started in with my rifle. That was all right until I shoved in an American cartridge clip—it was a French gun—and it jammed.

There was nothing to do but use my rifle as a club and jump into them. I banged them on the dome and the side and everywhere I could land until the butt of my rifle busted. One of the Germans hollered, "Rush him! Rush him!" I decided to do some rushing myself. I grabbed my French bolo knife and slashed in a million directions. Each slash meant something, believe me. I wasn't doing exercises, let me tell you.

I picked out an officer, a lieutenant I guess he was. I got him and I got some more of them. They knocked me around considerable and whanged me on the head, but I always managed to get back on my feet. There was one guy that bothered me. He climbed on my back and I had some job shaking him off and pitching him over the head. Then I stuck him in the ribs with the bolo. I stuck one guy in the stomach and he yelled in good New York talk: "That black _____ got me."

I was still banging them when my crowd came up and saved me and beat the Germans off. That fight lasted about an hour. That's about all. There wasn't so much to it. (quoted in Sweeney 1970, 147)

Dawn revealed four dead Germans laid out in Johnson's and Robert's hole, with evidence of at least thirty having been carried off by the retreating Germans. For holding off the raiding party, the two men were awarded the Croix de Guerre. Johnson also received the Gold Palm. Their actions were chronicled widely in the press. The 24 May 1918 edition of *Stars and Stripes* announced in bold type: "Two Black Yanks Smear 24 Huns; Big Secret Out. Station Porter and Elevator Boy Win Croix de Guerre." The article continued:

Their decoration let one of the darkest cats out of the A.E.F. bag. For some time past, a black American unit has been part and parcel of the French Army, eventually taking over front line trenches. The secret has been so well kept that only a few of the all-wise at G.H.Q. had even a suspicion, and the negroes themselves have been so completely absorbed that a German scout would have to come within ear-shot and be something of a linguist to be able to report that the terrifying *soldats noirs* in that sector were not the long-familiar French Colonials from down Morocco way.

Now the secret is out and all the testimony from the French commanders and from the French folk of the village where they have been billeted is in praise of the *soldats noirs de l'Amerique*. They know what it is to go over the top, to drop into the German trenches under barrage and emerge with prisoners, to scour no-man's-land every night even up to the Boche wire. There is nothing about no-man's-land they don't know, and it is their favorite joke and their great pride that unlike the white patrols, they do not have to make-up their tell-tale faces with lamp black before venturing on these excursions. (*Stars and Stripes*, 24 May 1918, 1).

The other three infantry regiments of the 93rd Infantry Division enjoyed similar success under French command. The 370th Infantry Regiment was attached to two French outfits, first the 73rd Infantry Division, and later the 59th Infantry Division. Called *Schwarze Teufel* ("Black Devils") by the Germans, and *Les Perdrix* ("The Partridges") by the French, the men of the 370th were well respected by both sides from the time they entered the line during the summer near the Saint Mihiel salient. The 370th took part in the last combat engagement of the war. Ten minutes after the Armistice was announced a small party of the 370th Infantry conducted a raid against the Germans, capturing fifty wagons.

The 371st and 372nd Infantry Regiments enjoyed similar reputations, gained at terrible cost. In the final week of September 1918, these regiments were attached to the reserve of "The Red Hand" (the 157th Infantry Division) before its assault on Ripont in support of the Meuse-Argonne offensive. After a long and hazardous overnight journey past the dead and wounded of the past two days' fighting, they jumped off at 6:45 A.M. on 28 September. Their target was the heavily defended Hill 188, one of the redoubts in the vaunted Hindenburg Line. Private James P. McKinney of Headquarters Company, 371st Regiment, described the fighting:

The day we went over the top we took our positions early in the morning and waited until our barrage had smashed the German defenses pretty well. About the time our barrage lifted, the Huns sent over a counter-barrage, but we went right through it and over the slopes commanded by their machine guns. They turned loose everything they had to offer, and the storm of lead and steel got a lot of our men. A few of the Germans tried to fight with the bayonet. A few feints and then the deathstroke was the rule. Most of the Huns quit as soon as we got at them. Even the ones that had been on the machine guns yelled for us to spare them. I guess in the excitement some of them fared poorly. (quoted in Scipio 1985, 83)

After five hours advancing under heavy fire, the men of the 371st took Hill 188. They got no rest, however; eight days of relentless advance against the Germans followed before they were relieved. During that time, the two regiments took at least three key towns and defended their gains against repeated German counterattack, suffering more than 1,400 casualties in the process.

After redeploying to the quieter Vosges sector of the front and some rest and refitting, the regiments returned to the field for the next big push. Just as they got ready to go, on 11 November 1918, word came of the Armistice. Lieutenant Bardin recalled the feeling:

After having spent several glorious days in Paris, I returned to join the Division down in Alsace. I had started up the mountain side before dawn on the morning of November 11th, 1918, hearing continuous firing up where we knew my Regiment was, from some bends in the roads we could see the smoke from shells as they exploded. We felt sure there was an attack on in our front. Just then a French officer rode as hard as he could up the mountain, stopped and told us that the Armistice had been signed. No more firing after 11 a.m. Was it a thrill when we reached our companies [and] we found the order was true and the battle we expected to take part in was only the Germans destroying hand grenades and shells before evacuating? (Scipio 1985, 95)

Their war over, the soldiers of the 92nd and 93rd Divisions returned to American control. They were immediately reminded of their status as second-class citizens. General Pershing's staff set about scheduling their return to the United States with exceptional haste, fearing the effect of their continued deployment among a French population indifferent to the racial question. They boarded transports bound for Hoboken in January and February 1919. Their reception was mixed. The 369th—the Harlem Hellfighters—were feted with a parade up Fifth Avenue; the other regiments went quietly out of service.

Despite the record of African Americans in the fighting, the First World War proved to be a disappointment for African Americans who hoped that selfless participation in the war effort would open the way for greater equality and respect at home. At every turn in training and in active service, black soldiers were abused, insulted, and misused. White officers assigned to lead black combat and labor units were frequently more engaged in preserving peacetime racial inequality and preventing their soldiers from developing a greater sense of self-respect and self-reliance. The Wilson administration did little to deflect racial intolerance in the military, opting instead to preserve the status quo. With the fighting over, all of the contributions and sacrifices made by the African-American community were quickly forgotten. If anything, World War I fostered an increase in racial intolerance. The renewed rise of the Ku Klux Klan immediately after the war can be seen as a reaction by bigoted whites to the perception of a rising level of empowerment among blacks after the war.

—Bob Wintermute

References and Further Reading

American Battle Monuments Commission. 1938. *American Armies and Battlefields in Europe: A History, Guide, and Reference Book.* Washington, DC: Government Printing Office.

Bullard, Robert Lee. 1925. *Personalities and Reminiscences of the War.* Garden City, NJ: Doubleday, Page, and Company.

Harris, Stephen L. 2003. *Harlem's Hellfighters: The African-American 369th Infantry in World War I.* Washington, DC: Brassey's Inc.

Keene, Jennifer D. 2001. *Doughboys, the Great War, and the Remaking of America.* Baltimore and London: Johns Hopkins University Press.

Little, Arthur W. 1936. *From Harlem to the Rhine: The Story of New York's Colored Volunteers.* New York: Covici Friede.

Pershing, John J. 1931. *My Experiences in the World War.* New York: Frederick A. Stokes Company.

Roberts, Frank E. 2004. *The American Foreign Legion: Black Soldiers of the 93rd in World War I.* Annapolis, MD: Naval Institute Press.

Scipio, Albert L. 1985. *With the Red Hand Division: The Black American Regiments in the French 157th Division.* Silver Spring, MD: Roman Publications.

Scott, Emmett J. 1969. *Scott's Official History of the American Negro in the World War.* New York: Arno and *New York Times.*

Sweeney, W. Allison. 1970. *History of the American Negro in the Great World War.* New York: Johnson Reprint Corporation.

U.S. Army War College. 1918. 1923. *The Ninety-Second Division, 1917–1918: An Analytical Study.* Washington Barracks, DC: Army War College.

"OVER THE DIRTY WATERS"

The Experience of
British Indians in World War I

———————— ◆ ————————

WHEN THE FIRST WORLD WAR ERUPTED, the leaders of the British government had no real thought of bringing the forces of its large empire to bear. It quickly became apparent, however, that they had no choice. The German army had pushed almost to Paris, and though British and French counterattacks reduced German gains, it was clear that the war would not end quickly. By the end of September 1914, all the forces on the western front were digging the ditches that presaged the trench systems of the next four years. If Britain wanted to stay in the fight, it needed soldiers who were equipped, trained, and ready to be thrown into the conflict. It had those soldiers in the Indian army.

Most Indian groups sprang to Britain's aid. This was no surprise for the princely states, but even nationalist leaders such as Mohandas K. Gandhi pledged their support for the British war effort. Money, supplies, and men poured into the British coffers. In London, Gandhi—then a lawyer—and his fellow Indian residents formed the Indian Voluntary Aid Contingent to give medical help in the conflict. The *Lahore Times* wrote,

Postcard of the cavalry of the army of India in France. (Rykoff Collection/Corbis)

We are prepared to make these sacrifices and more at the proper time. . . . If any troops are to leave this country for active warfare in Europe, let Indian as well as British soldiers be sent without distinction of race and creed to serve side by side in defense of our united cause. (Visram 1989, 17)

On 8 August 1914, therefore, only a few days after Britain had declared war, the Lahore and Meerut infantry divisions, with 16,000 British and 28,000 Indian soldiers, loaded on troopships and sailed for France to reinforce the British Expeditionary Force (BEF). After standing on the defensive through the winter of 1914–1915, the Indians moved to the offensive in March 1915 as part of a major attack by the British at Neuve Chapelle. The attack met with some success but also incurred heavy casualties. The Indian divisions remained in the line in France for several months until they were pulled out in the fall and sent to the Middle East, where they made up the core of a British force fighting the Ottomans. After that move, although Indian cavalry units remained in France, the preponderance of Indian forces fought in the Middle East and helped the British eventually overwhelm Ottoman forces there.

The Indian army was an imperial army designed to keep the peace in India itself and to garrison and defend the Northwest Frontier of India, where the Russian Empire loomed. Like the British army, it was a career, long-service army of professional soldiers; also like the British army, it was a small army. It had not fought in a major war for decades. At its core was a force of Indian soldiers, known as sepoys, with a reinforced spine of British units. The larger share of those British units had been in the Indian army only since 1857, when a mutiny by the native Indian soldiers had almost upset Britain's dominance. The British soldiers were thus both comrades-in-arms and watchful guardians. To emphasize the subordinate position of the Indians, the Indian soldiers were armed with weapons a generation old, and officers in the Indian army drew their authority from the viceroy of India, not the monarch of England. Seemingly a small difference, in reality it meant everything, as those officers were not considered the equals of officers in the British army back home.

To refer to the sepoys as "Indian" soldiers, however, would be a mistake. They were less Indian soldiers than soldiers of various tribes, castes, and religions, specially chosen by the British to be warriors. These so-called martial races were believed to be more aggressive and more warlike than the ordinary Indian. Only some of the martial races were actually races. Gurhkas were a separate tribe, as were Dogras. Some, like the Sikhs, were part of a religious sect. The forces that ended up on the western front came largely from the Punjab and were mostly Sikhs and Muslims.

They were organized into units by caste or class and were commanded by British officers. They did not think themselves Indian. Late in 1914, one sepoy teasingly mocked his British officer by telling him, "If the Germans allied themselves with us Afridis we could lick the world" (Greenhut 1983, 57). Another spoke of the honor that had accrued and would continue to do so through good service, not to India, but to his caste, the Jats: "Nowadays, the officers and men who go to England hear praise of the Jats from the lips of great men, and it is our duty to show that we are worthy of the praise" (VanKoski 1995, 46).

Thus, the sepoys lived in several worlds. For those who conceived of India as a nation, the sepoys were Indian soldiers, representing the larger nation abroad. For others they were representatives of their class, caste, race, or religion. For the British, they were at once soldiers and imperial subjects, and they stood in contrast and comparison not only to their German and Ottoman enemies but also to the British themselves. The sepoys, the British thought, should defeat their enemies, but in so doing, they should not surpass their allies.

Whatever symbolic roles may have been assigned to the sepoys, they were also men, and young men at that. They had volunteered for service in their homeland for a kind of war they understood and for a kind of honor they understood. Like so many soldiers in 1914, they were sent to places they did not know, to fight a war they did not understand, for an honor that, as the war stretched ever on, was increasingly unforeseeable.

The sepoys fought to understand this new world, and they fought to survive in it. They sought to explain it to those at home, through letters mostly—some 10,000 to 20,000 a week in 1915. Because most sepoys were illiterate, they relied on scribes who, for a small fee, would write their letters for them. They knew that censors were reading their letters; one soldier admonished his chatty wife to "never write again such things in your letters as before. . . .Our letters are read before they reach us, and if such things are written in a man's letters, it is not well for him" (VanKoski 1995, 49).

Their words and attitudes may have been shaped by this knowledge, though they showed a curious innocence about it. One sepoy wrote a friend to chastise him for mentioning that he was sending opium to the sepoy because letters both ways were read. The sepoy then went on to say that "when you send opium, you should mention it, but say that you are sending a preparation for the beard." Needless to say, the censor inked out this part of the letter (VanKoski 1995, 47–48). The records of their views are thus fragmentary, seen through the lenses of scribe and censor.

Arrival in France was a shock. When the sepoys arrived in Marseilles, they were "showered with flowers" by the locals (Visram 1989, 18). General Willcocks, the commander of the Indian corps, reported to Sir John French, the British Expeditionary Force's head, that "The condition, health and spirit of Indian troops now in France is excellent, and all are eager for the war" (Greenhut 1983, 62).

Desperate to hold the line against the Germans, the British high command immediately thrust them into the line around Saint Omer. They reached their positions in the trenches in October 1914 and were thrown into the fighting. The war was far different from the frontier wars they were

Indian troops marching through France, 1914. (Bettman/Corbis)

accustomed to and prepared for in its violence and requirements. Like the rest of the BEF and the French army, the Indians suffered substantial casualties almost immediately.

They nonetheless earned the respect of both the Germans and the British. One German soldier spoke of being attacked by the Indians thus:

> The devil knows those brown rascals are not to be underrated. At first, we spoke with contempt of the Indians. Today, we learned to look at them in a different light. . . . Thousands of these brown forms rushed upon us as suddenly as if they were shot out of a fog. . . . In no time, they were in our trenches, and truly these brown enemies were not to be despised. With butt ends and bayonets, swords and daggers we fought each other, and we had bitter hard work. (Visram 1989, 18)

An English soldier echoed the German's words. "They fight like tigers," he said of the Indian soldiers (Visram 1989, 18). Some Indian soldiers knew it. They had suffered heavy casualties, but they had proven themselves. A bit of swagger crept in: "What are the Germans in the face of Indian troops? They do nothing but run away in front of us" (Visram 1989, 23).

The fighting ate away at the strength of the Indian units. On average, each Indian unit had lost 200 men by the beginning of November. Some units had lost much more than that; the 47th Sikhs were down to 385 men (out of 764), and the 58th Rifles could muster only 461 (Greenhut 1983, 56).

The French climate also sapped the strength of the sepoys. The bitter winter of 1914 was, for most Indian soldiers, their first experience with snow, ice, and cold. "The cold here is intense, and it rains every day. The wind is terrible and the water is very cold," wrote Muhammad Ali Khan, a Punjabi (Omissi 1999, 121).

Morale plummeted along with the temperature. "May the dear God be merciful and release me from the climate of this country. . . . It is difficult to endure the trials of winter," one sepoy wrote home (Visram 1989, 23). When General Douglas Haig visited the Indian corps on 29 November 1914, he noted "an air of dejection and despondency" (Greenhut 1983, 59). This did not surprise Haig's chief of intelligence, Brigadier-General Charteris. With a typical sense of imperial superiority, he noted of the Indians:

> They are not, of course, as good or nearly as good as British troops. How could they be? If they were, we could not have held India with the small forces we have there. This kind of fighting is quite new to them. They have not been trained for it.(Greenhut 1983, 60)

One result of this lack of preparation and poor morale was an increasing number of self-inflicted wounds. Individual sepoys took to shooting themselves in the left hand in order to get out of the trenches. By 9 November 1914, more than a thousand men had been admitted to hospital with wounds of the hand. The 47th Sikhs and the 129th Baluchis led the way, with 479 and 318 hand wounds, respectively (Greenhut 1983, 57).

At first the British did not realize what was happening. Officials wondered whether there was perhaps a cultural difference that might cause the Indians to be wounded in the hand more frequently than British soldiers. They soon realized what was afoot though, and warned medical officers to be on the lookout for such self-inflicted wounds. There was, however, an imperial silver lining in this for the British, as Austen Chamberlain, a government minister, explained: "One cannot help wishing that the Indian troops could stand the strain of modern warfare better, and yet there is some compensation in the thought that British superiority is as marked as ever" (Martin 1986, 101).

Still, when the spring of 1915 came, the Indian corps were involved in the first major and concerted British push of the war, the attack at Neuve Chapelle. Originally mounted as a way to distract the Germans from an impending French offensive, the Battle of Neuve Chapelle, launched on 10 March 1915, was marked by a successful penetration of the German lines that was only contained when a combination of German stubbornness and less-than-rapid reinforcement on the British side held up the attackers. The battle petered out with the British having recaptured a bit more territory, but with the lines in essentially the same position as they had been at the end of 1914. The 47th Sikhs lost 575 officers and other ranks in two days of fighting. This was the worst, but other units were not far behind.

Those who survived, however, left a record not of bitter resentment but one that reflects a curious mixture of fascination, gratitude, and confusion. Living in France itself was strange. The sepoys may not have served in their home provinces during their earlier service in India, but they had at least found familiar religions, customs, and languages. France provided none of these.

The sepoy reaction to this strangeness was, for many, attraction rather than repulsion. Many found themselves in love with France. There was, for one sepoy, "no country like the country of France"(Visram 1989, 24). This extended to such things as farming methods. Many of the sepoys had come from rural areas of India, and French agricultural techniques drew their attention and admiration.

French women, however, fascinated the sepoys perhaps most of all and, despite some fear of the reaction of the French to interracial relationships, the soldiers seemed to have chased and won a fair number of women. "If you want any French women, there are plenty here, and they are very good looking. If you really want any I can send one to you in a parcel," wrote Umed Sing Bist, a Gurkha, to a friend at home (Omissi 1999, 123). A veterinary assistant named Chattar Singh, it was reported by the censor, went not a day for several months without a letter from local women (VanKoski 1995, 51). Another sepoy wrote to a friend at home about the opportunities for a soldier on leave:

In every village there are four or five hotels, and each of these today is an
ample realization of the paradise of which we have read in books and heard
from Mullahs. . . . I send you a picture of a girl. When you see it, you will understand what beauty there is in France. (VanKoski 1995, 51)

Besides the obvious, relationships had their advantages for the Indian soldiers, as one recounted: "Remion, Marguerite, and Nini . . . send their
greetings. I am lying on a bed in their house, and I have learnt French very
well" (VanKoski 1995, 51).

French women provided comfort for the soldiers on levels other than
physical, though, and vice versa. One sepoy on leave, for instance, was
lodged in the home of a French mother whose sons were dead, wounded, or
fighting at the time. She welcomed him graciously and for the brief period
of time that he was there, acted as mother to him while he acted as a son to
her. When he left, the separation was perhaps as painful as any between a
real mother and son. He wrote later: "When we had to leave that village, the
old lady wept on my shoulder. Strange that I had never seen her weeping for
her dead son and yet she should weep for me" (VanKoski 1995, 52).

Other sepoys expressed similar admiration for the continued endurance
of the French women. "They brace themselves up and show greater pluck
even than the men. . . . My mother and wives ought to show courage like
this," another noted (VanKoski 1995, 52).

In this way and many others, the experience of living in France made
them question life in India. The modernity of European technology and society made some sepoys look back at their home and despair at its poverty
and lack of progress. As one soldier noted thoughtfully,

When the English call us uncivilized they are right; our philosophy, our religion, and our morality, what has it done for us? It has merely made us the
slaves of others. When the spirit of man is destroyed it cannot be called civilization. (Visram 1989, 24)

France seemed the home of equality and liberty, much superior to India.
In a sentiment that might well have made a lower-class European smile in disbelief, some Indians wrote home lauding the equality of European society:

I was utterly disgusted to learn that the Indians can be ashamed of traveling
in the same compartment with their fellow countrymen! What progress can

you expect in a people like this! God has made all creatures equal. . . . In Europe, [the people] are all one and sympathize with each other. . . . Here, labor is not a disgrace, but a glory. (Visram 1989, 24)

To Indian eyes, the French lived graciously and were superior to the Indians. Not, as perhaps the British and French might insist, through natural inborn merit, but through virtue of their behavior. Wrote one sepoy, "The people here do not get blind drunk as they do in India. In the smallest villages there are schools in which boys and girls are taught. Women work in just the same way as men" (VanKoski 1995, 53).

Behavior made civilization, and behavior—the sepoys thought—could be changed through education. As one soldier put it, the French "appear to be superior to us solely because of education" (VanKoski 1995, 53). This was particularly the case concerning women. "When I look at Europe," one sepoy wrote, "I bewail the lot of India. In Europe, everyone, man and woman, boys and girls, are educated. . . . [India] ought to educate your girls as well as your boys and our posterity" (VanKoski 1995, 52–53).

Not every Indian soldier saw it that way, of course. For some sepoys, France seemed largely unreal, so distant was it from their experience. A sepoy named Pokhar Das wrote home to his brother, a soldier who had been sent back to India: "You are indeed fortunate that you have reached home. There is no doubt that Fairyland is here, and there are many to console us, still our hearts are disturbed. From your dear brother who is solitary and alone in Fairyland" (VanKoski 1995, 46–47).

Religion presented a particular problem for the sepoys living in France. They found French Christianity strange, and they found it difficult to keep to their own religious practices, whether Hindu, Muslim, Sikh, or other. Something as simple as eating in private, as Hinduism required, was nearly impossible in the conditions of the trenches. On a more dangerous level, later in the war, Sikhs had to decide whether to wear their turbans, as their religions required, or don the steel helmets upon which the army insisted.

In such difficult situations, the sepoys held on to what they could. Religious celebrations were treated with great seriousness, a fact that British officers frequently recognized, as Ghufran Khan wrote on 4 August 1915: "Colonel Southey Sahib . . . has made excellent arrangements [for Ramadan] and takes great trouble for us Muslims. His arrangements for our food during the fast are very good. . . . I cannot describe how good his arrangements have been" (Omissi 1999, 88).

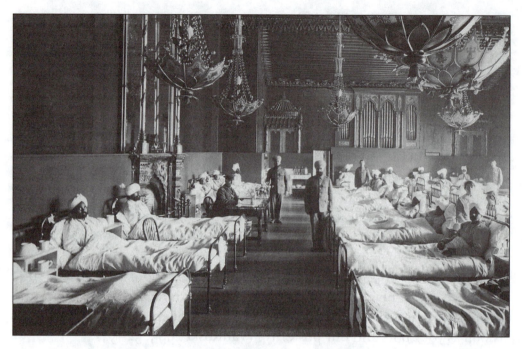

Injured Indian soldiers of the British Army at the Brighton Pavilion, converted into a military hospital, 1915. (Hulton Archive/Getty Images)

Food, in fact, was not as much of a problem as it might have been. The Indian government saw to it that soldiers of the various religions were provided with the proper diet. Sepoys often had to go to great lengths, however, to get and keep personal religious artifacts and holy books, such as the Koran. A Pathan's letter from October 1915 provides a stirring example:

> By all means get me a Holy Qu'ran of the same pattern as your own, even if it costs ten rupees, and send it to me. You can send it by the hand of any man who is coming to the front, or by parcel post. . . . Make every effort to get me a Holy Qu'ran. Never mind the price; I will pay it.(Omissi 1999, 116)

Such measures were required more frequently as the sepoy presence in Europe lengthened. Even as the Indians fought on the western front, a tiny village of Indians was growing up in England itself. Wounded Indian soldiers were treated by the Indian Voluntary Aid Detachment organized by Gandhi and by Indian medical personnel brought in from India. They formed a small enclave of India itself in the city of Brighton, on the south coast of England. King George set aside the Royal Pavilion at Brighton to serve as the hospital, and there Indians encountered their imperial masters with less of the pomp and ritual than in India.

The British—perhaps to undercut the nationalist independence movement, perhaps to encourage continued cooperation, or perhaps out of simple respect for those fighting alongside them—showed particular care for the soldiers. Within the hospital they created nine kitchens, each dedicated to a specific dietary pattern of different Indian soldiers, whether Hindu, Muslim, high caste, low caste, or no caste. The king and queen, among other royal personages, paid the Indian patients visits. "Yesterday," one wounded sepoy wrote, "some Royal princesses came from London to see us. They spoke to each one and treated us kindly as if we had been their children" (VanKoski 1995, 54).

When the soldiers were recovered enough to move about, they were often taken—in groups of twenty-four—on driving tours of London, and shown the sites and sights of British imperial splendor: Buckingham Palace, Trafalgar Square, the Tower of London, and more. As one of the tour guides wrote,

> One is able, while giving them a pleasant day, so to direct their attention and with it their minds that they obtain an impression of England's greatness, wealth, and power . . . [which] will also through them, react on other Indians of their class.(Visram 1989, 21)

The sepoys were perhaps not as impressed, however, with the imperial splendor as the British might have hoped. One sepoy wrote home to sum up his experience of England: "[They] have their food cooked by gas and electricity. Sanitation is excellent, and you never see flies or mosquitoes. There is any amount of milk. The people of the country are most friendly. What more can I say?" (VanKoski 1995, 55).

While this would have sorely disappointed the Buckingham Palace tour guides, the ordinary English life could be beguiling to the Indians. Some found it superior to what they had waiting at home. "Here there is neither thievery nor lying. Further, whatever one man wants . . . he can buy from another," wrote Natha Singh. Because of this, Jagindar Singh decided that "I really do not want to leave this place and come back to India, because this country of our king is a very beautiful one and all the people are learned"(VanKoski 1995, 56).

He was not alone in this feeling. Another sepoy wrote to his family, "We mean to live and die in this country. . . .We have no intention of returning to India. . . . When the victory comes, I intend to live in this country. I never even dream of India. My heart is quite estranged from it" (VanKoski 1995, 56).

At the same time, this Indian enclave created problems for the British. They had long run their empire on a strict exclusionary principle, which limited the native peoples to their spheres, ruled over, by not touched by, the British sphere. Now there were Indian sepoys, wounded in a battle to protect Britain itself, recovering on British soil. They could still be treated as imperial subjects and subject to a barrage of the evidence of imperial greatness, but even the simple question of whether to have them treated by British nurses sent the high command into a state of confusion.

At first, the British adhered to the idea of, as the commander-in-chief of British forces in India put it, "no nurses for Indians." As part of the campaign to show equal treatment for all soldiers of the empire, however, that was not sustainable, and eventually the British put some nurses into the Indian wards (Visram 1989, 21).

The British nonetheless remained obsessed with controlling the Indians. They wanted to treat them as regular British soldiers, but only in places and at times that the British themselves decided. The hospital at Brighton Pavilion was surrounded by fences of barbed wire and armed guards. Sepoys were only allowed out if escorted by a British soldier. Further, the British relied on the "very efficient plain clothes police system in Brighton" if the first two lines of defense were breached (Martin 1986, 105).

British administrators were particularly worried about Indian soldiers and British women consorting with each other. As one Indian soldier wrote, "If anyone is seen talking to a woman, young or old, he is severely punished" (Visram 1989, 22). This was despite the fact that as Sir Walter Lawrence, Kitchener's special commissioner for the Indian hospitals, reported, the "convalescents who are allowed out for exercise have behaved themselves like gentlemen" (Martin 1986, 111).

The Indians protested this treatment bitterly. They were the king's soldiers, they had traveled long distances to fight for that king, and they had been wounded in his cause. Yet now they were treated almost as prisoners. An Indian subassistant surgeon named J. H. Godbole wrote a letter of protest, noting that "These men have left their country and came here to die for the sake of the Kingdom," but they are denied the "right to go about." After receiving no satisfactory answer, he found himself a revolver and went to kill the commander of the hospital. He was stopped before he could do so, however, and sent to prison for seven years (Visram 1989, 22).

Yet Godbole was not the only one to be enraged at the double standards the British employed. Another sepoy wrote,

> We took no oath in Europe. We have crossed the seven seas and left our homes and our dear ones and our parents, and for the honor of such an unjust and false-promising King. We have sacrificed our lives. And now this is the honor we get in this Council. No doubt before them we are regarded as inarticulate animals, but who can say that to oppress and dishonor us is good. (Visram 1989, 25)

A convenient solution to this peculiar problem was not long in coming. Neuve Chapelle had been the swan song of the long-service regular army. That force of professionals, already greatly damaged by the inconclusive battles of 1914, was utterly worn down by the assault at Neuve Chapelle. By the end of spring 1915, all the units of the original British Expeditionary Force had been reduced to fading echoes of the units that had come over in 1914, including the Indian corps. The Indian army, despite India's millions in population, could not easily replace those losses. It was a professional force, deliberately limited in size by the British, and one could not simply wave a wand and create trained soldiers. On 1 May 1915, the Indian military headquarters warned that it could not send replacements to France without denuding India itself of soldiers.

Replacing the British junior officers, who had suffered extremely high casualties, was even more difficult. These officers were expected to speak the language of their unit and understand their soldiers' culture. Such men were few and far between in Britain. The obvious solution—to create commissioned Indian officers—was never really a possibility in the British mind. They simply did not believe Indians were capable of being good officers. General Willcocks wrote, on 31 January 1915, that "the Indian is simply not fit to lead his men against Europeans. . . . It is the presence and instincts of the white man which the Indian Officer can *never* replace" (Greenhut 1983, 66).

At the same time, it was now clear to the British that they were in a war that would not soon end, and that the only way it could be fought was by bringing as much of the manpower of the empire to bear as possible. Because of the climate and the difficulty in replacing the heavy casualties in officers and men, the British high command decided to send the Indian forces to the Middle East, a place that was thought to be more welcoming both in culture and in climate. Wounded Indian soldiers could be shipped back to India proper for treatment. It would relieve the pressure on the Indians, and perhaps also relieve the pressures on the British of being properly regal for their subjects.

The sepoys did, for the most part, find the Middle East much more congenial than they had France. Their morale, at least, appeared to hold up better—though this was perhaps as much due to an increased sense of internal community as anything else. Whereas the maximum number of sepoys on the western front was 138,000, more than 675,000 served in Mesopotamia. It was here that India's great manpower pool showed its true depths.

Fighting the Ottomans opened another issue, though, as the sepoys now faced Muslims. For some Indians, these were the traditional foe; for others, however, these were co-religionists. Many Hindu soldiers reacted to their Muslim surroundings with immediate suspicion and dislike. Sowar Jivan Mal, a Jat, wrote to a friend in France,

> The country in which we are encamped is an extremely bad place. . . . All the inhabitants are Muslims and the customs of the country are very evil. There is a great deal of coquetry and their complexion is fair and they are very pretty. They have wicked eyes; at any rate this is true of fifty out of a hundred of them. (Omissi 1999, 120)

Many Muslim sepoys were reluctant to fight their fellow Muslims; they felt the bindings of religion quite strongly. There was often even a sneaking sense of admiration for the Turks. This was heightened because of the contrast of the Ottomans with the Russians—now the Indians' putative ally, but also a prewar bogeyman looming over the Northwest Frontier. As on the eastern front, Russian forces did not always fare well in battle, and the sepoys took note. One wrote:

> We used to hear at home that the King of Russia was a great king. But this one has knocked facts out of him and smashed him and taken much of his country. . . . The Turks smashed and bashed the whole lot, and the losses are very heavy. The Turks are the bravest of all. (Visram 1989, 24)

A fair number of Indian units consequently indicated their reluctance to fight against the Ottomans to their British officers. Some incidents rose to the level of mutinies; most, however, did not.

News reports of the mutinies grieved other Indian soldiers greatly. When one Punjabi Muslim, still in France, heard that the 15th Lancers had refused to attack in the Middle East, he wrote:

> This is the time to show loyalty and give help to the Government and not to be false to one's salt. It was to work for the government and not for disobedience that they girded their loins and left their nearest and dearest. . . . Our duty is loyalty and bravery. (VanKoski 1995, 47)

Another put it more bluntly: "You should not do things of which you will be ashamed afterward" (VanKoski 1995, 47).

The British leadership in Mesopotamia did not use the Indian soldiers effectively at first, though its forces met with initial success. In April 1915, the British shattered a force of Ottomans at Shaiba and secured the main British port of Basra. The very ease of the victory made the British greedy, however, and they pressed the advance along the river valleys with their sepoy units. On 29 September 1915, General Townsend and the 6th (Poona) Division captured the town of Kut, opening the way to Baghdad. The British, looking for a victory to offset the continuing disaster that was the Gallipoli campaign, ordered Townsend to continue his assault.

Townsend advanced his forces to within a day of Baghdad itself, stretching his supply lines greatly in the process. There he was defeated. Though his forces remained intact, they were forced to retreat, with Ottoman forces in pursuit. The British forces ended up in Kut once again, besieged.

A hurriedly assembled relief got to within several days' march but was there hammered by an Ottoman army and forced to retreat. The siege stretched into the new year. The plight of the soldiers in Kut fired other sepoys, many of whom "were hopeful of being sent to join the relieving force," as Gunga Singh, a cavalryman in Lucknow wrote (Omissi 1999, 178). On 29 April 1916, however, Townsend surrendered his forces. "The one bright spot," the Mesopotamian Commission's later report said, "was the bearing of the troops" (Latter 1994, 100). Risalder-Major Kalander Khan Bahadur agreed with that later conclusion, writing on 5 May 1916, "They fought to the last with the greatest gallantry. . . . It was a great grief to all that relief could not reach them and that all our efforts were in vain" (Omissi 1999, 181).

The captured troops—around 13,000 men—were quickly marched northward by the Turks. Their captors had little in the way of food and supplies for themselves, let alone for their prisoners, and hundreds, if not thousands, of sepoys died along the way. The survivors eventually wound up in Turkey. Townsend was assigned to live at a villa by the sea, and his wife and family were allowed to join him. In contrast, the sepoys were used as forced labor, with the Muslims among them offered blandishments to join the Ottoman side. Some did, but most remained loyal.

Even in the Middle East though, away from the slaughter of the western front, the sepoys grew tired of the war. Durga Prasad of the 16th Cavalry wrote to his uncle in France that his "constant wish is that God will put a stop to this bloody war, and bring back the days of peace." Prasad had no doubt who was at fault. "What evil spirit has possessed the German nation? May God speedily and utterly destroy them" (VanKoski 1995, 45). There was the normal soldierly hope for the "days of peace," but there was, at least in Prasad's mind, no doubting the rightness of his and the empire's cause. This was not an uncommon sentiment. Another sepoy wrote, "Pray that our king and the British Empire may be victorious so that we people in safety and renown may return to our dear country" (VanKoski 1995, 45).

Weary but loyal, the majority of the sepoys soldiered bravely on. Risalder Mir Jafar Khan wrote on 25 April 1916,

> This is my thirty-third year of service, and I am the oldest soldier in the Army in Europe. My youth and old age are given in the service of the government; and if the government can be served with the dust of my bones, it is theirs. . . .
>
> If in this war I were to lose my life for my King . . . I would count it as gain. . . . During a railway journey when two people sit side by side for a couple of hours, one of them feels the absence of the other when he alights: how great then must be the anguish which I feel at the thought of having to sever myself from the regiment! (Omissi 1999, 179, 188–189)

In the same vein, Ganda Singh wrote a friend on 5 May 1916 with a profound sense of necessary martyrdom and of earning his salt:

> This is the time when he who desires to do so may illuminate his name and his clan and country by sacrificing himself. Do you pray in the temple . . . that the enemy may never see my back, but may always be faced by me as by a lion. We soldiers have been fed with money, which we have now to earn, with

our lives if necessary. . . . We must all die some day. It is best that we should die in this great war. (Omissi 1999, 182)

Sham Singh, a Sikh cavalryman in France, wrote of the fighting there in July 1916: "We do not wish the war to stop yet; we want it to continue. In our village, the fair is held once a year only; here there is a continuous fair" (Omissi 1999, 212). Waryam Singh, a private in the Canadian Expeditionary Force who had thus remained in France, even wrote of a major assault in November 1916 with some gusto:

Shells and bullets were falling like rain and one's body trembled to see what was going on. But when the order came to advance and take the enemy's trench, it was wonderful how we all forgot the danger and were filled with extraordinary resolution. We went over like men walking in a procession at a fair, and shouting, we seized the trench and took the enemy prisoner. (VanKoski 1995, 46)

Most sepoys, however, seem to have been more resolute. *Izzat,* or honor, had a lot to do with it. Their sense of patriotism was less, perhaps, than it would be in decades to come, but their sense of personal responsibility—to family, clan, caste, and religion—was powerful indeed. It often drove them to demonstrate their valor and their vigor. Mahomed Mazafar Khan wrote on 21 October 1917 that he was "suffering for one end only—*izzat.* My duty is to help Government and increase the reputation of our family" (Omissi 1999, 328). The loss or gain of *izzat,* after all, was lifelong. As Hoshiar Singh of the 16th Cavalry wrote to a friend in another unit in November 1915,

Remember that the work you do now will gain for you a good name or a bad name, which will last you the rest of your life. . . . You must always bear in mind your own honor and the honor of your family. There is nothing else in life better than honor. (VanKoski 1995, 46)

There was also a sense of the imperial in the Indian consideration of honor. *Izzat* had to be seen and acknowledged to be truly an achievement. Mahomed Usuf Khan, a Punjabi Muslim, spoke of how his achievements would have "illuminated" the family name. Later, he noted that

This is the only opportunity we have had for coming to this European war, and our brothers have shown such bravery in the war that the world rings with praise for them. What we have done [has] impressed not only our King and country, but also . . . our Allies. (Omissi 1999, 182)

There was no more public way of receiving that respect, for most Indians, than being awarded a medal. Sepoys wrote home ecstatically about the experience. Alam Sher Khan, a Punjabi Muslim, started his letter of 22 April 1917 to his father with "Congratulate your servant on having won the 2nd Class of the Indian Order of Merit!" (Omissi 1999, 288). It was a lasting public triumph, though none was more so than the ultimate medal, the Victoria Cross. Bigya Singh wrote in 1915 of a comrade who had won this award, using glowing terms: "One of the Garwhalis, a havildar, has won the honor of the Victoria Cross, and having made the reputation of his family for three generations, has arrived in Lansdowne" (Omissi 1999, 41–42).

Just as they believed that *izzat* could be won through great deeds and could bring honor and prestige not only to the soldier but to his family through several generations, so too did the sepoys believe that cowardly acts could bring public derision and ruin to a soldier and his family. In October 1917, Man Singh, a Sikh, discussed "a matter which I am very loath to write about, which has inflicted a great stain on us." Two of his comrades had failed to keep up their sentry duty and left the unit unprotected. They were summarily court-martialed and sentenced to death (though the sentence was commuted to a year's imprisonment). Singh's verdict on them was that "these two men have disgraced the caste and the squadron" (Omissi 1999, 297).

Some sepoys, though, did not seem to believe in their mission, regardless of honor—a development seen already after the heavy casualties the Indian troops had suffered on the western front. On 20 May 1915, for example, Havildar Abdul Rahman wrote to a friend in a unit still in India:

For God's sake don't come, don't come, don't come to this war in Europe. . . . Tell my brother Muhammad Yakub Khan for God's sake not to enlist. If you have any relatives, my advice is don't let them enlist. . . . Cannons, machine guns, rifles, and bombs are going day and night. . . . Those who have escaped so far are like the few grains left uncooked in a pot. (Omissi 1999, 61)

Rahman was able to send his letter because he was the Indian officer who translated letters for the censor. Yet others also wrote home in something like desperation, hoping for anything to break or loosen the bonds of carnage.

Metaphysical despair was perhaps less common than a quiet war-weariness, an acceptance that death was inevitable and out of the sepoys' control. Kasim Ali Khan wrote a friend on 27 December 1916,

> We think of you with every breath we breathe. Otherwise we are dead, and should not be thought of as living. Death stands before us at all times, even in the shape of shells, bullets and bombs, and by whichever of these means I am destined to die, my life will be extinguished forthwith. (Omissi 1999, 262)

The weary dedication of Hazur Singh, however, may have been closer to their feelings than either elation or utter despair. Singh wrote home in November 1916 that

> I am unlikely to get leave, nor do I wish to go, even if I could succeed in obtaining permission, till the war is finished. Because if I were to go on leave, it would be very hard to return. When I used to go on leave before, I used to be very disinclined to return to the cantonment—how much more disinclined then would I be to return to the war. When I return, I will tell you all about the war. It is impossible to write about it. The war will not be finished before 1918. . . . I have pledged myself not to return (on leave or ill) until I return with the entire regiment. (VanKoski 1995, 48–49)

On the whole, the concerns of the Indians remained resolutely small-scale. The sepoys seem to have thought little of the larger empire, or of Europe, or of the political questions of the war. They knew of, and mostly revered, the king of Britain, but paid little attention to other leaders. Neither of the British prime ministers during the war, Herbert Asquith and David Lloyd George, merited much attention. The single exception was the secretary of state for war, Horatio Kitchener. Kitchener had commanded the Indian army ten years previously, and he remained a revered figure in those circles. When he died in June 1916 on his way to Russia, his ship a victim of a German mine, many sepoys were distressed. One was the Hindu Ghirdari Lal:

We are greatly grieved to hear that our Lord Kitchener has been killed. See how a great man, who has done so much good work for the country, has had to meet death! It is not we only who are grieved, but the entire people of Hindustan are grieved. (Omissi 1999, 195)

Indian minds concentrated not on the world at large, naturally, but on the world they knew: India. The longer the war stretched on, the more the absence from home began to wear on the soldiers. They worried about their families and homes. They worried that their wives were straying while they were gone. "All the women are rampant . . . and the only thing to [do] is to send them out to join their husbands," heard Ghulam Hasain Khan from a friend at home. And Mashsud Mahomed heard from his father Fakir that

Abdul Hamid has given your wife to someone else in Chikar Village. When I heard of this and asked Abdul Hamid for an explanation as to why he had given my son's wife to another, he said, "Take back your [money]. I won't give my sister in marriage to Mashsud because he has gone to war . . . and no one has yet returned alive from that war." (Omissi 1999, 207)

Things were no easier for the wives, parents, and children the sepoys left behind. Their families rarely, if ever, saw them on leave. Most had to wait the long years until the war finished, with only the occasional letter to sustain them. Without their father, husband, or son, families had to figure out how to lead their everyday lives all over again. As the years stretched onward, it became more and more wearing. Nasab Ali Khan's wife wrote to remonstrate in November 1916:

Your mother has gone out of her mind, so I am alone all night. The winter and dark nights are ahead and how can I, a lone woman, stay by myself? . . . You write that you have been made Lance Dafadar. I don't care a rap whether you are made a dafadar. If you were a man, you would understand, but you are no man. (Omissi 1999, 248)

Prayg Singh's wife wrote to him in February 1917:

It is now three years since I was last blessed with your presence—what then must my heart suffer! I am wandering alone in the wilderness of this world. . . . You write to me about money, but what care I for money. I need you alone! (Omissi 1999, 277)

In a sense, Prayg Singh's wife was lucky, for her husband did eventually return home. Many sepoys, of course, did not, and the effect was often devastating, as this mother's letter reveals:

All your letters have come thrusting fresh spears of grief into my heart. . . . The fatal news reached me on the 17th October . . . My dear, only son (for whose sake alone we seven women live) . . . fell in France. Let his body quickly be sent home, that his grave may be made here and we may spend the rest of our lives weeping over it. (Omissi 1999, 118)

Those who did return—as most survivors did quickly when the war ended in November 1918—found a different India. The soldiers who came back could be called, perhaps for the first time, Indian. They had gone to war representatives of a region, a religion, and a caste. Now, many of them returned to a nation. The war also made the veterans feel that they had earned reward from the British. Surely some of that would be individual reward: pensions, property, and respect. As Bishan Singh wrote to his son on 10 April 1916, "Those subjects of the British Government who have served in this war, will, together with their families, certainly be remembered by the Government as to the fulfillment of their rights" (Omissi 1999, 172).

Just as much, however, sepoys expected the reward of independence. The veterans of the war returned to India and demanded something more than to be imperial subjects. In coming years, this would be fertile ground for the recruiting of the newly aggressive Indian National Congress led by Jawaharlal Nehru and Gandhi.

Across the empire and at home, the British government faced the same demands from a range of sources. The Irish argued and fought for independence. The working classes of Britain, who had made up the lion's share of the army, insisted on a land fit for kings to which to return. Women, who had underpinned the home front, demanded the vote. All of these groups in one way or another gained something of what they desired.

India was different. India was the jewel in the crown, the part of the British Empire that justified all the other parts. The British could not give it up; they could not believe that they might have to give it up. In 1917, they had allowed that an Indian government elected by Indians might be permitted to run India's internal affairs, but no more than that.

Sepoy dreams of independence had to endure more bloodshed, including the slaughter at Amritsar in 1919. If, however, the seeds of nationhood had been planted in the late nineteenth century as the British eagerly reorganized a territory into India and trained the natives to run it as such, the first profuse tendrils from those seeds sprouted in 1914–1918. Those years gave rise to the idea that Indians who had fought with and for Britain could no longer be merely subjects. The one unanswerable fact that they could throw in the face of any British politician, officer, or bureaucrat who denied this was: They were India, and they had fought.

—David J. Silbey

References and Further Reading

Farwell, Byron. 1989. *Armies of the Raj: From Mutiny to Independence, 1857–1947.* New York: Norton.

Greenhut, Jeffrey. 1983. "The Imperial Reserve: The Indian Corps on the Western Front, 1914–1915." *Journal of Imperial and Commonwealth History* 12, 1: 54–73.

Latter, Edwin. 1994. "The Indian Army in Mesopotamia." *Journal of the Society for Army Historical Research* 72, 290: 92–102.

Martin, Gregory. 1986. "The Influence of Racial Attitudes on British Policy Towards India during the First World War." *Journal of Imperial and Commonwealth History* 14, 2: 91–113.

Moreman, T. R. 1998. *The Army in India and the Development of Frontier Warfare, 1849–1947.* New York: Norton.

Omissi, David. 1994. *The Sepoy and the Raj: The Indian Army 1860–1940.* London: Macmillan.

———, ed. 1999. *Indian Voices of the Great War: Soldiers' Letters, 1914–1918.* New York: St. Martin's.

VanKoski, Susan. 1995. "Letters Home, 1915–1916: Punjabi Soldiers Reflect on War and Life in Europe and their Meanings for Home and Self." *International Journal of Punjab Studies* 2, 1: 43–63.

Visram, Rozina. 1989. "The First World War and Indian Soldiers." *Indo-British Review* 16, 2: 17–26.

THE WAR ON
THE PERIPHERY

The Experience of

Soldiers Fighting in

European Colonies, 1914–1918

———— ◆ ————

T HE POPULAR MEMORY OF WORLD WAR I largely concerns the western front. The mud and filth of the trenches; the apocalyptic battles of Verdun, the Somme, and Passchendaele; the war poetry of Wilfrid Owen and Robert Graves; the seemingly endless rows of poppies commemorating the waste of a "lost generation"—these are the popular touchstones of the Great War. There were other engagements, of course—Gallipoli figures prominently here—but the armed encounters beyond the western front have for the most part been referred to as "sideshows," confined to chapters on "the periphery" in textbooks on the war. To the people who experienced these "sideshows," however, they were anything but peripheral. The war brought wide-ranging change to the peoples of Africa, the Middle East, and India; disrupting families, villages, and nations; heightening national sentiments; and spreading death and disease. Indeed, the global nature of World War I set it apart from past conflicts as much as did its intensity.

French colonial soldiers at Mudros. Senegalese troops from the French possessions in Africa waiting at Mudros to embark for Gallipoli. (Reynolds, Francis J. and C.W. Taylor. Collier's Photographic History of the European War. *P.F. Collier & Son, New York. 1916)*

Colonial conflict occurred in the main in Africa. German-Allied conflicts occurred in Togoland, the Cameroons, southwest Africa (the modern-day country of Namibia), and German East Africa (the present nation of Tanzania). In the Middle East, British and French armies fought their Turkish enemies (who benefited from German aid) at Gallipoli, in the Arabian desert, on the Sinai Peninsula, and on the vast, windswept steppes of eastern Anatolia and the Caucasus. These battles had little in common save for the fact that they were fought by men who had, by and large, never set foot in Europe. There were few white faces on colonial battlefields during the First World War.

The conflict first came to most colonial peoples through recruitment, a process that took men far away from their families, often never to return. Born of internecine conflict in Europe, the war was difficult for many colonial peoples to understand. They saw little relevance to their own existence and, as a result, did not volunteer in large numbers. This sense of detachment and bewilderment is illustrated by a white Natalian, who recounted a conversation he overheard between two blacks, whom he identified as "A" and "B":

> A—How are things your way?
>
> B—Oh, all right, but there is a lot of talk about the natives the Government wants to go and work over the sea . . .
>
> A—Yes? . . . Why do they want our young men to go and help them?
>
> B—I don't know. I don't know what to think.
>
> A—I thought the white people could not be beaten. Why then do they call upon us to help them?
>
> B—I don't know what to think. Why do the white men want to take them . . . ?
>
> A—I won't go and our people won't go.
>
> B—I hear the white people will . . . take our boys if they don't go.
>
> A—Yes, then if they do that, there is going to be trouble.
>
> B—The white people will humbug us about this.
>
> A—Yes, they are a clever people. (Grundlingh 1987, 72)

Such reticence necessitated recruitment, a practice Europeans pursued with the help of native rulers. As one Nigerian man who was drafted as a carrier remembered,

> We came back one night from our yam farm. The chief called us and handed us over to a Government messenger. . . . After three days we reached the white man's compound. Plenty of others had arrived from other villages far away. The white man wrote our names in a book, tied a brass number round our neck, and gave each man a blanket and food. Then he told us we were going to the great war to help the king's soldiers. The Government police led the way, and allowed no man to stop behind. (Killingray 2001, 429)

Native rulers cooperated with European recruiting efforts out of a sense of self-preservation, as a result of bribes, or out of fear. Whatever their motivations, they helped raise large numbers of "volunteer" armies to prosecute the war in Africa.

Although some men did volunteer out of a sense of adventure, for material gain, or because they were influenced by propaganda from recruiters, most colonial soldiers were in fact pressed into service against their will. As a result, many understandably sought to slip the recruiting noose and escape into the bush. Vmande Kaombe, a Malawian boy, was one such case: "I escaped and hid in a river and my parents, since I had not married yet, secretly brought food to me. They were [asked about my absence] but they said they did not know what had become of me. They even accused the whites for my disappearance"(Page 2000, 50).

Similar tales occurred in British East Africa, especially after Britain's mass levy there in 1917: "After the first [conscription], Waitha fled and lived like a wild animal for the duration of the war in the inaccessible vastnesses of the banks of the Tna River, below Tumutumu Hill. Thence he came out like the hyenas . . . to seek his food and scurry back" (Hodges 1986, 105).

Despite such successes, however, it proved difficult to escape the recruiters' grasp, if only because the administrative structure of colonial governments meant that it was increasingly difficult for people to simply disappear. The work of one Raphael Simigini Osodo, of Bunyala, who served under a Wanga chief who recruited for Britain, illustrated this new reality:

> My work was to record the names of all the people that were . . . sent to war. I did all the correspondence with the Government because I could read and write. Letters used to come to me stating the number of men we were supposed to send. . . . At the beginning of the war the number we were required to produce for war ranged from 50 men to about 150 men; but at one time, about 500 men. . . . Many of these young men used to run away and hide in the trees from us. They would only come down by night for meals when we had gone away. . . . Some were very courageous and just joined without being forced into it. In those days there was a rumour that those who went to the war were eaten by the white men [so no more volunteered]. It was very hard for anyone to escape . . . because I had his name down and knew exactly where he came from.(Hodges 1986, 104)

If African responses to the coming of the war ranged from circumspection to confusion to fear, Indian soldiers, or at least their political spokesmen, were more positive. The Indian press reassured Great Britain that "Now that England is at war with a foreign enemy she may absolutely depend upon the loyalty of the people of this country. They may have their grievances, they may have their differences with the Government, but they are firmly attached to British rule" (Sydenham 1915, 58).

Such support, however, also reflected Indians' burgeoning sense of national identity. The *Lahore Tribune* wrote, "Let there be no question of 'prestige' or the inadvisability of employing brown against white soldiers. Prestige must be based on conduct and on no other considerations" (55).

Colonial troops served in two main roles: active and auxiliary service. Though some aspects of this service mirrored that of soldiers in Europe, the colonial perspective was different because of the issue of race. European views of colonial troops to a degree shaped how and where those troops were used during the war, and colonial peoples in turn came into contact with a world much broader than most had previously known. In practice, though, the demarcations between soldiers and their support services were often blurred; no distinctions were made, to be sure, when casualties were taken.

The war in the colonies was one of sheer physical endurance. If soldiers in Europe were forced to accustom themselves to a static war, almost becoming themselves part of the landscape, soldiers in Africa were cast into a mobile war. Allied recruits and German *askaris* fought campaigns that swept across the vast expanses of East Africa, the desert of southwest Africa, and the jungles of the Cameroons. The experience of the men serving under the German general Paul von Lettow-Vorbeck was a quintessential case in point. Though the general never had more than about 14,000–15,000 men under his command, he kept his enemies occupied by being constantly on the move (Tucker 1998, 193). After raiding the British territories of Uganda and Kenya, confronting the British on Lake Victoria, and repulsing the attempted Allied landing at Tanga—a port on the Indian Ocean—Lettow-Vorbeck took his men into the interior. They alternately harassed, pursued, and fled from Allied troops for the rest of the war. When his forces finally surrendered, two weeks *after* the war ended in Europe, they were in northern Rhodesia.

Because colonial armies were not well supplied with transport vehicles, all of this movement was carried out by forced march, usually under a searing sun. Unsurprisingly, the forced march figures prominently in colonial troops' experience of the war. One gets a sense of the physical and psychological struggle they endured in this Malawian marching song:

> *When I die, bury me at Zomba*
> *So that my heart should pain.*
> *Hunger, hunger is painful.*
> *Yes, when I die, bury me at Zomba,*

So that my heart should pain.
Hunger, yes, hunger is painful.
When I die, when I die,
Bury me at Zomba.
There rest my soul.
Hunger, I feel hungry.

In Africa, men always fought at the behest of the climate and terrain. Europeans found these factors particularly troublesome. Extremes of heat and cold took their toll, as did disease. The latter was spread above all by the dreaded tsetse fly, a common enemy for all colonial troops. Francis Brett Young, a Rhodesian officer serving in East Africa, described the travails of fighting a war while battling heat and dust:

> In the middle of the day, when there was no shelter from the vertical sun, the air above the sandy flats swam with heat, and the dust from our moving cavalcade dried upon our faces and parched our lips. I think that we felt the heat less than did our cattle. (Brett Young 1938, 50–51)

The horrors of war provided a stark contrast to the physical beauty of the land itself. Brett Young spelled this out when he described the dominant sights and smells of the battlefield: a combination of the dwarf scrub, "dusty purple flowers [that] spreads all over this inhospitable heart of Africa," iodine, and blood (Brett Young 1938, 42). A war of movement was made that much more difficult under such conditions.

If the forced march was an awful physical ordeal, it was often made worse by a deep hunger caused by lack of resources. The men on the Rufiji River in 1917, it was said, looked like "a collection of heart-broken skeletons" (Osuntokun 1979, 255). It also, however, gave rise to a heightened sense of group camaraderie and morale. The King's African Rifles (KAR), the main British armed contingent in East Africa, were notable for such a sense of collective identity. One KAR marching song highlights the group bonds that developed in the line:

The Big Bwanas
Stop away behind
We others have fighting and hunger

What kind of business is this?
The Portuguese are no good
When they hear a shot they run
Nor will they stop
Until they reach the sea
The KAR askaris
Are fierce to fight
But go carefully
There are lions [Germans] in the bush. (Miller 1974, 317)

Real lions were an occasional menace to troops in the bush, but it was the presence of the enemy that most occupied men's minds.

Though trench combat did occasionally occur, such as at the Rufiji front in 1917, the African war was one of movement and surprise. This meant that the actual fighting tended to be sporadic and reactive. The encounter of one Baluchi force with a German redoubt was typical:

As usual, when our forces stumbled on a prepared position in the bush—and indeed the first evidence of its existence was generally a burst of maxim fire—they had lost heavily in the first minute. There was no way out of it; these were losses which were inherent in the type of warfare and not to be avoided. (Brett Young 1938, 136)

Even when combat could be anticipated, colonial soldiers were often forced to fight in ways quite foreign to them. Nowhere was this fact more apparent than in regard to technology. As Young noted, "Even in this bush warfare, where man, one would think, is matched against single man, the machine-gun has become the most important weapon" (Brett Young 1938, 214).

The use of airplanes, a new tool Europeans turned to especially in Africa as a means of coping with a war over such vast distances, proved particularly troubling to many colonial troops. The usual reaction was a mix of fear and awe, as was clear in the interrogation of one captured German *askari* by the British. General Jan Smuts's chief of staff recorded that:

He [the prisoner] says that when they see "the bird" coming they run for their lives into the bush. The askaris who drag the big guns about are chained to them for that reason. . . . He says this Lukiguru River is full of crocodiles, but they'd go into that to get away from "the bird." . . . You see it isn't merely physical terror. They think it is magic. (Brett Young 1938, 224)

Alongside the fact that most colonial troops were forced into service, the fear attendant to war meant that maintaining discipline was a priority for European officers. The Germans' *askari* tended to be more loyal because General Lettow-Vorbeck and his subordinates treated their men better. It also did not hurt that much of the actual fighting occurred on the lands of these men, as this fostered a sense of self-preservation.

The Allies—particularly the British—had a more difficult time maintaining order and cohesion. After their initial successes in Togoland and the Cameroons, the British were reticent to use their West African troops against the Germans in East Africa, fearing that battle-hardened men would revolt. As a colonial office staff note put it, "It must not be forgotten that a West African native trained to the use of arms and filled with a new degree of self-confidence by successful encounters with forces armed and led by Europeans was not likely to be more amenable to discipline than in peace time" (Osuntokun 1979, 238).

As with their European counterparts serving in the trenches, colonial soldiers were not, officially, to be motivated by force. Unofficially, however, colonial soldiers were often disciplined by the sjambok (a long, stiff whip, usually made out of rhinoceros hide), the infamous tool of colonial oppression. As one British officer observed,

> Though indiscriminate flogging of natives . . . is prohibited, I have reason to know that the practice is indulged in to a considerable extent. . . . Flogging would seem to be the only recognized method of punishing the native who receives his 25 cuts with a sjambok for the most trivial offence, in most cases without any pretence of a trial, proving his guilt or otherwise. (Grundlingh 1987, 91)

Although the Germans, relatively speaking, were less harsh on their own troops, they could be bullies and brutes when it came to overseeing prisoners. The story of one notorious German officer, nicknamed Tsetse by his charges because his "bite" was as feared as that of the ever-menacing fly, bears out this observation. Tsetse had been in charge of Hausa prisoners of war in East Africa until he himself was captured by the British. His callous and sadistic treatment of his own prisoners came back to haunt him in a particularly acute case of poetic justice:

> One of [Tsetse's] prisoner's ankles was damaged by the leg-iron, and a sore developed that at first only lamed him. Instead of handing him over to the medical authorities he was forced by Tsetse to continue working till the ankle became so bad that he became a drag upon the other prisoners on the same chain. He was therefore taken out of the chain and forced to go on working by himself. When, owing to the bad state of his leg, he was forced to sit down and rest, he was beaten and kicked by this gentle son of the Fatherland. The sore became worse, so that frequently the Hausa fell down exhausted, only to by driven on again with blows. At last death, in the shape of gangrene, released the wretched man from further suffering . . . but Fate had a surprise in store for friend Tsetse. When he was in turn made a prisoner of war, his escort to Lindi consisted of a few of his ex-prisoners. (Downes 1919, 248–249)

Suffice it to say that Tsetse's former charges returned his earlier "kindness" with interest.

If colonial troops nonetheless frustrated European officers by not always following orders, perhaps it was for the obvious reason that they couldn't understand the language. The linguistic divide was perhaps the most striking problem when white men commanded black troops. An additional difficulty was the fact that colonial troops themselves came from innumerable different tribes, most of which did not speak a common language. It is little surprise that they did not find time to master European tongues. This elementary difficulty was not lost on the British, though they proved unsympathetic to their charges' frustration. As a British resident in Yola (then in Nigeria) recorded in his diary, "Men who served in the Cameroons are still talking of hardship they endured through having to serve under white men who did not speak their language" (Osuntokun 1979, 252).

Language was less of a problem for the other main group of colonial soldiers in Africa: Indians. Over 17,500 men made up Indian Expeditionary Group B, sent by the British in August 1914 to help capture German East Africa. As trained soldiers, these men were inferior to those sent in Group A to fight in France. The Indian army was divided into two branches, combatant (infantry, artillery, cavalry, sappers and miners, and signals) and noncombatant (supply and transport corps, medical services, ordnance services,

and remount and veterinary services). Indian soldiers were limited, however, by their poor training (Pradhan 1978a, 50–51, 73). They had no experience with advanced weaponry, lacked proper coordination of supply and
communication (e.g., no electrical services or mechanized vehicles), and
suffered (like Europeans) in the tropical climate.

Even more than their African cobelligerents, Indians found themselves
awash in a new and strange environment. Indian soldiers likened airplanes
to "the great bird Vishnu [Garuda]." They also suffered intensely at the
hands of gas attacks, the topic of one soldier's war poem:

> *He blows poison darts down our throats,*
> *And as we writhe in agony*
> *He laughs at us and gloats.* (Ellinwood 1978, 195)

The modern nature of the war challenged traditional notions of valor for
many Indians. One soldier, a Punjabi Muslim, wrote: "It is sad to see the
wounds inflicted by scraps of bombs, and the weapons used just now are
such that it is impossible for men to show their bravery" (Ellinwood 1978,
196).

Despite the challenges, Indian troops acquitted themselves well in Africa.
Major General Deventer, commander of British troops in East Africa in
1918, wrote in his diary that

> The troops sent from India have borne their full share of the campaign in
> which the fighting has been severe and the physical difficulties enormous
> and have played a gallant part in the conquest of German East Africa. I am
> proud to have had them under my command. (Pradhan 1978a, 72)

His use of the term *conquest* serves to reiterate the imperial nature of the war
in Africa.

Indian soldiers also saw active duty in Mesopotamia, where they in fact
made up the majority of Allied troops. The 588,717 Indians in that theater
performed admirably, though the outcome was not as favorable as in Africa
(Ellinwood 1978, 183). Britain was humbled at the siege of Kut, where
Turkish propagandists encouraged Indians to murder their British officers
and turn sides, writing: "Oh Dear Indian Brethren, You understand the fact
well that God has created this war for setting India free from the hands of
the cruel English" (Millar 1969, 303). Such appeals fell on deaf ears. After

A Turkish gun captured by British Indians. An 18-pounder Krupp field gun taken from the Turks by British Indians of the Indian Expeditionary Force, who operated with other British forces in the campaign against Baghdad. (Reynolds, Francis J. and C.W. Taylor. Collier's Photographic History of the European War. *P.F. Collier & Son, New York. 1916)*

Kut fell, many Indian troops were taken captive by the Turks and interned in POW camps. Some 11,300 perished. They were perhaps the lucky ones, considering the following description of conditions at the Shumran POW camp, where Kut prisoners were taken on 30 April 1916:

> The first group of prisoners to arrive had found that the "camp" was a stretch of dry ground near the river. Most of the men [British and Indian] were without tents and therefore exposed to the full force of the sun. No food had been provided other than Turkish service biscuits. These were five inches in diameter by three-quarters of an inch thick, of a brown rock-like substance interspersed with bits of husk and a considerable quantity of earth. Many had not eaten since the previous day and they attacked the biscuits furiously.

Indian troops with the British army wash camels in the sea off Rafa, Palestine, ca. 1914. (Hulton-Deutsch Collection/Corbis)

One procedure was to pound them into small pieces which were then soaked in river water until a sort of porridge was obtained. Others who could wait boiled the water first. The first method was responsible for an outbreak of cholera which claimed about a hundred lives while the troops were at Shumran. Turkish soldiers walked among the hungry men trying to sell onions, dates, chapatis and bread but very few had money and they had to barter their clothes and boots for food. (Millar 1969, 282; see also Fromkin 1989, 201–203, 369)

The experiences of Indians in Mesopotamia illustrate the great dislocation brought by the war, particularly for colonial peoples forcibly sent around the world. Indian ex-prisoners, for instance, were still showing up in their native villages in 1924.

Alongside colonial soldiers worked an even larger group of "volunteer" labor, the carrier battalions, or *tengatenga*. In Egypt and Mesopotamia, a good deal of physical transport could be done by pack animals, especially camels (Killingray 1998, 99). The Germans also employed this system to a more limited degree in southwest Africa. The Camel Transport Corps, the "unique creation" of the British, was organized in the winter of 1914–1915. While they should be given full credit for effort, the British, alas, were less adept at using their new transport than were the Egyptians. One Egyptian wryly observed that the average Briton "never succeeded entirely in ridding his mind of the strange obsession that a camel possessed the endurance of a motor-car" (Elgood 1924, 243).

Pack animals, however, could not be used south of the "tsetse line," which stretches across East Africa, as they did not survive long. This twist of fate meant that Europeans relied on huge numbers of human carriers. These men were the "hands and feet" of European armies; or rather, literally, they were the "heads," for most adopted the traditional female practice of carrying loads on their head. Carriers first used a convoy system to move supplies, much as they had done throughout the nineteenth century when pressed into service by their colonial masters. H. M. Stanley, the famous African explorer who, as his press had it, "discovered" much of central Africa on his own, was in fact accompanied by scores of African carriers.

The convoy system, however, did not always work without a hitch. Supplies often went bad before they reached their destinations, and the men themselves often could not physically endure the grueling physical labor. This is unsurprising, considering that the average load of each carrier was 50 to 60 pounds—and this did not include his own belongings, such as blankets, cooking pots, and so on. The task of carrying this heavy burden was made more difficult by the terrain over which carriers had to move. On the Dodoma-Iringa line (stretching from the border of the Belgian Congo east into central East Africa), porters "had to carry nine miles mostly waist-deep in water, much of it on raised duck walls made of undressed poles laid side by side" (Hodges 1986, 142–146). The system was changed in 1916, with carriers now laboring under a "dumping" system. Each unit would work between bandas (huts) along the line, moving supplies between its assigned stations much as would a fire-line moving water from the river to a burning house.

The carriers' difficult work was not offset by adequate wages. The British paid according to skill, a model followed by their German counterparts. An unskilled African laboring for the British could expect 5 or 6 Rs (approximately $1.65) per month. Men with the harrowing task of carrying batteries and machine-gun parts made an average of 15 Rs, and pier gangs 10 to 12 Rs. The most highly skilled laborers, such as cooks or interpreters, could make upwards of 25–30 Rs per month (Hodges 1986, 77).

The workers did not always get their money. The logistics of pay were difficult, as men moved from unit to unit, and some simply disappeared. European administrators tried to keep tabs on their charges through registration, but this process was anything but foolproof. The case of Bakari bin Salimu, a deserter arrested in 1915 at Mombasa, illustrates some of the problems of registration. Oscar Watkins, a district commissioner in the East African Protectorate administration and the originator of the carrier system, said of his case: "I do not think you will be able to substantiate a single story of men discharged without pay. Deserters of course sing a sad song when they go back, but for that there is no remedy but an application to the deserter" (Hodges 1986, 73).

There were also cultural problems, some as elementary as the laborers' names. Nicknames were common in African communities. They often commemorated a community or personal event, meaning that it was difficult to ascertain a person's "true" identity for purposes of registration. Name choices were also limited in some tribes—Njoroge, for instance, was a common name among the Kikuyu (Hodges 1986, 83). The registration system did achieve some successes. It was particularly effective, for example, in facilitating the payment of death benefits to the families of deceased laborers.

The difficulties attendant in organizing and paying for the mammoth carrier corps that trudged to and fro across the African landscape during the Great War point to two further aspects of the colonial perspective of the war; namely the social impact of war on colonial troops and the relationship during the war between colonials and their European masters. Perhaps the greatest challenge many colonials faced was dislocation. They moved, usually against their will, far away from their families and familiar surroundings, with little idea of what to expect. Tales of disaster abroad, such as circulated among black South Africans after the SS *Mendi,* a troopship carrying black recruits to the war in Europe, sank off the Isle of Wight in the English Channel in February 1917, only compounded matters. Over 600 men drowned in frigid 38-degree F waters (Grundlingh and Clothier 1987).

A sense of dislocation could also be brought on by more day-to-day concerns, such as food. As anyone who has traveled well knows, the most "foreign" thing in a foreign land is often the food. Colonial troops had to adjust their dietary requirements and expectations when they found themselves in strange new places. Such adjustments were particularly difficult for Muslims and Hindus serving in the war. A Hindustani Hindu in Egypt wrote that

> Not only I but a number of other Hindus—some of whom would formerly have rejected their food, if only the shadow of a passerby had fallen on it, have eaten from the hands of sweepers. Had we not done so there would have been no alternative but starvation. . . . Along with me is a doctor Lieutenant, by caste a Brahmin, who abstains from nothing. Moreover if anyone tries to abstain he advises them against doing so and as being immaterial, and indeed it is immaterial. (Ellinwood 1978, 190)

Indians serving in the British army in Mesopotamia also had to choose between their religious beliefs and their physical survival:

> The Indian troops and followers are now in a state of semi-starvation. The reduction of the grain ration to five ounces per man, which has of necessity been commenced, will reduce them to a state of great debility and emaciation. . . . I would consider that the universal use of horse-flesh by Indians would materially keep down the death and sickness rates, ameliorate a vast amount of human suffering, assist in preventing the progress of the effects of starvation, and maintain a large share in such a physical state as will enable them to carry on their duties. (Millar 1969, 225)

Food was important because it was quite literally the fuel of an army. European officers were acutely aware of the necessity of maintaining the strength of their charges. They endeavored to disabuse their men of ideas about food they found odd and counterproductive, perhaps forgetting that the Indian "Mutiny" of 1857 had been precipitated in part by British insensitivity about these very views. (The immediate spark for the revolt, known by the British as the Indian Mutiny, was the British government's decision to import new Lee Enfield rifles for use by the Indian army. The cartridge for these rifles was greased with pig or cow fat, seen as polluting by both Muslims and Hindus.) Major General Charles Townshend conveyed this mix of military utilitarianism and cultural ignorance in a desperate communiqué to his Indian soldiers at Kut:

> You have already received permission and every encouragement from your ruling princes and your religious leaders also to eat flesh in the dire emer-

gency. . . . I wish it to be clearly understood that I shall replace all non-meat eaters who become too feeble to do their duty efficiently as officers or non-commissioned officers, by other men who eat meat and remain strong. (Millar 1969, 107)

This issue of food neatly illustrates the social divide between European and colonial men during the war. In one camp, "The first meal of the day was partaken of at 10:30 AM; for the Europeans it was tea and various tinned foods provided by the C.O., whose cook box had arrived at the firing line; and for the men it was rice and bully beef" (Downes 1919, 155).

And the question of food taboos was not just apparent in the colonies. In Europe, too, colonial troops had to adjust to circumstance. Many Indians serving on the western front, for instance, were forced by want to eat whatever was available. As Jemandar Abdul Khan related in a letter to a relation in India, "Now my inner man begins to prompt me and I am afraid of falling. Many distinguished people here have given up making any distinction between clean and unclean things" (Omissi 1999, 284).

The colonials' war experience was not all suffering and struggle. African and Indian soldiers had an opportunity to meet other Africans and Indians, no doubt broadening their horizons. Colonial soldiers filled their leisure time with football (soccer), discussions, dances, and songs. In engaging in these activities, they differed little from European soldiers. The British encouraged their Indian troops to play sports—both traditional Indian ones, like wrestling, and European team sports. Rajput men serving in Mesopotamia spent their downtime playing football (soccer): "Outside one could hear the thuds and shouts of the enthusiastic Rajput footballers and see their breath in the cold air" (Millar 1969, 107).

The "games ethic" of fair play, cooperation, and manliness were seen as transferable traits, equally applicable to football and war. Sports were particularly important in the colonial soldiers' experience because colonials and whites often competed together, a rare display of cooperation and equality. Colonial troops took great delight in besting their European opponents during these encounters.

The war did not get in the way of other perennial interests, either. The Kamba *askari* Mbwika Kivandi defiantly sang:

Iuvi Nzama! Iuvi Nzama!
You Council, maliciously taking me from home,

You thought I was going to die,
Council; that I will not do, but
Will go back home to enjoy the company of beautiful women!
(Hodges 1986, 150)

Unfortunately for colonial soldiers, the beautiful women they had left behind sometimes were not there for them when and if they came back. Such
a decision is perhaps easy to understand, for village life was difficult with the
men away. Many women did attempt to donate food and supplies to their
husbands who were away, but the aid did not always reach its destination.
Villagers were primarily concerned with providing for their own family,
meaning that the continent's economy became one defined more than ever
by subsistence needs. Europeans had a less charitable view of self-sufficiency.
As one put it,

> There are no men in the villages to press the women to work in their gar-
> dens, and the women are having a good time, never dreaming of working in
> their gardens, and all are expecting their husbands back with money to buy
> the food, and nobody is taking the trouble of producing. (Page 2000, 134)

Much of the relationship between Europeans and their colonial troops is
revealed in this critique. While European powers necessarily relied on colonial peoples to fight the war, they continued to perceive them with a mixture
of paternalism, contempt, and racism. Europeans believed that differences
in temperament, character, and national origin meant that some colonial
peoples would make better soldiers than others. This theory of "martial
races" was held most firmly by the British, though the French, Germans, Belgians, and Portuguese also subscribed to their own variations.

Colonial peoples, particularly Indians, also attached prestige to the concept of caste and racial identity. Men of the so-called martial races, such as
Rajputs and Sikhs, sometimes found the mixed nature of colonial fighting
meant they had to perform duties "below" their station. As one Rajput soldier wrote to a friend,

> You were pressing me to join the infantry, and I am sorry that I did not take
> your advice and that I joined the artillery instead. It is an easy job, but all
> classes are mixed up in it, and no one pays attention to class. For us, therefore,
> it is not pleasant, as we have to perform work which is derogatory for Rajputs

to do. The business of a Rajput is to fight, and I love fighting. (Omissi 1999, 383)

Although the "fighting nature" of the colonial recruit was important, physical strength and fitness was a more immediate concern given the harsh climatic conditions under which combat took place. Mulei Nguyo, who was recruited as an *askari,* remembered that "A European came to a place called Kwa Kithembe on a horse, and the people were called out name by name [from a tax register]. They selected strong men, but not fat ones, who then walked to Nairobi" (Hodges 1986, 104).

Europeans were selective about which colonial peoples would serve under their command because they could be. They viewed their colonial charges as human capital rather than as people with individual concerns. This position is well illustrated by the description of the Swahili-speaking peoples by Angus Buchanan, a Scots captain with the 25th Royal Fusiliers in East Africa: "They were simple, good nature people, those blacks, and very easy to deal with if one took the trouble to understand them and their language, and ruled with a strong yet considerate hand" (Buchanan 1969, 28).

Buchanan believed Africans lacked "vigour" and were more "fearful" than Europeans, lessons he drew from an encounter in the bush:

> On outward journey ran across a rhinoceros, who charged on hearing a stick break under foot. . . . Self and companion, at the sound of the rushing crash of the charge, had backed behind stoutish trees, with rifles ready, but the natives, in an incredibly short moment, had squirmed frantically into the bushed overhead. They were fully frightened, poor wretches—but they were low-caste porters. (Buchanan 1969, 201)

Other Europeans held to milder forms of paternalism. After perceiving a sense of homesickness among a regiment of Kenyans from the shores of Lake Victoria, Brett Young confided to his diary that

> What intrigued me . . . was to realise that these primitive people, who, only a few years ago, were walking around in nakedness, were not only afflicted with the same nostalgia as myself, but found some relief from its twinges in thinking of places which they had loved and left, and in speaking of them too. (Brett Young 1938, 83)

The experience of war, however, could sometimes break down the cultural divide between black and white. Many colonial soldiers exhibited great bravery, earning the respect of their European brethren. Abudu Dinga, for instance, a Nigerian carrier working for the British at the Battle of the Nyengedi stream, carried supplies to and from the line for hours under intense German fire (Downes 1919, 159–161). His courage was far from an isolated case. The very intimacy of active service also meant that cultural barriers sometimes fell away, at least in the field. White Europeans, after all, "dressed and undressed, washed and shaved in the presence—usually the very near presence—of the multitude."

Colonial peoples also found some humor in the strangeness of many Europeans. Karanja, a character in *Red Strangers* (a 1939 novel by Elspeth Huxley) who observed Europeans throwing away grass cuttings instead of giving them to cows, is made to say: "They have no sense, and do many foolish things without reason" (Hodges 1986, 147–149). Many real Africans would no doubt have had similar stories of their own to tell, though few were recorded in a culture that relied on oral tradition.

A sense of cross-cultural amity should not, however, be overestimated. The relationship between Europeans and their colonial troops remained an unequal one, a fact not lost on either party, though for different reasons. One debate that has captured historians' interest is whether the experience of war encouraged in the colonies feelings of nationalism. The evidence is not decisive on either side. No colonial nation attained its independence coming out of the war. Nationalist uprisings, however, were not uncommon, and many eventual colonial nationalist leaders took their first steps during the conflict.

Europeans certainly feared nationalist uprisings, and they took steps to quell such sentiment. They understood that onerous service heightened unrest, as did agricultural failings caused by the absence of the men at war. These fears intensified late in the war. The British district commissioner in Kiambu reported in 1918 that "A gloom spread over the native population . . . any spark might have caused a dangerous outbreak; the headmen were obviously perturbed and afraid" (Hodges 1986, 109).

Colonial leaders had seen the outbreak of war as an opportunity to assert their own sense of identity. John Chilembwe, a Baptist reverend and Malawian (then British Nyasaland) nationalist leader, believed that

> The masses of our people are ready to put on uniforms ignorant of what they
> have to face or why they have to face it. . . . It is too late now to talk of what

might or might not have been. Whatsoever be the reasons we are invited to join in the war, the fact remains, we are invited to die for Nyasaland. (*Nyasaland Times*, 26 November 1914)

Chilembwe led a nationalist uprising against the British in 1915. The uprising failed, and Chilembwe was killed.

The fate of Chilembwe's uprising is indicative of the colonial soldiers' broader perspective on the war—possibility unfulfilled. The war stimulated change for colonials by exposing them to peoples they would never otherwise have encountered, both Europeans and other Africans and Indians. Colonial people also developed through their war experiences a sense of pride. Nationalism intensified, and colonial societies developed a greater sense of identity and belonging. The modernizing nature of World War I had its negative consequences, too. Indians were better able to adapt to these forces than were Africans; everywhere in the colonial world, however, the Great War in fact led to the intensification of imperial rule.

In the final account, warfare in the colonies was a minor aspect of World War I. Allied victories in Africa and the indecisive fighting in Mesopotamia did not turn the tide. World War I was ultimately decided in Europe. We must not, however, therefore conclude that the service of colonial soldiers and auxiliaries was inconsequential. While Europeans may have abhorred their service in the colonies—("Ah, I wish to hell that I was in France! There one lives like a gentlemen and dies like a man, here one lives like a pig and dies like a dog"; Buchanan 1969, vii)—the fact remains that much of the actual fighting, and all of the labor, was performed by their colonial subjects. These men fought, labored, and died in the same manner as did the men on the western front. Unlike the men of the western front, they did not record their experiences for future generations to read. Given the struggle endured by many of these men during the First World War, and the fact that so many of their voices will remain forever silent, lost to histories reliant on the written word, it is appropriate to conclude with the inscription on the War Memorial on Kenyatta Avenue in Nairobi (written by Rudyard Kipling):

> *This is to the memory of the native African troops who fought, to the Carriers who were the feet and hands of the army, and to all other*

men who served and died.
If you fight for your country
Even if you die, your sons
Will remember your name.

—Daniel Gorman

References and Further Reading

Brett Young, Francis. 1938 [1917]. *Marching on Tanga (with General Smuts in East Africa)*. London: Collins.

Buchanan, Angus. 1969 [1919]. *Three Years of War in East Africa*. New York: Negro Universities Press.

Downes, W. D. 1919. *With the Nigerians in German East Africa*. London: Methuen and Company.

Elgood, Percival G. 1924. *Egypt and the Army*. London: Oxford University Press.

Ellinwood, DeWitt. 1978. "The Indian Soldier, the Indian Army, and Change, 1914–1918." In DeWitt Ellinwood, ed., *India and the First World War*. New Delhi: Manohar.

Fromkin, David. 1989. *A Peace to End All Peaces*. New York: Deutsch.

Grundlingh, Albert. 1987. *Fighting Their Own War: South African Blacks and the First World War.* Johannesburg: Ravan.

Grundlingh, Albert, and N. Clothier. 1987. *Black Valour: The South African Native Labour Contingent, 1916–1917, and the Sinking of the* Mendi. Pietermaritzburg, South Africa: University of Natal Press.

Hodges, Geoffrey. 1986. *The Carrier Corps: Military Labor in the East African Campaign*. New York: Greenwood.

Killingray, David. 1998. "The War in Africa." In Hew Strachan, ed., *The Oxford Illustrated History of the First World War*. Oxford: Oxford University Press.

———2001. "African Voices from Two World Wars." *Historical Research* 74, 186 (November): 425–443.

Millar, Ronald. 1969. *Kut: The Death of an Army*. London: Secker and Warburg.

Miller, Charles. 1974. *Battle for the Bundu*. New York: Macmillan.

Mwina, Maulidi. Interview 15 August 1972, and Kildon Wajiusa, interview 2 August 1973, p. 117.

Omissi, David, ed. 1999. *Indian Voices of the Great War: Soldiers' Letters, 1914–1918*. London: Macmillan.

Osuntokun, Akinjide. 1979. *Nigeria in the First World War*. London: Longman.

Page, Melvin E. 2000. *The Chiwaya War: Malawians and the First World War*. Boulder: Westview.

Pradhan, S. D. 1978a. "Indians in the East African Campaign—A Case Study of Indian Experiences in the First World War." In DeWitt Ellinwood, ed., *India and the First World War.* New Delhi: Manohar.

———. 1978b. "The Indian Army and the First World War." In DeWitt Ellinwood, ed., *India and the First World War.* New Delhi: Manohar.

Sydenham Clark, George. 1915. *India and the War.* Introduction by Lord Sydenham of Combe. London: Hodder and Stoughton.

Tucker, Spencer. 1998. *The First World War.* Bloomington: Indiana University Press.

"IN A STUPID CAP
AND A GREY JACKET"

Soldiers' Experiences

of World War I in

the Neutral Netherlands

———————— ◆ ————————

FRIDAY, 31 JULY 1914, DAWNED A BEAUTIFUL, SUNNY SUMMER'S day in the Netherlands. Unlike previous Fridays, however, there was tangible tension in the air. Rumors of imminent war spread like wildfire across Europe. People worried that if neighboring Germany went to war, its armies might pass through the Netherlands to reach Belgium and France. Fear inspired panic. On Thursday, shops throughout the country had emptied of preserved goods, meat, and bread, while long queues of people appeared outside banks to withdraw their life's savings. By Monday, 3 August, silver money had become so scarce that the government and municipal councils had to print and circulate emergency "silver coupons" to ensure employers could pay staff, and that families could buy vital necessities.

This particular Friday morning also saw the Dutch cabinet assemble, as it had each day during the past week, to assess the risks of war. The ministers raised the national security status to "war danger" and authorized what they had been preparing for several days: general mobilization of 200,000 con-

scripts (out of a total population of about 6.7 million people). At 1:30 P.M.,
Queen Wilhelmina called her citizens to arms. The Dutch were the first people in Western Europe to fully mobilize.

The mobilization was fundamentally defensive in aim: namely, to keep
the country out of any potential war by protecting its neutrality. Only if they
were invaded would troops be used in combat roles. For the average Nether-
lander, this rationale of mobilization as a precautionary measure did not sit
easily as they emptied into the streets, read mobilization posters, hailed
down local messengers, or heeded the call of church bells announcing a
town meeting that afternoon. P. H. Ritter described the heightened sense of
anxiety at one such meeting:

> The whole town gathered in the burning sun, in front of the white pillars of
> the town hall. The mayor stepped to the front onto the high steps, and
> started to read out the mobilization declaration. Such a deadly silence hung
> around the packed-together crowd, that one could hear the birds chirping
> in the gardens behind the houses. When it was announced that fifteen mili-
> tary intakes would be called up, a breath of dismay, like a sudden wind surge,
> spread through the crowd. One woman fell unconscious. Other women
> started to cry silently, and buzzing and stumbling the crowd parted into the
> small streets, where their dull footsteps echoed from the walls of the houses,
> which absorbed an unrest never known before. (Ritter 1931a, 81)

The everyday normality of Friday afternoon quickly evaporated. Frightened by the prospect of impending invasion, people left work early and
talked with friends and neighbors in stunned whispers. Ritter described how

> the first moment was ominous and fearful. A panic, as had never been
> known, captured the masses. . . . In front of every shop window which had
> bulletins pasted to it, fearful, silent crowds formed, and yet even in this ut-
> terly despairing moment people tried to talk courage into each other. . . .
> Everybody was hoisted from their normal path of life, and saw the fruit of
> their life's work disappear; expectations for the future collapsed . . . the ma-
> jority of the population plunged into dismay. (Ritter 1931a, 32–33)

That evening the first conscripts appeared at the mobilization depots.

The Dutch armed forces consisted of a large army of mostly conscripted
men, a smaller navy of predominantly career sailors, and a fledgling air

branch, incorporating four airplanes and a few officers. All Dutch males were eligible for conscription at age twenty. Once picked by a lottery, they received compulsory military training for anywhere between six to eighteen months. After training, the soldier returned to civilian life but remained available for military duty in a variety of forms until he turned forty years of age. On 31 July 1914, most of the Netherlands' eligible conscripts received their mobilization summons.

On the first day of mobilization, Saturday, 1 August, chaos ruled in households around the country. Men frantically sought, cleaned, and repaired long-disused, moth-eaten uniforms, retrieving them from the back crevices of cupboards and attics. Many had outgrown the clothing issued to them at age twenty, and a substantial number had lost their boots or worn them through. In a country where military service was seen as a "necessary evil"—disliked but endured—and where the expectation of going to war featured only dimly in conscripts' minds as they passed through their basic training, it was little wonder that they answered the call to arms in various states of unreadiness (Blom 1990, 84–104).

Overnight, this once-peaceful nation was overrun by soldiers. Unlike elsewhere in Europe, however, there were no elated crowds wishing troops well. Almost everywhere, dour faces and anxious eyes dominated the scene.

Soldiers took whatever route available to reach the depots. Train stations were overrun, roads clogged, and trams filled to overflowing. In the space of three days, the national rail network carried nearly 180,000 troops, 6,600 horses, and 500 vehicles (Snijders 1932, 18). It was a massive operation that, amazingly, succeeded with very few setbacks, no doubt aided by strict bans on alcohol consumption by soldiers and the general apprehension of possible war. Some journeys were arduously slow, but by late Monday evening most soldiers had reached their depots, ready for their first defense assignment.

At this stage, officers worried about the readiness of their men to fight a war. Many troops had forgotten what they learned at their initial training all those years ago. Marching proved difficult to coordinate, rifle shooting proved even more problematic, and discipline was lacking, although not universally. One brigade commander described his motley group of conscripts stationed at the border in the following terms: "The people in my brigade will look like beggars when they are compared with the soldiers of brigades, which are billeted in garrisons or others lodged in fortifications" (Burger 1922, 390). Regardless of readiness, they all awaited an invasion.

Guards at the Dutch-Belgian border, 1914. (Hulton-Deutsch Collection/Corbis)

But on Tuesday, 4 August, German armies entered neutral Belgium and Luxemburg, carefully avoiding the Dutch border. Netherlanders everywhere heaved a sigh of relief. It looked more than likely that their country would be spared the prospect of immediate military conflict. Yet while the Dutch would remain neutral as their immediate neighbors fought each other, they could not avoid the presence of war. This was especially true in the southern provinces bordering Belgium. Few geographic barriers separate the two Low Countries; at times towns cross right over the border, with even houses, farms, churches, and convents cut in half by the invisible frontier. In the early days of the war, people could and did cross the border indiscriminately. Some ventured to see for themselves what the war was about; others checked on relatives or fled from the destruction of the fighting in Belgium (Ritter 1931a, 84–85).

The lack of obstacles at the Dutch-Belgian border provided an all-too-alluring incentive for Allied spies to reach the German side of the western

A sign at the Belgian-Dutch frontier during World War I reads "Achtung" or "Attention" and alerts people to the danger of the high voltage electric fence, ca. 1916. (Topical Press Agency/Getty Images)

front, and an even easier way for Belgians and Dutch to smuggle information, persons, and goods. Even though the border was patrolled around the clock by German troops on one side and Dutch patrols on the other—both under orders to shoot anyone suspicious on sight—transgressions continued almost unabated, forcing the German authorities to consider alternatives for blocking access. From April 1915 onward, they erected an electric fence, some two meters (6.6 feet) high, that stretched for 180 miles from the town of Vaals, where the Dutch, Belgian, and German state lines met, to the eastern bank of the Scheldt River. The authorities hoped that the fence would deter people from smuggling and spying.

The fence admittedly made the task of Dutch border patrols easier, since it was much harder for illicit crossings to occur. It also made their task more gruesome. It is estimated that anywhere up to 3,000 people—including a few soldiers, some civilians, no doubt several spies, and numerous smugglers—died upon touching the wires (Vanneste 1998, 315).

Safety measures, especially in the first few weeks, were inadequate. In many places, no barriers existed between passersby and the "devil's wire," as locals soon came to call it (Feith 1915, front page). Because the fence crossed through towns, sometimes over the tops of houses and across canals and streams, it was not unusual for accidents to occur. Pets, livestock, and fowl also fell victim to the deadly structure. It proved to be one of the more sobering realities of this neutral country's war experience.

The realities of war came all too close to home in other ways as well, especially for troops stationed in the south. Their primary responsibility was to uphold the territorial integrity and neutrality of the border by preventing foreign soldiers from entering the country. A few German and Belgian soldiers strayed onto Dutch soil in the opening weeks of war, including two German officers whose car took a wrong turn and ended up in the Dutch city of Maastricht rather than in Belgium (Wolf 2001, n.p.). Most of the foreigners would be disarmed and subsequently interned in camps set up for that purpose.

Significantly more disturbing for border troops were the many casualties from nearby battles brought into the country by the Dutch Red Cross (Van der Mandere 1917, 128). Once treated—and if they survived—most of the wounded also found themselves recuperating in an internment camp, a visible reminder to locals of the war's proximity.

The battles themselves passed dangerously close to the Netherlands in the opening weeks. Southern residents soon became used to the rumbling of distant cannon barrages. Even further away in The Hague and in Zwolle, the air would shake with the booms from heavy artillery. As one soldier reported from the Belgian border late in 1917, the cannon thunder "has now grown to a fire of almighty drum rolls, that lasts sometimes for hours or days, and at night mysterious red, green, blue and white flares ascend out of the occupied area" (Erkens 1926, 41).

The experience was as much exhilarating as harrowing. As renowned Dutch author Albert Verwey explained,

> There is something breathtaking in the expectation [experienced] during large battles. Europe listens. And while we—foolishly—catch ourselves with the desire to strain our ears to listen if perhaps the rumble of cannon thunder on the borders of France can be heard here, and to stretch our eyes from

the Dutch dunes to see a fleet off the Belgian coast, we are taken up in the
universal speechlessness and know no longer what to think or how to express
ourselves. (Verwey 1916, 10)

Occasionally, stray shots and shrapnel landed on Dutch soil, at times in-
juring locals. Once aircraft featured regularly in battles on the western
front, the Dutch had a new threat to face: bombs. By November 1918, sixteen towns and villages had been hit by bombs thrown from British and German airplanes (VanLith 2001, 266). Such raids caused considerable
damage to property, several injuries, and at least three deaths (VanLith
2001; Vandenbosch 1927, 81).

It was also all too common for dislodged sea mines to wash up on Dutch
beaches. More than 6,000 such landings were reported between 1914 and
1918 (De Bles 1991, 78). Sometimes the mines exploded, causing damage,
injury, and death. Casualties from the war at sea also washed up on the
Dutch coast. Twenty-three corpses landed on the small island of Ter-
schelling during the war; most of them now lie in unidentified graves
(Kelder 1997, 4). It was the responsibility of troops and coast guards to deal
with all these consequences of the not-so-distant conflict.

As early as 4 August 1914, Belgian refugees sought to escape the destruction in and around their homes by fleeing into the Dutch province of Limburg. The trickle became a torrent over the following weeks, and in the first
week of October, during the German siege of Antwerp, it turned into a tidal
wave. Nearly a million destitute Belgians escaped their beleaguered city
northward in the space of two or three days (Tallier 1998, 23).

This was a humanitarian crisis well beyond the capabilities of a small nation to deal with effectively. All roads and railway routes into the country
were clogged, filled with clusters of human misery. Border troops, the first
to encounter these anxious masses, could do little but move the refugees in-
land as fast as possible and distribute them among towns and cities. They set
up temporary shelters, helped local charities and city councils organize and
find housing for the visitors, cooked for them, and provided medicinal care,
bedding, and shelter. It was barely enough.

At the same time as the wave of refugees, nearly 35,000 Belgian and
British troops found themselves cut off from the rest of the Allied armies
around Antwerp on 9 October (Van Lier 1967, 52). They had little choice
but to escape northward as well. Arriving at the Dutch border, the foreign
soldiers all had to be disarmed and interned under military guard. Amidst

Scene among the thousands of Belgian refugees who have sought refuge in Holland until even the hospitable Dutch are taxed to the utmost capacity. They sit about the streets with their names written on the walls. They occupy railway carriages and sleep in the parks, 31 October 1914. (Bettmann/Corbis)

the anarchy already present in the south, the internees only created more pandemonium. Yet somehow, by December 1914, the Dutch army had built secure and well-guarded camps for the new arrivals.

A dreary existence of drab dullness awaited many of the foreigners for the next four years. One British officer described his internment, in a fictional account based on his wartime experiences, as follows:

> Here we are—shut up . . . we can't escape; we can't help in any way, even as civilians in England can help. We are as much out of the world as if we are dead. What we do or don't do makes no difference to a living soul. As long as we live, we shall never again be responsible to ourselves alone. And we don't know how long it will last—years perhaps; or Holland may come into the war next week and we find ourselves in the trenches the week after. It gives me a feeling, as far as the war is concerned, of absolute fatalism. (Morgan 1932, 92)

The lengthy time spent in one place ensured internees created a special place for themselves within local communities. British soldiers, in particular, were very welcome. They were deemed a "desirable catch" by some Dutch women, earning many an officer the unhappy title of "maiden robber," bestowed by their Dutch counterparts (Ritter 1931a, 157).

By December 1914, most of the civilian refugees had moved back to Belgium; some had been forced out of towns by city councils unwilling or unable to house or feed them, others were attracted by promises of peaceful conditions in Antwerp, and yet others left to avoid a bleak future in refugee camps set up in the Dutch countryside (Bossenbroek and Kruishoop 1988, 25–28). Even so, between 100,000 and 200,000 Belgians remained in the Netherlands until the end of the war (De Roodt 2000, 173). They would prove especially burdensome when significant shortages occurred beginning in late 1916, as the German U-boat campaigns and the Allied blockade severely hampered deliveries of foodstuffs and coal into the country.

By December 1914, the most exciting time of Dutch soldiers' war experiences had passed. The thrill of mobilizing and the early crises of war had been resolved. Even civilians who had busily knitted undergarments, scarves, socks, and gloves for troops had difficulty maintaining the same level of enthusiasm after Christmas 1914. For conscripts, the next four years, though interspersed with the occasional national emergency, would be characterized by endless training exercises, patrols, and long days doing little of importance. Boredom and a stifling malaise set in quickly. As a popular verse put it all too clearly,

> *Piet spends months at the border,*
> *has nothing to do, sees no one;*
> *Piet stands still there and vegetates*
> *They say: Piet is mobilized!*
> (Haags Gemeent Museum 1986, 13)

Another soldier-writer described his mobilization more eloquently:

> If only there was blood to purge for Fatherland and Monarch, that would be fairer, than chocolate, cabbage, and sausage. If only there were other dangers in the game than fleas, or sighing in a stuffy cell. . . . Then I would shout cheerfully and would sharpen my bayonet on the purest grindstone. . . . Unfortunately, fighting does not apply [here], instead [we] march in step in a stupid cap and a grey jacket. (Stoke 1917, 9)

Morale dropped markedly through the course of 1915. Soldiers soon demanded better leave provisions, better living conditions, and better pay. The country had inadequately prepared, in the years leading up to 1914, to house, feed, and clothe so many thousands of men for such a long period of time. Often troops slept in abysmal conditions: in old factories, large barns, even tent camps, which were far from adequate to withstand the depths of a Dutch winter. At one typical location in the town of Tilburg, a soldier noted that "Even the cavalry would think twice about lodging their horses here. Imagine returning from duty, numb from the cold and misery, to a drafty hole, to lay down on a morsel of straw" (Van de Vrande n.d., 152).

The government and military authorities were slow to respond to soldiers' complaints. Inevitably, riots broke out in many of the main billeting centers, including Tilburg. When, during Easter 1916, the government revoked all leave entitlements due to an unfounded rumor of a pending British attack, five thousand conscripts went home anyway (Kleijngeld 1983, 86). Going AWOL (absent without leave) was a serious offense, and as a result, many of the wayward conscripts ended up in military prison. The Easter fiasco did, however, ensure that leave provisions improved markedly and other privileges increased. The authorities heeded German general Helmuth von Moltke's warning: "An army without discipline is a costly, in time of war useless, and in time of peace a dangerous institution" (Thomson 1916, 4).

Throughout the country in 1915 and 1916, troops and civilians called for a partial, if not general, demobilization. The stalemate on the western front looked to be permanently entrenched, and the threat of invasion by either Germany or Great Britain had seemingly ebbed. Antiwar organizations, conscientious objection campaigns, and peace movements gained in popularity at this time. A call for an end to the war, mixed with political movements urging soldiers to refuse to serve and the rise in the number of radically inspired "mobilization clubs" among troops, heightened the sense of impending crisis within the armed forces.

Many soldiers had had enough of the war by 1917. As one wrote, "A strong longing for peace is visible everywhere, among soldiers too. Three years from home, situated far from their place of residence, remarkably bad clothing and food, it has also taken too long for civilians" (Erkens 1926, 30). In reality, only a small number of conscripts ever seriously thought about protesting against their conscription status, but the minority certainly made themselves heard.

Ironically, just as the government decided to give in to demands for more long-term leave late in 1916, the changing international situation warranted increasing security at the borders. Rumors of Germany's imminent resumption of indiscriminate U-boat attacks and a buildup of German troops on the Dutch border (Germany worried that the Netherlands and Denmark might declare war if it targeted their merchant marine, something that neither neutral nation could afford to do) led to a need for expanded rather than decreased military preparedness in the Netherlands (Frey 1997, 551). Certainly calls for complete demobilization diminished in the last two war years, although a vocal antiwar movement remained.

By early 1918, most of the men mobilized in 1914 had received long-term leave, with the provision that they could be recalled to service at a moment's notice. To replace them, nearly 200,000 new conscripts had been forced into uniform. Most of these men had missed out on the conscription lottery at the age of twenty, seen as a lucky escape at the time, for which they were now being punished with service in the reserves (*Landstorm*).

Many new *Landstormers* were far from happy with their lot, and blamed the minister of war, Nicolaas Bosboom, for their plight. Although on paper, training new troops raised the total size of the Dutch armed forces above 400,000 and alleviated low morale among those mobilized in 1914—who now returned home—it did very little to enhance relationships between commanders and their charges, let alone between the families of new conscripts and the military institution. The First World War did much to aggravate the belief that armed service was unduly burdensome, even if it may prove necessary. One popular newspaper columnist who was mobilized into the *Landstorm* explained this feeling toward conscription in revealing terms:

> That [preconscription happiness] was then, in the long ago past, when you were allowed to work, were useful and lived. Terribly long ago, so long that your memories are becoming very, very vague. A civilian claims of course that it was only a few months ago, in other words, quite recently. But this person has jog-trotted on in his dull daily routine, he hasn't passed through the gate, above which is written in field-gray letters: "abandon hope, he who enters here." (De Jong 1975, 19)

The frustrations of the mobilization experience for everyone became exacerbated in areas where soldiers were billeted with civilians for long years upon end. Southern provinces, again, bore the brunt of billeting, with the inevitable consequence that previously sleepy towns were "enlivened" by young men seeking predictable entertainment, in the form of alcohol and women. With so many troops from different regions and with different religious and social backgrounds interacting with locals from strictly religious communities, it sparked concerns from town elders and, not uncommonly, from parents whose daughters had fallen for a soldier from "the wrong part of the country" or with the "wrong beliefs." The military authorities worried too, resulting in the erection of temporary Protestant churches in Catholic towns, and the commissioning of field preachers and pastors for a variety of religions into officer ranks. These were entrusted with keeping the souls of impressionable young men on the "right path" (Kleijngeld 1983, 184–185; Ritter 1931a, 159).

The most exciting posting for Dutch soldiers during the Great War certainly was border patrols. Such patrols became increasingly more important in attempting to stem the vast amount of smuggling between the Netherlands and Germany. In 1915, for instance, 37,000 persons throughout the Netherlands faced charges of smuggling; in 1917, the city of Arnhem alone nearly met that total with 25,000 cases before the courts (Abbenhuis 2002, 317). Patrols also shot at numerous smugglers, sometimes killing them.

One local newspaper reported 300 such deaths in the province of Limburg alone in 1916 (Moeyes 2001, 131).

Smugglers came in many forms, from children hiding items under their clothing, to sophisticated operations that hollowed out logs and filled them with contraband materials. Even in areas where the electric fence operated, crossings continued. People used ingenious contraptions to pass through, over, or underneath the high-voltage wires.

The nation had to be extraordinarily strict on smuggling to placate the demands of the Allies, who believed illicit neutral trade interfered with their blockade of Germany. The Dutch government also hoped that by making smuggling unattractive, it could keep vital foodstuffs in the country. Even with considerable efforts from military personnel and customs officials, however, the campaign against smugglers was unsuccessful. In all, it is estimated that only 5 to 10 percent of smuggled goods were ever intercepted (Smidt 1993, 51; Frey 1998, 195). It is most likely that only a general decline in the availability of supplies caused a significant dent in smuggling levels.

Soldiers, of course, were not incorruptible. It was quite common for them to turn to smuggling themselves. There were considerable profits to be made, which supplemented their meager wages nicely. It was also not unknown (although it was highly illegal) for patrols to sneak over the border to visit their German colleagues. One soldier recollected such a clandestine episode:

> Many of us crept, along a detour path, across the border and stepped with a "guten Abend" [good evening] into the guard house of the Germans. It looked far nicer than our barracks! A beautiful villa, with splendid furniture. Everywhere you noticed beautiful tapestries, armchairs and whatever you could name. I could stick it out here! . . . When we visit them we take cigars, sugar, white bread or cheese with us. They are always quick to respond. They pour us a delicious glass of wine or beer, just what we needed. By midnight the mood is certainly pleasant, we drink to each other's health, and sing cheerful songs. (Van de Vrande n.d., 206–207)

Despite not fighting in the war, by 1918 the Netherlands had reached crisis level. People suffered from the cold and from hunger. Although they were better off than most civilians in Germany, the Dutch endured far

greater food and coal shortages than Britons and French civilians. Like rioters in Germany, many Netherlanders were discontented enough to take to
the streets in protest. In the words of one commentator, "Due to the long
period of rationing, an army of workers, with hunger in their eyes and with
faces gray like potato peelings, protested, with pent up bitterness, against a
government that . . . was deficient in its measures to provide the material
needs of its people" (Ritter 1931b, 350).

On several occasions, protests turned into riots. At times, police and troops
were sent in to quell the unrest; on at least two occasions this led to several
deaths when they opened fire on crowds in Amsterdam and in The Hague.
This in itself caused disquiet, as soldiers were rumored to have greater sympathy for the rioters than for their commanding officers, although no serious
cases of military insubordination have been linked with the riots. Quite understandably, the nation's leaders were on edge throughout 1918.

Soldiers also suffered heavily from the supply crisis in 1918. Although
they always received more food and greater rations than civilians—based on
the old adage that "an army marches on its stomach"—these supplies could
not be maintained at 1914, or even 1916, levels. The lack of foodstuffs,
along with epidemics of Spanish influenza, which resulted in the cancella-
tion of almost all unnecessary leave through the summer months of 1918
and caused deaths, took their toll on morale.

When, in October 1918, fears of a German retreat through the Netherlands surfaced and the high command felt it absolutely necessary to cancel
all leave, disquiet among soldiers rose to levels not seen since the 1916
Easter fiasco. On 25 October 1918, soldiers in the Harskamp barracks, situated in the lonely heaths of the Veluwe, protested en masse about their living conditions: they were hungry, bored, and wanted weekend leave to visit
their families. Due to mismanagement of the situation by commanding officers, as well as general bedlam when a fire began in one of the mess halls,
large numbers of troops rioted and then fled the camp that night, sparking
what was seen by the press at the time as a serious mutiny (Kleijngeld 1983,
144; Fasseur 1998, 543). In fact, the level of insubordination was probably
no higher than that of Easter 1916; almost all troops returned the following
evening. Given the tense revolutionary situation in neighboring Germany
though—news of the Kiel mutiny reached the Netherlands on 30 October—many Dutch perceived the makings of a revolution.

The sense of crisis only intensified when news reached the public on 9
November 1918 of the resignation of Dutch commander-in-chief General

C. J. Snijders after a dispute with the government over Harskamp. When the German Kaiser, Wilhelm II, arrived on the Dutch border that same day seeking refuge, the country had a true emergency. "No other event," in the words of the leader of the main socialist-democratic party, P. J. Troelstra, "made such a huge impact in our country" as the arrival of the kaiser (Troelstra 1931, 187). It looked like the Netherlands would tread the same revolutionary path as Germany.

Even though the Armistice had not yet been signed, the Dutch government refused to take any chances, ordering the speedy demobilization of troops for fear they would take up arms and join potential revolutionaries. A massive antirevolutionary movement grew overnight, consisting mainly of civilian militia groups who announced their allegiance to Queen Wilhelmina and vowed to protect their homes from socialist insurrectionists. Troelstra, in turn, declared on 12 November that revolution was nigh, calling all workers to take up arms and overthrow the regime (Van As 1919, 42 – 55).

In fact, most soldiers and civilians had no desire to revolt. They liked their queen and feared what would happen if the nation emulated Russia. This fear, mixed with a series of unfortunate and alarming events at home and abroad, had spiraled the nation into a seemingly uncontrollable situation. Within two days, however, the supposed revolution, which saw a far greater number of royalists take up arms than revolutionaries, fizzled out. Troelstra declared he had made "a mistake" on 14 November (Scheffer 1984, x). By this time, the Armistice had been signed, and the Dutch had survived World War I without engaging in a military campaign.

The end of the war came none too soon, for the conflict had taken its toll on the Netherlands. The country now faced an insecure future on a continent reeling from the impact of more than four years of devastating conflict. For Dutch soldiers and civilians, the mobilization ended ingloriously. As one commentator all too aptly described the situation, "The spirit left . . . the appreciation of the army was no longer especially great and there is much truth in the following verse . . .

> *When need arises and war arrives*
> *People cry for God and army.*
> *But when war passes, and peace thrives*
> *People forget God, and despise the army."*
> (Van Linden Tol 1922, 914–915)

It was a lesson that would haunt the nation at the outset of the next world war.

—*Maartje Abbenhuis*

References and Further Reading

Abbenhuis, Maartje. 2002. "Rustig te midden van woedende golven: De moeilijke verdediging van de Nederlandse neutraliteit." In Hans Andriessen, Martin Ros, and Perry Pierik, eds., *De Grote Oorlog: Kroniek 1914–1918*, vol. 1. Soesterberg: Aspekt.

Blom, J. C. H. 1990. "A Necessary Evil: The Armed Forces and Society in the Netherlands." In G. J. A. Raven and N. A. M. Rodger, eds., *Navies and Armies: The Anglo-Dutch Relationship in War and Peace 1688–1988*. Edinburgh: John Donald Publishers.

Bossenbroek, Martin, and J. C. B. Kruishoop. 1988. *Vluchten voor de Groote Oorlog: Belgen in Nederland 1914–1918*. Amsterdam: De Bataafsche Leeuw.

Burger, J. 1922. "Fragmenten uit het dagboek van een brigadecommandant." *Militaire Spectator.*

De Bles, H. 1991. "De Koninklijke Marine mobiliseert." In W. Klinkert, J. W. M. Schulten, and Luc De Vos, eds., *Mobilisatie in Nederland en België: 1870–1914–1939*. Amsterdam: De Bataafsche Leeuw.

De Jong, A. M. 1975. *Notities van een landstormman*. Edited by Johan van der Bol. Amsterdam: Em. Querido's Uitgeverij.

De Roodt, Evelyn. 2000. *Oorlogsgasten: Vluchtelingen en krijgsgevangenen in Nederland tijdens de Eerste Wereldoorlog*. Zaltbommel: Europese Bibliotheek.

Erkens, J. 1926. *In het Grijsgroen: Schetsen uit het Soldatenleven*. Heijthuijsen: J. Beijnsberger and Zonen.

Fasseur, Cees. 1998. *Wilhelmina: De jonge koningin*. Amsterdam: Uitgeverij Balans.

Feith, Jan. 1915. "Langs de electrische draadversperring." *Soldatencourant* 192 (7 November), front page.

Frey, Marc. 1997. "Trade, Ships, and the Neutrality of the Netherlands in the First World War." *International History Review* 19, 3: 541–562.

———. 1998. *Der Erste Weltkrieg und die Niederlande: Ein neutrales Land im politischen und militärischen Kalkül der Kriegsgegner*. Berlin: Akademie Verlag.

Greven, H. B., ed. 1928. *The Netherlands and the World War. Studies in the War History of a Neutral*. vols. 2–4. New Haven: Yale University Press.

Haags Gemeente Museum. 1986. *Den Haag '14–'18: Fragmenten uit een dagboek*. The Hague: Haags Gemeente Museum.

Kelder, Albert. 1997. "Tastbare herinneringen." *De Groote Oorlog* 3, 2 (October): 4.

Kleijngeld, A. M. P. 1983. *Gemobiliseerde militairen in Tilburg tijdens de Eerste Wereldoorlog*. Tilburg: Stichting Zuidelijk Historisch Contact.

Kossmann, E. H. 1978. *The Low Countries 1780–1940*. Oxford: Clarendon.

Moeyes, Paul. 2001. *Buiten Schot: Nederland tijdens de Eerste Wereldoorlog 1914–1918*. Amsterdam: De Arbeiderspers.

Moore, Bob, Susanne Wolf, and Paul M. Binding. 2001. "The Netherlands and Sweden: The Experience of Neutrality." In Peter Liddle, John Bourne, and Ian Whitehead, eds., *The Great World War, 1914–45: Volume 2, The People's Experience*. London: HarperCollins.

Morgan, Charles. 1932. *The Fountain*. New York: Alfred A. Knopf.

Ritter, P. H. 1931a. *De Donkere Poort*, vol. 1. The Hague: D. A. Daamen's Uitgevers-maatschappij.

———. 1931b. *De Donkere Poort*, vol. 2. The Hague: D. A. Daamen's Uitgevers-maatschappij.

Scheffer, H. J. 1984. *November 1918: Journaal van een revolutie die niet doorging*. Utrecht: De Bataafsche Leeuw.

Schulten, C. M. 1984. "The Netherlands and Its Army (1900–1940)." *Revue Internationale d'Histoire Militaire* 58: 73–95.

Smidt, H. A. R. 1993. "De bestrijding van de smokkelhandel door het leger tijdens de Eerste Wereldoorlog." *Mededelingen van de Sectie Militaire Geschiedenis* 15: 43–72.

Snijders, C. J. 1932. "Twee mobilisatiën." *Militaire Spectator* 101, 1 (January): 11–23.

Stoke, Melis [pseudonym]. 1917. *Van Aardappelmes tot Officiersdegen: Kantteekeningen van den Landstormplichtige*. Amsterdam: Van Holkema and Warendorf.

Tallier, Pierre Alain. 1998. "De Belgische vluchtelingen in het buitenland tijdens de Eerste Wereldoorlog." In Anne Morelli, ed., *Belgische Emigranten: Oorlogsvluchtelingen, economische emigranten en politieke vluchtelingen uit onze streken van de 16e eeuw tot vandaag*. Brussels: EPO.

Thomson, Gustaaf Henri Eugene Nord. 1916. *Militaire Straf- en Tuchtklassen*. Amsterdam: A. H. Kruyt.

Troelstra, P. J. 1931. *Gedenkschriften: Vierde Deel Storm*. Amsterdam: Em. Querido's Uitgevers Maatschappij.

Van As, G. G. 1919. *November-Alarm: De Revolutie-Bedreiging in Nederland, November 1918, Gedenkboek*. Kampen: J. H. Kok.

Van de Vrande, F. n.d. *Grensleven: Met de 3e Compie aan de Nederlandsch-Belgische grens tijdens de mobilisatie van 1914*. Velsen: Schuyt.

Van der Mandere, H. Ch. G. J. 1917. *Geschiedenis van het Nederlandsche Roode Kruis (1867–19 Juli–1917)*. Amsterdam: Algemeene Uitgevers-Maatschappij.

Van Lier, F. J. 1967. "Internering van vreemde militairen in Nederland tijdens de eerste wereldoorlog." *Ons Wapen*.: 50–57.

Van Linden Tol, P. A. R. C. 1922. "De Stelling van Amsterdam." In J. Kooiman, ed., *De Nederlandsche Strijdmacht en Hare Mobilisatie in 1914*. Arnhem: Herman de Ruiter.

Van Lith, Hans. 2001. *Plotseling een vreselijke knal: Bommen en mijnen treffen neutraal Nederland, 1914–1918*. Zaltbommel: Europese Bibliotheek.

Van Tuyll van Serooskerken, Hubert. 2001. *The Netherlands and World War I: Espionage, Diplomacy, and Survival.* Leiden: Brill.

Vandenbosch, Amry. 1927. *The Neutrality of the Netherlands during the World War.* Grand Rapids, Mich.: Wm. B. Eerdmans Publishing.

Vanneste, A. 1998. *Kroniek van een Dorp in Oorlog: Neerpelt 1914–1918,* vol. 1. Deurne: Uitgeverij Universitas.

Verwey, Albert. 1916. *Holland en de Oorlog.* Amsterdam: Maatschappij voor Goede en Goedkoope Lectuur.

Wolf, Susanne. 2001. "International Law and Internment in the Netherlands, August to December 1914." Unpublished paper presented at NIOD WOI workgroup, 6 April, Amsterdam.

"GOOD LUCK [. . .] DIG IN!"

The Experience of
Trench Warfare during World War I

———————◆———————

Monday Dec. 25, 1916. Up betimes and by 9.30 A.M. were on our way to trenches. Talk of mud! Unless one has experienced this they wouldn't believe it. One was literally covered by the time we were billeted. No food all day from 7 A.M. to 6 P.M. On guard tonight. Only hope I can stand the racket until I've done 'my bit'. Under fire from shells and trench mortars for the first time in my life and our dugout fairly shook one shell burst so close to us. So did my nerves. (Burrell 1916)

THIS DIARY ENTRY BY CANADIAN PRIVATE HERBERT BURRELL is a fairly typical description of life in the trenches. It describes the mud, fear, boredom, and sometimes hunger of front-line life during World War I. For the most part, trench life was in fact highly routine—particularly between battles and in quiet areas. Time was divided into "tours" of a few days, although in extreme cases when the front lines could not be relieved, soldiers were forced to stay for periods of several weeks. "Tours" to the front lines alternated with periods in the support trenches, or with "rest" periods behind the lines. Rest periods were not exactly rest, as soldiers underwent training, drilled, and worked, repairing railways, cutting wood, or building roads (Simpson 1993, 10). In historical perspective, this was the norm for

91

World War I; every diary, every novel, every poem, and every story of World War I mentions the trenches.

At the time, however, it was so far from what soldiers, commanders, and indeed the public expected as to be bizarre. Most European military commanders looked on the Austro-Prussian War of 1866 and the Franco-Prussian War of 1870 as the instructive cases for "modern" warfare. Future wars, they thought, would be like those: highly mobile and over relatively quickly. Indeed the initial months of World War I demonstrated all the characteristics they might have expected. On the western front, a strong German offensive swept through Belgium and into France, threatening Paris. Only the "Miracle of the Marne" halted the German drive and forced the invaders back to the Aisne River. French efforts to reclaim their territory by outflanking the Germans created a "race to the sea"; it ended, however, in a dead heat, with the French and German armies facing each other along a line that stretched from the North Sea to Switzerland.

In the east, the ponderous Russian advance was stymied by the rapid deployment of the German Eighth Army, which whirled on its interior lines to destroy two Russian armies. A lack of further resources on the German part combined with an understandable caution on the Russian side to induce a virtual standstill by mid-1915, however. Further south, the Russian and Austrian forces initially met in a confusing swirl of battles along the plains in front of the Carpathian Mountains. Here too, though, the initial movement soon gave way to a stalemate on both fronts that drove soldiers on all sides to dig in. Instead of glorious charges and flowing battles, there were everywhere trenches and carnage.

The trenches had a geography all their own. According to historian Paul Fussell, theoretically it should have been possible to walk underground from the coast of Belgium to the Swiss border, through a meandering trench system so jagged as to be almost equal in length to the circumference of the earth (Fussell 1975, 37). Improved artillery and machine guns, rather than facilitating movement, rendered it almost impossible. Trench warfare, almost unheard of before this, became the defining factor of World War I.

To some degree, this was a matter of choice for the Germans. Having penetrated into enemy territory, they were able to choose suitable defensive locations where they might hold and, conceivably, force the opposition to negotiate, if not surrender. German trenches, therefore, tended to be elaborate, almost permanent fortifications. German soldiers excavated not only trenches but also huge dugouts that served as kitchens, meeting rooms, and full-sized living quarters. In the 1916 issue of *Architectural Digest,* no less, an Allied officer described one captured German trench near Mametz that

> was designed to house a whole company of 300 men, with the needful kitchens, provisions and munitions storerooms . . . an engine-room, and a motor room; many of the captured dugouts were thus lighted by electricity. . . . [In] the officers' quarters there have been found full-length mirrors, comfortable bedsteads, cushioned armchairs, and some pictures, and one room is lined with glazed "sanitary" paper. (Booth 1996, 75)

Henry Gregory, a British private with the 199th Machine Gun Company, recalled his first sight of the enemy fortifications as well:

> Infantry bombing squads began to work their way along a maze of enemy dugouts, which were palaces compared to most of those we had occupied in the British Lines. I remember one German dugout in particular; it had forty steps leading down to a veritable home from home, with bread and bottles of wine on tables. There was also a piano, the top of which was covered with picture postcards of places in Germany where, apparently, the occupants of the dugout came from. (Simpson 1993, 49)

Once the Germans dug in on the western front in late 1914, the Allied troops had to follow suit. Private Leonard Wood of the First East Lancashire Regiment recalled the situation:

> At the first part of the war there were not any trenches to speak of. We had to dig them. Dig out the dirt and throw it in a pile; then throw sandbags on top; and then we'd nicely have the trench ready, when two of those "bottle-busters" [shells] came along and ruined our work. (Reid 1985, 45)

Fussell suggests that the Allies had much more haphazard trenches because of an official injunction that read, in part: "The choice of a [defensive] position and its preparation must be made with a view to economizing the power expended on defense in order that the power of the offense may be increased" (Fussell 1975, 43). Because the British believed that the offensive breakthrough would come, their trenches were built as a temporary measure, a stopgap until the expected war of movement broke out again.

The recollections of George Coppard, a British soldier engaged in those early battles, support Fussell's thesis:

> The whole of our trench warfare seemed to be based on the concept that we, the British, were not stopping in the trenches for long, but were tarrying awhile on the way to Berlin and that very soon we would be chasing Jerry across the country. The result, in the long term, meant that we lived a mean and impoverished sort of existence in lousy scratch holes. (Coppard 1969, 87)

The typical British trench consisted of three roughly parallel lines—forward, support, and reserve—connected by a perpendicular communication line. All of the trench lines zigzagged, a design feature intended to reduce the effectiveness of enemy artillery fire and to offer defensive positions in case any portion of the trench was overrun. The first, or forward line, was most often little more than a ditch, not even deep enough to provide cover to an upright soldier. It was augmented by sandbag parapets with machine-gun posts built in, and fronted by layers of barbed-wire obstacles. The supporting and reserve trenches were increasingly more comfortable, as Ian Hay recalled:

> The firing [forward] trench is our place of business, our office in the city, so to speak. The supporting trench is our suburban residence, whither the weary toiler may betake himself periodically (or, more correctly, in relays) for purposes of refreshment and repose. (Hay 1916, 97)

There were, of course, variations in style created by prevailing conditions, terrain, and intent—what Fussell refers to as "national styles" (Fussell 1975, 43). The French, for instance, usually constructed only two lines of trenches. The front line, which was used as a firing base, consisted of strongly fortified positions separated by unpopulated and only thinly defended segments. The area between positions was regarded as a "kill zone," where enfilading fire could be brought to bear on the enemy. Austro-Hungarian forces, in comparison, concentrated their strength in the forward line, leaving only a small reserve in the support trenches. Their first lines resembled those of the Germans, with deep bunkers housing kitchens and soldiers' quarters. The Russians tended to concentrate their reserves in the rear, where they huddled in cavernous dugouts out of sight of the enemy

Germans in their well-protected trenches on the Belgian frontier aiming at the enemy.
(National Archives)

and, theoretically, out of danger from artillery fire. Like the French, they usually constructed only two lines of fortifications.

The trench systems thus differed significantly in terms of proximity to the enemy, danger, and environmental quality. In some cases the trenches were in "quiet sectors," areas of the front line where attacks, artillery fire, and flooding were uncommon. And yet everywhere the trenches and the experience of the trenches was roughly the same. Saps (small trenches) led out into no-man's-land for reconnaissance and behind the trenches into latrines. No-man's-land, the area between opposing trenches, was protected by barbed-wire entanglements sometimes up to fifty meters (165 feet) thick (Fussell 1975, 41). Behind the front-line trench were the equally twisty communication trenches leading back to the support trench, which incorporated dugouts housing section or company headquarters. And behind the support trench was the reserve trench, housing battalion headquarters and advance dressing stations. Divisional and corps' headquarters lay yet further behind all this.

Wireless and telephone communications existed, but due to the noise, the shelling, and destruction of wires, they were often unreliable in the front lines. The planned jaggedness combined with artillery damage to make huge mazes in the ground. Guides were thus indispensable, and trenches were often named in order to aid directions. Names also often reflected familiar streets, landmarks, towns, or in some cases danger: Petticoat Lane, Regent Street, Hyde Park Corner, or Dead Man's Corner, for instance (Fussell 1975, 43).

Messages often had to be carried by runners, soldiers notable for their speed and dexterity, who would run between the lines delivering messages and instructions. As runners were often out in the open, in full view of the enemy, the job was a particularly dangerous one. One runner described his job:

> Many were the shocks that a runner would get in the night, as each rustle of trees made him think it was the enemy. He would strain his eyes and ears on those night runs to near bursting point, as every little sound in the night seemed to magnify itself many times over, and at every sound his hold on his rifle would tighten. (Simpson 1993, 19)

For the most part, however, life in the trenches—like military life almost everywhere—consisted of routine. Because of the cover afforded by darkness, nights were often busier than the days. Troop and supply movements were usually effected by night, and those soldiers not shuttling from one place to another were commonly occupied with patrols and wire repair (Heyman 2002, 45). Both sides consequently sent patrols out during the night as well, hoping to gain intelligence about the enemy's position or intent by listening in on work patrols or capturing some forward sentries for interrogation. German patrols usually consisted of eight enlisted men, unaccompanied by an officer; the Russians did not dare to send enlisted men out without an officer present. For all sides, though, these patrols were the most common form of action seen by the men at the front, as large offensives were difficult and costly to mount as well as generally unsuccessful. One French sergeant, with the 161st Infantry Division, described the experience of a night patrol thus:

> We slid forward imperceptibly, moving on our elbows and knees, our left hands gripping the handle of our bayonets. I scoured the enemy trenches

with an intense gaze, but not fixedly, for if you keep on staring into the pitch blackness, vague shadows seem to appear, immobile objects seem to move, and imagination takes over from precise observation. (Ellis 1976, 74)

Day and night were separated by a "stand to" at dawn and at dusk, the times when the troops were most likely to attack or be attacked. "Twice a day," Fussell writes, "everyone stared silently across the wasteland at the enemy's hiding place and considered how to act if a field-gray line suddenly appeared and grew larger and larger through the mist and the half-light. Twice a day everyone enacted this ritual of alert defence that served to dramatize what he was in the trench for and that couldn't help emphasize the impossibility of escaping" (Fussell 1975, 51).

For some soldiers this routine was comforting, but for others, such as Harold Harvey, the very routine was trying. He noted that

More trying—more wearing and tearing to the nerves—than anything that in my experience ever followed it was the stand to itself. The moments, minutes, even hours that followed the old familiar order, "stand to," were the worst I ever went through. As every eventide comes on I still feel just a little—just a very little—of what I felt then. (Harvey 1920, 82)

Once the sun was fully up, and the danger of an attack in the half-light had passed, soldiers were allowed to descend from the fire step, start breakfast, and begin the "normal" day (Fussell 1975, 46). For the most part, this consisted of repairing the trenches and creating new dugouts or improving old ones. Philip Gibbs, one of the official British reporters in World War I, recalled:

There was always work to do in the trenches—draining them, strengthening their parapets, making their walls, tiling or boarding their floorways, timbering the dugouts, and after it was done another rainstorm or snowstorm undid most of it, and the parapets slid down, the water poured in, and spaces were opened for German machine gun fire. (http://www.firstworldwar.com/bio/gibbs.htm)

Except in rare circumstances, soldiers in the front lines had to stay underground, with their heads well below the parapet, or they risked being shot by a sniper. One soldier recounted his "typical" day in a quiet sector:

The day is long, so long. Bored . . . stiff from sitting or crouching on the ground all the time . . . we try to amuse ourselves . . . reading . . . playing cards . . . soon give up . . . try less wearisome positions . . . stand up . . . watch the aircraft and their maneuvers through binoculars . . . not much of a distraction . . . go back into the shelter . . . bored as ever . . . write something . . . sleep. (Gibbs 1920, 261)

Of course, performing duties could often be worse. One of those instances, almost universally loathed, was sentry duty. One French soldier described it in the following terms:

One hour, two hours, three hours, the time crawls as if paralyzed. This guard duty will never end. Weariness turns into stupor. The man who was determined not to sleep can feel his eyes about to close, but he will not sleep. He will feel the cold and the rain, he will slip occasionally into swift unconsciousness, but he will not escape completely into good, deep, animal sleep, dreamless and uninterrupted. There is always the rain, always the winter, always the shadow. (Audoin-Rouzeau 1992, 38–39)

The slow tedium of sentry duty must still have been preferable to the sounds of war, however. Artillery posed a constant threat, and even an occasional shell could wreak havoc. One French soldier recalled that he was

walking along, happy despite everything because of the sunshine, when I stopped short at the edge of a shell hole. At the bottom, in the freshly upturned earth, five bodies were spread out so symmetrically that you could see that the shell had burst right in the middle of a little group of men, sending each one flying in a different direction so that these poor bodies looked like the five arms of a macabre review.

The force of the explosion had buried them in the earth; three were almost completely buried in the sides of the pit, like wisps of rag. The arm of one of these flattened bodies stuck straight out of the clay; the hand was intact, with an aluminium ring still on one finger. (Audoin-Rouzeau 1992, 78)

When fire was sustained in long barrages during battle, often referred to as "drum fire" (*Trummelfeuer*) by the Germans, the noise could induce that condition peculiar to World War I: shellshock. After the war almost 6 percent of British soldiers drew disability pensions for "neurasthenia," many of them permanently affected by the combination of abject fear and deafening noise (Ferguson 1998, 341). John Patrick Teahan, a military policeman on the front lines in France, described one relatively small artillery attack: "Shells pour across the sky from British batteries behind us. . . . They sound like anything from a rocket to an express train. Others scream like huge sheets of heavy wrapping paper being torn apart" (Teahan 1999, 81). It was, of course, much worse on the receiving end. A German soldier watched the effect of artillery during a British attack:

> Whole sections appeared to fall. All along the line, Englishmen could be seen throwing their hands in the air and collapsing, never to move again. Badly wounded rolled about in their agony, while other casualties crawled into shell holes for shelter. . . . The noise of the battle became indescribable. . . . With all this were mingled the moans of the wounded, cries for help and the last screams of death. (Lloyd 1976, 88–93)

Both sides eventually developed strategies for avoiding such disastrous bombardments. The Germans and Russians, for instance, would retreat to their deep bunkers and wait until the barrage stopped, then rush out to man their machine guns and defensive positions in anticipation of a coming assault. To counter this, the "creeping barrage" developed, where the artillerists would move the range of fire back at predetermined intervals to allow the infantry to advance accordingly.

Artillery thus became more deadly for both sides, and as the war dragged on the continuous shelling turned the battlefield into a nightmare landscape. Lieutenant Bernard Pitt noted one tour of no-man's-land as follows:

> I climbed into the field, which of course consists of shell holes, and had a look 'round. . . . Along by the high banks of the trenches thousands of tins are lying: bully beef, jam, soup, cigarette, sausage, etc. Bits of iron and bits of shell are everywhere, and here and there are canonical fuses, our own and the enemy's, since this ground was once in German hands. . . . I found a dugout that had got lost and took some crockery out of it. Corpses had been uncovered, and I had some men out to rebury them. Every heavy shell hereabouts disturbs some wretched, half-decayed soldier. . . .
>
> Farther back on the other side of the German wire—all smashed to bits— there were a dozen dead men, two of them lieutenants. I got a party of men and buried the poor fellows. They were all blackened, and the hands were al-

Canadian troops going "over the top" during training near St. Pol, France, October 1916. (National Archives)

most fleshless. Over each man's mound we stuck a rifle and bayonet—heaps were lying about—and his cap on the rifle butt. (Simpson 1993, 36)

Once out of the trenches, soldiers were exposed to a myriad of weapons, the most feared of which was the machine gun. A relatively new weapon, the machine gun was estimated to be equal to somewhere between thirty and sixty individual riflemen. Because it was such a small target, moreover, it was difficult to put out of action (Heyman 2002, 29). A few enemy men operating a machine gun could destroy the ordered rows of soldiers crossing no-man's-land, inflicting terrible damage and injury. Trying to move across such terrain in the heat of a battle, and in the face of machine guns, was a horrific experience. A sergeant of the 3rd Tyneside Irish at the Battle of the Somme, 1 July 1916, remembered seeing

away to my left and right, long lines of men. Then I heard the "patter, patter" of machine guns in the distance. By the time I'd gone another ten yards there seemed to be only a few men left standing around; by the time I had gone twenty yards, I seemed to be on my own. Then I was hit myself. (Keegan 1998, 295)

That opening day of the Battle of the Somme was the worst of the war: of 100,000 men, 20,000 were killed and 40,000 were wounded. Some units, such as the 1st Newfoundland Regiment, sustained such a loss of life that they simply ceased to exist (indeed, 1 July remains a day of mourning in Newfoundland) (Keegan 1998, 295).

As bad as the Somme was, it was not atypical of the battles between trenches in World War I. The diary of Gordon Howard, a British artillery man, provides an overview of how such a battle might unfold:

Just as a curtain is rung up at a theatre, so things began. Directed from the dugout, invisible batteries began thundering. We watched their shells bursting all around the distant ridge, churning it up like water—an irruption [*sic*] of dirty brown earth and dense smoke.

It went on for forty minutes or so. Behind us the aide was digging his pegs into the switch-board, talking all the time, controlling the fire, giving ranges, warning unseen regiments to be ready to advance. And all the while not a man showed between us and the horizon. It was the uncanniest panorama imaginable, a storm of projectiles coming out of the unseen and converging on what looked like a deserted hillock.

Then, just as abruptly as the guns had opened, the firing ceased, and simultaneously men, the size of dots, rose in long lines out of the plain and crept (as it seemed, though I knew the fellows were going at the double) nearer and nearer to the smoke-topped ridge.

I could hear the continuous rattle of rifle fire and the quicker purr of machine guns, though whether they were ours or the Germans' or both it was impossible to tell. Nor could I at that distance have told how the affair ended, but for the voice on the telephone. "Righto! Good luck! Splendid! Dig in!" (Howard 1970, 95–96)

One French soldier rendered a more detailed account:

At the prescribed hour our officers gave us the usual pep talk, with last instructions, and then enquired if we were ready. At our response in the affirmative, there was a moment's silence and contemplation, and then suddenly the shout "Advance!" . . .

Without hesitation, officers and men humped on to the parapet and ran to the front line to take the place of friends who were already close to the Boche line. We hardly stopped before we heard the cry again, "Advance!"

We scrambled over the next parapet and ran forward after the first wave, shouting whatever came into our heads—"Vive la France! Get at them! Come on, boys!" The guns were crackling away ahead of us, the machine guns spitting out their ribbons of death, tack-tack-tack-tack-tack.

We caught up to our friends but—to our horror—we met a barbed wire barrier that was still intact and more than thirty metres deep. And all the time the enemy machine guns went on—tack-tack-tack-tack-tack—while we could see our friends on our left, falling, covering the ground with their blue uniforms, red with blood where they were hit.

Now the third and fourth waves arrived in their turn. Up ahead a few men had managed to slip under the wire and reach the troublesome trench. They jumped in, but sadly we did not see them again. There were not enough of them. It was impossible to get across the wire en masse anywhere else, and our position became more and more critical.

The shout went up: "Tools!" We dug into the ground furiously and were soon dug in right against the Boche wire. Shots whistled over us and we hung onto the ground we had won. (Audoin-Rouzeau 1992, 70–71)

Ground won was usually minimal and frequently lost just as quickly, and this constant back-and-forth contributed to not only the misery of the men but to the casualties. As Philip Gibbs recalled,

It was very annoying—using a feeble word—to battalion officers and men of the 3rd Division Suffolks and King's Own Liverpools, Gordons and Royal Scots who had first come out of the salient, out of its mud and snow and slush and shell fire to a pretty village far behind the lines, on the road to Calais, where they were getting back to a sense of normal life again. Sleeping in snug billets, warming their feet at wood fires, listening with enchantment to the silence about them, free from the noise of artillery. . . . They were hugging themselves with the thought of a month of this. . . .

Then, because they had been in the salient so long, and had held this line so stubbornly, they were ordered back again to recapture the position lost by new men. (Gibbs 1920, 261)

Trench warfare clearly was, to understate conditions, a wrenching experience. Billy Gray, a subaltern in the Canadian army, described his feelings immediately after a battle:

> But the aftermath—the vacuum at the stomach—the palpitating heart—the deep breaths you needed, that, if you did not take, it seemed as if you'd choke, the feeling you must sit down—the desire for a drink—the insatiable way in which you ate up cigarette after cigarette in long deep inhales—the hope they would not start bombarding again—the cheery voice you forced as you walked along a bath mat and jokingly curbed your own desire to shout by praising the men and belittling "the show"; all these when your emotions that had bubbled to the boiling point again simmered down. (Gray 1916, 144–145)

Gray's "cheerfulness," and that of so many others, covered for the often-terrible destruction that took place, here described by another soldier:

> After a battle there would be some men lying around seriously wounded. I saw men without arms and legs or with their stomachs hanging out. Then stretcher bearers picked up any man with wounds, but the dead were just left where they fell. A mortally wounded man was not touched. I turned my guts when I saw these things. I once looked in a dugout . . . up against the wall there were some dead men with their brains and stomachs splattered all over the place. I got used to it, thinking nothing of it after awhile. We used to say, "When your time comes—you go." That's all. (Reid 1985, 66)

During the Battle of Verdun in the French sector of the Allied trenches, half a million French soldiers had been killed by 1916, leading one soldier to comment that "All day long they lie there, being decimated, getting themselves killed next to the bodies of those killed earlier" (Ferguson 1998, 340).

The perpetual presence of rotting corpses brought more than just sheer, spectacular horror, however; as Stuart Cloete found out:

> The first experience I had of rotting bodies had been at Serre, where, as a battalion, we dealt with the best part of a thousand dead who came to pieces in our hands. As you lifted a body by its arms and legs they detached themselves from the torso, and this was not the worst thing. Each body was cov-

ered inches deep with a black fur of flies which flew up into your face, into your mouth, eyes and nostrils, as you approached. The bodies crawled with maggots. (Simpson 1993, 42)

The dead bodies also attracted rats, and the rodents quickly extended their domain to the trenches, providing the soldiers there with a more annoying, if less deadly, enemy. One captain in the British army noted of his dugout, "I can't sleep in mine, as it is over-run with rats. Pullman slept here one morning and woke up to find one sitting on his face" (Simpson 1993, 29).

Even more prevalent were lice and other insects. Soldiers could not often wash while in the trenches, or change their clothing for the duration of their time at the front (a few days to over a week), so lice bred extremely quickly. Private Burrell noted in his diary the prevalence of the insects:

Our trenches here are in the midst of the scene of some great battle where the French lost 60,000 men. One sees evidences quite often by bodies protruding through the trench walls. . . . My companions are busy hunting lice on their shirts and Lee tells me he has had scabies for months and that they are very catching. Pleasant news as he sleeps close to me. So far I've escaped these trench pests. (Burrell 1916)

Henry Gregory, a private with the 199th Machine Gun Company, likewise told of a friend's torture with lice:

All at once he said "Damn this, Gregory, I cannot stand it any longer!" He took off his tunic—we slept in them—then he took off his jersey, then his shirt. He put his shirt in the middle of the dugout floor and put his jersey and tunic on again. As we both sat up in bed watching the shirt he had taken off and put on the floor, it actually lifted; it was swarming with lice. (Simpson 1993, 39)

A soldier posted to the Dardanelles wrote home about similar conditions there:

There are so many flies in my dug-out that I am obliged to write in almost complete darkness. . . . The heat is pretty bad, but it is nothing to the flies. The country is dried up beyond all expression. The roads, with huge ruts from the heavy gun-carriages and ammunition cases, are rivers of white dust, which flies up at the least breath of wind. (Vassal 1916, 154)

Most soldiers on the European fronts, both east and west, likely would have given anything to have to deal with "only" dust. The norm in Europe was mud, mud, and more mud. The transit of thousands of heavy guns following hundreds of thousands of soldiers and their provisions to the lines stripped the rear ground almost bare. The constant artillery barrages churned up the ground even more, rendering the front an eerie, lunar landscape devoid of trees and crisscrossed with the earthen homes of the soldiers. As the chorus of a popular song at the time put it,

> *It's mud, just mud; a-sticking and a-clinging to all;*
> *Yes mud, just mud; it comes when the rain starts to fall;*
> *Oh it's hell for the soldier, and worse for the truck;*
> *The whole army wades to its knees in muck;*
> *The cannons and the wagons and the men all get stuck;*
> *In the mud; that's all.* (Gibbons 1918, 162–164)

The weather certainly played a part, as one might expect. This was especially true on the eastern front, where ice and snow were more common and lasted longer. Those phenomena were not unknown on the western front, however, as Philip Gibbs noted: "It was so bad in parts of the line during November storms that whole sections of trench collapsed into a chaos of slime and ooze. It was the frost as well as the rain which caused this ruin, making the earthworks sink under their weight of sandbags" (Gibbs 1920, 208).

The mud, however, was a year-round fact of life for all combatants in trench warfare. From the moment that soldiers began to dig in, they had to deal with the constant strain of mud, as Private David Shand, 2nd Gordon Highlanders, relates: "Water came pouring in when digging down only a few feet. We had to do a lot of riveting to the sides of the trenches to keep them from falling in. The country was so flat that the water couldn't be drained away" (Reid 1985, 65). Another soldier in the same unit wrote:

As Highlanders, we suffered the most as we wore kilts, low shoes, khaki spats and thick hose. The suction of the mud was so great that it pulled everything off our legs. Some men sank to their waist or their knees and had to be pulled out. . . . We spent many days in our bare feet when the snow was on

British soldiers discuss their options as a horse is stuck in the mud during the Battle of Flanders. Weather was an important element in many of the battles of World War I. (The Great War in Gravure: the New York Times Portfolio of the War. *The New York Times Co., 1917)*

the ground. Then we were issued with fur-lined leather waistcoats. We put our legs through the sleeves so the jackets covered out feet. We would have frozen otherwise. (Reid 1985, 67)

A third wrote:

Another trying day's work in the mud. . . . We are like the rats which infest the trenches burrowing in the ground; sleeping by day; grovelling in the mud at night. Mud in your bed; in your mess tin; on your food. We seldom wash. No water to spare. (Burrell 1916)

Such conditions bore heavily on the soldiers and, in many instances, led to physical afflictions, as Gibbs noted:

Another misery came to tortured soldiers in the line, and it was called "trench-foot." Many men standing in slime for days and nights in field boots or putties lost all sense of feeling in their feet. These feet of theirs, so cold and wet, began to swell, and then go "dead," and then suddenly to burn as though touched by red-hot pokers. When the "reliefs" went up scores of men could not walk back from the trenches, but had to crawl, or be carried pick-a-back by their comrades to the field dressing stations. (Gibbs 1920, 210)

Commanders often thought cases of trench foot to be just another form of malingering at first, or attributed the problem to carelessness and poor personal hygiene. The issuance of foot oil and rubbing drill to soldiers in the trenches reduced the incidence of trench foot by early 1916, but the mud remained a constant burden to the soldiers.

In one case at least, however, the mud saved lives, according to Sergeant Howard, a gunner in the Canadian army:

One morning at dawn we were in action to repel an attack and the Germans turned a really heavy gun on us. They dropped three in front and the fourth landed between our two guns. The crater was so wide that both guns slipped into the crater. The mud deluged down on the remaining guns and ammunition making it unfit to use until cleaned, so we were all out of action. The mud rained down on me and I was plastered from head to foot; you could hardly see my buttons. No one was hurt. The shell went in so deep that the mud saved us. (Howard 1970, 24)

What is perhaps surprising is how well—sometimes even cheerfully—the fighting men on all sides bore up under these conditions. John Horace Brown, a Canadian soldier, wrote almost fondly of his experience:

There is a kind of charm about the life that one will look back to when it is all over. There is not so much excitement as you might think. Sometimes it makes me think of being out hunting. The other morning when we stood-to, which we always do at dawn and in the evening, I couldn't help but think of duck hunting. It was something the way the sun rose and the mists, rising out of the long grass . . . that reminded me of it. I'd love to be up at the lake and get out in the canoe again. (Brown 1915)

A French soldier who was headed out on patrol recorded the conditions more laconically:

It is time to go. With tent canvas slung across one's shoulders, haversacks at our sides, full of water bottles and our cafard [a cafard is literally a cockroach, in this case perhaps a euphemism for dirtiness, stench, or lack of hygiene in general] drowned in cheap wine, we wait to set off when night has fully covered everything with its dark camouflage. After barely ten minutes' walking, it begins to rain. This is when you must arm yourself with patience, determination, and strength. (Audoin-Rouzeau 1992, 39)

The struggle against the elements seemed somehow to bring the men who shared such hardship even closer together, as John Gallishaw, a Newfoundlander stationed in the Dardanelles, recalled:

The men all did their best to make the work of the non-coms [noncommissioned officers] easy. . . . The men called their corporals and sergeants Jack or Bill or Mac, but there was never the slightest question about obeying an order. Everybody was overworked, underfed, and every man tried to give as little trouble as possible. (Gallishaw 1916, 90)

The French newspaper *Le Periscope* reported similar conditions prevailing on the western front in 1916:

Having shared the odd green apple gathered with difficulty during the days of retreating without bread, having laboured together, marched together, suffered at the same places, having been buried by the same mine, stuck in the same mud, having bent their heads under the same rain, having suffered the blast from the same heavy shells, they have developed a deep friendship for each other. From their shared memories and pains has come an indestructible bond which keeps them always together.

You see them like this, in pairs, in the squads, two by two, as if friendship could not be extended to include more people without weakening, and would lose its intensity by being shared. . . .

You never see one without the other. Their lookout points are side-by-side in the trench; they march in the same rank and the more weary of the two hands his rifle over to the other; at dangerous points along the trenches, they keep close together, helping each other along difficult stretches. On fatigue duties they carry the same bit of wood or hurdle; one shifts the earth dug out by the other. They practice the most brotherly communism and share their money; the contents of one bag belong equally to the other; they share parcels, drink from the same water bottle and take it in turns to pay for their drinks.

They read their letters to each other in the evenings in rest camps, before blowing out their candle, they chat about very quietly to each other their families, their affairs, and go to sleep exchanging plans for the future. They are known as *camarades*. (Audoin-Rouzeau, 1992, 95)

On rare occasions, the mutual suffering even extended camaraderie across no-man's-land, as Gibbs noted in 1916:

There, at Hooge, Germans and English talked to one another out of their common misery.

"How deep is it with you?" shouted a German soldier. His voice came from behind a pile of sandbags which divided the enemy and ourselves in a communication trench between the main lines.

"Up to our blooming knees," said an English corporal who was trying to keep his bombs dry under a tarpaulin.

"So? You are lucky fellows. We are up to our belts in it." (Gibbs 1920, 208)

When there was anger about the conditions of life in the trenches, it was often aimed at officers and at the high command. Many soldiers felt their lives were being risked by people who had no idea of the conditions at the front line and could not understand the danger into which they were putting the infantry. Private Burrell, for instance, noted in his diary,

We seldom see our officers here. They are down in a comfortable dugout; are warm and fed on the best; while the men are going hungry and have to carry the rations for the damned officers wherever we go. They play a baby warfare compared to the men & with a few exceptions are a useless bunch. (Burrell 1916)

The food, or the lack of it, was also a common complaint for soldiers in the trenches. The logistics of war became particularly complicated in terms of the delivery of food rations. All food had to be transported to the soldiers in the front lines, and bringing in hot food was often difficult and dangerous work. One soldier remembered:

On one occasion our mid-day meal . . . was very late, and we had become exceptionally hungry. At last the ration orderly arrived, but alas, in coming up the communication trench he had trodden on a loose duckboard, which had sprung up and tipped him into a few feet of icy water. The Dixie containing the stew was also upset, and all that was rescued were a few carrots and a little gravy! (Simpson 1993, 18)

Soldiers were meant to receive rations of fresh meat, bread, cheese, and fresh vegetables each day, but in the front lines this was rarely possible. The British diet at the front was highly unvaried; for instance, usually consisting of bully beef (a tinned meat somewhat like corned beef), canned stew, bread, jam, and biscuits known as "hard tack." One soldier reported that when wood for the fire ran out "war biscuits make dandy fuel" (Teahan 1999, 86). Regarding a friend, he added, "He has so far escaped without injury except for the loss of six teeth through chewing war biscuits" (Teahan 1999, 97).

All of this the soldiers bore with great patience and fortitude. Though the postwar literature is rife with tales of the horrors of trench warfare, few cared to let on how hard it was at the time. A "typical" letter home, from A. G. Heath, a British officer of the 6th Royal West Kents, carried only veiled hints at the true nature of the conflict:

Just a few loving lines in answer to your kind and loving letter, and thanking you for the two beautiful parcels that have come in very handy. The cake was quite unbroken, and me and my mates enjoyed it very much in the trenches.

Dear Mrs. We have been six days and nights under fire, but the Germans will never advance near; they are afraid of our rifle fire. . . .

We are back now for a bit of rest, and we can do with it too, but every night we dig trenches under fire. We shall go into the trenches again soon, and after that we come on leave, so I shall see you and the two dear babies again. Ho, what joyful times we shall have when this is all over. (Reid 1985, 78)

When the horror of the war and the shock of the conditions of trench warfare—the mud, the rats, the lice, the shelling, the sickness, the death, and yet more mud—have worn off, it is this sense of duty and determination that remain fixed in the literature of World War I. It is a sense perhaps best summed up by the words of a soldier's diary, penned in the course of the hopeless fighting at Gallipoli:

In this incomparable scenery, when shells have stopped raining down on us, when the infernal noise ceases, when the wounded have been carried away and their groans forgotten, delicious visions offer themselves to us soldiers.

I look to the future with joy and courage; I do not linger over the past. If the soldier at war gave time to thoughts of love and caresses, little by little he would become incapable of struggling on up the slope. He prefers to keep going, and drives away every soft thought. (Vassal 1916, 151)

—Kirsty Robertson
—Shaun M. Jones

References and Further Reading

Allen, E. P. S. 2005. *The 116th Battalion in France, 1914–1918*. Ottawa: CEF.

Ashworth, Tony. 1980. *Trench Warfare, 1914–1918: The Live-and-Let-Live System*. Basingstoke, N.H.: Macmillan.

Audoin-Rouzeau, Stephane. 1992. *Men At War, 1914–1918: National Sentiment and Trench Journalism in France during the First World War*. Providence: Berg.

———. 2002. *1914–1918: Understanding the Great War*. London: Profile.

Barbusse, Henri. 2004. *Under Fire*. New York: Penguin.

Barton, Peter. 2005. *Beneath Flanders Fields: The Tunnellers' War, 1914–1918*. Montreal: McGill-Queen's University Press.

Bird, Will R. 2000. *The Communication Trench: Anecdotes and Statistics from the Great War, 1914–1918*. Ottawa: CEF.

Booth, Allyson. 1996. *Postcards from the Trenches*. New York: Oxford University Press.

Brown, John Horace. 1915. Diary. Ottawa: Canadian War Museum, 58 AI 7.9 acq 19830003–026.

Brown, Malcolm. 2001. *The Imperial War Museum Book of the Western Front*. London: Pan.

Bull, Stephen. 2002. *World War I Trench Warfare*. 2 vols. Oxford: Osprey.

Burrell, Herbert Hecford. 1916. Diary. Ottawa: Canadian War Museum, 58A 1 92.11 acq 1992 018700z.

Cassar, George H. 2004. *Kitchener's War: British Strategy from 1914 to 1916*. Washington, D.C.: Brassey's.

Cochrane, Peter. 2004. *The Western Front, 1916–1918*. Sydney: ABC.

Coppard, George. 1969. *With a Machine Gun to Cambria: The Tale of a Young Tommy in Kitchener's Army, 1914–1918*. London: HMSO.

Ellis, John. 1976. *Eye-Deep in Hell: Trench Warfare in World War I*. New York: Pantheon.

Ferguson, Niall. 1998. *The Pity of War: Explaining World War I*. London: Allen Lane.

Frantzen, Allen J. 2004. *Bloody Good: Chivalry, Sacrifice, and the Great War*. Chicago: University of Chicago Press.

Fussell, Paul. 1975. *The Great War and Modern Memory*. London: Oxford University Press.

Gallishaw, John. 1916. *Trenching at Gallipoli: The Personal Narrative of a Newfoundlander with the Ill-Fated Dardenelles Expedition*. New York: Century.

Gibbons, Herbert Adams. 1918. *Songs from the Trenches*. New York: Harper and Brothers.

Gibbs, Philip Hamilton S. 1920. *Now It Can Be Told*. New York: Harper Brothers.

Granatstein, J. L. 2004. *Hell's Corner: An Illustrated History of Canada's Great War, 1914–1918*. Vancouver: Douglas and McIntyre.

Gray, Billy. 1916. *A Sunny Subaltern: Billy's Letters from Flanders*. Toronto: McClelland, Goodchild, and Stewart.

Harvey, Harold. 1920. *A Soldier's Sketches under Fire*. Toronto: Thomas Allen.

Hay, Ian. 1916. *The First Hundred Thousand*. Boston: Houghton Mifflin.

Heyman, Neil M. 2002. *Daily Life during World War I*. Westport, Conn.: Greenwood.

Holmes, Richard. 2004. *Tommy: The British Soldier on the Western Front, 1914–1918*. London: HarperCollins.

Howard, Gordon S. 1970. *The Memoires [sic] of a Citizen Soldier*. Regina, Saskatchewan: Gordon S. Howard.

http://www.firstworldwar.com\bio\gibbs.htm (accessed December 2004).

Johnson, J. H. 1995. *Stalemate! The Great Trench Warfare Battles of 1915–1917*. New York: Sterling.

Jünger, Ernst. 1988. *Copse 125: A Chronicle from the Trench Warfare of 1918*. New York: Howard Fertig.

Keegan, John. 1998. *The First World War*. New York: Alfred A. Knopf.

Lloyd, Allan. 1976. *The War in the Trenches*. New York: David McKay.

Mills, Scott. 2002. *Trenches*. Marietta, Ga.: Top Shelf.

Moore, Christopher. 1998. *Trench Fever*. London: Little, Brown.

Parker, Ernest W. 1994. *Into Battle: 1914–1918*. London: Leo Cooper.

Rawling, Bill. 1992. *Surviving Trench Warfare: Technology and the Canadian Corps, 1914–1918*. Toronto: University of Toronto Press.

Reid, Gordon. 1985. *Poor Bloody Murder: Personal Memoirs of the First World War*. Oakville: Mosaic.

Saunders, Anthony. 2000. *Dominating the Enemy: War in the Trenches, 1914–1918*. Stroud, U.K.: Sutton.

———. 2000. *Weapons of Trench Warfare, 1914–1918*. Stroud, U.K.: Sutton.

Saunders, Nicholas J. 2003. *Trench Art: Materialities and Memories of War*. New York: Berg.

Simpson, Andy, ed. 1993. *Hot Blood and Cold Steel: Life and Death in the Trenches of the First World War.* London: Tom Donovan.

Smith, Leonard V. 2003. *France and the Great War, 1914–1918.* Cambridge: Cambridge University Press.

Teahan, John Patrick. 1999. *Diary Kid.* Edited by Grace Keenan Price. Ottawa: Oberon.

Thompson, Hugh S. 2004. *Trench Knives and Mustard Gas: With the 42nd Rainbow Division in France.* College Station: Texas A&M University Press.

Vassal, Joseph M. J. 1916. *Uncensored Letters from the Dardanelles.* London: W. Heinemann.

Veronesi, Sandro. 2003. *No-man's Land.* Milan: Bompiani.

VICTIMS OF
A GREENISH CLOUD

The Experience of
a Gas Attack during World War I

───────── ◆ ─────────

T HE HISTORIAN ALBERT PALAZZO WROTE OF THE USE OF GAS as a weapon in the First World War, "All warfare and weapons are by definition morally offensive, but gas . . . occupies a special niche that society identifies as beyond the pale of acceptable human behaviour" (Palazzo 2000, 2). When chlorine gas was used as a weapon for the first time on the western front in 1915, it signaled an escalation in the war of attrition. The horror aroused by the use of gas in the war was like that of no other weapon. The highly visible effects of gas poisoning, combined with the ominous nature of the gas cloud floating across no-man's-land (the unoccupied land between the opposing armies) and the ethical problem of introducing biological weapons, made it appear as a particularly malevolent and feared tool, in spite of the questionability of its effectiveness.

Unlike traditional weapons of war, a cloud of poisonous gas completely erased the individuality of its victims, rendering bravery utterly useless and destroying long-held notions of war as a glorious and romantic pursuit (Richter 1992, 1). These very qualities, however, were exactly what made it attractive to those using it. The greatest problem presented to those running the First World War was that it was essentially a defensive war—a barrage of bullets and shellfire made crossing no-man's-land and breaking through into enemy territory virtually impossible. Gas seemed to offer a solution to this impasse. If it could silently kill the enemy troops on the other side of the battlefield, then a break would be made in enemy lines, possibly transforming the war into an offensive one fought by mobile troops on open battlefields (Palazzo 2000, 6).

A return to an open style of warfare was the great hope of many of the Great War generals who felt that the only way to win was to break through the opposite lines. It was thought, particularly by the British and French armies, that trench warfare was a stopgap. Breaking out of the trenches was one of the most important goals of many of the huge and deadly battles fought between 1915 and 1918. The British general Sir Douglas Haig, in particular, clung to the notion through much of the war that the cavalry could still be used once the battle had opened up (Palazzo 2000, 20–21). Gas seemed to be one way to break the lines of the enemy and create a war of movement.

Gas was actually used for the first time on the eastern front, at Bolimov, Russia, in January 1915; the gas used, however, was lachrymal—irritating, but not lethal (Keegan 1998, 197). Beyond this, there were problems with delivery. Conditions on the Russian front were so cold that the gas froze and dropped to the ground at some points, becoming totally ineffective. Shortly afterward, German efforts produced chlorine gas. Chlorine is not always lethal, but extended exposure stimulates too much production of fluid in the lungs, leading to death by drowning (Keegan 1998, 197). The gas used by the Germans against the Allied troops in 1915 was a by-product of the German dye-stuff industry. IG Farben, the main company involved in manufacturing these products, had already saved the German war effort through its experiments to produce synthetic nitrates—an essential component of explosives, and available in natural form only in Allied-controlled territory (Keegan 1998, 197–198).

On the western front, gas was used for the first time in April 1915, at Ypres in Belgium against Algerian and Territorial troops, who were supported by the Canadian army. The Allies were caught completely by surprise, as is shown in this account by Lieutenant Ian Sinclair, 13th Battalion of the Canadian army:

About four o'clock in the afternoon, Captain George MacLaren, Captain Burt Daniels, Tod Bath and myself enjoyed a glorious tea of Scottish short-

Early German gas masks, Ypres, France. (Ridpath, John Clark. Ridpath's History of the World, Volume X. *Jones Bros. Publishing Co., Cincinnati, OH. 1921)*

bread and chocolate biscuits outside Bath's dugout; all of us were very cheerful. After tea we retired to our respective parts of the trench. Shortly afterwards about five o'clock we noticed a heavy greenish cloud hanging over the French lines on our left. We could see the French running back, but owing to the very heavy shelling to which our trenches were now being subjected, we could find out nothing more. (Reid 1980, 79)

At first Sinclair did not make any account of the danger of the gas. He was instead quite taken with the beauty of the spectacle and almost completely fearless, as neither he nor any of his comrades had any experience of gas. His admiration quickly turned to fear, though, as he began to take in the effect on the soldiers of the "greenish cloud":

As we watched it, four red flares were dropped making it quite a pretty sight. Our gaze must have been lingering on this a little too long for when I turned, men were leaving the trenches on our right. A great wall of green gas about fifteen to twenty feet high was on top of us. Captain MacLaren gave an order to get handkerchiefs, soak them and tie them around our mouths and noses. (Some were able to do that and some just urinated on their handkerchiefs.) Some managed to cover their faces. Others, myself included, did not, owing to a scarcity of the necessary articles. Even with these precautions it was hopeless to try and stand up against the stuff, so we retired choking, coughing and spluttering . . .

Anyway the Germans couldn't see us owing to the gas . . . For about seven hours they shelled us most unmercifully: the shells dropping all around, some hitting the parapet, some just going over causing a great many casualties. As far as the Highlanders were concerned we were worthless anyway because we just lay in bundles at the bottom of the trench, choking and gasping for breath. (Reid 1980, 81)

The fact that the Germans were unable to follow up this opportunity demonstrated another of the problematic qualities of gas: it tended to linger in the target area, making attack as difficult as defense. Nonetheless, chlorine gas proved effective enough for the Germans to continue its use. The German gas attack at Langemarck in Ypres had opened an 8,000-meter gap in the Allied line. The Algerian and Territorial troops (the 87th Territorial and 45th Algerian Divisions) were forced to retire. The 1st Canadian Division was heroically able to hold the line. Private David Shand of the 1st Gordon Highlanders, Canadian army, described his first encounter with the aftermath of the gas attack at Ypres, and his shock at the use of the weapon:

We never heard the word *gas* before because the Germans had never used it. So we moved along the railway tracks around Ypres and stopped at a ditch at a first aid clearing station. There were about two hundred to three hundred men lying in that ditch. Some were clawing at their throats. Their brass buttons were green. Their bodies swelled. Some of them were still alive. They were not wearing their belts or equipment and we thought they were Germans. One inquisitive fellow turned a dead man over. He saw a brass clip bearing the name CANADA on the corpse's shoulder and exclaimed "These are Canadians!" (Reid 1980, 82)

The Canadians only managed to hold because the Germans dug in instead of pressing on (Keegan 1998, 198).

Evidence shows that Fritz Haber, the scientist in charge of gas warfare in Germany, believed (even after conducting experiments on himself) that chlorine gas incapacitated rather than killed, and thus the Germans did not foresee their advantage (Richter 1992, 8). Furthermore, because the Canadian command quickly figured out that the gas was water-soluble chlorine and were able to instruct that cloths soaked in water be tied around the face, enough soldiers were able to remain in their places to defend the trenches (Keegan 1998, 198).

Often, though, there was not enough water available. Two weeks later, when the Germans launched their final gas attack of this battle, for instance, this time against the 1st Battalion of the Dorset Regiment, the British troops were caught off guard and were only able to maintain the line through a superhuman effort. Second Lieutenant Kestell-Cornish, with only four men remaining of his platoon of forty, picked up a rifle and fired into the gas cloud to hold off the German attack (Keegan 1998, 199).

After the battle in Ypres, word spread quickly about the use of chlorine gas, and it quickly became a feared and menacing weapon. The psychological impact of gas—a weapon that made dugouts and shelters useless—was perhaps even more threatening than its physical impact (Palazzo 2000, 42). Furthermore, gas could come on very quickly and at any time, as military police officer John Patrick Teahan recalled:

> [The gas] was used in darkness, and the men did not perceive it until it was rolling over them. Many were found this morning with one hand inside the pocket of their tunics; they had been overcome while reaching for their respirators. (Teahan 1999, 83)

Once gas had been established as a weapon, both sides quickly began to use it in the conflict. Following the 1915 battle, British scientists began to experiment. They sent various substances, including an extract of hot peppers and even sneezing powder, over to the other side, before settling on chlorine gas. Later, however, the British developed an even more lethal weapon: mustard gas (Palazzo 2000, 44). Throughout the war, however, the British displayed a sense of moral superiority because the Germans "had done it first" (Richter 1992, 2). In the wake of the first German attack at Ypres, British field marshal H. H. Kitchener noted that the use of gas demonstrated "to what depths of infamy our enemies will go, in order to supplement their want of courage in facing our troops" (Palazzo 2000, 43).

Picture posed in France, near front-line trenches, to illustrate effects of phosgene gas, 1918. (National Archives)

It should be noted, though, that by August 1916 the Germans had discontinued their use of gas whereas the British and Americans continued to use it (Richter 1992, 224).

By early 1916, Allied soldiers were being regularly sent for training in working with and coping with gas. Private Donald Fraser of the Canadian army complained, "The smoke helmets are not very comfortable . . . [and] owing to leaky helmets a few of our fellows got slightly gassed" (Fraser 1985, 96). Fraser was lucky to have been issued a gas mask at all. For some time after the first gas attacks, soldiers were encouraged to use "any loose fabric, such as a sock, sandbag, woollen scarf . . . soaked in urine, wrung out, sufficient to allow free breathing through it, and tied tightly over the nose and mouth" (Richter 1992, 10). One captain even recommended a ladies' sanitary napkin soaked in soda (Richter 1992, 12).

One of the most hated aspects of gas was actually carrying it to the trenches. One soldier remembered that the cylinders

> were horrifying things to handle. They weighed 180 pounds and were slung on a pole between two men. Everyone had to wear his gas helmet all the time

in case the cylinders leaked, and that meant most of the time we were stifled and half suffocated. . . . We tramped through the warm thundery summer rain, the shining wet cylinders swinging between every swearing group of men knocking their knees and trapping their fingers. (Richter 1992, 123)

Even that was not the worst, though; gas canisters frequently leaked or came open without warning in the conditions of the trenches. Soldier Anthony Eden recalled an incident in 1916:

The worst assignment that summer was to carry gas cylinders up communication trenches and install them in our front line. This took many weary and exhausting hours. The most disagreeable part of the business was that we had to wear gas masks rolled up on top of our heads under our tin hats all the time. These masks . . . were damp and impregnated with some unpleasant-smelling stuff which, as we were soon to learn, could bring out an ugly and itching rash on the forehead. (Simpson 1993, 18)

The difficulties of bringing gas into the trenches were compounded by the fact that gas never proved particularly effective—primarily because it was so unpredictable. The first time the British used gas was at the Battle of Loos in 1915. The result was a disaster as company commanders, unwilling to override orders, allowed gas to be released in unfavorable weather. The wind was blowing back on British trenches, and many British soldiers were gassed by "friendly fire" as a result. J. B. Plautnauer remembered:

The noise seemed to increase and they brought a lot of gas casualties along the trench . . . yellow-faced men coughing their lungs up. . . . Most of them were wearing the red, green and white brassards of the Royal Engineers. The German shells had thrown the gas pipes back into the trench and smashed the gas cylinders that had been dug into the parapet. Instead of gassing the Germans they gassed themselves. They lost 58 men out of 64. (Richter 1992, 134)

Occasionally gas did work in the way it was supposed to, as is clear in the following description:

The gas attack was on and I saw it rise from those cylinders, form into a white cloud, and this cloud rose to about 6 to 8 feet from the ground. The whole lot joined up together, and with a west breeze behind it, just went towards the German lines. Behind the gas, walking in an orderly fashion, was the infantry, but they were keeping behind the gas and not belting into it. (Richter 1992, 96)

In spite of some successes, however, after Loos gas was rarely used as a central weapon. Instead it gained a role in the war of attrition. Commanders hoped that the use of gas would wear the enemy down by increasing his misery and making him unwilling to continue. In this the British did have a small advantage, as even though gas was never proven to be a particularly effective killing agent, the British had better respirators than their German counterparts. Because the British knew that German gas masks could only keep out gas fumes for approximately four hours, German soldiers were faced with the disconcerting knowledge that their enemy might be able to produce a threat that could outlast the protection of their masks (Palazzo 2000, 33).

For some soldiers, the use of gas on the enemy was as repugnant as the use of gas on themselves. For most, however, it was simply another weapon. Eventually gas became so familiar as to even remind soldiers of home. John Horace Brown noted in his diary,

We had a smell of our friends' gas. I know the smell but could not place it. It smelled somewhat like an old barrel of apples. There was just a smell of it drifted here today from an attack. It was not strong but it hurt the eyes a little. (Brown 1915)

Lieutenant Billy Gray of the Canadian army even managed to find a bit of ironic levity in the face of German gas attacks:

Well, we started out, the thirty-two all being present at roll call, each one a soldier (private) except his breath which was and still is and likely will be (from the ribald glee emitting from the bar) an admixture of gin and beer, (not at all like the fragrant rose of old England). The breath when breathed upon one in conjunction with a sweet scented odor of gasoline which leaks through the floor of the bus, only convinces me that I have nothing to fear from German gas. (Gray 1916, 58–59)

Another soldier found some humor in the situation as well:

When the alert went off you had to urinate on the cotton waste, tear pieces off to plug your nostrils, shove the rest in your mouth and tie the lot on with a strip of lace curtain. Everyone obliged, but the gas was away to our left and we had the all-clear. However, about 15 minutes later the alert went again and as the lads had made such a good effort in the first instance nothing was forthcoming at such short notice and it was funny to see us all making desperate efforts. (Richter 1992, 12)

And at the extreme, there was a soldier who remembered at least one welcome side effect of the gas:

The trench swarmed with rats, big rats, small rats, grey rats, tall rats in every stage of gas poisoning! Some were scurrying along scarcely affected while others were slowly dragging themselves about trying to find a corner in which to die. A most horrid sight—but a very good riddance! (Richter 1992, 137)

Gas did indeed have horrible effects. As often as not, they were temporary. Nonetheless, the sight of gas victims was often enough to produce fear—which only encouraged both sides to continue their use as a weapon in hopes of making their enemies give in. Lieutenant Colonel G. W. W. Hughes recalled the scene clearly enough:

I shall never forget the sights I saw up at Ypres after the first gas attack. Men lying all along the side of the road between Poperinghe and Ypres, exhausted, gasping, frothing yellow mucus from their mouths, their faces blue and distressed. It was dreadful and so little could be done for them. One came away from seeing or treating them longing to be able to go straight away at the Germans and to throttle them, to pay them out in some sort of way for their devilishness. Better for a sudden death than this awful agony. (Richter 1992, 6)

As soon as gas masks were invented, gas became less effective as a weapon, although the animals used in the First World War suffered terribly. Even though gas masks were made for horses, they fit badly, and many died (Richter 1992, 138). It was also highly difficult to keep gas a secret. By the time most British gas attacks were underway, the Germans were fully prepared. By lighting fires along their own front lines, they were able to create

Gas masks for man and horse demonstrated by an American soldier, ca. 1917.
(National Archives)

a current that lifted the gas up and over their front lines (Richter 1992, 89). Thus, both sides could defend themselves effectively against gas and usually had adequate warning of when it would be used. Further, more than 75 percent of those exposed to gas made full recoveries. Most suffered only temporary eye irritation, though this was often mistakenly thought to be permanent blindness. In the end, then, gas failed even to contribute significantly to the attrition on either side.

Being gassed was nevertheless a terrifying and horrific experience. The encounter of H. S. Clapham and his friend Robertson with gas is fairly representative for soldiers in World War I:

> The next day Robertson was worse, and had to be led to the Aid Post with a bandage around his eyes, for he could not bear the light on them. There was a continuous stream of water running from my eyes, and they were extremely inflamed and very sore. I was in chronic pain, as my head, throat, eyes and lungs ached unmercifully. In addition, the mustard gas had burnt me severely in a delicate part of my anatomy that is usually not displayed in public! (Simpson 1993, 52)

This was undoubtedly unpleasant, to say the least, but Clapham survived, as did many others. Gas, for all its terrifying psychological effects, never proved effective as a weapon in the First World War.

—*Kirsty Robertson*

References and Further Reading

Brown, John Horace. 1915. *December 19, 1915*. Ottawa: Canadian War Museum, 58 AI 7.9 acq 19830003–026.

Fraser, Donald. 1985. *The Journal of Private Fraser, 1914–1918*. Reginald H. Roy, ed. Victoria: Sono Nis.

Gray, Billy. 1916. *A Sunny Subaltern: Billy's Letters from Flanders*. Toronto: McClelland, Goodchild, and Stewart.

Heyman, Neil M. 2002. *Daily Life during World War I*. Westport, Conn.: Greenwood.

Keegan, John. 1998. *The First World War*. Toronto: Key Porter.

Palazzo. Albert. 2000. *Seeking Victory of the Western Front: The British Army and Chemical Warfare in World War I*. Lincoln and London: University of Nebraska Press.

Reid, Gordon. 1980. *Poor Bloody Murder: Personal Memoirs of the First World War.* Oakville, Ontario: Mosaic.

Richter, Donald. 1992. *Chemical Soldiers: British Gas Warfare in World War I.* Lawrence: University Press of Kansas.

Simpson, Andy. 1993. *Hot Blood and Cold Steel: Life and Death in the Trenches of the First World War.* London: Tom Donovan.

Teahan, John Patrick. 1999. *Diary Kid.* Grace Keenan Price, ed. Ottawa: Oberon.

"LIKE GETTING INTO THE WITCH'S OVEN"

The Experience of
Tank Combat in World War I

———————————— ◆ ————————————

Looking back on it now, I don't think I was frightened. I've
been very frightened indeed, both before and after that day;
but on that particular morning the whole thing seemed so
unreal.

—Captain H. W. Mortimore *(Foley 1963, 190)*

At a quarter past five on the morning of 15 September
1916, German troops occupying a forward pocket along the Somme
battlefront between Ginchy and Delville Wood heard a strange mechanical
noise emerging from the smoke-filled haze in front of their positions. The
Germans, who had been shelled incessantly for over seventy-two hours, were
anticipating a fresh British infantry assault that day, and the activity along
the enemy line was not in itself surprising. What was more difficult to understand was the distant but disturbing groan of some kind of machine,
moving slowly but inexorably toward them.

Suddenly, an iron rhomboid eight feet high and over thirty feet long appeared from the gloom, mounted on caterpillar tracks that extended along

127

its entire hull and spitting fire from Hotchkiss machine guns and two six-pounder barrels mounted in side sponsons. It crawled closer to the German position, effortlessly flattening the bracelets of barbed wire that girded the trench; retaliatory rifle and machine-gun fire seemed to simply bounce off its metal plating. The reaction of the battle-hardened German troops is exemplified by this account from a captured Bavarian veteran, whose section encountered more of these extraordinary war engines that morning: "One stared: one stared and stared as if one had lost the power of one's limbs. The big monsters approached us slowly, hobbling, rolling, rocking, but always advancing. Someone shouted 'the devil is coming,' and the word passed along the line" (Foley 1963, 23).

This diabolical agent was in fact His Majesty's Landship "D.1," a Mark I model commanded by Captain H. W. Mortimore of the Heavy Branch of the British Machine Gun Corps. The unfortunate German soldiers it had chanced upon had, however reluctantly, participated in a military milestone: the first armored vehicle engagement in the history of warfare. Throughout 15 September, thirty-five more of these exotic metal contraptions would take part in operations against the German defenses along the Somme, in most cases provoking widespread panic throughout the enemy line. The psychological effect of the landship—soon universally known as the "tank"—was undisputable.

The subsequent fate of D.1 on 15 September 1916, however, is testament to the mixed fortunes of the new weapon. Three tanks were actually supposed to have attacked Ginchy-Delville that morning, but one had broken down beforehand and another had ditched along the way. Later in the day Captain Mortimore's own vehicle was struck by a shell that wrecked its steering gear, and it had to be abandoned. For all their veneer of invincibility, tanks would soon prove to be dangerously vulnerable to natural and man-made obstacles.

Nonetheless, the attack of 15 September was truly epochal in its influence, for its measured success convinced the British military authorities that a large-scale investment in tank technology might yet break the trench stalemate that had paralyzed their strategic bid for victory. For the next two years, tanks would be one of the principal bludgeons used by the Allied powers to batter away at the sophisticated German fortifications along the western front. The results varied—a reflection of the primitive mechanical systems available to tank designers and the as-yet-uncertain tactics that field commanders needed to use to best exploit the advantages of their new, but brittle and often unpredictable, weapon. Yet, the long-term significance of the British, and later French and American, landship war was revolutionary; and the story of the men who created and crewed the Great War tanks is one of inspiration, disappointment, ingenuity in the face of disaster, courage, endurance, and an unflappable belief in the potential of their unwieldy new tin chariots to change the world.

In 1919, still flush with victory, a Royal Commission on Awards to Inventors sat to try to determine which person, in their judgment, had the right to be called the inventor of the tank. That honor, the Royal Commission eventually decided, best belonged to Lieutenant-Colonel E. D. Swinton, who began the war as the press officer attached to the British Expeditionary Force in Flanders. In October 1914 he wrote to Maurice Hankey, the secretary of the Committee of Imperial Defense, suggesting the creation of an armor-plated fighting vehicle equipped with guns and mounted on caterpillar tracks. Hankey's influence persuaded the lukewarm War Office, in February 1915, to review a trial using an American Holt tractor—it bogged down in the mud. The idea was officially dropped, but Swinton did not give up, and in July his exhortations paid off when a combined army and navy committee agreed to sponsor the construction of a custom-designed test model.

This prototype tank, "Little Willie," performed much better in test conditions than the Holt tractor had, and a more advanced follow-up model designed by Royal Navy lieutenant W. G. Wilson and creatively named "Big Willy" was ordered. Its test driver, Charlie Maughan, recalled the first trial on 29 January 1916, when he took the tank up a parapet over four feet high: "She went up it like a bird. I could tell there was a lot of people hoping we would fail on this demo, but the old bus just clawed her way on this big step beautifully. Then I remember rightly, we had to cross a trench five feet wide" (Foley 1963, 7). Big Willie went across it easily. The observers were impressed. One hundred fifty copies of Big Willie, now rechristened the Mark I, were ordered for operational use.

It was also Swinton who gave the tank its enduring name. The new vehicles were officially designated "landships," but as this hinted at their operational use it was decided as a security measure to create a cover story and a code name, pretending that the machines under construction were mobile water-carrying vats to be sent to the Russian front. Winston Churchill recommended that these be called "Water Carriers for Russia," but when another member of the Landships Committee pointed out that this would likely be shortened to "WCs," Swinton threw in the more edifying sugges-tion of "tanks" instead. The nom de guerre stuck long after the authorized title of landship had fallen into disuse.

Swinton was now tasked with recruiting and training men for this fledg-ling arm of the services, beginning with six companies of twenty-eight offi-cers, 255 men, and twenty-five Mark Is each. Both processes were chaotic and remained so right up to the Armistice. A premium was set on volunteers with high engineering and technical competency. Among the first batch of men recruited were trained Army Service Corps "grease monkeys" from the motor transport pool, who made excellent drivers and mechanics. As the number of vehicles and the demand for men expanded, however, Swinton and his eventual replacement, General Sir Hugh Elles, had to take whomever they could get. Such a peculiar fighting branch inevitably at-tracted its share of eccentrics and malcontents. As historian Patrick Wright has noted,

> Very few of the recruits were trained soldiers. There was a music hall propri-etor; a Scottish baker; a plebeian-looking auctioneer, said once to have been the Mayor of Cromer, who was often puce with drink. The Equipment officer in C Battalion was the best-known bee-keeper in Wales . . . the Medical Offi-cer had previously spent two years with [explorer Ernest] Shackleton at the South Pole. (Wright 2000, 71)

Captain D. E. Hickey, who led a tank company at Ypres and Cambrai, re-membered, "My senior tank commander was a man of some forty-four years . . . he had participated in a revolution in Paraguay; he had prospected for gold in Canada; he had been torpedoed by the Germans" (Hickey 1936, 43–44). Infantry, cavalry, navy, and Royal Flying Corps uniforms were dotted around indiscriminately.

Training itself was an exercise in educated guesswork. Not only was it un-clear just how the new weapons ought to be used in combat, but there was also a chronic shortage of models with which to practice tactics. The last-ditch resort was dummy canvas tanks carried by their crewmen, which they paraded around like pantomime horses, much to the amusement of local children. Major W. H. L. Watson recalled that

> The men hated [those dummies]. They were heavy, awkward, and produced much childish laughter. . . . One company commander mounted them on

wagons drawn by mules. The crews were tucked in with their Lewis guns, and each contraption, a cross between a fire engine and a triumphal car in the Lord Mayor's show, would gallop past targets which the men would recklessly endeavor to hit. (Cooper 2002, 49)

The testing ground for authentic vehicles developed a peculiar toxic quality from the combination of gasoline, oil, and mud, which gave the men sporadic and painful inflammations all over the body.

While training continued in mid-1916, word of the new weapons—now deployed in France and awaiting commitment in one of General Haig's offensives—spread around the rest of the army. Despite their supposed secrecy, it became fashionable for senior officers from other units to visit the camp and request "a show." This often damaged equipment and wasted time that was already in dwindling supply. Swinton complained that

> Some of the machines were asked to force their way through a wood and knock down trees—tricks which they had not been designed to play and which were likely to damage them severely. I protested against these "stunts." . . . In addition to the almost continuous work of repairing, cleaning and tuning up their tanks, the men barely had time to eat, sleep and tend themselves. (Liddell Hart 1959, 66)

Already there were troubling indications of how difficult it was going to be to keep the tanks' brittle mechanical systems serviceable in the uncongenial mud and rain of the western front, a problem that—perhaps even more than enemy countermeasures—would dog the armored service throughout the Great War.

The decision to commit the tanks of Captain Mortimore and his companion officers to the Somme battle on 15 September was controversial. Some, including the then-war minister, David Lloyd George, who had taken a keen interest in the development of the new weapon, complained that a piecemeal introduction of tanks would waste their power of surprise and dilute their psychological impact upon the unsuspecting German army. The need to revivify the faltering Somme offensive overtook larger calculations, though, and so forty-nine landships were delegated for the opening attack.

Their performance on the first day was generally impressive, though with worrying caveats. The appearance of the tanks caused widespread panic in the enemy lines, and three vehicles attached to the British and New Zealand

XV Corps managed to help take the strategically important village of Flers. Of the total number of tanks originally assigned to the operation, however, only thirty-six actually made it into battle. The others all broke down or ditched en route to the starting line. As the offensive progressed, more tanks succumbed to engine problems and enemy shellfire. By the time the Somme campaign was officially called off in November, only a handful of landships remained operational. Many of the original proponents of the tank were disappointed that it had been hurriedly misused. General Haig was nonetheless impressed enough with the new weapon's performance to request 1,000 additional tanks with better armor and armament.

By this time, rumors about the tank had reached the British home front, and the news of this audacious addition to the Allied war arsenal piqued the interest of a public dismayed by mounting casualty lists and a depressing inertia in the fighting. Because war correspondents were forbidden to describe tanks in any detail, they fell back on vague prehistoric metaphors—"Saurian monsters" and "primeval beasts," among others—that only titillated the civilian audience. Some troops played on the hyperbole by providing mock-narratives of tanks in battle to send to naïve relatives and sweethearts, as in this soldier's account recorded by Lieutenant-Colonel Albert Stern, who was in charge of tank supply:

> They can do prisoners up in bundles like straw-binders, and in addition, have an adaptation of a printing machine which enables them to catch the Huns, fold, count, and deliver them in quires. . . . [T]hey can chew up barbed wire and turn it into munitions. As they run they slash their tails and clear away trees, horses, howitzers, and anything else in their vicinity. They turn over on their backs and catch live shells in their caterpillar feet. (Stern 1919, 98–99)

Throughout the winter of 1916–1917, the survivors of the Machine Gun Corps Heavy Branch—which would shortly become the Royal Tank Corps—transferred to Bermicourt, near Arras, their permanent depot in France. They did not enter action again until the Battle of Arras in April 1917, when sixty tanks were assigned to support the advance. The same problems of organization and terrain encountered on the Somme arose once more, though; the tanks were scattered too thinly among the various infantry units to have any effective weight, and the marshy ground incapacitated so many vehicles that a mere twenty-six struggled onto the battlefield. These were quickly knocked out by artillery or sank in the wet soil.

Worse was to come at the Third Battle of Ypres in August, when the tanks, operating in deep mud churned up by thousands of shell bursts, became hopelessly bogged down. One crewman who fought at Passchendaele recalled vividly the miseries of the tankers:

> Our sister tank ["Iron Rations"] got ditched. This often happened with the tanks. The track would cut through soft earth, wet earth, and sink in until the ground was tight up under the belly of the tank. Then the track just spun round without gripping anything . . . we took the strain and then pulled "Iron Rations" out. But we knew that we were disobeying orders in going close together. Apparently they would rather have had the two tanks ditched, unable to do anything, than orders be disobeyed. (MacDonald 1993, 48)

By the autumn of 1917, many in the tank corps had become exasperated by the British high command's insistence in committing tanks to battle under conditions for which they were not designed. Then, at last, a real opportunity seemed to present itself in November 1917. Lieutenant-Colonel J. F. C. Fuller, the corps' chief general staff officer and a future tank theoretician whose work on armored warfare tactics would become world famous, proposed an eight-hour raid on the town of Cambrai. Surrounded by firm, chalky uplands that had not been whipped into muddy gruel like the Somme and Ypres battlefronts, Cambrai would be perfect for tank operations; and, for the first time, landships would be used en masse, with 474 of the latest Mark IV models attacking simultaneously. The logistical complexities of bringing such a large number of vehicles together in one place is indicated by their supply requirements: 165,000 gallons of gasoline, 75,000 pounds of grease, 500,000 six-pound shells, and five million rounds of machine-gun ammunition.

The battle began on 20 November 1917, and it was initially a stunning success for the tank. The British army advanced five miles along a six-mile front, further than it had gotten in months of futile slaughter during any of its earlier operations, and captured sections of the redoubtable "Hindenburg Line." One tank commander later recalled his first encounter with its layered defenses on the morning of the attack:

27th New York Division smashing the Hindenburg Line. (Ridpath, John Clark. Ridpath's History of the World, Volume X. *Jones Bros. Publishing Co., Cincinnati, OH. 1921)*

Emerging out of the gloom, a dark mass came before us—the German wire. It appeared absolutely impenetrable. It was certainly the thickest and deepest I had ever seen, stretching in front of us in three belts, each about 50 yards deep. It neither stopped our tank nor broke up and wound round the tracks as we had feared, but squashed flat. (Cooper 2002, 98–99)

For the first time since the outbreak of war, church bells were rung in Great Britain to celebrate a victory.

The euphoria did not last. Fuller had envisioned the plan as a brief smash-and-grab raid, with a rapid withdrawal back to the starting position after less than a day. As the prospect of a large-scale triumph grew, though, more and more troops were committed to the Cambrai attack, and its scale and objectives became more ambitious. This proved unwise. No landships had been kept in reserve on the opening day, and so by 27 November, most of the tank corps' vehicles were out of action. An aggressive

German counterattack quickly pushed back the British salient and in some places captured ground held by the Allies at the start of the battle.

Cambrai was an important watershed in the history of the tank, with valuable tactical lessons learned. Its disappointing outcome, however, reinforced the limitations of the new weapon at this protean stage of development. Even with greater numbers, advances in tank materials and equipment, and more sophisticated coordination between infantry and armored units, the poor endurance and marginal reliability of Great War landships persisted. At the Battle of Amiens in August 1918—perhaps the Royal Tank Corps' greatest success in the First World War—72 percent of all vehicles were disabled through various causes after five days of fighting. The corps ended its war with exactly eight tanks still operable.

Certainly some far-seeing strategists could see that—in principle, if not yet demonstrably—the landship had the potential to alter ground warfare forever, and its more efficient and dependable offspring would become masters of the battlefield. Many jaundiced infantry officers who had seen broken-down tanks abandoned by the score along roadsides and dumped unceremoniously in shell-holes might have been forgiven in 1918, however, for echoing the British field marshal Lord Kitchener's earlier comment that the new weapon remained "a pretty mechanical toy" (Liddell Hart 1959, 50).

The British army used seven tank models during the Great War. The first, a straight copy of the original "Big Willie" (later also known as "Mother"), was the Mark I. It came in two varieties, a "male" version with two six-pound guns and four Hotchkiss machine guns, and a "female" with one Hotchkiss and four heavier Vickers MGs. This became a standard pattern for all British heavy tanks of the period. The Mark I was protected by a third of an inch of allegedly bullet-proof high tensile and nickel-steel plate—experience would show this to be wishful thinking—and had a set of large wooden gun-carriage wheels connected to the rear for steering. Fully laden, it weighed twenty-eight tons, and in its fastest gear and under optimum conditions, it could manage about four miles per hour. Marks II and III, which only had short production runs, were minor variants on the Mark I that abandoned the steering wheels and had slightly thicker armor and better-quality rollers for their tracks.

The Mark IV, which was the tank used at Cambrai, had still better armor and replaced the Hotchkiss MGs with Lewis guns. In 1918, two final wartime versions of the original "Mother" design were produced. The conventional

With the Americans northwest of Verdun, France. The skipper and gunner of a "Whip-pet" tank, with the hatches open, 1918. (National Archives)

Mark V had five-eighths of an inch of plating, a superior gear system, and a more powerful engine; its cousin, the Mark V Star, was longer, designed for crossing broad trenches and carrying small numbers of infantry. There was, lastly, the so-called Whippet light tank, which at a mere fourteen tons could race across the battlefield at a mercurial seven miles per hour.

When tank models became obsolete for combat purposes, they were often adapted for support roles. Among the duties that second-line tanks accrued were gun carrying and supply, wireless communication, and the transport across the battlefield of towing gear and wire grapnels, bridging materials, and telephone wire. Individual tanks were given colorful names by their crews—Autogophaster, HMS Lucifer, Our Emily, and Rumblebelly, to name a few—or christened according to a standard pattern within a unit, sharing, for example, the same initial letter. One flamboyant company of tanks sported the titles of popular dance shows then playing in London's West End.

All conventional vehicles had a crew of eight "tankers": a commanding officer and a driver in the front, a left and right gunner positioned in each of the side sponsons, with a loader behind them, and two gearsmen, who controlled the movement of the tracks on either side. On their first introduction to battle some landships were provided with an additional occupant: an infantry sniper. This unfortunate passenger, usually bilious and vomiting after a few hours in the squalid conditions of the tank interior, proved redundant because the shaking vehicle was a useless platform for a marksman.

For the crewmen, the experience of being in a moving tank under fire on the western front was an extraordinary sensual excess—a violent barrage of heat, noises, smells, gases, motions, and objects within a dark and claustrophobic shell that, quite apart from their physical danger, could prove psychologically overwhelming. One veteran of the Heavy Branch's attack on the Somme in September 1916 recalled that

> The nervous strain in this first battle of tanks for officers and crew alike was ghastly. Of my company, one officer went mad and shot his engine to make it go faster; another shot himself because he thought he had failed to do as well as he ought; two others had what I suppose would be called a nervous breakdown. (Terraine 1992, 149)

There was, first of all, constriction. The small amount of space within the tank's cocoon not already taken up by the engine, the radiator system, and the gears was packed with the ephemera of battle—supplies, ammunition, tools, and spares. A tank's full complement of equipment typically included gas helmets, sidearms, water bottles, haversacks, field dressing kits, signaling equipment, thirty tins of food, sixteen loaves of bread, cheese, tea, sugar, milk, canisters of grease and engine oil, a spare machine gun with replacement barrels, 324 six-pound shells (for the male), and 6,272 rounds of small arms ammo (or 31,232 rounds for the female). In addition to this panoply, the walls bristled with wrenches, hammers, screws, and other mechanical components separated into small pigeon-hole compartments. Although there were twin gangways a foot wide running along the sides of the tank, in practice these were so clogged with paraphernalia that it was extremely difficult, if not impossible, for a crewman to move from his own position. Even getting into the tank was difficult:

> The doorway was only two feet by four feet. In the male tank one entered in a more or less upright position, for the door was vertical. But the door of the female tank was placed horizontally, so that the only way to get in was to lever oneself in on one's stomach. It was like getting into the witch's oven of Grimm's fairy tales. (Hickey 1936, 50)

Once inside, even shorter men could not stand completely upright. "The tanks are so badly constructed," wrote Wilfred Bion, a landship commander whose diary provides an invaluable glimpse into the experience of early armored warfare, "that to take off the cylinder heads and exhaust, we had to remove the roof" (Bion 1997, 41–42).

In addition, tankers could scarcely see anything. With the doors closed, the interior was almost pitch black, and the only visual aid available was a dim electric light bulb that hovered uncertainly above the engine. Seeing out of the tank was difficult as well, especially under fire. The first models were equipped with "bullet-proof" rectangular glass prisms, but these often shattered when hit, sending splinters into the faces of the unfortunate driver and commander. Later tanks had narrow hinged observation flaps that were closed when approaching enemy lines, leaving the men to peer through tiny pinholes in the plating bracketed with leather padding so that crewmembers could rest their heads against the hull without suffering concussion. This restricted field of vision made driving treacherous, especially at night. Tank compasses, encased in metal, gave false readings, so establishing direction was difficult. In preparation for battle, "tank commanders went out on foot under cover of darkness and laid white tapes through the maze of trenches to the points behind the front lines" to guide the vehicles to their starting points.

It was a dangerous operation for the commanders, who had to walk in front of their tanks to guide the drivers. The greatest hazard was barbed wire, for if a commander got caught up in this the chances were that he would be crushed down by his own tank (Cooper 2002, 86).

Great War tanks had no suspension systems. Crewmen had to ride every rise and dip of the vehicle's forward motion, which would throw them violently forward or backward as the tank sank into a trench or staggered over the crest of an escarpment. The vibration from the tracks and the engine caused the hull to shake uncontrollably. Wilfred Bion wrote that

> Tanks were expressly forbidden to take back wounded if limbs were broken. In a previous action they had been ordered, on coming out of action, to carry back all they could. The result was a tragedy. At the end of half an hour's ride, after an otherwise perfect performance, every wounded man that had been picked up with broken bones turned out to be dead. (Bion 1997, 60)

The noise was infernal. Soldiers could easily hear a landship approaching over 1,000 yards away; inside the tank, it was much, much worse. Captain Hickey recalled that the clamor inside his vehicle, "Hadrian," was "deafening; it almost drowned the noise of the barrage, and speech was practically impossible. . . . [T]he rattle of the tracks and machinery produced the illusion of tremendous speed; but we were not moving faster than a mile an hour" (Hickey 1936, 102).

Communication between both crewmen and fellow tanks had to be done by nonaudible means. The commander would bang on the transmission casing to indicate a change in direction to his gearsmen, or make suggestions with a pat on the head or a less-polite kick. Because radio reception quickly proved impossible due to noise and vibration, tankers had to rely on lamps, flags, semaphore, colored discs, or even carrier pigeons (if they survived the journey within the tank long enough) to send messages. There were cases of tanks running into steam locomotives because they could not hear the sound of the approaching train above their own din.

And then there were the temperature and the dust. A tank's six-cylinder Daimler sleeve-valve engine, running at 1,000 rpm and producing 105 horsepower, generated an enormous amount of waste heat that could not be adequately vented by the rear-mounted cooling fan. After a short period of firing cannons and machine guns, the smoke and fumes of spent cartridges, combined with the engine's residue stench of oil and gasoline, made the air almost unbreathable inside a tank. This actually got worse in the later model Mark V, when the radiator was inexplicably mounted inside the hull. Tankers grew used to spending battles stripped down to vests and pants as the tank slowly cooked. The exhaust pipe attached to the manifold typically got so hot that a crewman could hang a kettle of cold water from it and quickly bring it to a boil for making tea. There were less benign aspects as well. Corporal J. L. Addy wrote:

> We had to stand by with a pyrene fire extinguisher and get ready to shoot it at the engine if it got too hot, because we had 20 gallons of petrol on either side of the tank and all round the sides there were racks of ammunition. If you had a fire in a tank you hadn't an earthly [chance]. (MacDonald 1993, 163)

Exhaust fumes could be dangerous outside the tank as well, as Wilfred Bion discovered when his fellow tankers dug sleeping trenches beneath their landships for protection.

> When we awoke next morning, we found the crews apparently dead under their tanks. We hauled them out and to our intense relief they began to show signs of life. . . . What had happened was this: the tank engine had been run and had simply poured petrol fumes and carbon monoxide from its exhaust into the hole it was over. (Bion 1997, 60)

The effects of enemy fire only multiplied the misery. Bion recalled that

> Bullets hitting the tank sound like sledgehammers in your ear. Also they knock off tiny pieces of red-hot metal. These fly off and cut you about . . . the worst thing was that the bullets began coming in through the gaps in the armor plate and ricocheted around the tank. Some rivets were driven in, thus leaving holes in the armor. (Bion 1997, 48)

Although the Mark I's metal plate was designed to be resistant to small-arms fire, German model K armor-piercing bullets could penetrate it at close range, sometimes exiting through the other side of the tank. Even with the improved Mark IV, bullets sometimes found their mark through cracks in the sponsons. The effect of "splash," or iron chips broken away from the inside wall of the armor plating by impact on the external hull, was unforeseen by tank designers. Splash tore at crewmen's faces, sometimes leaving them drenched in blood at the end of an action. To compensate, tankers were forced to adopt leather helmets and chain-mail visors, restricting their vision and hearing even further.

Despite their initial panic at the appearance of landships, German troops soon began to realize the limitations of this new enemy weapon and devised effective countermeasures to disable and destroy British tanks. Though a single hand-grenade was usually not powerful enough to pierce tank armor, a cluster of grenades tied together in sackcloth could blow off a track or—if placed in the path of an advancing tank with luck and timing—could explode beneath the vehicle, perforating its weaker floor plating. The rear face, with its exhaust funnel, gas tank, and radiator, was also vulnerable. Enemy fire could reduce a landship to a moving scrap heap. One tank commander at Cambrai noted after the battle that

> We found the tank was an extraordinary sight. One unditching rail had been cut right through and was hanging down in front, the front flap was at an angle of 30 degrees, the beam had great grooves cut in it, and the hull had innumerable pitmarks all over it from point-blank machine-gun fire. The front gun was bent, and battered in its port, looking rather like a splayed-out, rusty cigarette-end stuck on a ball mounting. (Cooper 2002, 121)

Most dangerous of all for the tankers was the discovery of how vulnerable their ponderous machines were to artillery fire. In one notorious incident at Flesquieres Ridge on the opening day of the Battle of Cambrai, sixteen tanks lumbering over the horizon in perfect silhouette against the November skyline were picked off one by one by German field guns. No tank armor could stop a direct hit by an enemy shell. Bion remembered,

> The worst of it was that the splinters would usually kill or wound the crew and set the tank alight. The wounded couldn't get out and simply were burned to death. The petrol [gasoline] would catch at once and then the oil. After that the ammunition kept on going up, as the sides are just honeycombed with it. They look like large squibs going off when they are burning as you get the continuous 'pops' of the 6-pounder shells. (Bion 1997, 35)

At Ypres, Corporal A. E. Lee of "Iron Rations" experienced a shell hit while clambering outside his tank trying to unditch it.

> The next I knew I was laying eight or nine yards away, completely unhurt. I staggered up and there was Iron Rations, a complete wreck. Everyone within

yards was either dead or badly wounded. By some freak I'd been thrown off by the blast before the splinters had a chance to spread out. . . . It took me a few minutes to realize that Iron Rations had gone and that these were all my own chums lying there. (MacDonald 1993, 118)

What disabled far more landships than enemy fire, however, were simple mechanical failure and the viscous Flanders mud. Tanks were clumsy and slow under even the best of conditions. To turn, a tank of Great War vintage had to stop, shift one track out of gear, and make a stationary pivot to left or right, a time-consuming and imprecise art. They would meander across country in a protracted, semi-blind crawl, picking up whatever battlefield flotsam they encountered on the way. After one engagement, Sergeant Jim Allison recalled,

As we were crossing an open field, the steering became very sluggish and the engine began to lose power. . . . [T]here were two wounded Germans lying in our path, and I could see by the expressions on their faces that they were absolutely terrified. But they didn't seem to be terrified of the tank: they were staring past it at something behind us. . . . [W]e had somehow picked up the barbed wire and were dragging behind us a mass of the stuff as big as a house. (Foley 1963, 124–125)

Even unencumbered, a Mark IV had only a 35-mile maximum range before its small gas tanks were exhausted and its engine and tracks needed extensive maintenance. Many tanks broke down long before they came within range of the enemy.

If they did not run out of gas or seize up, tanks often got hopelessly stuck—sinking into mud, sliding into ditches, or impaling themselves on tree stumps. One commander noted that "Our tanks had only a very small clearance between the fly wheel and the hull, and if one ran onto a stump which could not be cleared, the belly of the tank stuck on it, the hull buckled and fouled the fly wheel, and the tank was a salvage job" (Cooper 2002, 121).

The broad earthworks of the Hindenburg Line were a particular hazard: tanks often carried large bundles of wood called "fascines" that they dumped into enemy foxholes too wide to cross normally, but misjudgments and collapsing dugouts sent them capsizing into trenches, wedged beyond extraction. After a particularly bloody action these abandoned landships would be found scattered across the battlefield, impromptu dressing stations and mortuaries for their crews and passing infantry. An officer who witnessed such a macabre scene wrote:

> As I neared the derelict tanks, the scene became truly appalling; wounded men lay drowned in the mud, others were stumbling and falling through exhaustion. . . . [T]he nearest tank was a female, her left sponson doors were open, out of these protruded four pairs of legs, exhausted and wounded men had sought refuge in this machine and dead and dying lay in a jumbled heap outside. (Fuller 1920, 124)

It was images like these that, ironically, discouraged the German army from seriously developing armored vehicles itself during World War I. Although during the 1920s and 1930s German military theorists would come to embrace the possibilities of the tank—with spectacular results during Hitler's 1940 campaign in France and the Low Countries—the Imperial High Command in 1916–1918 saw only the disadvantages of the awkward new weapon, and downplayed successes as the temporary result of "tank panic" within its own ranks.

Other than a few captured British Mark IVs that were used with limited effectiveness, the single German contribution to First World War tank technology was the A.7.V *Sturmpanzerwagen,* which debuted in combat during the great March 1918 offensive on the western front. This was a curious beast, which on paper—with thicker armor, sprung tracks, and twin engines giving greater horsepower and speed—was superior in several respects to its British rivals. It was poorly constructed, however; its ground clearance was far too small to make it stable on a shell-pocked battlefield, and its extraordinarily large crew—eighteen men packed into a space only twenty-four feet long—was more of a liability than an asset.

On 24 April 1918 the first tank-versus-tank battle in the world took place on the Cachy-Fouilloy road along the Somme estuary between an A.7.V and a male Mark IV (which, appropriately enough for such a foundational moment, happened to be No. 1 Landship of No. 1 Section, A Company, 1st Battalion Royal Tank Corps). Despite the circumstances, it was not an encounter of great drama. The British tank hit the German, which in trying to maneuver out of the line of fire struck a bank and toppled over. This was enough to help dampen the already lukewarm German enthusiasm for the tank, and the production run of A.7.Vs dwindled to a trickle. Only twenty

German-built tanks were completed before the Armistice.

By contrast, the U.S. Army, despite the relative brevity of its involvement in the First World War, was keenly interested in forming an armored wing. It is one of the curious details of history that two of America's greatest generals of the war to follow—George S. Patton and Dwight D. Eisenhower—were both involved in commanding and training that embryonic unit. Patton, a captain in the American Expeditionary Force, received a posting to the U.S. First Army's light tank school at Langres in November 1917. The training camp began with scarcely a machine gun to its name, never mind a tank, but by July 1918 it had expanded sufficiently to produce a brigade of two battalions led by Patton himself. He commanded the American Expeditionary Force's tankers through their principal combat actions at Saint Mihiel and the Meuse-Argonne until being wounded on 26 September.

Captain Eisenhower's war was an altogether more tranquil affair, for he commanded a tank-training center at Camp Colt in Gettysburg, Pennsylvania. Although he never saw action in the Great War, Eisenhower did establish the principles of armored warfare instruction in the U.S. Army that, though sorely neglected in the locust years of the 1920s and 1930s, would be revived to great effect in the war of 1941–1945 (Wilson 1997).

American tankers joined the service for much the same reasons as their British counterparts—novelty, glamour, a liking for machinery, the hopes of expedient promotion, and perhaps a vague sense that their oily tin boxes represented the way of the future. Imported British tanks were used to great effect in war-bond and recruitment drives in U.S. cities. The image of tank warfare as the toughest branch of the army—the U.S. tank corps' "Treat 'em Rough!" wildcat campaign was an inspired marketing decision—encouraged volunteers to think of armor as a particularly exciting and hard-hitting choice. The emphasis on the egalitarian basis of promotion also touched a peculiarly American nerve. In its recruitment literature, the U.S. tank corps portrayed itself as "a highly democratic organization in which every man begins at the bottom and works up—every opportunity for advancement . . . the bars are down" (Harris 1998, xii).

Lieutenant Harvey L. Harris, whose letters from France contain a wealth of information about conditions for early American tankers in the AEF, gave his reasons for joining as these:

1) The wonderful possibilities of the tank.
2) The desire for blood.

American troops in French Renault tanks going forward to the battle line in the Forest of Argonne, France, 26 September 1918. (National Archives)

3) The fact that I would have a hand in it from its first inception. Practically among the first in the Tank Corps of the United States—a unique and desirable situation.

4) And, I admit it, the romance of such a service which is a combination of all branches. (Harris 1998, 60)

More sheepishly, he confessed that the expected low casualty rate for tank crews (which proved to be barely 15 percent of that for the infantry) also contributed to his decision to transfer.

As with almost all heavy military equipment, the Americans were forced to rely on Allied tank models to supply their armored battalions. A few late-war units used British Mark V and Mark V Stars, but the bulk of American tankers were equipped with French designs, particularly the Renault FT-17 light tank. The "Mosquito," as it was known, was a versatile little vehicle very different from the stocky rhomboids used by the British. Although its modest 35-horsepower engine made it no faster than larger tanks, it weighed only 7.4 tons and required just two crewmen—a driver and a commander who also loaded, aimed, and fired the 37mm cannon or Hotchkiss machine gun mounted in a fully traversing turret.

Physical conditions inside the Renault, although cramped, were far superior to those in the "Mother" variants. Harvey Harris wrote to his father,

> You ask about the temperature in a tank. Not so bad. Not much worse than in the front seat of a closed automobile. The fan sucks the air out of the compartment. We two stand in the engine compartment to cool the engine. We get air through slits generously placed through which we also see. (Harris 1998, 92)

There was an element of play about the American preparations for battle, expressed by Harris in his effusive descriptions of training in his Renault.

> This is a wonderful branch, and I consider myself lucky. . . . [W]hen you hit about five miles per hour over undulating country it's like sailing, and when you climb up the edge of a shell-hole until perpendicular and you are sure you are going over backwards and then come down gently. Oh Boy it's a grand feeling! (Harris 1998, 50)

The reality of fighting was of course rather different. The citations of the Great War tank corps' two Medal of Honor recipients—one posthumous—give a flavor of the authentic dangers of armored combat. Corporal Donald Call was the first winner for his actions near Varennes on 26 September 1918. During an operation against enemy machine-gun nests,

> Call was in a tank with an officer when half of the turret was knocked off by a direct artillery hit. Choked by gas from the high-explosive shell, he left the tank and took cover in a shellhole 30 yards away. Seeing that the officer did not follow, and thinking that he might be alive, Cpl. Call returned to the tank under intense machinegun and shell fire and carried the officer over a mile under machinegun and sniper fire to safety. (http:\\www.army.mil\cmh-pg\mohwwi.htm)

Another corporal, Harold Roberts, received his award under more tragic conditions in the Montrebeau Woods on 4 October 1918.

Roberts, a tank driver, was moving his tank into a clump of bushes to afford protection to another tank which had become disabled. The tank slid into a shell hole, 10 feet deep, filled with water, and was immediately submerged. Knowing that only 1 of the 2 men in the tank could escape, Cpl. Roberts said to the gunner, "Well, only one of us can get out, and out you go," whereupon he pushed his companion through the back door of the tank and was himself drowned. (http:\\www.army.mil\cmh-pg\mohwwi.htm)

The American tank war, like the British, ended in November 1918 on a note of disillusionment. Mechanical failures had been so endemic in Patton's brigade that scarcely fifty operable vehicles remained in the order of battle at the time of the Armistice. Traditionalists scornfully suggested that although the tank had had its temporary uses in the unusual trench conditions of the western front, its persistent unreliability made any more general application of armored tactics in future wars unlikely. The independent tank corps was dissolved in June 1920 in a round of demobilization cost-cutting. Its more ambitious staff—including both Patton and Eisenhower—transferred to other army branches shortly afterward.

The landship could not be uninvented, though, no matter how much some dogmatic cavalry commanders might have wished it so. Despite doctrinal neglect in the two decades preceding World War II, the tank would reemerge in that conflict as the prime arbiter of ground combat. The experiences of the Great War crews had to be relearned by a new generation of tankers, now; however, equipped with machines of vastly better endurance and firepower.

—Alan Allport

References and Further Reading

Bion, W. R. 1997. *War Memoirs, 1917–1919*. London: Karnac.

Cooper, Brian. 2002. *The Ironclads of Cambrai*. London: Cassell.

Foley, John. 1963. *The Boilerplate War*. London: Frederick Muller.

Fuller, J. F. C. 1920. *Tanks in the Great War*. London: John Murray.

Harris, Harvey L. 1998. *The War as I Saw It: 1918 Letters of a Tank Corps Lieutenant*. St. Paul, Minn.: Pogo Press.

Hickey, D. E. 1936. *Rolling into Action*. London: Hutchinson.

Liddell Hart, B. H. 1959. *The Tanks: A History of the Royal Tank Regiment*, vol. 1. New York: Frederick and Praeger.

MacDonald, Lyn. 1993. *They Called It Passchendaele*. London: Penguin.

Stern, A. G. 1919. *Tanks, 1914–1918: The-Log Book of a Pioneer*. London: Hodder and Stoughton.

Terraine, John. 1992. *The Smoke and the Fire*. London: Leo Cooper.

Wilson, Dale. 1997. "American Armor in the First World War." Proceedings of the Fourth Annual Great War Interconference Seminar, Shippensburg, Penn.

Wright, Patrick. 2000. *Tank: The Progress of a Monstrous War Machine*. London: Faber and Faber.

LIFE IN A TIN CAN

The Experience of Submarine Personnel during World War I

———————————◆———————————

L IKE THE TANK, AIRPLANE, AND POISON GAS, THE SUBMARINE was a weapon used on a large scale for the first time during the First World War. The submarine, however, was more than a mere weapon of war: it was home for a small group of pioneers willing to risk their lives in the most dangerous manner in pursuit of victory. These men, too many of whom were never destined to see the end of the war, lived and worked in conditions that ranged from uncomfortable to abysmal. Even with quantum leaps in technological and material improvements in submarines over the course of the war, life in a "tin can" remained nasty, brutish, and short.

The submarines of World War I were not true submarines because they were incapable of running indefinitely underwater. They needed to run on the surface frequently in order to recharge the electric batteries used to propel the engines while submerged. Early submarines were propelled by a variety of means—gasoline, paraffin, or even steam power. Within the first year of the war, the motive power of choice came to be diesel engines, although some British and French submarines continued to be built with steam engines.

Some captains preferred to remain on the surface as much as possible, submerging only when necessary to achieve surprise or evade pursuit. Running on the surface provided opportunities for the crew that they would not be able to enjoy while submerged—swimming, smoking, and breathing fresh air, for example. These may seem like small things, but it was these little pleasures snatched during quiet times that made the anxiety and terror of action less unbearable. One U-boat, sent from Germany to the Mediterranean, took advantage of lax Allied patrols and balmy Atlantic weather to run on the surface nonstop from Cape Finisterre to Gibraltar. As one crewman recalled, "[Four] days of sunshine and placid sea they were. We idled away the hours, sleeping or playing cards on deck, and did not have to submerge once" (Thomas 1929, 59).

There were many reasons why crews preferred the opportunity to spend as much time as possible on deck. The air inside a submarine was frequently fouled with oil and vapors, surfaces were coated in condensation, and the smell of a submarine was a mixture of oil, stale cooking, human excrement, and the ripe odor of unwashed men wearing dirty clothing in close quarters. Living in early British submarines, propelled by gasoline engines, was described as "like living under the [hood] of a motor car," due to the oil and gasoline vapors in the air. The only compensation for the sailors on board was that, somehow, this unsavory concoction sharpened the appetite (Compton-Hall 1991, 160).

The conditions inside a submarine affected the relationship between the officers and the crew. On surface warships, a sharp class distinction existed between the officer corps and the sailors. Officers ate in separate messes, enjoyed certain privileges of rank, and were held to a different code of conduct. The intimate confines of a submarine, however, all but eliminated the opportunities for officers to maintain that line between themselves and their men. Some officers let that distinction slide and allowed discipline to be lax; although this made for greater camaraderie on board because the officers and men now shared hardships, it also meant the commander risked losing control of his crew in a crisis. Other officers maintained a rigid discipline, convinced that only strict adherence to protocol would keep the crew in control. This worked for some commanders but risked creating an atmosphere of unhappiness on board, and this could be equally dangerous during a long patrol.

Privacy was nonexistent in a submarine; its very nature precluded getting away from fellow crewmates. Even sleeping accommodations were at a premium. Crews were forced to hang hammocks wherever possible, including such unlikely and uncomfortable locations as the torpedo rooms and the engine rooms. In the event of action, sleeping crewmen had to act quickly

Sailors at work in the interior of a British submarine. (NMPFT/Daily Herald Archive/SSPL/The Image Works)

to remove their hammocks. Furthermore, crews often used the "hot–bunk" method, whereby one sailor relieved another on duty, and the relieved sailor took his place in the still-warm hammock (Compton-Hall 1991, 27).

Sometimes circumstances and the cramped quarters of a submarine necessitated improvised sleeping accommodations, as one junior U-boat officer found on his first cruise:

> I had a very strange bedfellow. We were short of room, and when the boat was fully loaded there was one torpedo more than there was place for. I accommodated it in my bunk. I slept beside it. I had it lashed in place at the outside of the narrow bunk, and it kept me from rolling out of bed when the boat did some of its fancy rolling. At first I was kept awake a bit by the thought of having so much TNT in bed with me. Then I got used to it, and it really made quite a comfortable "Dutch wife." (Thomas 1929, 89)

The notion of a submarine as a cruising warship was new. Early submarines were built with harbor or coastal defense duties in mind. Endurance was secondary, as were properly designed crew accommodations. The first two classes of British submarines did not even have toilets on board. When toilets (or "heads," in nautical parlance) were installed, they were pressure-operated and could only be flushed when the ship was not in danger of being detected. If the sailor operating the flushing mechanism made a mistake, the pressure flush could produce the opposite effect from what was intended, and the unfortunate sailor ended up "getting his own back"—another unappealing element to life under the sea (Compton-Hall 1991, 23).

Cleanliness was a luxury few submariners were able to enjoy while on patrol. Precious water was rationed for drinking and cooking, with little left for bathing. Alternatives such as sand and pumice were tried with mixed results. When the men were especially desperate, the dregs of their tea could serve as shaving-water. Personal hygiene aboard submarines left much to be desired, and the stench of sweaty bodies mingled with all the other odors on board ship (Thomas 1929, 155; Niemöller 1939, 63, 93). Oral hygiene proved paramount to at least one British officer, however. The German *UB-15* attacked and sank the British *E-20*, then stopped to rescue the survivors. One officer pulled aboard seemed disoriented by events, and disconcerted that his submarine had been sunk while he was brushing his teeth. When his German rescuers asked him if there was anything he wanted, he requested a toothbrush, and then resumed cleaning his teeth from where he had been interrupted (Thomas 1929, 139).

Discomfort was also a standard feature when submerged. Even at depths of one hundred feet, a submarine could experience "bumping"—rolling in the swells created by a heavy storm. Even experienced sailors were not immune to the effects of seasickness from the constant, three-dimensional swaying and bucking of the ship. Veteran captains would often ride out storms by allowing their sub to settle on the bottom, minimizing movement. This maneuver, however, could be accomplished only in areas where the bottom was sandy and not too deep for the ship's hull to withstand the pressure (Gray 1972, 47, 26). One U-boat captain described the effects that a Force-10 storm had on his submarine, even after he gave the order to dive:

In the steep seas the dive was a neck-breaking manoeuvre. *UB-2* headed precipitately for the sea bed and struck heavily. The effects of the storm were violent even at 28 metres [around 91 feet] and could only be countered by giving the boat a nose-heavy trim so that the bow rested on the bottom while the remainder of the hull was balanced at an angle upwards. As much of the seawater ballast as possible was expelled to reduce the jarring movement of the swell: it could not be eliminated completely but was transformed into a relatively light feathering kind of motion. (Fürbringer 1999, 13)

It was impossible to prevent the interior of a submarine from getting wet under any conditions. Spray and wash coming down from the conning tower from surface running in choppy seas or from rapid diving flowed down into the bilges. Bilgewater was a fact of life aboard a submarine, and in it could be found floating all the effluvia washed down from the crew and ship—vomit, blowback, oil, and food particles. Worse, if the saltwater in the bilges got into the batteries, it could react with the sulphuric acid in the batteries to create choking clouds of poisonous chlorine gas, forcing the crew to surface and vent the ship's atmosphere (Niemöller 1939, 149–150). Even without this, condensation tended to build up inside the hull, a reflection of the temperature difference between the sub's interior and the water outside. Condensation also could prove to be dangerous, making electrocution or short-circuits a constant threat. The damp also posed long-term health risks for crews, with rheumatism being one ailment commonly affecting surviving submariners (Compton-Hall 1991, 28; Thomas 1929, 50).

Water posed an even greater threat in the winter, but for a different reason. A submarine surfacing in sub-zero temperatures soon found itself encased in a sheet of ice. This created a whole series of problems. One submariner described his experience in just such a situation:

When we were ready to trim down we found we couldn't lower the radio masts. The supporting wires were coated in ice and would not rove through the blocks. We knocked away the ice with hammers. The conning tower hatch wouldn't even close. Finally we melted the ice with a blow torch. When we did contrive to get below surface I stared at the instrument board in amazement. We went down by the stern and stuck fast at seven metres. Then I understood. The instruments were all frozen. When we ran the periscope out *it* froze. A thick layer of ice covered the objective lens. Our one eye was put out and we could not see while below surface. In short, when the temperature gets down to twenty below [Celsius; just under zero Fahrenheit] a submarine is a submarine no longer—we had to run on the surface. (Thomas 1929, 43–44)

Even air pressure could pose a threat to the submariner. Many of the submarine's internal workings relied on pressurized systems, and the air pressure inside a submarine therefore continued to build as long as the submarine remained underwater. The flotation tanks, the torpedo launchers, and the heads were all pressure-operated. As a result, when the submarine finally did surface and hatches were opened, there was often a great rush of air escaping the submarine. It was necessary to grasp hold of the captain's legs as he opened the hatch as a precaution; sometimes the escaping air could catch and propel him with the same force used to launch a torpedo, out of the submarine and even into the ocean (Compton-Hall 1991, 30).

Given such circumstances, it is hardly surprising that submariners were also a superstitious lot. Some submarines were considered to be "jinxed" or "cursed," and it took a great deal of persuasion to convince crews that their vessels were seaworthy and fit for action. Mine laying was a particularly dangerous job for submarines, as many things could go wrong when performing that onerous chore. A good number of mine-laying submarines were lost through mischance or accident, so much so that the Germans referred to their mine-laying submarines as the "sisters of sorrow" (Gray 1972, 195). British submariners equally detested mine-laying duty. The rumor was once spread that the admiralty would issue decorations to personnel completing eight mine-laying patrols; one old salt's comment was simply: "God! Ain't they generous? The odds are 100 to 1 they'll never have to decorate anybody" (Gray 1971, 191).

Another superstition was to avoid setting out from harbor on certain days: Fridays, the thirteenth day of a month, and especially a Friday the thirteenth. It seemed that there was always a story someone knew of an ill-omened submarine that had defied custom and set forth on one of those accursed days, only to run into some form of bad fortune. Even the number 13 was believed to be cursed. When the crew of a British submarine learned they were being transferred to a new boat, *K-22,* a surprisingly large number of them came down with a mysterious ailment that prevented their reassignment. The reason for this malady was that *K-22* was really *K-13,* which had sunk while in harbor and then been raised, repaired, and renumbered. A mere coat of paint and an assumed name were not enough to ward off the bad luck, or to fool the submariners (Gray 1972, 226).

The *K* class of submarines was known in the Royal Navy as the worst of all classes of submarines. They were unreliable and accident-prone, and their steam engines were a nuisance to deal with when the submarine needed to make a sudden dive. Furthermore, they were difficult to control; on one occasion when trying to dive, an exasperated commander telephoned his first lieutenant, stationed in the bows, and asked him: "I say, Number One, my end is diving: what the hell is your end doing?" (Everitt 1963, 5).

Probably the worst example of such luck was that which beset three U-boats that set off together on a Friday the thirteenth. The first, *U-32*, got off fairly lightly—it ran into a series of storms and spent its entire patrol being tossed around the North Sea. As a result, a number of crewmen returned from the voyage with broken limbs.

The second, *U-22*, came across a potential target—a submarine sitting quietly in the water. *U-22* maneuvered itself into position and torpedoed the other craft, only to discover that its victim was a fellow German craft, *U-7*. Worse still, the captains of the two boats were best friends: "The two men had been inseparable for years. When you saw [one] you always looked for [the other]. They ate together, drank together, and what belonged to one belonged also to the other" (Thomas 1929, 170–172).

The third U-boat, *U-31*, went off on patrol and did not return. This was not surprising to the Germans, for the British had taken to not announcing U-boat kills in order to provoke anxiety in the Germans. The Germans, therefore, simply assumed *U-31* was just another casualty of British antisubmarine activity. This, however, was not the case; it was even worse. Six months after setting out, the submarine ran aground on the east coast of England. When opened up, it was discovered that the entire crew was dead, all lying peacefully in their bunks. What had probably occurred was that the commander had ordered the boat to be rested on the bottom for the night, to allow all hands an opportunity to get a good night's sleep before action. Instead, while the crew slept, they were asphyxiated by poisonous fumes, possibly saltwater in the batteries. For months *U-31* sat on the bottom of the North Sea, its cargo of dead men carefully sealed away. Eventually, the ballast tanks leaked, allowing the sub to rise to the surface, after which the tide washed it ashore. The story of *U-31* helped fuel rumors of a "phantom submarine," manned by a ghostly crew, forever on patrol (Thomas 1929, 172–174).

Submariners could never tell what kind of patrol they would have. This was truer of the German U-boats, which were more likely to put themselves in harm's way, than for Allied submarines. The submarine could spend three weeks on patrol and see nothing, or spend the entire voyage dodging enemy attacks. Uneventful patrols could have a greater effect on crews be-

The crew of a U.S. Navy submarine, March 1917. (Hulton-Deutsch Collection/Corbis)

cause of the stress of waiting for something to happen, and because this meant lengthy periods where there was nothing to do. One German commander described the effects of anxiety:

> Submarine men were likely to break down with nerve strain of some kind or other and were constantly being sent away to recuperate. The ordeal of life aboard the U-boats, with the constant stress of peril and terror, was too much for human flesh to bear for long stretches. Some men went mad. Others, after periods of rest and medication, came around and were, or perhaps were not, fit for undersea service again. All felt the grinding pressure. (Gray 1972, 180)

There were few ways to relieve the stress while on patrol. For most, the calming effect of a cigarette was nearly impossible, due to the fetid air in the submarine; that was why opportunities to run on the surface were prized by crewmembers. A few submariners turned to narcotics as a substitute, but this practice was frowned upon both by command and by fellow crewmates—an incapacitated sailor was a liability in a crisis (Thomas 1929, 257; Compton-Hall 1991, 29).

Ultimately, submarine crews had to find a way to laugh at themselves and the lot fate had thrown at them, good or bad. One U-boat captain, for instance, was frustrated to find that the bearing indicator on his periscope had not been reset by the coxswain while on patrol, causing him to miss his target with his last torpedo. Angrily, he demanded why the coxswain had not performed his duty.

> The small portly warrant officer answered calmly, his voice reproachful. "When the *Herr Oberleutnant* kept swivelling with the periscope, he crushed me so much against the bulkhead that I couldn't get round to the compass. Also when I was squashed I got caught on a hook and tore open the seat of my pants." In the control room somebody spluttered. Then we all laughed. (Fürbringer 1999, 18)

On another occasion, the same commander attacked and sank a British steam trawler, then rescued its crew of eight.

> One stepped forward from the group . . . and demanded to be taken to the commander. I motioned for him to approach the conning tower and asked

what he wanted, to which he adopted a semi-military bearing and shouted up, "I would like to inform you, sir, that this is my third time on your submarine, and I thank you for your good treatment."

"And I hope to see you many more times in the future," I responded with a beguiling gesture, at which the other fishermen all broke out in roars of laughter. (Fürbringer 1999, 50)

There was, of course, a darker side to the life of a submariner as well. Death was a constant part of the hazards of submarine duty, either the death of the hunted or the hunter. Some submariners were able to turn themselves away from the carnage and not feel what they were doing. Most others were affected by what was happening and had to find ways of dealing with their emotions. A sailor on *U-39* wrote about one incident while attacking a merchant vessel: "It was an extremely sad day for me. . . . In the morning I saw dead on the deck, two poor Norwegians who had unhappily fallen victim to our gunfire. . . . The day will be engraved on my memory in letters of blood" (Gray 1972, 175).

It could be even worse if there was no way to save doomed men. The German boat *U-30*, for instance, sank in Emden harbor with no way to rescue the trapped crew. For three days, as other U-boats passed by the shipwreck, they could hear hammering coming from *U-30*, from the men who could do nothing but wait to die at the bottom of the ocean (Gray 1972, 89).

Life on board a World War I submarine was not always the worst life imaginable; every now and again the monotony or terror was broken by some unusual event or some carefully planned celebration, ideal for lifting the spirits of the crew. For Christmas 1914, the crew of *U-20* gathered together and celebrated the holiday: a green wreath stood in for the Christmas tree, but without the traditional candles—which would have been a fire hazard. The crew drank tea mixed with rum and ate a Christmas dinner of canned food. After dinner they were entertained by the submarine's band, which consisted of a violin, a mandolin, and an accordion. "The Berlin Philharmonic does better, but our concert was good," a junior officer reminisced a decade later (Thomas 1929, 83–84).

It was not a life for everyone. The forced intimacy, the smells, the cramped nature, the damp, and above all the uncertainty—would it be kill, or be killed?—made it perhaps the most difficult and dangerous assignment in any of the combatants' navies. Despite the high death tolls, men continued to volunteer for the "Silent Service" and continued to perform their duties in what were, even by the war's end, still primitive and dangerous technological marvels.

—*David Olivier*

References and Further Reading

Compton-Hall, Richard. 1991. *Submarines and the War at Sea, 1914–18*. London: Macmillan.

Everitt, Don. 1963. *The K-Boats: A Dramatic First Report on the Navy's Most Calamitous Submarines*. London: George G. Harrap.

Fürbringer, Werner. 1999. *Fips: Legendary U-Boat Commander, 1915–1918*. Translated by Geoffrey Brooks. Annapolis: Naval Institute Press.

Gibson, R. H., Maurice Pendergast, and Earl Jellicoe. 2004. *The German Submarine War, 1914–1918*. New York: Periscope.

Gray, Edwyn. 1971. *A Damned Un-English Weapon: The Story of British Submarine Warfare, 1914–18*. London: Seeley, Service, and Company.

———. 1972. *The Killing Time: The U-Boat War, 1914–18*. London: Seeley, Service, and Company.

Gunton, Michael. 2003. *Submarines at War: A History of Undersea Warfare*. London: Carroll and Graf.

Niemöller, Martin. 1939. *From U-Boat to Concentration Camp*. Translated by D. Hastings Smith. London: William Hodge.

Stern, Robert C. 1999. *Battle Beneath the Waves: The U-Boat War*. London: Sterling.

Thomas, Lowell. 1929. *Raiders of the Deep*. Garden City, N.J.: Doubleday, Doran, and Company.

"IT'S ONLY THE ONES WHO MIGHT LIVE WHO COUNT"

Allied Medical Personnel
in World War I

❖

DUE TO THE USE OF NEW WEAPONS THAT RESULTED IN NEW levels of devastation, World War I proved to be the most destructive war to date. One outcome of that destruction was that medical care at the front took on a new priority; another was that several important, long-reaching medical advances were made. From the outbreak of the conflict in the summer of 1914 to the Armistice in November 1918, over sixty million men were mobilized worldwide, over seven million were killed, and over nineteen million were wounded. Additionally, millions of civilians died or had their health compromised by the conflict.

Yet new methods of disease prevention developed over those years virtually eliminated illnesses that had been common in earlier wars. During the early years of the fighting there was a high rate of infection, resulting in a wound mortality rate of 28 percent and an amputation rate of 40 percent for bone wounds involving extremities. New treatments lowered the amount of infection and, in turn, the death rate. By the end of the war, the overall wound mortality rate had dropped to 8 percent (Gabriel and Metz 1992, 239–240). As U.S. general John J. Pershing noted near the end of the war,

> Our Medical Corps is especially entitled to praise for the general effective-
> ness of its work both in hospitals and at the front. Embracing men of high
> professional attainments, and splendid women devoted to their calling and
> untiring in their efforts, this department has made a new record for medical
> and sanitary proficiency. (Pershing 1919, 24)

At the onset of the fighting Germany was, medically speaking, the most prepared nation for war. The Germans were well organized and had learned lessons about the importance of first aid kits, forward surgery, casualty clear-ing stations, speedy transportation of the wounded, antiseptics, and aseptic surgery from their involvement in the Franco-Prussian War. Russia was the most medically ill-equipped nation, as general conditions in that country were already collapsing, and the war exacerbated the situation. France, where most of the hostilities took place, had begun reorganizing its Sanitary Service in 1910, and the changes were not complete in 1914. French med-ical officers were under the command of the line officers, and the quarter-master controlled medical supplies; emphasis was on military needs rather than medical ones. Great Britain, although facing military medical prob-lems of its own, managed to expand its medical corps from 20,000 in 1914 to over 180,000 by 1918 in order to adequately care for the over four mil-lion British and Commonwealth soldiers fighting on the European conti-nent. The United States, recognizing the need to be prepared, began expanding its capabilities to provide medical care for its military in 1916 (Gabriel and Metz 1992, 243–249; Church 1918, 34–37; U.S. Surgeon Gen-eral vol. 1, 344–346).

Long before the United States entered World War I in April 1917 though, and while the government was still proclaiming its official policy of neutrality, many Americans were involved in providing medical care for the sick and wounded soldiers and the affected civilians of the various nations involved in the fighting. Some were individuals living in Europe who wanted to assist their host nation, providing money or property, or by giving of their own time and efforts. Some volunteers were medical personnel; others had no medical training but wanted to be of service in some way. Glenna Bigelow, for instance, was working as a private duty nurse in Belgium when the Germans invaded. She immediately went to work assisting with the care of the wounded at a nearby convent. Four years later, she was still in Europe nursing at an American mobile hospital (Bigelow 1918, 45–53; 1919, 753). Edward Coyle was an ambulance driver with the French army before the United States entered the conflict; he volunteered because everyone was talking "war" and he felt some type of allegiance to France (Hansen 1996, 129). Many of these untrained volunteers ended up doing administrative and support work in hospitals and sometimes even actual patient care.

A young woman studying in France wrote about her experiences as a nurse's aid and later a certified nurse in a French military hospital in 1914 and 1915. Mary Needham was living in France with her journalist husband when he was killed in an accident. Rather than returning home, she volunteered at the American Military Hospital as an aid. In early August 1914 Mrs. C. Mitchell Depew, wife of an American entrepreneur and a fifteen-year resident of France, converted part of her home into a forty-bed hospital complete with operating room and X-ray equipment. Sculptor and socialite Gertrude Vanderbilt (Mrs. Harry Payne) Whitney opened a hospital in a converted sixteenth-century seminary in Juilly, a site close to the front, utilizing volunteers from the College of Physicians in New York. Frances Huard, an American married to a Frenchman, had no medical experience but converted her home to a French military hospital under the auspices of the French Red Cross in the fall of 1914 (*Mademoiselle Miss* 1916; Needham 1915, 258; Hansen 1996, 7–8, 18; Cushing 1941, 34–35; Huard 1917). Eight American nurses who were vacationing in England volunteered when war was declared and went to Serbia two days after the British troops went to France.

The conditions these volunteers found were often less than ideal. The nurses who volunteered to go to Serbia in August 1914, for instance, arrived there to find a barracks hospital of 1,000 beds with 1,200–1,300 patients and no modern conveniences, not even running water. Surgeries were performed without the benefit of anesthesia. Lack of fuel was also problematic at General Hospital No. 9. Nurses were allotted one pint of kerosene per room every forty-eight hours, which provided heat for about two hours out of every twenty-four. Some mornings they used the water from their hot water bottles for bathing when the pipes froze solid during the cold winter (Allison 1919a, 356).

One of the American Red Cross (ARC) units that arrived later in Serbia used an old tobacco factory for a hospital. All water had to be carried in, and all waste was carried out in buckets to a cesspool several hundred yards away. Straw mattresses were the norm for patients, doctors, and nurses. One of the nurses wrote home to describe the work:

> For four days the staff spent its entire time in dressing wounds and getting all the seriously wounded into one ward, averaging four hundred dressings per day; many of the patients had not had their wounds dressed since the temporary first-aid dressing on the field, from ten days to two weeks previous. Badly infected wounds were the rule, not the exception.(Krueger 1915, 1015)

The other ARC unit in Serbia had a modern and well-built hospital, but it was in terrible condition when they arrived. In one day the three doctors and twelve nurses had 9,000 patients arrive. There was not enough food, beverages, medicine, or supplies. There was not even time enough to carry out the dead. Oftentimes the staff had to step over the corpses on the floor (Gladwin 1916, 908). In fact, most hospitals at the front did not have complete supplies as needed. One nurse recounted the situation at her hospital:

> Cotton, gauze and bandages don't always come with the asking. Drugs and lotions must be used sparingly. . . . Surgical requisites and appliances such as dressing bowls, syringes and splints may be conspicuous in their absence. . . . Your help may be limited; sometimes you may have none. (Sumner 1915, 825)

Conditions at a French hospital near the front, staffed by American, French, and English women, were no better, as one nurse recalled:

> We had barely the necessities for a hospital. Our buildings, being temporarily constructed, were little protection against the snowy weather of December. . . . The wind blew down the stovepipes, putting out the fires, and almost tearing the roof off. Snow sifted into the ward through cracks in the ceiling and around the windows. I had to rearrange the beds every day, pulling them into the centre at all angles to avoid drips, giving the room a demoralized aspect. (Black 1922, 75)

An ARC unit that went to Germany in 1914 and 1915 served in a military hospital set up in the city theater. The lower foyer, screened off by sheets pinned over coat racks, was used as the operating room and dressing room. The surgical table was made from two carpenter's horses with boards,

This shattered church in the ruins of Neuilly, France, furnished a temporary shelter for American wounded being treated by the 110th Sanitary Train, 4th Ambulance Corps, September 1918. (National Archives)

padded by a blanket. A hat tree served as an irrigating stand, and old newspaper had multiple uses, including replacing sputum cups and rubber sheets (Burgar 1915, 1095–1096). Some ARC hospitals established in England and France were homes on large estates converted for medical use. At the other extreme was the Royal Naval Hospital in England, built in 1735, with ninety-nine wards of twenty-eight beds each. In Austria and Russia, converted school buildings were used. In the desert of Wadi-el-Arish, the staff worked in hospital tents ("The Red Cross" 1915, 1112–1115; Davison 1920, 79).

Medical personnel in the United States who were anxious to be of service traveled to Europe individually or in groups to provide care. Doctors volunteered with the Red Cross to serve in Europe, for instance, as well as in such out-of-the-way places as northern Persia and Siberia, where there was also fighting and need for medical personnel and supplies (Speer 2002; Hazlett 1917, 445–449; Howe 1916, 61; Burr 1915a, 364–365; 1915b, 459–461; 1915c, 35–36). Nurse Elsie Burr decided in November 1914 to go and be of help; she sailed the next day for Paris, where her services were accepted at one of the hospitals. The American expatriate community had opened a hospital for its own use in 1910, in the Paris suburb of Neuilly-sur-Seine. When the war began, the organizers made plans to treat the French wounded, setting up tents on the grounds of the hospital. The French government offered them an unfinished school building about one-half mile from the American hospital for use as a military hospital, known in France as an *ambulance*. The Americans finished the construction of the building and set up a 600-bed hospital to treat French and British wounded, who began arriving in early September 1914. When the United States entered the war three years later, the capacity was expanded to two thousand. The board of governors of the American Military Hospital at Neuilly read like a *Who's Who*—mainly the wives of American diplomats, politicians, and businessmen (Gray 1974, 60; McCallum 2001, 54–59; Hansen 1996, 3; "Base Hospital No. 1, Neuilly, France" 1919, 134–135).

There were also those who organized civilian groups in the United States, raising the funds along with the personnel, and traveling to the war zone together. Some were sent by the U.S. government or agencies based in the United States with quasi-official governmental status. Just before the outbreak of the war, for example, a registry of American nurses had been established in Paris for the benefit of Americans traveling in France who might have a need for a trained nurse. In August 1914 the superintendent of the newly established American Military Hospital in Neuilly, France, called the registry asking for volunteers. Many came to work at the hospital immediately, along with nurses from a similar English registry (Robinson 1918, 298–302).

In the spring of 1915 the medical school at Harvard University sent a surgical unit to the American Military Hospital at Neuilly for a period of three months. A unit from Western Reserve University of Cleveland, Ohio, was already there when the Harvard Unit arrived to take over the University Service, a 162-bed unit of the hospital. These units were privately financed, and the doctors were all volunteers. Some stayed on long after their initial commitment ended. George Benet of the Harvard Unit went from the American Military Hospital to serving at a French hospital about three miles from the front line. A second and third Harvard Unit went the next year to serve at a

British hospital in France. A complete medical unit from Chicago traveled to France in early summer 1915 at the request and expense of the British government (Howe 1916, 32, 55; Laskin 1996, 3; Cushing 1941, 12–18; Quandt 1918a, 388–390; 1918b, 454–458).

From the earliest days of the war, the Medical Department of the U.S. Army sent observers to the front to learn from the French and British military medical support. These men reported to the surgeon general on medical care and the projected number of hospital beds and personnel that would be needed if the United States became involved in the fighting. Many of these doctors became leaders in the American Expeditionary Force (AEF), incorporating lessons learned from the Allies into planning for the care of sick and wounded American soldiers (Jaffin 1991, 174; U.S. Surgeon General vol. 1, 347–348).

Ambulance services were set up in France, hospitals were organized in several countries, and funds were started to collect monies to assist the various countries. Recognizing the need for a transport service to move the sick and wounded to the new American Military Hospital, for example, philanthropist Anne Harriman Vanderbilt arranged for Ford chassis from the French assembly plant to be outfitted as ambulances. Agreeing on the importance of getting the wounded from the front lines to the hospital, the hospital board formed a transportation committee to fund and manage the new ambulance service (Hansen 1996, 6–7).

In the early months of the fighting, Americans formed three major volunteer ambulance organizations. H. Herman Harjes, a senior partner of the Morgan-Harjes Bank in Paris, established the Harjes Formation, often referred to as the Morgan-Harjes Section. The American Ambulance Field Service was organized by future U.S. congressman A. Piatt Andrew to meet the need at the American Military Hospital at Neuilly, and businessman Richard Norton formed a unit called the Anglo-American Volunteer Motor-Ambulance Corps, sponsored by the British Red Cross (BRC) and the St. John Ambulance Association of London.

The Morgan-Harjes ambulance service started with six cars, two surgeons, and equipment, and began transport and hospital work in the autumn of 1914. Eventually the focus of the work was narrowed to transport only, and the unit became known as the *Section Sanitaire* American No. 5, attached to the French Red Cross.

Edward Toland left his job as a banker in Philadelphia and sailed to Europe in August 1914. He ended up at a small hospital unloading the wounded and later working as a surgical assistant. He was offered a job driving ambulances, and by October he was with the Harjes helping to set up a field hospital near the front (Hansen 1996, 14–15; McCallum 2001, 79–89).

American Francis Thompson Colby traveled to Belgium shortly after the war began with a load of clothing, chocolates, and a completely equipped operating room. He was driving for the American Military Hospital when he met with Richard Norton in late September 1914. Together they planned to run an ambulance service for the hospital. After the hospital decided to organize its own transport service, the British Red Cross agreed to sponsor the group, the Anglo-American Volunteer Motor-Ambulance Corps, in October 1914. By mid-January 1915 the organization had eight cars and twelve American drivers. By April 1917 the combined group had thirteen sections with over 100 ambulances and more than 200 men (Hansen 1996, 21–37; Gray 1974, 90–92).

A. Piatt Andrew went to France with plans to help the war effort by driving an ambulance for the American Military Hospital. His first duty was in Dunkirk working the night shift, meeting trains full of wounded and taking them to hospitals or boats. Andrew soon received permission from the French military to establish a ten-car ambulance service and got the unit attached to divisions of the French army, while still being the official ambulance service for the American Military Hospital. The service performed admirably during the first battle of Verdun.

By the time the United States entered the war, the organization had over thirty complete sections with nearly 1,200 drivers and 1,000 vehicles. In October 1917, the U.S. War Department authorized the formation of the United States Ambulance Service with 160 sections. Twenty-eight of the sections were made up of the already existing American ambulance services and their 3,500 drivers. Eventually, 137 sections were organized and 120 were sent overseas (Gray 1974, 61, 88; Hansen 1996, xvi–xvii, 19–20, 46–54; U.S. Surgeon General vol. 1, 355).

The French and British governments requested assistance with medical care as soon as the United States officially entered the war. England appealed for six completely equipped and staffed base hospitals and 1,000 additional doctors to serve with British troops. France requested that the American Military Hospital at Neuilly be taken over by the military and expanded. The American government granted these requests (Ashburn 1929, 322).

Base Hospital No. 4, organized at Cleveland, Ohio's, Lakeside Hospital in 1916, was the first ARC base hospital unit to be mobilized in May 1917, just one month after the U.S. declaration of war. With only ten days notice, the well-prepared unit sailed for Europe. In late May, it took over General Hospital No. 9 of the British Expeditionary Force (BEF), five miles outside of Rouen, France. The hospital continued to be known as General Hospital No. 9, caring mainly for English, Scottish, Welsh, Irish, Canadian, Australian, New Zealand, and South African patients. General Hospital No. 9 was located forty to sixty miles behind the front, but during the summer of 1917, the bombing along the Ypres-Messines sector was easily heard at the hospital.

In twelve months of service the hospital treated over 80,000 patients, with the heaviest day being 27 March 1918, when 1,125 patients were admitted and released during the course of the day. The operating room had six tables that were often in use twenty-four hours a day for weeks on end. The average number of surgeries reached over 100 in a twenty-four-hour period (Base Hospital No. 4, USA, and Mobile Hospital No. 5, USA 1919, 4, 15–17; Allison 1919a, 356).

In August 1918, Mobile Hospital No. 5 was organized from Base Hospital No. 4 (General Hospital No. 9) to care for the seriously wounded in the American sector. Six officers, twenty nurses, and thirty-five enlisted men— along with some reinforcements from the BEF—moved closer to the front and treated those from the Meuse-Argonne offensive. This small unit had a laundry, X-ray equipment, sterilizer, operating rooms, tents, and equipment for 245 beds, with expansion capabilities to 300 beds. Expansion eventually totaled 700 beds. The operating rooms had two to three tables per team, each doing twelve-hour shifts (Base Hospital No. 4, USA, and Mobile Hospital No. 5, USA 1919, 23–25).

Base Hospital No. 9, located in Bitray, France, consisted of thirty-four buildings with 500 beds, a capacity that increased to 2,250 in early 1918. The need to enlarge forced the hospital to requisition buildings in the town, taking over a school and equipping it for 200 patients and another barracks for 400 beds. From August 1917 to January 1919, the hospital admitted 15,219 patients, with a death rate of only 0.87 percent (Brown 1920, 55–63, 137, 149).

Setting up a base hospital was no easy matter. Base Hospital No. 32, a unit from Indianapolis, Indiana, arrived in the summer resort village of Contrexeville, France, in late December 1917. Just a few months later the staff could report on the work needed to create a hospital out of hotel buildings.

In the two months that elapsed since the hospital's arrival an almost incredible amount of work had been done. Dirty, unsanitary hotels had been transformed into clean, shining hospitals. More than fifty carloads of supplies and equipment had been unloaded and installed. One thousand beds were standing, made up ready to receive patients. Kitchens, laboratories, pharmacies, surgeries, dressing rooms and X-ray and special departments were equipped, organized and ready for service. . . . Streets had been cleaned, truckloads of accumulated refuse around the various buildings had been hauled away and the grounds had been thoroughly policed. (Hitz 1922, 57)

This surge in the need for medical personnel sparked a recruiting drive for doctors and nurses at home. In April 1917, the *Journal of the American Medical Association* ran articles every week lamenting the need for more volunteers in the medical corps. Writers called for over 1,000 more doctors, whether the United States went to war or not ("The Immediate Emergency" 1917, 1044; "The Civilian Doctor in Military Service" 1917, 1123–1124; "The Current Need of Young Men for the Regular Medical Corps" 1917, 1265). In similar fashion the surgeon general requested 1,000 nurses a month be recruited in August 1918, then raised that number to 1,000 a week in September of the same year. The demand for graduate nurses was so great that the need would not be met for the duration of the war. The shortage of American nurses in Europe increased from over 1,000 in July 1918 to almost 7,000 by November 1918.

Articles in professional journals, magazines, and newspapers carried titles such as "Nurses of America, Your Country Needs You!" and statements such as: "No more urgent need exists to-day [*sic*] and no factor can be more important in the winning of this war than adequate care of our sick and wounded" and "without a sufficient number of trained nurses, America's young men will languish and die" (Ashburn 1929, 330; "Nurses of America, Your Country Needs You" 1918, 215–218; "A Call for Women to Volunteer" 1918, 30). Age requirements for all nursing applicants were originally between twenty-five and thirty-five, but due to the shortage these were changed to twenty-one and forty-five. An army school of nursing was established to help meet the need for trained nurses. Many African-American nurses volunteered to serve, but their applications were rejected on the grounds that the AEF lacked the perceived necessary separate quarters ("Nursing News and Announcements" 1916, 1137; U.S. Surgeon General vol. 1, 333; vol. 7, 441–445; vol. 13, 291–292). A more real problem was the

Scottish Territorials being examined in a dressing station during the Battle of Menin Road, Belgium 1914. British Bureau of Information. (National Archives)

lack of ships to transport both troops and medical personnel. In June 1918, there were about 4,000 nurses serving overseas and 1,200 waiting in New York. At the time of the Armistice there were about 8,500 nurses with the Army Nurse Corps, when 15,000 were needed (U.S. Surgeon General vol. 2, 127–128).

Much of the system of American military medical care was based on the French and British systems noted by the American medical observers in 1914–1917. Treatment stations had various names, depending upon whether they were under U.S., British, or French control, but followed the same general pattern. Treatment of the wounded began at the *abri du blesse,* an area of the trench that sheltered the wounded, with initial first aid possibly from the soldier's own kit or that of a comrade. U.S. soldiers were issued hermetically sealed first aid kits for this purpose. Next, a wounded man would be moved to the advanced dressing station, also underground and about fifty yards behind the line. He was then transported through the trenches, by stretcher-bearers if too severely injured to walk, to the battalion dressing station—called casualty clearing stations by the British—about one mile behind the lines, the furthest forward point accessible to ambulances.

Here there were surgical facilities and a trained surgeon. A doctor would clean wounds, apply dressings, set fractures, apply splints, perform any emergency surgeries and amputations, then prepare the patient for transport. Further back were field hospitals and evacuation hospitals for those patients who needed extended care. Even further back were hospital centers made up of several base hospital units, where thousands of sick and wounded got treatment and recuperated (Mason 1917, 92–93; Jaffin 1991, 178; American Red Cross, *War-Time Manual*, 86; Ashburn 1929, 340–341; Ford 1918, 203; "The French Military Hospital System" 1917, 120–122).

Rates of survival for the wounded depended on the time that elapsed from injury to treatment, so the work of the stretcher-bearers and ambulance drivers was just as important as that of the doctors and nurses. The ambulance companies' purpose was to gather sick and wounded, give temporary treatment as needed, and transport these patients as quickly as possible to the next unit toward the rear. Moving the wounded was often done at night to prevent exposing stretcher-bearers to any more danger than absolutely necessary (Gray 1974, 61; Allison 1919b, 430–432; Mason 1917, 23).

Leslie Buswell drove an ambulance and in describing one night's work showed that fighting soldiers were not the only ones facing danger:

> Last night I was on duty all night . . . and it was a great strain riding backward and forward in pitch darkness up and down the very steep and narrow road. . . . This road is in full view of the Germans and much bombarded, and shrapnel burst close by, which reminded me that a lovely moonlight night with trees and hills and valleys dimly shaping themselves *can* be other than romantic. (Buswell 1916, 36–37)

By regulation, AEF field hospitals were supposed to be organized at four per division, with a capacity of 216 patients, and located about five miles from the front, outside the range of fire. It was not always possible to meet these requirements. Female nurses were supposed to serve only in large hospitals to the rear, but many were sent much closer to the front (Mason 1917, 24, 142; Ashburn 1929, 341; Black 1922, 210–212; Ford 1918, 67–68, 204;

First aid nurses of the British Yeomanry Corps at work in the trenches, placing a wounded soldier on a stretcher, January 1915. (Underwood & Underwood/Corbis)

Ginn 1997, 42; U.S. Surgeon General vol. 2, 876–879; vol. 13, 334–345). Field hospitals were to provide emergency care only: resuscitation, stabilization, and needed surgery while preparing patients to be moved further to the rear. Cases were triaged, or sorted by categories, here. This French concept of triage was considered one of the most important steps in the care of the sick and wounded, and it was repeated at every location through the chain of care, creating a system that accounted for every sick and injured soldier.

Regulations also stated that beds were not required at this level, so patients often were placed on straw on the floor. If the receiving room could only handle a few patients at a time, the others would lie in wait in the next room. Upon being carried into the room, the men were quickly washed and given an anti-tetanus injection. Doctors or medics would check any previously applied dressings to assure they had not loosened, which could cause hemorrhaging. The patients were numbered consecutively from one upward, in order of need for prompt evacuation to rear. Diagnosis tags were attached to all patients (dead or alive). A list of sick and wounded was kept daily by the regimental surgeon, and monthly reports were sent to the surgeon general.

Specific rules about the disposition of those tags were spelled out in army regulations. At the field hospital patients were classified as (1) fit for return to service; (2) not fit for two to three weeks, send to rear; (3) fit to return to service in near future, send forward when next big battle; and (4) serious, evacuate as soon as able to travel. Another way of categorizing the patients was: those who would die soon, no matter the treatment; those needing immediate treatment to live; and those whose treatment could be delayed. One nurse mentioned the attitude that had to be taken about the dealing with the sick and injured soldiers: "In a war, the ones who are going to die don't matter. It's only the ones who might live that count" (Boylston 1927, 75).

Evacuation hospitals were further to the rear, ideally about eight to ten miles but sometimes as far as twelve to twenty miles, and located near a railroad. They were usually allotted at one per division, with a 500- to 1,000-bed capacity. This was the first place that had the necessary equipment, physicians, and enlisted personnel to provide complete medical care for the patients. Evacuation hospitals were moveable units, self-contained and usually set up in pairs. They were organized without female nurses, but once the units were sent overseas, females were frequently detached to them. Additional teams, such as operating teams, gas teams, and splint teams, were often sent to the unit during heavy fighting.

Evacuation hospitals again divided the patients into categories of (1) seriously wounded and not transportable; (2) seriously wounded, but transportable; and (3) slightly wounded, needing seven to ten days for recovery. With a shifting front, the distance from a field hospital to the evacuation hospital could shorten or grow to as much as fifty miles (U.S. Surgeon General vol. 1, 352–356; vol. 2, 854–861; vol. 13, 334–345; Mason 1917, 454–455; Gabriel and Metz 1992, 250; Ashburn 1929, 342). American nurse Elizabeth Black described the French hospital near Cugny, France, where she began serving in 1917:

The hospital is a town of its own, with a railroad-station from which the *blesses* are sent to the interior as soon as they can travel to make room for others who are constantly arriving from the trenches. Rows and rows of sheds stretch away on every side, connected by plank walks. The corridors have floors of earth, and suggest subterranean caves or catacombs, as they are dark at night. There are twelve wards, wooden huts, connecting the corridor on each side. Each has room for forty-six or fifty beds. (Black 1922, 48)

Once they were far enough behind the lines and had received initial treatment, the men were transported by rail to the larger and better-equipped base hospitals in the rear. In the early days of the war freight cars were used, but these had the distinct disadvantage of having no heat or light. Freight cars were soon replaced by passenger coaches adapted for this purpose. These cars were definitely more comfortable for the patients but proved difficult to load due to the small size of the doorways. Special hospital trains were then manufactured to specifications, with ten cars each, with eight for patients and a capacity of 200. Hospital trains were normally staffed by three doctors, three noncommissioned officers, two cooks, twenty-two privates—or twenty nurses—and two orderlies.

The ward cars were Pullmans, stripped of lower berths that were replaced by hospital beds. One car was a completely equipped operating room and surgical ward. Capacity totaled eighty beds for patients and 120 berths for sitting patients. Occasionally hospital barges were used for transport, each with thirty beds and a staff of two nurses and one doctor. The advantage of the barges was the smoothness of transport for the seriously wounded, but they were slow, and waterways were not always conveniently located near the front or hospitals (Ford 1918, 235–252; Mason 1917, 2).

Rather than tents or temporary structures that housed evacuation hospitals, base hospitals were usually located in permanent buildings and had a much larger staff. Thirty-five officers, 200 enlisted men, and 100 female nurses, along with adequate equipment to give complete medical care, were the norm. Base hospitals were frequently shorthanded as special medical teams, such as surgical teams, splint teams, and shock teams were created from personnel at base hospitals to serve closer to the front during times of increased fighting. A casual operating team, for example, consisted of one surgeon, one assistant surgeon, one anesthetist, two nurses, and two orderlies attached to a base hospital and sent to front lines when needed. In December 1918, there were 2,662 American personnel serving on 447 teams ("Personal Experiences of World War I Nurses" 1957a, 7–8; 1957b, 9).

Hospital centers were made up of several base or general hospitals, with 10,000–25,000 beds, and resembled full-fledged, yet temporary, cities. By November 1918, the AEF operated twenty such hospital centers. One such center covered 172 acres and included thirteen sections and a cemetery. There were ten general hospitals, each with 1,000 beds within fifty-five buildings. There was also a quartermaster camp, a convalescent camp with a capacity of 2,000, and a psychiatric hospital.

The Mars Center in France began operation when the first patients arrived on 2 August 1918. Base Hospitals No. 68 and 48 had arrived on 24 and 25 July, and other units continued to arrive until February 1919. It was originally designed to be a 40,000-bed hospital center with a 5,000-bed convalescent camp. It was just over half-completed on 11 November 1918, when it consisted of 700 buildings on a thirty-three-acre site, complete with roads, a sewage system, and lighting facilities. Those stationed there organized an orchestra, a theater, a newspaper, a Masonic society, and athletic events. In its short existence, the Mars Center cared for 37,774 patients. Only 438 of those are buried in the center's cemetery (American Red Cross, *War-Time Manual*, 86–87; Ashburn 1929, 333–334; U.S. Surgeon General vol. 2, 488; Dearborn 2002).

Convalescent hospitals and camps were needed for those men who no longer needed to be in a base hospital but still needed some care. These were the soldiers who were not permanently disabled but also could not immediately return to their unit. Convalescent camps were usually attached to base hospitals, and each hospital group was assigned one convalescent camp. There were also hospitals at some of the divisional training camps for local admissions only, and most of these had a 300-bed capacity. Anyone seriously sick or wounded at these hospitals would be transferred to a base hospital (U.S. Surgeon General vol. 1, 354; vol. 2, 286–288).

For those too seriously injured to be moved and to take some of the pressure off of the field and evacuation hospitals, the military also had mobile surgical hospitals. A mobile hospital was a

Well equipped, standardized surgical hospital that is easily transportable, and can be brought forward close to the division field hospital used as triage, to provide prompt surgical care for these cases and obviated a long ambulance haul to larger hospitals placed of necessity further to the rear. (U.S. Surgeon General vol. 1, 872)

Although considered transportable, a description of one of these hospitals, which had a 250-bed capacity and occupied twenty-two tents, shows that even though it admitted only those nontransportable wounded, otherwise it functioned much the same as an evacuation hospital (U.S. Surgeon General vol. 2, 873).

Early in the war, typhus proved to be a problem on the eastern front. The disease was carried by lice, and so medical personnel had to protect themselves from being infected with this disease, which brought headache, fever, rash, delirium, and depression. The doctors and nurses in Serbia wore louse-proof clothing, head coverings, and rubber gloves, making sure that there were no openings for lice to invade their clothing. Methods of lice control included having large bathing facilities, so that all soldiers could have a bath at least once a week, and having their clothing disinfected (Howe 1916, 63, 68; U.S. Surgeon General vol. 6, 1005).

In the fall of 1917, the French *Service de Santé* invited some Americans to send operating teams to some of their hospitals to see firsthand how the French were caring for their wounded soldiers. The teams from the Johns Hopkins Unit (Base Hospital No. 18), the New York Hospital Unit (Base Hospital No. 9), and the Roosevelt Hospital Unit (Base Hospital No. 15) visited a 4,000-bed French hospital center located seven miles behind the lines. In October during a major offensive, the French were averaging eight hours from the time a man was hit to getting him on the operating table. Of special note were the speed of the stretcher-bearers, the importance of X-rays, the connection between bacteriology and surgery, and the use of the new Carrel-Dakin method of cleaning wounds. Before the war, only the larger military hospitals had X-ray equipment, but its use in diagnosis proved the value of it in all hospitals. By November 1918, over 700 sets of X-ray equipment had been shipped overseas (*The History of Base Hospital No. 18, AEF* 1919, 94–95; Ashburn 1929, 315).

The major cause of severe injuries was shrapnel, a metal shell encasing bullets and carrying an explosive charge that burst upon contact with a hard object. This type of projectile goes easily through soft tissue and upon hitting bone flattens, causing multiple injuries and immense pain. Wounds were invariably infected by the time patients arrived at a hospital for care. Trench fighting in France and Belgium was conducted on richly fertilized land, filled with bacteria from fecal matter. Wounds from exploding shells were ragged and gaping, with contaminated mud and muddy clothing driven deep into the wounds. The bacterial infections—either aerobic (requiring oxygen for existence) or anaerobic (those that cannot live in the presence of oxygen)—required different kinds of treatment (Black 1922, 165; Schwartz 1995, 5; Barkley 1918, 161–162, 166).

The major problem with infected wounds was gas gangrene, a "spreading, moist gangrene produced by gas-forming anaerobic bacteria in extensively traumatized tissues" (U.S. Surgeon General vol. 12, 407). English researchers at a mobile laboratory in France were able to determine that gas gangrene was basically a muscle disease after examining microscopic changes that occurred in the muscles. The symptoms, which might be delayed, included pain, swelling, fever, rapid pulse, a crackling sound when pressure was applied to the area (caused by gas accumulating in tissues), change in color, and a discharge with an offensive odor. Edema, or swelling, appeared in the region four to six hours after being wounded, then traveled to the abdomen within six to eight hours along with the crackling sound. The effects on the nervous system included tremor, convulsions, and bowel paralysis (U.S. Surgeon General vol. 12, 409; Schwartz 1995, 6; Barkley 1918, 185).

At Base Hospital No. 36, in the spring of 1918, the wounded were arriving directly from the front with dressings that had been untouched for days.

> Gauze had grown to the flesh, and even with the utmost care the removal of this, and the packing, caused untold agony to the soldier. . . . Doctors and nurses worked far into and sometimes all night bathing the patients and dressing wounds in the wards, while four or five tables in each operating room would be going for the removal of shrapnel, amputations and more complicated wounds and fractures. (Cooper 1923, 145)

George R. Baker served as a medic at General Hospital No. 18 at Camiers and CCS No. 48 at Brie, France. In mid-September 1918 he described the heavy workload facing the medical staff and the amount of infection they faced resulting from what he called "the big Cambrai affair":

> I certainly feel sorry for the poor fellows who lose an arm or leg. They never can get them back. If they were in any other place but a lousy, bacteria-infected front, a great many of them would not suffer these losses, but here infection starts as soon as a man has been hit and it works fast. We have gas gangrene in nearly every case. (Baker 1999, 97)

Nurse Helen Boylston described the difficulty of caring for a wound when gas gangrene had set in:

> Frightful arm; elbow joint smashed, and the whole arm stiff and swollen, and full of gas gangrene. In getting off the dressing I had to move it some, and though I was as careful as I could be, I could hear the bones crunching and grating inside. Then I had to pull off hard, dry sponges, and haul out yards of packing that kept catching on the splintered bone. (Boylston 1927, 149)

Caring for head injuries proved to be especially problematic. Noted Harvard physician Harvey Cushing stated that, even in the absence of external symptoms, all head wounds from projectiles had to be taken seriously because it was easy to overlook serious head trauma. Although well established by 1914, the field of neurology made important strides in diagnosis and treatment of brain injuries and acute diseases. Treatment for head injuries required shaving and X-raying the head, then opening the wound and removing all infected tissue, bits of bone, and foreign bodies. Symptoms of brain injury could include a slowed pulse, headache, irregular pupils, muscle twitches, unconsciousness, stupor, and paralysis. Recuperation required bed rest with the head elevated (Keen 1917, 101–102; Boller and Duyckaerts 1999, 882–885).

Due to the nature of trench warfare, the fighting during World War I resulted in more facial injuries than any previous war. The British began doing new and innovative work in the field of maxillofacial surgery at a time when there was no established science for the treatment of facial wounds. An American military medical observer commented that "some very wonderful work was done, and is being done, in the restoration to a semblance of something human to those suffering from the terribly disfiguring wounds of the face." He went on to describe the work in detail:

> They borrow pieces of rib and bits of shin-bone and make new noses of them; they twist and pull and coax adjacent tissue until it covers the gaps, and they bridge in vacant areas by skin grafts. (Church 1918, 73–74)

Dental surgeons arrived with the first Harvard Unit at the American Military Hospital in Neuilly to provide specialized work on jaw fractures. Eventually the Americans opened four hospitals that focused on this type of treatment and introduced the team approach for reconstructive surgery. The dentists were also able to diagnose other dental troubles that were the cause of many medical problems plaguing the soldiers, such as arthritis, gastritis, and ear and sinus infections (Gabriel and Metz 1992, 242; Howe 1916, 180–183; Ring 1999, 105–106).

Abdominal wounds were often multiple wounds involving more than one internal organ and were almost always infected. Wounds of the buttocks were especially difficult to deal with because, just as with other abdominal wounds, amputation was not an option as it was with extremities, and high mortality rates were the rule if the rectum was involved (Keen 1917, 101–102; Barkley 1918, 178–183; Davis 1917, 1689).

A major medical problem during the war was a vasomotor condition called trench foot, caused by cold and wet conditions combined with pressure interfering with circulation. First the veins in the feet began to constrict, then the feet felt cold. Next came loss of feeling, followed by swelling, then pain around the ankles and up into the calves. When the soldier's boots were removed the feet might be bright pink or already black and gangrenous. With treatment, circulation would gradually return to the site, the swelling would go down, and pain would begin, sometimes severe enough to require morphine. Those with a mild case needed a warm footbath daily, followed by massage. If there was swelling present, the foot was elevated, powdered with boric acid, and wrapped with cotton wool. Mild cases took about three weeks to recover. In severe cases the foot was also elevated and wrapped, but the patient was evacuated to a base hospital. Severe cases could take three months to recover, and if the foot was already gangrenous, amputation was required.

Although some sources claimed that trench foot was not a severe problem for American soldiers, accounts from medical personnel tell another story. An American nurse described a patient with trench foot in February 1918:

We are getting in a lot of trench feet now. Horrible things! One lad struggled in here the other night, slightly wounded in the leg, but with fearful trench feet. His trousers had been nearly shot off and hung in ribbons, pinned here and there with nails. He was soaked to the waist from lying in a shell hole full of water, and he had not slept for four days and nights. His feet, which were hideously swollen and purple, were raw with broken blisters and were wrapped in muddy, dripping bandages. He *walked* into my ward. I got him to bed and warm blankets as quickly as I could, filled him full of hot drinks and morphine, and left him in peace and [with] clean bandages. He fell asleep while I was putting them on. (Boylston 1927, 25–26)

An American medic also wrote about soldiers coming in with trench foot in March 1918, stating that oftentimes they could not get circulation to return to the purple and black extremities, forcing amputation as the only alternative. Waterproof boots decreased the incidence of this painful condition, as did having soldiers oil their feet or their socks and the wearing of hip boots. The army made it a punishable offense if soldiers did not take care of their feet, expecting them to remove their boots daily, clean their feet, dry their boots out if possible, and carry extra dry socks ("Trench Foot" 1917, 598–607; Ashburn 1929, 353; Baker 1999, 65).

In May 1915, British doctors noticed a new illness that seemed to defy identification. For want of a better term they called it "trench fever" when it began as an epidemic on the western front. Once exposed, there was a latent period of anywhere from eight to thirty days, followed by sudden faintness, headache, leg pain, shivering, possible rash, and recurring fever. There were muscle pains that mimicked meningitis and appendicitis. Following remission, the illness usually recurred within five to six days. This course might be repeated up to twelve times. Complications included rapid heartbeat, and though few died, the majority of victims were unfit for duty for three months.

Doctors tested for bacteria but found this to be a viral, infectious disease and not a form of typhoid or paratyphoid. Because there was no laboratory test for the illness, diagnosis had to be made by the process of elimination. Doctors compared the disease to influenza, recognized that it was transmitted by whole blood, and believed that it was carried by lice. Infestation of men in trenches ran about 97 percent, making this very difficult to combat. Yet as suddenly as it appeared, this epidemic disappeared from the western front by 1918 (Schwartz 1995, 9; Miller 2003; American Red Cross 1918, 11–21; Ashburn 1929, 353).

Also first recognized during the First World War was a new kind of mental condition labeled "shellshock." Entire books were written on the subject, including Lewis R. Yealland's *Hysterical Disorders of Warfare,* written and published in 1918. Patients suffering from shellshock might appear dazed, and could even be unconscious. Symptoms varied but included delirium, amnesia, confusion, hallucinations, and sleep disturbances. Speech disorders such as stammering, mutism, and difficulty in expressing thoughts often appeared as well. Many victims suffered from sensory and somatic symptoms, such as anesthesia, pain, or hypersensitivity to touch. Other indicators could include blindness, deafness, paralysis, trembling, loss of motor control, extremely rapid heart rate, incontinence, and diarrhea.

All of these were symptoms of other physical and mental conditions, but they were showing up in greater concentration and variety than in civilian life. Doctors found it difficult to distinguish between malingerers and those who were truly ill while they searched for an explanation. Some claimed that trench life and trench warfare caused a nervous stress that was specifically exhausting. Treatment consisted mainly of bed rest and offering the patient reassurance (Salmon 1917, 683–686; Starr 1918, 183; Barkley 1918, 195–196).

Another condition common early in the war was tetanus, an anaerobic bacterium. Conditions that favored gas gangrene also contributed to tetanus. The symptoms included rigid muscles, sensitivity to light and noise, increase in muscle reflexes, and lockjaw. An anti-tetanus serum was developed and routinely given to all patients upon arrival at a treatment station, virtually eliminating the disease by the end of the war (Barkley 1918, 186–188).

Many soldiers suffered burns for which the traditional treatments were fairly simple and nontoxic but not optimum. These included covering the burn with gauze soaked in an Epsom salt solution to relieve pain and reduce inflammation, bathing in saline or sodium bicarbonate, and putting alcohol on fresh burns. A much-heralded new treatment called "the ambrine treatment" was developed by Dr. Barthe de Sanfort. Ambrine was a liquid preparation of paraffin and oil of amber, with the exact proportions kept as the doctor's secret. His treatment consisted of washing the wound with sterile water, drying it, then spraying or brushing the mixture onto the burned area. The wound was then covered with a thin layer of cotton wool, followed by a second layer of the paraffin mixture. This was left on the burn for two to three days, removed, and applied again every two days until it healed. At the second dressing, the dead layers of skin were cut away. These steps sealed the burned area so it could heal, resulting in less scarring and deformity than in the past. This same treatment was found to be effective on trench feet as well (Barkley 1918, 188–195; Church 1918, 101–102; Black 1922, 150–153; Keen 1917, 122–124).

World War I saw the first use of chemical or gas warfare when the Germans used it at Ypres in 1915. Soldiers affected by that first gas came into the hospitals with swollen eyes, blistered skin, and serious respiratory problems, and they were spitting blood. In 1917 American medical observers were sent to the French army's School of Asphyxiating Gases. They then prepared the first report to the U.S. War Department on gas warfare, and from this report came the creation of the Gas Service, later renamed the Chemical Warfare Section, which was in charge of offensive and defensive chemical warfare in the AEF (Barkley 1918, 197; Allison 1919b, 432; U.S. Surgeon General vol. 14, 39–40).

Gases were classified not by their chemical composition but by the effects on the human body. Lacrimators, or eye irritants, commonly known as "tear gases," could immediately produce tearing and temporary blindness. Sternutators, or nasal irritants, caused irritation of the nose, throat, and eyes, leading to headaches and nausea. Inhalation of suffocants or lung irritants resulted in edema (swelling) of the lungs, asphyxiation, and even death. The effects were immediate and in high concentrations caused spasms, violent coughing, and vomiting. A soldier suffering from exposure to this type of gas would have ashen skin and lips and possibly a bloody, thin liquid foaming from the mouth and nose. There would be damage to the small air pockets of the lungs, and the lobes would enlarge, becoming dense and doughy. Pulse and respiration would be rapid but weak. Although the gas did not directly affect the heart, the blood would become thick and dark, and the right chambers of the heart would dilate due to the composition of the blood. Exertion could cause death from asphyxia. If the patient lasted seventy-two hours, he was usually out of danger but still in need of complete rest. Although deadly, these gases dissipated quickly, so it was difficult for the enemy to keep an effective concentration for any period of time.

The most commonly used gases had a high density with little irritation to eyes and none to skin, making detection difficult (U.S. Surgeon General vol. 14, 89–92). Wearing a gas mask protected the eyes, nose, and throat from the vesicants, or skin irritants, but since they were odorless it was easy to be unaware of their presence. Unlike some of the other gases these penetrated clothing, causing burning of the skin. This gas was latent upon discharge for anywhere from thirty minutes to eight hours, but then it was effective for hours and even days after use, making it a very effective weapon. Symptoms of exposure included skin lesions, blisters, nausea, vomiting, headache, fatigue, inflamed eyes, and temporary blindness. These usually became more severe on the second day after exposure. Death could occur anywhere from the fifth to twenty-first day after exposure (U.S. Surgeon General vol. 14, 89–92).

The treatment for gas victims began with removing the patient from the area and attempting to identify the type of gas. Then these men were separated from the nongassed patients, moved to a specialty hospital, and divided into wards according to the type of gas they had encountered. Oxygen was given if needed, and blood was drawn at a first aid or dressing station. The victim might even require artificial respiration. Those believed to have been exposed to lung irritants and mustard gas were not allowed to walk. If the gas was no longer present, the patient was given something to bring on coughing at regular intervals.

Those exposed to skin irritants were evacuated. They could not be wrapped or covered in any way until their clothing was removed, their skin lesions opened and cleaned, and their hair clipped. Then they were bathed. Alkaline dusting powder was used on the skin, and the ambrine treatment was used for deeper burns. Eyes were irrigated and protected from light. With any burn, every precaution had to be taken to prevent secondary infection (U.S. Surgeon General vol. 14, 265–270).

According to the U.S. surgeon general, gas poisoning was the cause of 31.49 percent of the battle injuries, and almost 9 percent of fatalities were from gas. The average treatment time per gassed patient was almost forty-two days; thus almost three million man-days were lost due to hospitalization. More than 2,800 soldiers, some 14 percent of all those disabled during the war, were discharged with disability due to gas.

Medical personnel were also exposed to the gases, not directly, but from the clothing of the patients. Inhaling these lingering gases or getting it on skin could cause them to have the same respiratory problems and skin lesions. From March to November 1918, Base Hospital No. 32 treated 6,000 gas cases ranging from slight exposure to complete poisoning, 28 percent of which were considered serious. Fatalities were caused mainly by the effects of the gases on the respiratory tract. There was no treatment available other than oxygen, and the hospital had no oxygen tanks at that time. The Allied Gas Service recommended an alternative treatment when oxygen was not available: a medication to bring on coughing that would expel the contents of the bronchi and trachea, making breathing easier and thereby getting more oxygen to the patient (U.S. Surgeon General vol. 14, 273–274; Boylston 1927, 137, 163; Hitz 1922, 133–136).

In the spring of 1918, the fighting troops along with the rest of the world were affected by the pandemic of flu, commonly known as the Spanish Flu or the "Spanish Lady." The disease spread quickly around the world, incapacitating its victims but actually killing few of them. Sometimes the symptoms were not even severe enough for a soldier to report to sick call. This flu continued to spread throughout the summer, but most patients recovered. With bed rest and an enema, most symptoms were gone in twenty-four to seventy-two hours. There were few aftereffects except mild weakness.

A second wave of the flu hit in late August and continued into the autumn. This second wave attacked its victims with a new vengeance and a sudden onset of headache, backache, fatigue, sore throat, collapse, and often death within a few hours or days. The pandemic hit its peak in September and October, and a third wave followed in February 1919. The major targets of the disease were people between the ages of fifteen and thirty-five, such as the military troops, and not the very young or the elderly as one might expect (U.S. Surgeon General vol. 12, 187; Parsons 2002; Patterson 1920).

Research was conducted at military labs in France, but no cause of the flu was discovered. Autopsies showed laryngeal, tracheal, and bronchial swelling and hemorrhage; the presence of frothy, bloody sputum; and involvement of all of the lobes of the lungs. Various species of microbes were found to be present, including influenza bacilli, streptococci, and pneumococci, but it was not until 1933 that the culprit, the influenza A virus, was finally identified (U.S. Surgeon General vol. 12, 189–192). George R. Baker, at CCS No. 48 in Busigny, Belgium, in November 1918, wrote:

> All kinds of men are dying every hour with the flu. They cannot get them buried fast enough. It is a shame to die just as the war is about ended. An ambulance is loaded at the front with flu stricken patients but before it can get to the train just a few miles away, most of the men are dead. They are lying in rows, each covered with a blanket. I sure feel sorry for these war-torn Tommies who have to die from flu when the war is about over. (Baker 1999, 117)

Venereal disease was another issue that caused concern for the military. Although the rate of infection in American troops was considered low, there were still over 57,000 primary hospital admissions and 1.7 million days lost from duty due to venereal disease. American military leaders opposed the French solution of licensing prostitution to prevent and control venereal disease, but the AEF did set up prophylactic stations, enforced compulsory treatment if exposed, and penalized those who did not use preventative measures or seek treatment when they contracted the disease. Separate camps were established for those recuperating from any form of venereal disease, and no one was allowed to return to the United States until he was considered "clean" (Ashburn 1929, 336–337; U.S. Surgeon General vol. 6, 934–935, 965).

Prevention of all types of disease was recognized as a priority and fell under the responsibilities of the Division of Sanitation of the Medical Department. The work of this division included making policies on sanitation, inspecting military camps, collecting and studying statistics on illness, and assigning sanitary personnel. Sanitary corps carried out the day-to-day work of the division. The U.S. Army had learned an important lesson from the Spanish-American War, when typhoid caused immense difficulties. A vaccination was developed to protect against the disease, with its symptoms of rash, fever, bronchitis, and intestinal hemorrhage. Serious efforts were made to eradicate carriers and bad water supplies that harbored the typhoid bacillus (Ashburn 1929, 310; Jaffin 1991, 181).

Sick and wounded soldiers usually arrived at the hospital filthy and infested with vermin. After being checked by a doctor in the reception area, they were bathed and their clothing disinfected to kill any lice. Bathing facilities were built at all hospitals. Lice were annoying as well as being carriers of disease, and they were a major problem. Over two hundred insecticides were tested from 1914 to 1918, but nothing proved effective in killing lice and their eggs (nits) except kerosene, gasoline, ordinary petroleum jelly, and extreme heat. Lice and nits lived mainly in the soldier's clothing, so a method of using dry or steam heat to disinfect uniforms and bedding was implemented. Other parasitic problems encountered by the soldiers and the doctors treating them included itch mites (causing scabies), hookworms (causing anemia and fatigue), and other intestinal parasites (causing diarrhea) (Hall 1918, 108–110).

The traditional treatment for open wounds was to clean out the wound and then suture it closed. This was resulting in a large rate of infection and amputation as anaerobic bacteria were being trapped inside the wound. French surgeon R. LeMaitre introduced a new technique called "debridement." He advocated that within twelve hours of injury flesh in and around the wound be excised, while the wound would be closed at a later time. The removal of multiple bullet fragments was made easier by the use of high-powered magnets. The magnetic pull would actually cause pieces to move slightly, indicating location to the surgeon. For removal, a long, thin steel rod might be inserted into the wound until it touched the bullet. The other end of the rod was then connected to a large electric magnet. The rod was slowly withdrawn, pulling the bullets from the deep recesses of the human body (Kerr 1915, 712–717; Church 1918, 91–92).

A wounded soldier often needed treatment to prevent or retard infection before he could reach a location where surgery was available. French physician and Nobel Prize–winner Alexis Carrel showed that within six hours of injury, various bacteria appeared near the site of the wound, and that within twenty-four hours, the bacteria had spread throughout the body. When dressing a wound was delayed, the blood would dry and form a scab, sealing the wound and creating a perfect environment for anaerobic bacteria to multiply.

Carrel and English chemist Henry Dakin came up with a system of treatment that contributed greatly to saving many lives. They tested almost two hundred compounds and decided the best antiseptic solution was sodium hypochlorite combined with boric acid as a neutralizer, mixed at an exact strength. If it was too weak, it was ineffective; if too strong, it was irritating to the skin and tissues. They also noted that the compound lost its strength after about an hour, so a new supply had to be added every two hours. The wound would be cleaned and then Carrel's irrigation system of continuous bathing and draining with the Dakin solution would be administered. The "guiding principle [was] to place the tubes so that the liquid will come into contact with every portion of the wound" (Keen 1917, 50).

Dakin's solution was placed in a one-liter flask with long rubber tubes extending from the lower end of it, joined to the ends of drains by small glass tubes. The drains were perforated at 5, 10, and 15 centimeters, using one to four holes according to the size of the wound. The end was tied with string to keep the solution flowing where needed, and a metal clasp on the long tube was opened every two hours to disinfect and moisten the wound. The wound would be closed after the patient maintained a low enough bacteria count for two days in a row. This could happen as early as the fifth day, with the average being the seventh to ninth day (Keen 1917, 31–61, 89–92; Black 1922, 104–105; Schwartz 1995, 7; Barkley 1918, 167, 185).

The field of anesthesiology also made great advances during the war. British anesthetists used only chloroform in the early months, with ether becoming available soon after. While some doctors complained about the quality of the available ether, Canadian Dr. William B. Howell began using a small amount of chloroform prior to administering ether, which seemed to solve the problem of the slow effect of ether. American surgical shock expert Dr. George Crile also reported the successful use of nitrous oxide and oxygen. Doctors began to recognize that the correct choice and administration of anesthesia could be the difference between life and death for many of the patients. The problem of a shortage of nitrous oxide was solved when the ARC bought, disassembled, shipped, and then reassembled in Europe a plant that manufactured the gas. The use of spinal and regional anesthesia also became more popular for brain surgery and amputation, since so many patients had respiratory complications, making the use of general anesthesia dangerous (Courington and Calverley 1986, 644–649).

An innovative concept in military medicine during the war was the organization of a Division of Physical Reconstruction and the use of reconstruction aids in the rehabilitation of the thousands of wounded. The need for physical and occupational therapists to work with the disabled patients was recognized as early as December 1917, but few of these individuals actually arrived in Europe before the Armistice. The first group sent by the surgeon general's office arrived in France in October 1918. At the end of the year, 200 therapists were serving at twenty base hospitals with the AEF, and at least thirty served with the occupation army in Germany in 1919. In the United States, a Harvard professor of educational psychology developed a program in occupational therapy for returning injured at Walter Reed General Hospital and published a protocol for other hospitals to develop similar programs (U.S. Surgeon General vol. 2, 128–129; Ginn 1997, 72).

Another innovation in medical support during the war was the use of mobile laboratories. This was the first time that laboratories were used near the front with combat forces. The staff in these mobile units was able to examine local water supplies and prepare cultures to be sent to fixed laboratories. By the end of the war there were thirty-one operational laboratories with the American forces, with nineteen more in the process of being organized (Ginn 1997, 71–72).

Arriving in the war zone, the medical units found conditions to be unusual at best and difficult at worst. In many cases, whereas medicine had advanced significantly, facilities had not. The French and British had already been at war for three years and had utilized most of the available, suitable buildings for hospitals already. Supplies were also very scarce by this time. The units negotiated with the French government for sites that could be used, often adding large tent wards or huts to existing buildings. Large hospital centers needed open ground near a railway, and that was not always easy to find.

Working conditions ranged from excellent to terrible for American medical personnel. Hospitals were set up in chateaus, hotels, and schools that may have been architecturally attractive but difficult to work in. Other times, hospitals were tents or quickly erected barracks buildings. Even in beautiful surroundings there was usually a lack of central heat, running water, and electricity, and sewage disposal was a major problem. For supplies and equipment, the medical staff creatively reused materials: petrol cans became stoves, boxes were cut up for latrine covers, and tin cans were cut up for utensils (Barclay 1923, 99).

When busy, everyone in the hospital was very busy, but when things were slow, many were completely bored. Dr. Harold Barclay served with the Roosevelt Hospital Unit and the 42nd Rainbow Division in France. During a lull in September 1917 he wrote how "time drags interminably. . . . I feel as if my brain were jellifying" (Barclay 1923, 82). But the opposite was expressed by George Baker, who volunteered as a medic with Base Hospital No. 12 from Northwestern University Hospital, where his duties included shaving patients, changing dressings, making splints, and writing letters for patients. In March 1918 he wrote:

> Am all alone in ward as other man is in quarantine. All heavy surgical cases. I have many bad cases and all the worst kind—wounds in head, chest and stomach. Many have open wounds that are draining so they can heal up clean. It is the wreck of war. (Baker 1999, 62)

Six months later the staff at Base Hospital No. 12 was very busy, working through a barrage that lasted all day:

> We are almost crazy with so many wounded coming in but if they can stick it out, we can. My legs and feet are what bother me the most. They get almost paralyzed from standing so long. I have to bathe them in salt water every day when I get through. (Baker 1999, 97)

On 8 March 1918, Helen D. Boylston wrote that her hospital was so close to empty that one would not even know that there was a war on. However, sixteen days later after a major battle, she wrote:

> They've come! I've been working all night. . . . The field dressing-stations and casualty clearing-stations have all been destroyed, and we are getting the boys direct from the line. It's hideous! . . . As far as the eye could see they [ambulances] were coming. They came much too fast for us, and within fifteen minutes were standing twenty deep around the dressing table. As the hours went by we ceased to think. (Boylston 1927, 38, 60–61, 64–65)

On 27 March she wrote that the British hospital at which she served had admitted 4,853 wounded and done 935 surgeries, with only twelve deaths; and on 15 April she wrote that they admitted 1,100 in twenty-four hours, with ninety surgeries a night by three operating room teams (Boylston 1927, 67, 68).

> We rushed all our nurses to a certain point when one attack was on; they did magnificent, heroic work for two weeks in a hospital that was being shelled, and now for three weeks have had nothing to do as that sector has been very quiet. If they are withdrawn, tomorrow the sector may become the center of the conflict, and we would again be unprepared. (Ashe 1918, 102–103)

In July 1918, Elizabeth Ashe, a nurse with the ARC Children's Bureau in France, was spending her days off nursing at the American Military Hospital in Neuilly:

> The wounded continue to pour in night and day, it is impossible to handle them properly. I am on duty in the receiving ward (a big garage which holds about 100 stretchers, packed so closely together you can't step between). (Ashe 1918, 112)

Nurses from Base Hospital No. 21 were sent to a casualty clearing station in October 1917, one nurse and one doctor to each operating table.

> You can imagine what surgical work the nurse has to do, no mere handling of instruments and sponges, but sewing and tying up and putting in drains while the doctor takes the next piece of shell out of another place. Then

after fourteen hours of this, with freezing feet, to a meal of tea and bread and jam, and off to rest if you can in a wet bell tent in a damp bed without sheets, after a wash with a cupful of water. (Stimson 1918, 142)

The weather in France and Belgium can be cold and damp in the fall and winter, and the weather in 1917–1918 was especially miserable. "At times the medicines and the dressing solutions on the ward would freeze solid; night after night it was difficult to keep the dressings from freezing on the patients themselves" (*The History of Base Hospital No. 18* 1919, 18).

Besides the cold, it rained almost every day from September to January. Universally, the medical staff recorded the dismal weather in their letters home and in their diary entries. Anne Hardon commented that she could always see her own breath and that the warmest spot was near the stove, where it was 51 degrees Fahrenheit. It was still so cold in June that one needed to wear long underwear. Medical personnel—particularly the nurses—often complained of chilblains.

This form of frostbite resulted in inflammation and swelling of feet, toes, and fingers, followed by reddish patches on the hands and feet, and sometimes on the ears, with burning and itching. Severe chilblains correspond to second-degree burns. There were medical units in Siberia where temperatures averaged –25 degrees to –30 degrees and sometimes it got as low as –65 degrees. The ground there was snow-covered from September to June. There were also medical units in Turkey and Persia where the temperatures averaged well over 100 degrees. Dreary weather, long hours, and miserable conditions affected morale (Black 1922, 86, 165; *Taber's Cyclopedic Medical Dictionary* 1965, C-41; Hardon 1927, 20–21; Stimson 1918, 46–49, 92, 132–134).

Quarters for the staff were less than luxurious. Doctors and nurses were allowed better living quarters than enlisted men, but these could range anywhere from palaces to hotels to barracks to huts. Even those who were indoors did not always have centralized heat or running water. They slept often on cots with no mattresses (Stimson 1918, 28–29, 86, 182). Nurse Elizabeth Black developed the habit of putting her clothes in the bed each night so they would be warm enough to wear in the morning. Sometimes snow drifted into her quarters. Food was often less than palatable: "Tinned food, horse-meat, red wine that tastes like vinegar, mouse-trap cheese—we are so hungry we eat it all" (Black 1922, 90, 97).

To protect from nightly bombing raids, all interior lights had to be extinguished or all windows completely covered. Outside there could be no lights of any kind, not even matches or cigarettes, making the trip from quarters to the hospital and back again rather difficult. When aircraft or bombs approached, nurses who were off duty were rousted from their beds and sent to trenches or dugouts, sometimes several times a night. Those on duty remained in the wards caring for their patients.

Stretcher-bearers and ambulance drivers commonly worked under fire, and doctors, nurses, and orderlies worked right through barrages. One of the first Americans killed after the country's entry in the war was a doctor, Lieutenant W. T. Fitzsimmons, killed along with three privates at Base Hospital No. 5 in northern France in September 1917. In early November 1918 the personnel of Evacuation Hospital No. 4 were forced to completely evacuate the hospital under fire, with shells falling every three minutes. Another bombardment in July 1918 caused an evacuation just as an influx of patients arrived. Amidst dropping bombs, the medical staff worked to get the patients out. At 6 A.M., a shell hit the post-operative ward, killing two patients and wounding many others. In Belgrade in the early months of the war, there were few twenty-four–hour periods without firing of some kind (Allison 1919c, 514–515; "Personal Experiences of World War I Nurses" 1957b, 9; Hatch et al. 1920, 23; "Care of the Wounded under Fire" 1918, 121–122; Krueger 1916, 904–905). Designer Elsie de Wolfe was at Chemin-des-Dames, helping to care for the wounded during one offensive:

> We often administered the ambrine cure in tents while the shells shrieked over our heads. I wonder sometimes, when I think of those days, at my own courage, for I never felt fear of any kind, and I have come to the conclusion that in such moments the human ego loses all consciousness of itself as an entity and is concerned only with the need of relieving the pain of those around it. (De Wolfe 1974, 194)

Although there seemed to be a great need for doctors, female physicians were not allowed to serve in the U.S. Army, though their services had been accepted in the past during wartime as contract surgeons. Because of this, female doctors took things into their own hands. A group in New York state organized the Woman's Army General Hospital Unit in July 1916. Then, in 1917, the Medical Women's National Association organized the American Women's Hospital (AWH), and within one year over 1,000 female physicians had registered to serve. In July 1918, the AWH No. 1 opened in Neufmoutiers, Seine et Marne, France, for military and civilian patients, caring for residents from over one hundred villages. Some other American medical women went independently, like Alice Gregory, M.D., who had her service accepted by the French army. Gregory was stationed within a few miles of the front, where she and the few nurses were the only women for miles (Lovejoy 1918, 6; Gregory 1920, 1–2).

American women physicians were following the example of their counterparts in Great Britain who had organized the Women's Hospital Corps (WHC) and established a hospital in Paris in 1914. After turning down the women who volunteered to serve, the Royal Army Military Corps invited the WHC to establish a hospital at Wimereux, near Boulogne. This group later took over a large hospital in London.

The largest group of female physicians organized during the war, though, was the Scottish Women's Hospital (SWH), established by the Scottish Federation of the National Union of Woman's Suffrage Societies. When the British War Office turned down their offer of assistance, Dr. Elsie Ingils of the SWH went to the French government, who accepted her offer of a hospital. The group established a hospital at Abbaye de Royaumont in December 1914. The SWH sent units to Serbia, Salonika, and Corsica in 1915; to Russia in 1916; and to Villers Cotterets, France, in 1917. During the great German advance on the Aisne in mid-1918, the unit at Villers Cotterets was ordered to evacuate but stayed long enough to care for a large influx of wounded, later evacuating and reestablishing the hospital at Royaumont. Being the only hospital in the area, the unit there ran three operating rooms during the day and two at night. The excellence of the medical care is shown by the fact that the unit had lower amputation and mortality rates than most other hospitals. By 1916 the British had such a shortage of physicians that the War Office finally agreed to accept women doctors as contract surgeons, but with no rank, and sent them to hospitals in Egypt, India, Malta, and Salonika as well as in England (Whitehead 1999, 107–112).

Other American women, some with no medical experience, volunteered and ended up working with whatever group would accept their service. Elizabeth Black volunteered as an aid with an American medical unit but arrived in Paris in June 1917 to find the ARC had taken over all of the units. She then worked at a canteen serving meals to traveling soldiers. She soon managed to get assigned to a small hospital with the French army only seven miles from the front lines, where half of the nurses and aids were American women and the rest English army nurses and Voluntary Aid Detachments

(VADs). Black started her duties with taking temperatures and pulses, but she was soon assisting with dressing wounds.

Dorothy Cheney sailed to France in October 1917 to do relief work for children. When that did not work out, she did canteen work and then began assisting in a hospital. More than once, though she protested that she was neither a nurse nor up to such responsibility, Cheney was asked to take solo night duty in a ward. She was told that she was better than no one at all (Black 1922, 6–52, 78; Cheney 1930, 8, 49–50, 67–68).

Dr. James Robb Church served as a military observer in France from January 1916 to April 1917. He acknowledged that the medical personnel who served in the war zone were in a unique position.

> I think it cannot be difficult to understand that this front line work is hard work for the Medical personnel which carries it out. The Doctors who do it are really entitled to a different classification than that of "non-combatant." If "non-combatant" means just a man who does not fight, they fall within that category. But when you come to consider that they bear in common with their brothers of the line all the danger of these advanced positions; that they are subject to the same intense bombardment, the same shock of assault, of gas and all the nerve wracking terrors of life in the trenches, it seems as thought there ought to be at least a brevet title which would differentiate between the accepted meaning of the term and the actuality in these circumstances. (Church 1918, 245)

With the Armistice at the eleventh hour on the eleventh day of November 1918 came a cessation of fighting, but not an end to the duties of the medical personnel. In fact, although no troops were shipped overseas after that date, medical units that were waiting in port proceeded to Europe. They were needed to care for the large number of sick and wounded. There was an epidemic of influenza sweeping across the entire world, and there was a massive ill and undernourished civilian population in need of medical care. Medical units went into Germany, providing much-needed care for prisoners of war, German soldiers, and the German civilian population (U.S. Surgeon General vol. 1, 346; Turitz 1985, 291–292). A letter from a nurse at Base Hospital No. 102 in Italy told of the need that still existed. "Here as everywhere, the hardest work of the Red Cross will come with peace. If we are allowed to help, the work along public health lines will be tremendous, as the need here is appalling" (Noyes 1919, 371).

The work done by the countless doctors, nurses, ambulance drivers, and other medical personnel both during and after the war was crucial to the war effort, and to the development of modern medicine. Despite inadequate training, shortages of personnel and supplies, and the advent of new diseases and conditions, medical personnel forged ahead. Looking back at surgery in World War I from the perspective of over eighty years, Ira M. Rutkow, an esteemed surgeon, stated in November 2001,

> The greatest surgical achievements of World War I would be a better understanding of the pathophysiology of traumatic injuries and refinements in the treatment of wounds and their infectious sequelae. . . . From a technical standpoint, there were other far-reaching innovations, including unimaginable ingenuity in reconstructive maxillofacial surgery (this led to the beginnings of plastic surgery as a bona fide surgical specialty), and remarkable developments in the orthopedic treatment of gunshot wounds. (Rutkow 2001, 1328)

It would be difficult indeed to overstate the importance of the work of the medical personnel who served during World War I and the medical innovations that resulted from research at the front. The concept of triage, the use of X-rays, the importance of laboratories, the strides made in neurology and anesthesiology, speedy transportation of sick and wounded, modern wound treatment, the value of sanitation for health, rehabilitation methods, and maxillofacial surgery are just a few examples of the advances made in medical science as a direct result of military medicine during the years 1914 to 1918. As the Johns Hopkins Unit, otherwise known as Base Hospital No. 18, commented in its official history,

> The nursing staff was at many times entirely inadequate in numbers to cope with the volume of work in the hospital, and in consequence was at times reduced to a dangerous condition of exhaustion. Their devotion and untiring industry never slackened, and they earned the well-merited appreciation of all those who were thrown in contact with them. (*The History of Base Hospital No. 18* 1919, 20)

—*Katherine Burger Johnson*

References and Further Reading

Allison, Grace E. 1919a. "Some Experiences in Active Service–France." *American Journal of Nursing* 19 (February): 356.

———. 1919b. "Some Experiences in Active Service–France." *American Journal of Nursing* 19 (March): 430–432.

———.1919c. "Some Experiences in Active Service–France." *American Journal of Nursing* 19 (April): 514–515.

"American Girl in the French Army." *Literary Digest,* 12 August 1916, 366–367.

"American Hospital Work in France." *Literary Digest,* 18 November 1914, 615–616.

American Journal of Nursing. 1914–1919.

"The American National Red Cross." *Ladies Home Journal,* October 1917, 33.

"American Nurse and Her Blesses." *Literary Digest,* 15 February 1919, 56–68.

American Red Cross. *The First Year of the American Red Cross in France—Activities for the Year Ended July 1, 1918.* Washington, DC: American Red Cross, n.d.

———. 1918. *Trench Fever: Report of Commission, Medical Research Committee, American Red Cross.* New York: Oxford University Press.

———. *The War-Time Manual Describing the Organization, History, Works and Reliefs of the American Red Cross Society.* Chicago: The Service Publishers, n.d.

"America's Red Cross in Europe." *Literary Digest,* 9 October 1915, 778–779.

Ashburn, P. M. 1929. *A History of the Medical Department of the United States Army.* Boston: Houghton Mifflin Co.

Ashe, Elizabeth. 1918. *Intimate Letters from France during America's First Year of War.* San Francisco: Philopolis.

Baker, George R. 1999. *Heroes and Angels: A Medic Remembers World War I, France and Belgium, 1917–1919.* Baltimore: Gateway.

Barclay, Grace D. "Experiences with the Red Cross." *Johns Hopkins Nurses Alumnae Magazine* 14 (November 1915): 277–284.

Barclay, Harold. 1923. *A Doctor in France, 1917–1919: The Diary of Harold Barclay, Lieutenant-Colonel, American Expeditionary Forces.* New York: Privately printed.

Barkley, A. H. 1918. *Surgical and War Nursing.* St. Louis: C. V. Mosby.

"Base Hospital No. 1, Neuilly, France." 1919. *Modern Hospital* 12 (February): 134–135.

Base Hospital No. 4, USA, and Mobile Hospital No. 5, USA. 1919. *Album de la Guerre.* Cleveland: Scientific Illustrating Studios.

Beardsley, Edward H. "Allied Against Sin: American and British Responses to Venereal Disease in World War I." *Medical History* 20 (April 1976): 189–202.

Bigelow, Glenna Lindsley. 1918. *Liege, on the Line of March.* New York: John Lane.

———. 1919. "Before and After the Armistice." *American Journal of Nursing* 19 (May): 753.

Black, Elizabeth Walker. 1922. *Hospital Heroes.* New York: Scribner's.

Blech, Gustavus M. *Personal Memoirs of the World War.* Chicago: Reprinted from and by *The American Journal of Clinical Medicine,* 1924.

Boller, Francois, and Charles Duyckaerts. 1999. "1914 to 1917: The Great War Years." *Archives of Neurology* 56 (July): 882–885.

Bowerman, Guy Emerson, Jr. 1983. *The Compensations of War: The Diary of an Ambulance Driver during the Great War.* Mark C. Carnes, ed. Austin: University of Texas Press.

Boylston, Helen Dore. 1927. *"Sister": The War Diary of a Nurse.* New York: I. Washburn.

Brown, Raymond Shiland. 1920. *Base Hospital No. 9 AEF: A History of the Work of the New York Hospital Unit during Two Years of Active Service.* New York: n.p.

Burgar, Donna G. 1915. "In Gleiwitz." *American Journal of Nursing* 15 (September): 1095–1096.

Burr, Elsie Parkinson. 1915a. "My War Patients." Parts 1–2. *Nurse* 3 (November): 364–365.

———. 1915b. "My War Patients." Part 3. *Nurse* 3 (December): 459–461.

———. 1915c. "My War Patients." Part 4. *Nurse* 3 (January): 35–36.

Buswell, Leslie. 1916. *Ambulance No. 10: Personal Letters from the Front.* Boston: Houghton Mifflin.

Cabell, Julian M. *A Brief Sketch of Base Hospital No. 41 by the Commanding Officer.* Washington, DC: np, 1925.

"A Call for Women to Volunteer." 1918. *Literary Digest* (22 June): 30.

"Care of the Wounded under Fire." 1918. *American Journal of Nursing* 19 (November): 121–122.

Carter, Merle Wright, and Dean Gabbart. "Hospital Unit R in World War I: Fairfield to France." *The Palimpsest* 65 (1986): 142–161.

Cheney, Dorothy. 1930. *Memories, November 1917–March 1919.* Privately printed.

Church, James Robb. 1918. *The Doctor's Part.* New York: D. Appleton.

"The Civilian Doctor in Military Service." 1917. *Journal of the American Medical Association* 68 (14 April): 1123–1124.

Cooper, Alice, et al., eds. 1923. *A History of U.S. Army Base Hospital No. 36 (Detroit College of Medicine and Surgery Unit).* Philadelphia: n.p.

Coplin, William M. L. 1923. *American Red Cross Base Hospital No. 38 in the World War,* Philadelphia: E. A. Wright Co.

Courington, Frederick W., and Roderick K. Calverley. 1986. "Anesthesia on the Western Front: The Anglo-American Experience of World War I." *Anesthesiology* 65 (December): 644–649.

"The Current Need of Young Men for the Regular Medical Corps." 1917. *Journal of the American Medical Association* 68 (28 April): 1265.

Cushing, Harvey. 1941. *From a Surgeon's Journal, 1915–1918.* Boston: Little, Brown.

Davis, George G. 1917. "Wounds of the Buttocks in War." *Journal of the American Medical Association* 68 (9 June): 1689.

Davison, Henry P. 1920. *The American Red Cross in the Great War.* New York: Macmillan.

De Wolfe, Elsie. 1974. *After All.* New York: Arno.

Dearborn, Frederick M. *American Homeopathy in the World War.* http:// homeoint .org/books2/ww1/activities.htm (cited 27 June 2002).

Deland, Margaret. "The American Girl Over There." *Ladies Home Journal,* October 1918, 20f.

Dexter, Mary. 1918. *In the Soldier's Service: War Experiences of Mary Dexter; England, Belgium, France, 1914–1918.* Edited by her mother. Boston: Houghton Mifflin Company, 1918.

Dymond, Steve. "A Hell Call the Somme." *Nursing Times* 92 (3 July 1996): 48–49.

Foote, Katharine. 1919. *An American V.A.D. 88 Bis and V.I.H.: Letters from Two Hospitals.* Boston: Atlantic Monthly Press.

Ford, Joseph H. 1918. *The Details of Military Medical Administration.* Philadelphia: P. Blakiston's Sons.

Fowler, Maj. Royale H. M. C., ed. 1920. *The War History of United States Army Base Hospital No. 61 A.E.F.,* n.l., n.p.

"The French Military Hospital System." 1917. *Modern Hospital* 9 (August): 120–122.

Gabriel, Richard A., and Karen S. Metz. 1992. *A History of Military Medicine,* vol. II: *From the Renaissance through Modern Times.* New York: Greenwood.

Gaeddert, G. R. 1950. *The History of the American National Red Cross,* vol. IV, *The American National Red Cross in World War I, 1917–1918.* Washington, DC: American National Red Cross.

Geisinger, Joseph F., ed. 1924. *History of the US Army Base Hospital Unit No. 45 in the Great War (Medical College of Virginia Unit).* Richmond, VA: William Byrd Printing.

Gill, Janice. "The Origins of the Australian Army Nursing Service and Its Involvement in the First World War." *ANU Historical Journal* 15 (1981–1987): 58–70.

Ginn, Richard V. N. 1997. *The History of the U.S. Army Medical Service Corps.* Washington, DC: Office of the Surgeon General and Center of Military History, United States Army.

Gladwin, Mary E. 1916. "Experiences of a Red Cross Nurse in Serbia." *American Journal of Nursing* 16 (June): 908.

Goodnow, Minnie. 1917. *War Nursing: A Textbook for the Auxiliary Nurse.* Philadelphia: W. B. Saunders.

Gray, Andrew. 1974. "The American Field Service." *American Heritage* 26 (December).

Gregory, Alice. 1920. "Work at a French Army Dressing Station." *Medical Woman's Journal* 27 (January): 1–2.

Hall, Maurice C. 1918. "Parasites in War Time." *Scientific Monthly* 6 (February): 108–110.

Hansen, Arlen J. 1996. *Gentlemen Volunteers: The Story of the American Ambulance Drivers in the Great War, August 1914–September 1918.* New York: Arcade.

Hardon, Anne Francis. 1927. *43bis: War Letters of an American VAD.* New York: Privately printed.

Harper, George McLean. "U.S. General Hospital No. 9." *Scribners* 64 (October 1918): 410–415.

Hart, W. Lee. 1919. *History of Base Hospital Number Fifty-Three, Advance Section, Service of Supply. Langres, Haute-Marne,* France: 29th Engineers Printing Plant.

Hatch, J. Philip, et al., eds. 1920. *Concerning Base Hospital No. 5: A Book Published for the Personnel of Base Hospital No. 5.* Boston: Barta.

Hazlett, T. Lyle. 1917. "Experiences with the Russian Army of the Caucasus in Northern Persia." *Military Surgeon* 41 (October): 445–449.

Hine, Darlene Clark. "The Call that Never Came: Black Women Nurses and World War I, an Historical Note." *Indiana Military History Journal* 15 (January 1983): 23–27.

The History of Base Hospital No. 18, AEF (Johns Hopkins Unit). 1919. Baltimore: Base Hospital 18 Association.

History of the Pennsylvania Hospital Unit (Base Hospital N. 10, U.S.A.) in the Great War. 1921. New York: n.p.

A History of United States Army Base Hospital No. 36 (Detroit College of Medicine and Surgery Unit). 1922. Alice Evelyn Cooper et al. eds. Detroit: n.p.

A History of U.S.A. Base Hospital No. 115, A.P.O. 781, A.E.F. Vichy, Alliers, France: n.p., n.d.

Hitz, Benjamin. 1922. *A History of Base Hospital No. 32 (including Unit R).* Indianapolis: Edward Kahle Post No. 42, American Legion.

"Hospital Organization Under the War Department." *The Modern Hospital* 9 (August 1917): 88–89.

"How American Nurses Helped Win the War." *The Modern Hospital* 12 (January 1919): 7–9.

Howe, M. A. DeWolfe, ed. 1916. *The Harvard Volunteers in Europe: Personal Records of Experiences in Military, Ambulance, and Hospital Service.* Cambridge: Harvard University Press.

Huard, Frances Wilson. 1917. *My Home in the Field of Mercy.* New York: George H. Doran.

"The Immediate Emergency." 1917. *Journal of the American Medical Association* 68 (7 April): 1044.

Jaffin, Jonathan H. 1991. "Medical Support for the American Expeditionary Forces in France." Master's thesis, U.S. Army General Command and Staff College.

Johnstone, E. K. "From 'Over the Top' to the 'C.C.S.'" *Military Surgeon* 41 (December 1917): 694–702.

Journal of the American Medical Association. 1914–1919.

Kaletzki, Charles Hirsh. 1919. *Official History USA Base Hospital No. 31 of Youngstown, Ohio, and Hospital Unit "G" of Syracuse University.* n.l., n.p.

Kalisch, Philip A., and Margaret Scobey. "Female Nurses in American Wars: Helplessness Suspended for the Duration." *Armed Forces and Society* 9 (Winter 1983): 215–244.

Kauffman, Ruth Wright. "The Woman Ambulance–Driver in France." *Outlook* 3, October 1917, 170–172.

Keefer, Frank R. 1917. *A Text-Book of Military Hygiene and Sanitation*. Philadelphia: W. B. Saunders.

Keen, W. W. 1917. *The Treatment of War Wounds*. Philadelphia: W. B. Saunders.

Kerr, Katherine. 1915. "War Treatment of Wounds and Illnesses." *American Journal of Nursing* 15 (June): 712–717.

Krueger, Mathild. 1915. "Personal Experiences in Servia." *American Journal of Nursing* 15 (August): 1015.

———. 1916. "Personal Experiences in Servia." *American Journal of Nursing* 16 (June): 904–905.

LaMotte, Ellen N. "An American Nurse in Paris." *Survey,* 10 July 1915, 333–336.

Laskin, Lisa Lauterbach. 1996. "Here's to the Nurse: A Story of American Nurses in France with the Harvard Surgical Unit during World War I." Paper for History 2671, Harvard University, May; photocopy.

Lovejoy, Esther Pohl. 1918. *Certain Samaritans*. New York: Macmillan.

MacDonald, Lyn. 1980. *The Roses of No-Man's-Land*. New York: Athenaeum.

Mademoiselle Miss: Letters from an American Girl Serving with the Rank of Lieutenant in a French Army Hospital at the Front. 1916. Boston: W. A. Butterfield.

Mason, Charles Field. 1917. *A Complete Handbook for the Sanitary Troops of the U.S. Army and Navy and National Guard and Naval Militia*. 4th ed., revised. New York: William Wood and Company.

McCallum, Jack Edward. 2001. "*Les Sections Sanitaires:* American Volunteers in the Great War." Ph.D diss., Texas Christian University.

McCulloch, Champe C. "The Scientific and Administrative Achievement of the Medical Corps of the United States Army." *Scientific Monthly* 4 (May 1917): 410–427.

Millard, Shirley. 1936. Adele Comandini, ed. *I Saw Them Die: Diary and Recollections of Shirley Millard*. New York: Harcourt, Brace and Co.

Miller, M. G. 2003. "Of Lice and Men: Trench Fever and Trench Life in the AEF." http://raven.cc.ukans.edu/~kansite/ww_one/medical/liceand.htm (cited 25 January 2003).

Miller, Vern V. 1938. *The History of United States Army Base Hospital No. 22*. Milwaukee: Direct Press.

"Mobilizing an Army of Mercy." *Literary Digest,* 3 August 1918, 38.

"Mobilizing Women as Nurses." *Literary Digest,* 27 April 1918, 33.

Mortimer, Maud. 1917a. *Green Tent in Flanders*. New York: Doubleday.

———. 1917b. "What a Nurse Will Find at the Front: The Experiences of an American Woman in a Field Hospital in Belgium." *Ladies Home Journal,* 18 October .

Munger, Donna Bingham. "Base Hospital 21 and the Great War." *Missouri Historical Review* 70 (April 1976): 272–290.

Needham, Mary Master. 1915. "What a War Nurse Saw." *Independent* (23 August): 258.

Noyes, Clara D. 1919. "The Red Cross." *American Journal of Nursing* 19 (February): 371.

"A Nurse's Experiences—Incidents of a Life in a French Hospital." *Current Opinion,* February 1918, 64.

"Nurses of America, Your Country Needs You." 1918. *Touchstone* (June): 215–218.

"Nursing News and Announcements." 1916. *American Journal of Nursing* 16 (August): 1137.

On Active Service with Base Hospital No. 46, USA, March 20, 1918 to May 25, 1919. n.p., n.d.

Orcutt, Philip Dana. 1918. *The White Road of Mystery: The Note-book of an American Ambulancier.* New York: John Lane Co.

Parsons, W. David. 2002. "The Spanish Lady and the Newfoundland Regiment." http://raven.cc.ukans.edu/~kansite/ww_one/medical/parsons.htm (cited 10 October 2002).

Patterson, S. W. 1920. "The Pathology of Influenza in France." *Medical Journal of Australia* 1 (March 6). Available online at http://raven.cc.ukans.edu/~kansite/ww_one/medical/mja.htm.

Pershing, John J. 1919. *Report of General John J. Pershing, U.S.A., Commander-in-Chief, American Expeditionary Forces.* Cabled to the Secretary of War, 20 November 1918; corrected 16 January 1919. n.p.: A. G. Printing Dept., General Headquarters, AEF.

"Personal Experiences of World War I Nurses." 1957a. Part 1. *Carry On* 36 (May): 7–8.

———. 1957b. Part 2. *Carry On* 36 (November): 9.

Pottle, Frederick A. 1929. *Stretchers: Hospital Unit on the Front.* New Haven: Yale University Press.

Power, D'Arcy, Lieut. Colonel R.A.M.C. 1915. *Wounds in War: Their Treatment and Results.* London: Henry Frowde, Oxford University Press.

Quandt, Emma. 1918a. "Active Service on the Western Front." Part 1. *American Journal of Nursing* 18 (February): 388–390.

———. 1918b. "Active Service on the Western Front." Part 2. *American Journal of Nursing* 18 (March): 454–458.

"The Red Cross." 1915. *American Journal of Nursing* 15 (September): 1112–1115.

Ring, Malvin E. 1999. "The Life and Work of Dr. George Byron Hayes, Pioneer Maxillofacial Surgeon." *Journal of the History of Dentistry* 47 (November): 105–106.

Robinson, Caroline E. 1918. "Work Done by the American Nurses in Paris in 1914." *American Journal of Nursing* 18 (January): 298–302.

Roudebush, Marc Oliver. 1995. "A Battle of Nerves: Hysteria and Its Treatment in France during World War I." Ph.D. diss., University of California at Berkeley.

Rutkow, Ira M. 2001. "World War I Surgery." *Archives of Surgery* 136 (November): 1328.

Salmon, Thomas W. 1917. "War Neuroses ('Shell Shock')." *Military Surgeon* 41 (December), 683–686.

Savage, Clara. "Helping Out in France." *Good Housekeeping,* November 1918, 22.

Schwartz, Eric David. 1995. "Coming Together during World War I: Medicine's Response to the Challenge of Trench Warfare." *The Pharos* 58 (Fall): 5, 6, 7, 9.

Sergeant, Elizabeth Shepley. "American Women in France." *New Republic,* 19 October 1918, 333–336.

Shay, Michael E. 2002. *A Grateful Heart: The History of a World War I Field Hospital.* Westport, CT: Greenwood.

Shipley, Arthur M., and Agnes T. Considine. 1929. *The Officers and Nurses of Evacuation Eight,* New Haven: Yale University.

"Some War Impressions of an American Woman." *Outlook,* 15 March 1916, 632–637.

Speer, Robert E. 2002. "Charles E. Lewis: A Pioneer Surgeon in China." http://raven.cc.ukans.edu/~kansite/ww_one/medical/Siberia/SibDoc.htm (cited 27 June 2002).

Starr, M. Allen. 1918. "Shell Shock." *Scribner's* 64 (August): 183.

Stevenson, Sarah Sand. 1976. *Lamp for a Soldier: The Caring Story of a Nurse in World War I.* ND: North Dakota State Nurses' Assoc.

Stimson, Julia C. 1918. *Finding Themselves: The Letters of an American Army Nurse in a British Hospital in France.* New York: Macmillan.

Sumner, Irene K. 1915. "How Dressings Are Done at the Front." *American Journal of Nursing* 15 (July): 825.

Swan, John M., and Mark Heath. 1922. *A History of United States Army Base Hospital No. 19.* Rochester, NY: Wegman-Walsh Press.

Taber's Cyclopedic Medical Dictionary. 1965. Philadelphia: F. A. Davis.

Terriberry, Gladys. 1998. *Diary of Gladys Terriberry: American Army Nurse, 1918.* New Brunswick, NJ: David Joseph Riley.

Tjomsland, Anne, M.D. 1941. *Bellevue in France: Anecdotal History of Base Hospital No. 1.* New York: Froben Press.

Tobey, James A. 1927. *The Medical Department of the Army: Its History, Activities and Organization.* Baltimore: Johns Hopkins University Press.

"Transportation and Care of the Wounded at the Front." *Modern Hospital* 9 (December 1917): 442–444.

"Trench Foot." 1917. *Military Surgeon* 41 (November): 598–607.

Trumpener, Ulrich. "The Road to Ypres: The Beginnings of Gas Warfare in World War I." *The Journal of Modern History* 47 (September 1975): 460–480.

Turitz, Leo E. 1985. "Amelia Greenwald: The Jewish Florence Nightingale." *American Jewish Archives* 37 (November): 291–292.

Tyler, Elizabeth Stears. 1920. *Letters of Elizabeth Stearns Tyler.* Norwood, MA: Plimpton Press.

"A Unique American Hospital." *Literary Digest,* 4 November 1914, 516.

United States Army, AEF, 1917–1920, Base Hospital No. 10, Le Treport, France. 1921. *History of the Pennsylvania Hospital Unit (Base Hospital No. 10, USA) in the Great War.* New York: P. B. Hoeber.

United States Army, Base Hospital No. 26. 1920. *History of Base Hospital 26.* Minneapolis: D. D. Getchell.

United States Army, Base Hospital No. 50. 1922. *The History of Base Hospital Fifty: A Portrayal of the Work Done by this Unit while Serving in the United States and with the American Expeditionary Forces in France.* Seattle: Official Committee of Base Hospital Fifty.

U.S. Surgeon General's Office. 1921–1929. *The Medical Department of the United States Army in the World War.* vols. i–xv, Washington, DC: Government Printing Office.

U.S. Surgeon General's Office. 1921–1929. *The Medical Department of the United States Army in the World War.* vols. 1–13. Washington, DC: Government Printing Office.

Vedder. Edward B. 1925. *The Medical Aspects of Chemical Warfare.* Baltimore: Williams and Wilkins Co.

Villard, Henry S. "In a World War I Hospital with Hemingway." *Horizon* 21 (August 1978): 85–95.

Villard, Henry Serrano, and James Nagel. 1989. *Hemingway in Love and War: The Lost Diary of Agnes von Kurowsky, Her Letters, and Correspondence of Ernest Hemingway.* Boston: Northeastern University Press.

Volk, Katherine. 1936. *Buddies in Budapest.* Los Angeles: Kellaway-Ide Co.

"Volunteer Nurses One: VADs at War." *Nursing Times* 80 (August 1984):36–38.

Wagner, Agnes. 1917. *My Beloved Poilus.* St. John, NB: Barnes.

"War Letters of an American Woman." *Outlook,* 2 August 1916, 794–799; 9 August 1916, 863–868.

Whitehead, Ian R. 1999. *Doctors in the Great War.* Barnsley, South Yorkshire: Leo Cooper.

Wight, Otis B., Donald Macomber, and Arthur S. Rosenfeld. *On Active Service with Base Hospital 46, USA, March 20, 1918 to May 25, 1919.* n.l.:n.p., n.d.

"With the Suffrage Hospitals in the French War Zone." *Woman Citizen,* 13 July 1918, 128.

Yealland, Lewis R. 1918. *Hysterical Disorders of Warfare.* London: Macmillan and Co.

"SERVICE FOR SOLDIERS"

The Experience of American Social Welfare Agencies in World War I

———————◈———————

"I cannot define for you exactly what 'morale' is, but I can tell you it comes in many different ways," [said the staff officer]. "I have known 'morale' to be found in a cup of hot coffee. That sounds unromantic, but think what it means to a man who has had ten hours of consecutive shelling. I have seen 'morale' created by a man taking a big risk. I have seen it sustained by a man merely writing a letter home, just before he went into action.

"You can describe 'morale' in a score of ways, little and big. It may come from the faith in a future life or from the thought that one is protecting the loved ones at home. But if you want a short and easy definition of 'morale' you will find a good one in the four letters YMCA."

He took me to a window and showed me men trooping into a YMCA hut. "Those are men," he said, "who will be going up to the front line tomorrow. Some of them will be playing games, and let no man laugh at a game as a preparation for battle. Others will be writing home, others will be attending divine service, but each in his own way will be finding and strengthening his 'morale' in the comradeship of his fellows beneath the symbol of the Red Triangle and the inspiration for which it stands.

"All this is a thing which cannot show on my charts. But it is also a thing which is going to turn the balance in our favor. Go back and tell people at home that a dry soldier, concerned alone with military calculations, believes that the Young Men's Christian Association is playing a far bigger part in winning the war than any mere civilian can recognize. I do not speak to you as a philanthropist. That is not my job. But I want to see an end to this horrible business, and if a soldier's words have any weight, tell them to help the Association to carry on." ("The Secret Chart, by Junius" 1918, 3–4)

Durwng World War I, American social welfare organizations provided social, spiritual, and physical comfort to U.S. and Allied soldiers to maintain morale and keep them combat ready. The war sent millions of young men far from home to training camps and the front lines, where, no longer subject to traditional mores, they might succumb to social vices (drinking, gambling, and prostitution) that could undermine their military effectiveness. The fight against homesickness was critical in bolstering military morale in basic training camps and overseas. A wide range of social services in canteens and huts provided a little bit of "America" and reminded doughboys of the support of their friends and families back home. American social welfare organizations mobilized their resources to provide relief for soldiers that the U.S. government lacked the experience and resources to provide. This work was the precursor for the establishment of the United Services Organization (USO) for American troops in World War II.

When the war began in Europe in August 1914, private American charities rushed to aid victims of war. Welfare agencies such as the American Fund for French Wounded, the American Committee for Training in Suitable Trades the Maimed Soldiers of France, the Serbian Relief Committee of America, and the War Children's Christmas Funds emerged early in the war. For the most part, these organizations focused on particular groups or regions and relied heavily on wealthy benefactors for support. As the war spread across Europe, their ability to provide aid remained limited.

Some, however, grew from private philanthropic charities into government-sponsored relief organizations. In October 1914, Herbert Hoover became the director of the Commission for the Relief of Belgium, which provided food relief behind German lines. The commission received extensive funding from the U.S. and Allied governments. When the United

"Save Serbia our ally. Send contributions to Serbian Relief Committee of America." View of Serbian soldiers and civilians as they migrate into the mountains. The remains of the Serbian nation, approximately 700,000 people, who after a severe defeat by the Austro-German army, fled to the mountains of Albania in the winter of 1915 with many thousands perishing along the way. (Library of Congress)

States entered the war in April 1917, President Woodrow Wilson recruited Hoover to supervise American food relief programs as the United States food administrator. Hoover took charge of the American Relief Administration (ARA), which supervised American food relief operations overseas during the war to Belgium, Britain, France, and Italy. After the Armistice, the ARA extended food relief operations to Germany, Austria, Poland, Czechoslovakia, Romania, Finland, and the Soviet Union. By the end of 1923, the ARA had distributed over $5.2 billion in American food relief to European nations (for a general chronology of the efforts of American charities during the early days of the war, see the *New York Times Current History of the European War* vols. 1–3; see also Von Schrader and Jones 1920, 85–116; Surface and Bland 1931, 3–14).

Central to the relief services provided to American and Allied soldiers during World War I were the "Seven Sisters": the Young Men's Christian Association (YMCA), the Knights of Columbus, the Young Men's Hebrew Association (YMHA), the Salvation Army, the Young Women's Christian Association (YWCA), the American Library Association (ALA), and the War Camp Community Service. When the United States entered the war, these organizations offered their services for American troops to the government.

With the exception of the War Camp Community Service, a group of local organizations that united to serve recruits in basic training camps across the United States, all had emerged as a response to the Industrial Revolution. These agencies began to provide safe havens for rural young men and women driven to urban areas in search of employment in the nineteenth century. Their services included education, social functions, entertainment, athletic competition, and spiritual comfort. As these organizations grew in membership and financial support, they expanded their efforts to youngsters, railroad workers, soldiers and sailors, immigrants, minorities, and other groups deemed susceptible to "moral challenges."

Most of the organizations had religious roots; for example, the YMCA, YWCA, and Salvation Army were Protestant, the Knights of Columbus was Roman Catholic, and the Young Men's Hebrew Association was Jewish. Several were imported into the United States, and their international headquarters abroad were composed of national organizations in many countries. The YMCA, for example, was originally founded in London in 1844 and worked with the World's Alliance of YMCAs in Geneva. The YWCA was also established in London, in 1855, which remained the international headquarters until after World War I. The Salvation Army emerged in London in 1865 and spread around the world during the nineteenth century. The Knights of Columbus was organized in Connecticut in 1882 but had expanded into Canada, Cuba, Mexico, and the Philippines before the Great War began.

When the war broke out in Europe, the World's Alliance of YMCAs in Geneva found itself in a difficult situation. As a Protestant organization, the YMCA had strong national organizations in Britain, Germany, and the United States. The war in Europe was a catastrophe, and the World's Alliance had to evaluate the situation. By the end of August 1914, the World's Alliance had developed a relief plan whereby national associations served their soldiers at the front, and served wounded troops and prisoners of war of all nations behind it. The organization also sent a telegram to the American YMCA, the only large neutral association, requesting financial support and qualified secretaries. The American YMCA sent John R. Mott, its general secretary, to Europe that September to investigate the situation.

Mott had to develop a relief program that would not violate U.S. neutrality. After touring a number of belligerent nations, Mott met with the members of the World's Alliance in Geneva. The World's Alliance, with the support of the English and German YMCAs, recommended that the American Red Triangle provide relief services to prisoners of war (POWs). These men suffered in captivity beyond the assistance of their homelands and were a burden to their captors. Providing assistance to prisoners of war in both Allied and Central Power prison camps maintained U.S. neutrality policy.

In January 1915, Mott met with President Wilson, and the president approved the proposal (Latourette 1957, 76–77; "World's Committee of Young Men's Christian Associations Plenary Meeting of 1920 at Geneva" 1921, 193–195; Hopkins 1979, 439–440; International Committee, *International Committee Monthly Meeting Minutes* 1916; Taft, Harris, Kent, and Newlin 1922a, 56–57; 1922b, 217–230). The American YMCA dispatched Archibald C. Harte and Carlisle V. Hibbard to Europe in February 1915 to negotiate access to prisoners of war with the belligerent governments. The initial battles on both the western front and East Prussia resulted in hundreds of thousands of prisoners. Yet, expecting a short war, none of the belligerents had prepared for the massive infusion of dependents. Most governments concentrated large numbers of prisoners in camps, but the inmates had a great deal of time on their hands and little to do. "Barbed-wire disease" led to depression. The Allied blockade reduced rations to Entènte prisoners in the Central Powers, which led to physical problems as well. To compound the situation, people assumed that their troops held as prisoners received poor treatment and often demanded retribution against POWs held by their nations.

Harte and Hibbard met with the British government, which was reluctant to open its prison camps to a neutral organization. The two secretaries decided to split up; Harte traveled to Germany, and Hibbard went to France. Harte received support for the proposed operation from the German YMCA and the U.S. ambassador to Berlin, James W. Gerard. In March 1915, the German government agreed to allow the American YMCA to undertake welfare operations, if similar arrangements were made for German prisoners in Allied countries. In response to the German proposal, the French and British governments opened their facilities. Thus began the "Principle of Reciprocity," under which belligerent governments agreed to allow American Red Triangle secretaries to work in their prison camps if the same arrangements were available for their soldiers in enemy camps.

The true test was access to Russian prison camps. Both the German and Austro-Hungarian governments insisted that the YMCA start War Prisoner Aid (WPA) operations in tsarist prisons, especially since Russian POWs would have access to relief programs in German and Dual Monarchy camps. Harte encountered an interested but reluctant tsarist regime in Russia in June 1915. The Russians were suspicious of the objectives of this foreign Protestant organization but recognized that their government lacked the resources to provide relief to POWs. Harte extensively toured prison camps in Siberia and reported favorably on conditions. These reports helped quell the fears of tsarist officials, and the imperial authorities granted access to the American YMCA. By the end of the war, using the Principle of Reciprocity, the YMCA extended WPA operations to all of the belligerent nations, with the exception of the Ottoman Empire (Young Men's Christian Association National War Work Council 1920, 100–103; Taft, Harris, Kent, and Newlin 1922b, 231–240).

The American YMCA began WPA operations by building special huts in prison camps. The first hut opened in the German prison camp at Göttingen in April 1915, and was soon followed by huts in Britain, France, Austria-Hungary, Russia, Italy, and Bulgaria. One official recalled the process:

The YMCA Secretaries have gone into the different prison camps to help the prisoners help themselves. Lumber has been taken in to build YMCA huts. The prisoners are of all kinds. All that needs to be furnished is the material and the prisoners will do the work. But, once the building is up, the work of the YMCA in the prison camp is only commenced. Athletic equipment is provided so that the men can exercise. Musical instruments have been taken in with a view of organizing orchestras and bands. Educational classes have been formed in order that the prisoners may improve their minds; and in many instances food has been given to thousands of men who could not have endured the prison diet. Thousands and tens of thousands of men have been enrolled in the educational classes. . . . In many of the prison camps a full college curriculum has been introduced, because among the prisoners are college professors who can teach the classes. (Whitehair 1918, 110–111)

The steady influx of POWs and the establishment of new prison camps made hut construction expensive and of limited impact. The WPA secretaries then adopted the strategy of establishing associations, based on the American university model, inside prison camps. Secretaries organized committees by recruiting prisoners with YMCA experience, a relatively easy task among British and German POWs. These committees then implemented the YMCA's fourfold program of spiritual, physical, social, and educational relief for the prison camp population under the general supervision of the WPA secretary. Red Triangle workers strove to provide spiritual comfort to prisoners of all faiths. They worked with prison camp authorities to recruit local ministers, priests, and rabbis to conduct services or to transfer captured chaplains to camps with large populations of their denomination; they made the YMCA hut available for devotional services; they distributed Gospels, Testaments, and a wide range of religious materials to prisoners; and they promoted special religious festivals, especially Christmas and Easter. Conrad Hoffman, the senior American WPA secretary in Germany, always worked to raise POW spirits at Christmas:

It was my rare privilege to secure permission for our four-year-old daughter to accompany me to one of the camps near Berlin [Ruhleben] during the Christmas holidays. Never have I seen anything so pathetic, and so touching as the scene that took place when the little girl, very much like a fairy dropped from heaven, appeared in the midst of the big, stalwart, unshaven men, cut off from human society and family life for a year or more. How tenderly and timidly, lest they hurt her, they fondled her hands and her cheeks.

She seemed a revelation to them. They had forgotten that there were such creatures as little children. One after another asked permission to hold her on his knee.

I recall the man who three different times entered the room where she was, bringing a bit of chocolate each time as an excuse for seeing her. Another man humbly asked if he might kiss her on the cheek, and in the eyes of most men tears had gathered as they no doubt thought of their own little ones at home.

It was a wonderful experience and brought home to all of us the magical power of childhood, even with full-grown men. As never before all of us realized the meaning of the words, "And a little child shall lead them."

They showered her with figs from their stores of supplies—plum pudding, bonbons, chocolates and the like. We then went into the YMCA hall and the patter of her feet as she ran through the hall attracted others who came from the adjoining rooms to see this marvel, a baby in their midst.

As we left the camp the little one asked me why the men had cried, and I told her that no doubt they had been thinking of their own little girls and boys at home; and then she asked, as perhaps only a child would do, whether God was sorry for these men. How glad I was able to tell her, yes, God cared for these men; that that was one of the reasons, if not the chief one, why I was there. (Hoffman 1920, 92)

Education was also a high priority for WPA secretaries. They recruited prisoners with teaching experience to lead classes from basic literacy and arithmetic classes to advanced business, foreign language, and history courses. One secretary wrote, regarding the educational work in the camps, "You cannot imagine the joy of the men who for the first time in their lives are able to write their families. It is like making the dumb to speak" (Whitehair 1918, 111–112).

WPA secretaries worked with local universities to help incarcerated college students continue their education. The YMCA stocked prison libraries with books and prewar magazines, and every hut had a reading room. The demand for books often outpaced the available supply. The association also arranged for vocational training opportunities so younger men could learn trades or wounded prisoners could train for new professions (Hoffman 1920, 1–97; Colton 1940, 22–37; "A Shining Mark" 1919, 49; Potter 1919, 478–480; Von Schrader and Jones 1920, 302–310; Young Men's Christian

Association National War Work Council 1920, 103–105; Taft, Harris, Kent, and Newlin 1922b, 230–314).

Still, as a WPA official noted, not every need could be addressed:

> To the prisoners I have sent everything from a football to a black-board—including books (both for reading and school purposes), games (such as chess, checkers, dominoes, lotto), orchestra music, mouth organs and, in one instance, anatomical charts for a class of Russians, and I have at present unfulfilled commissions for playing-cards, ladies' wigs and decorations for the interior of a Catholic chapel.
>
> The conditions as I find them in the various camps are pretty constant for the three nationalities and may be summed up as follows: French, excellent (although they have the most wants); Russians, fair to poor; Serbians, invariably pitiably poor. Of course this must not be taken to refer to the treatment on the part of the German officials, it refers simply to the matter of the receipt of letters, parcels, and money from home.
>
> In the case of the Serbs, it seems highly desirable that a special fund should be devoted to their relief. So far I have had nothing from the Association that I could use for such a purpose. Many of them have been in the field for five years and have seen nothing of home or family in all that time. The country has forbidden the sending of food parcels outside the borders, were the families of the prisoners able to send anything.
>
> Among the prisoners are men of seventy and over, and in at least one camp several cases of death due purely of old age were reported to me by two different German officers. Especially in Traunstein, the civilians' camp, are clothes needed. I had brought some over with me from friends in America—two marks apiece to 120 of the oldest of them, those who could not go out to work and so earn a little something.
>
> It will be a relief to my mind if we are able to do something really to help these poor Serbs; the German commandants say, "Anything you can do will be most worth while," and to people in real distress a game of checkers or a mouth-organ affords after all scant comfort. (Lowry 1917, 47–48)

By February 1917, the American YMCA had 72 WPA secretaries working in prison camps across Europe. Yet when the Wilson administration broke off diplomatic relations with Berlin, the WPA program was in danger of collapsing. The United States declared war against Germany on 6 April 1917, and Mott offered the YMCA's service to the Wilson administration. President Wilson responded on 25 April 1917:

> The Young Men's Christian Association has, in the present emergency, as under similar circumstances in the past, tendered its services for the benefit of enlisted men in both arms of the service. This organization is prepared by experience, approved methods and assured resources, to serve especially the troops in camp and field. It seems best for the interest of the Service that it shall continue as a voluntary civilian organization; however, the results obtained are so beneficial and bear such a direct relation to efficiency, inasmuch as the Association provision contributes to happiness, content and morale of the personnel, that in order to unify the civilian betterment activities in the Army, and further the work of the organization that demonstrated its ability to render a service desired by both officers and men, official recognition is hereby given the Young Men's Christian Association as a valuable adjunct and asset to the Service. Officers are enjoined to render the fullest practical assistance and co-operation in the maintenance and extension of the Association, both at permanent posts and stations and in camp and field. (Wilson 1917, 478)

The government recognized that the military needed American welfare organizations to support American troops. In the Spanish-American War and the Mexican Border War of 1916–1917, the U.S. Army relied on the Red Cross and YMCA for relief services to American soldiers. By April 1917, the association already had over two years of overseas military experience in World War I ("A Shining Mark" 1919, 49; "What the YMCA Is Doing for Our Soldiers" 1917, 188–189; Young Men's Christian Association National War Work Council 1920, 3–5; Taft, Harris, Kent, and Newlin 1922a, 49).

The entry of the United States into the war threatened the collapse of WPA operations for prisoners of war. The Germans and Austro-Hungarians demanded the immediate withdrawal of American personnel from WPA service. Harte and the World's Alliance negotiated in Berlin and Vienna, and a compromise solution was reached: Hoffman would remain at his post in Germany, but the departing American WPA secretaries would be replaced by association workers from Switzerland, Denmark, Norway, Sweden, and the Netherlands. The WPA continued to provide relief services to both Allied and Central Powers prisoners. After the Armistice, American WPA secretaries returned to Germany to provide welfare assistance to Russian prisoners trapped by the Russian Civil War. The American YMCA maintained WPA operations in Germany until 1923, when the last Russians left the country (Hoffman 1920, 98–264;. Young Men's Christian Association National War Work Council 1920, 105–108; Taft, Harris, Kent, and Newlin 1922b, 302–304, 314–327).

On 28 August 1917, American Expeditionary Force (AEF) headquarters issued General Order No. 26 (1917), dividing relief work between the American Red Cross and the YMCA (*The United States Army in the World War* 1992, 61). As a result, the YMCA took the lead role in providing educational, social, and entertainment programs for American soldiers, whereas the Red Cross focused on wounded and sick troops. The YMCA International Committee organized the National War Work Council to meet the needs of the American armed forces. Mott became the chairman, and William Sloane, former chairman of the Army and Navy Department, became the general secretary, supported by four associate general secretaries. The council divided operations into two general spheres: relief for soldiers in the training cantonments in the United States (Home Service), and welfare operations for American and Allied soldiers overseas (Foreign Service) (Young Men's Christian Association National War Work Council 1920, 5–8, 109–112; Taft, Harris, Kent, and Newlin 1922a, 212–226).

The YMCA did not undertake these services alone. The other six "Sisters" provided welfare workers at military bases at home, and four also sent workers abroad. The Knights of Columbus provided 1,134 secretaries for home service in training camps and dispatched 1,075 others overseas to France (over half), Britain, and Italy and Dalmatia. The YWCA sent 289 secretaries abroad to operate boardinghouses and canteens for French munitions workers and American and British women serving in the auxiliary forces. The Salvation Army became famous for its "doughnut service" in canteens during World War I, providing 289 workers for the AEF. The YMHA assigned 189 secretaries to work with American soldiers in France.

The bulk of relief workers sent to support the Allied war effort, however, was provided by the YMCA. Over 200,000 Americans volunteered to support association work during the Great War, and the YMCA hired 25,926 paid secretaries. Of this total, the YMCA sent 12,955 workers overseas to work with the AEF (11,446 men and women) or with Allied armies or prisoners of war (1,509 secretaries) (Boyd 1986, 73; Brown 1919, 252–253; Chesham 1965, 161; Egan and Kennedy 1920, 297; Kauffman 2001, 55–57; Kennedy 1919, 665; McKinley 1995, 151–155; Von Schrader and Jones 1920, 328–339,

349–376, 379–389, 393–400; Young Men's Christian Association National War Work Council 1920, 112, 196–197; Wisbey 1956, 162–163).

In negotiating for access to prison camps, the YMCA often found belligerent nations reluctant to extend free access to prison camps because of the religious basis of the association. Darius A. Davis, an American in France, found the government suspicious of YMCA goals. To allay French fears, Davis offered comparable services to French soldiers. Emmanuel Sautter, a general secretary of the World's Alliance, left Geneva at the beginning of the war to serve French troops. He developed the *Foyer du Soldat* (Soldiers' Fireside) program; French soldiers could visit *foyers* for refreshments, reading material, and light entertainment. Sautter opened the first *foyer* at Baccarat in the Vosges in January 1915. Davis offered to support the *Foyer du Soldat* program and expanded operations with funding from the International Committee in New York. By September 1917, the YMCA supported seventy *foyers* across the western front.

Although this technically violated U.S. neutrality, the International Committee also provided financial support to war work services in Germany and Austria-Hungary for *Soldatenheimen* (Soldiers' Homes) and the distribution of religious tracts. A World's Alliance secretary reported:

> Four Soldiers' Homes have so far been opened in the capital cities of Austria, Bohemia and Hungary, viz., in Vienna, Prague and Budapest. Suitable rooms with games, literature, writing materials, refreshments, etc., have in each case been placed at our disposal. Four well-qualified Army secretaries have been called and duly appointed for a year, provided the war lasts so long.
>
> A large number of invitation cards have been printed (10,000 in Vienna alone) in the required languages—German, Hungarian, Czech, Polish, Slovak, Croatian and Roumanian—and are being widely circulated among the soldiers in the streets, in the hospitals and at the official Military Divine service by the secretaries, the army chaplains, as well as by the voluntary helpers from the ranks of the Young Men's Christian Association, both members and students. Lady friends also help in distributing these cards when ministering to the wounded and in the hospitals. The best propaganda for our work is, however, done by those who themselves visit our Homes, and are furnished with cards in order to enable them to invite their comrades and to bring them if possible with them.

In all these Homes our friends try to render a true social service in a Christian spirit to the soldiers who are all heartily welcomed there, of whatever nationality or of whatever creed. So one finds sometimes half a dozen different nationalities gathered together round the tea tables, all belonging to the same Imperial Army. ("Extracts from a Letter from a Secretary Who Has Recently Returned to Switzerland from Austria-Hungary" 1915, 15–16)

In Russia, YMCA secretaries assisted Russian soldiers by working in hospitals and major railroad stations. When Italy entered the war, the American YMCA helped develop a program for soldiers similar to the French system called the *Casa del Soldato (*Soldiers' Home*)*. In addition, the International Committee in New York funded British, Canadian, Australian, New Zealand, and South African association war work, based on the Principle of Reciprocity, which established huts for Commonwealth soldiers in France, Britain, Egypt, the Dardenelles, German Southwest Africa, German East Africa, Mesopotamia, and India. Before the United States entered the war, the British and Commonwealth associations operated more than 1,500 centers around the world, with the support of 150 American secretaries. For the American YMCA, work for the belligerent nations was highly controversial because it might violate U.S. neutrality, but it was deemed a critical service to young men facing death at the front (Young Men's Christian Association National War Work Council 1920, 3–4, 54–55; Taft, Harris, Kent, and Newlin 1922b, 335–339, 369–371).

The hut was the centerpiece of YMCA work for soldiers during World War I and the critical element of the association's social program. According to G. Sherwood Eddy, a well-known evangelist of the day,

The red triangle at the entrance gleams across the whole camp and stands for the three things the soldier needs most.

It stands, in the first place, as a pledge for supplying the *physical need* of these hungry, lonely and fiercely tempted men. A dry shelter, a warm fire, a cheerfully lighted room, the bursts of song and the hum of conversation make the men forget the wind and rain and mud outside. Supper and a hot cup of coffee satisfy their hunger. On the notice-board is the announcement of the outdoor sports, football tournaments, and the games where the thirty thousand men of the division will compete in open contest on the coming Saturday, under the direction of the YMCA. Whatever the soldier needs for his physical life, whether it is to eat or to sleep, a bed in London, a cool drink in the thirsty desert, or hot coffee in the trenches, it is furnished for him by the Association.

The hut also provides for the soldiers' *intellectual* and social needs. The piano and the phonograph, the billiard tables, draughts and chess boards, tables for games, library, and reading room keep him busy; and the concerts, stimulating lectures, moving pictures, educational classes, and debating societies provide him with recreational and mental employment.

The far deeper *moral and spiritual needs* of the soldier are also met. As the evening draws to a close, one sees the secretary in his military uniform stand up on the table; hats are off and heads are bowed at the call for evening prayers, which are held here every night. On Sunday the parade services of the different denominations take place in turn in the Association hut. Weekly voluntary religious meetings are also held. At one end of the building is the "quiet room," where groups of Christian soldiers can meet for Bible classes or for prayer. At regular intervals evangelistic meetings are held. On our last night at this hut, on a Sunday evening, twelve hundred men gathered to listen to the Christian message. (Eddy 1917, 34–36)

Every hut had a trained Red Triangle secretary who oversaw activities inside the facility and scheduled activities in the evening. The association provided stationery and envelopes for soldiers to write home, and volunteers to write letters for illiterate soldiers; the U.S. Army estimated that 16 percent of its recruits were foreign born and 25 percent were illiterate. Most important, the secretary served as a confidant for soldiers to discuss problems. The goal was to make the YMCA hut a "soldiers' home" and help them unwind from the rigors of military life (Perkins 1917, 421; "A Shining Mark" 1919, 49; Taft, Harris, Kent, and Newlin 1922a, 274–292).

The United States transported over two million troops to Europe during World War I. Secretaries accompanied troops on trains from training camps to their port of embarkation. Local associations set up relief operations at railroad stations to provide refreshment and recreation during stopover periods. The YMCA estimated that secretaries served 3,000 troop trains, or 1.5 million men, during the war. When troops arrived at the embarkation points, they could visit the YMCA facilities and enjoy the wide range of activities offered by secretaries. The association constructed two large buildings at the nation's two great embarkation points, Hoboken, New Jersey (the Hudson Hut), and Newport News, Virginia. The YMCA also established major huts for traveling soldiers in New York City (the Eagle Hut), Boston, Charleston, and Philadelphia. On the dangerous voyage across the Atlantic, secretaries implemented the Red Triangle program, offering entertainment, motion pictures, gramophones, stationery, cigarettes, chocolate, boxing, and "sour pickles for seasickness" (Young Men's Christian Association National War Work Council 1920, 15–17; Taft, Harris, Kent, and Newlin 1922a, 364–382).

Approximately half of the members of the AEF landed in British ports during World War I, and the American YMCA quickly set up operations to welcome them. The Americans pooled their resources with the British, Canadian, Australian, and New Zealand YMCAs in Britain to form the International Hospitality League and provide social services to all Allied troops. In July 1917, the American YMCA began relief operations in England by meeting a troop ship arrival in Borden. Initial services focused on money exchange, letter postings, and canteen services, especially since most American troops had spent only forty-eight hours in England before leaving for advanced training in France. As Sherwood Eddy, an American evangelist, pointed out,

> During the whole war it is the Overseas Forces, the men farthest from home influences, who have no hope of leave or furlough, who are far removed from all good women and the steadying influence of their own reputations that have fared the worst in the war. The Americans not only share this danger with the Colonials and other Overseas Forces, but they have an additional danger in their high pay.
>
> Here are enlisted men who tell us that they are paid from $35 to $90 a month, from the lowest private to the best-paid sergeants. When you remember that the Russian private is allowed only one cent a day, that the Belgian soldier receives only four cents a day, the French private five cents, the German six cents, and the English soldier twenty-five cents a day—most of which has to go to supplementary food to make up for the scantiness of the rations supplied—you realize what it means for the American soldier to be paid from one to three dollars a day, in addition to clothing, expenses and the best rations of any army in Europe. (Eddy 1917, 15)

As the number of U.S. troops in Britain increased, the American YMCA set up operations at embarkation points, rest camps, hospitals, aviation bases, city and town huts, leave centers, and lumber camps by organizing

YMCA workers at the Eagle Hut, London, 1915. (Hulton-Deutsch Collection/Corbis)

clubs, hotels, and recreation huts for Allied soldiers. The Red Triangle established the Eagle Hut in London, a "little piece of America," which served 3,000 men daily. In Eddy's words:

> It would be difficult to devise a more homelike or attractive place for soldiers. In addition to sleeping accommodations for several hundred men, the lounge and recreation rooms, the big fireplaces and comfortable chairs suggested the equipment of an up-to-date club, in marked contrast to the surroundings of a cheerless soldiers' barracks. (Eddy 1917, 19–20)

The YMCA assigned carefully selected young American women as secretaries to provide a wholesome social atmosphere in a number of huts, to remind soldiers of home. Secretaries also arranged sightseeing tours of historic interest for soldiers to introduce them to British culture. One notable service of the International Hospitality League was the London Street Patrol. The association sent out street-wise young women in pairs to deter prostitution and divert Allied soldiers to more wholesome activities (Hergesheimer 1918, 334; "Women's Work in the 'Y'" 1919, 35–36; Von Schrader and Jones 1920, 286–290; Young Men's Christian Association National War Work Council 1920, 18–22, 114; Taft, Harris, Kent, and Newlin 1922b, 67–92). One of the officials recalled the scene:

> The Strand had settled down to its midnight quiet. There were soldiers straggling here and there, some of them drunk, and women of the street moving noiselessly but stealthily in the quiet of shame. One of them accosted a colonel of a Canadian regiment, who stood lonely and aimless on the edge of the sidewalk in front of the Grand Palace Hotel. They were about to move away together when another woman, middle-aged and robust, approached the departing ones.
>
> She wore a uniform, not unlike the trim outfit of women welfare war-workers, with a peaked hat like that of an American soldier. "Good evening," she said, addressing them both; and then turning to the man, "Please tell me what time it is." The officer saluted. He recognized the woman by her hat. She was a New Zealander. That meant something. Whatever the lack of good-feeling may have been between the English Tommy and his cousin, from Canada, Australia, or New Zealand, among themselves the colonials had a strong bond of kinship that as a show of pride in democracy was exhilarating, not to say vigorously demonstrative. "It is ten minutes after one, madam," politely replied the colonel.
>
> The procuring woman had already been engaged in conversation with another "NZ" woman in uniform. But the interest was in the fighting man on leave. "Now you do not know this person," said the strong motherly New Zealander, when the officer with the characteristic defensive remark that he did know her, ill concealed his untruthfulness. "You are the eighth person she has accosted since she passed Wellington Street. (This distance is about two of our city blocks.) I am sure you will come to your senses," she added kindly, "when you think of your mother. Are you married? Have you a family? What if they knew?"
>
> The colonel, a man about forty years of age, well set up, clean-looking, a good countenance, broke down completely, hiding his face in his hands. He

cried in great grief, and poured out his gratitude to Mrs. F. McHugh, leader of the International Street Patrol. ("Women's Work in the 'Y'" 1919, 35)

The principal welfare work of the YMCA and the other six "Sisters," however, focused on the two million men of the AEF in France. Darius A. Davis met with American YMCA secretaries working with prisoners of war and the French army to plan activities for the AEF. The secretaries planned to implement the association's fourfold program' for American troops, and the U.S. Army entrusted the post exchange system in France to secretaries. By November 1918, 4,510 secretaries (1,138 women among them) maintained canteen operations on the western front. The canteen service consisted of warehouses; 48 factories for the production of chocolate, biscuits, and other supplies; a chain of banks; 100 hotels, dormitories, and cafés; 50 garages and machine shops for repair work; and a fleet of motor vehicles. It cost over $50 million to construct and was essentially the world's largest grocery store chain. (Mayo 1920d; Whitehair 1918; Eddy 1917; Young Men's Christian Association National War Work Council 1920, 25–27, 114; Taft, Harris, Kent, and Newlin 1922a, 119–135, 478–514; 1922b, 118–141).

The YMCA tried to establish a hut for every 500 American soldiers in France. If troops were assigned to a large city, such as Tours or Bordeaux, the association rented houses or hotels. The association established a Construction Department to build huts and an Equipment Department to supply the necessary material to operate the building. The operation, as Eddy recalled, was most efficient:

Just beside the present tent there is being rushed into position a big YMCA hut which will accommodate temporarily a thousand men, before it is taken in pieces and shipped to some new center. The Association has ordered from Paris a number of permanent pine huts, 60 by 120 feet, which will accommodate 2,000 soldiers each, and keep them warm and well occupied during the long, cold winter evenings that are to come. On the railway siding at the moment are nine temporary huts, packed in sections for immediate construction, and a score of permanent buildings have been ordered to be erected as fast as the locations for the camps are selected by the military authorities. Indeed, the aim is to have them on the ground and ready before the boys arrive and take the first plunge in the wrong direction. (Eddy 1917, 16–17)

French contractors built 65 percent of the American huts, and the association opened its own factory for prefabricated huts at Champagnole in the Jura Mountains in March 1918, with a second factory opening at Bordeaux in June 1918. Secretaries also employed specially equipped trucks to visit smaller, isolated units. When the Germans mounted their massive spring offensive in March 1918, the French demanded that American units join the front lines to stem the German onslaught. YMCA secretaries followed their units to the front lines. Eddy described his visit to the Somme:

> We duck into our little YMCA dugout, just under the crest of the ridge. It is an old, deserted German pit for deadly gas shells, which even now are lying about uncomfortably near, in heaps still unexploded. Here the men, going to and from the trenches, come in for hot tea or coffee and refreshments night and day. A significant sign forbids more than thirty men to congregate at once in this exposed spot, as sometimes these YMCA dugouts are blown to atoms by a shell. The one down below in "Plug Street" has been blown to bits, and the man in the one just up the line has been under such fire for several days that he will have to abandon his dugout. (Eddy 1917, 6–7)

Secretaries established relief operations in dugouts, tents, and abandoned buildings and served the men in the trenches. They continued to provide the full association program and, at the very least, distributed chocolate, cigarettes, biscuits, and hot drinks. Ford trucks resupplied these detachments every night. During the operation to stem the German advance, the YMCA even lost "huts" to enemy action. When the Allies launched their counteroffensive in August 1918, Red Triangle secretaries accompanied the advance, distributing relief (Mayo 1920a, 150–152; Von Schrader and Jones 1920, 271–277; Young Men's Christian Association National War Work Council 1920, 29–35, 120–124; Taft, Harris, Kent, and Newlin 1922a, 515–531). Secretaries attempted to implement the fourfold program to the best of their abilities, often under difficult combat conditions. As Eddy recalled,

> There are three types of work at the front:
>   First, the work of these huts, or buildings, which are in the part of the line the farthest removed from the actual front line trench. They are long, low, wooden buildings, which must be hidden under the trees, or camou-

flaged, so that the German balloons, which hang high in the heavens, and the German planes, that are constantly trying to pass over the British lines, cannot send a signal which will bring over a shell. Especially are they in danger of being bombed by planes on moonlight nights. Into these huts the men crowd by the hundreds, night after night, day after day, to write their home letters. Quite often it is their last farewell letter before "going in" to "go over the top." They get their cup of tea, smokes, etc., at the canteen. They pack the hut night after night to see the movies, hear the concerts, witness the wrestling and boxing matches, swap stories, [and] last, but not least, hear a religious message. . . .

In the devastated villages we find the second type of work that is being carried out by the YMCA at the front. In the cellar of some old building a Secretary has set up his canteen. Men flock into it by hundreds for a cup of hot tea, other little knickknacks or smokes. In one hut tens of thousands have received comfort and cheer. In fact, during the winter of 1916 and 1917, over 160,000 cups of cocoa were given away in this one cellar. . . .

The last general type of work being done by the YMCA is at the very front, in the dugouts, up in the forest of barbed wire, up where the great hounds of hell are always barking, up where the bullets always whine. The dugouts are so stationed that the men pass by going in and coming out of the front line trench. It is here that the YMCA reaches out and gives your boy his last helping hand before he goes into the front line to go "over the top." It is here the hand reaches out to give him the first human touch as he comes struggling painfully back from No Man's Land, tired and weary after his turn in the front line. (Whitehair 1918 71–78)

A new dimension of YMCA work in Europe emerged when the association took responsibility for U.S. Army leave areas. When French and British soldiers earned leaves, they could travel home and visit their families, but American soldiers did not have that opportunity. The army recognized that troops needed to escape from military life on an occasional basis. The command also recognized that they could not allow troops to disperse across France. To address the situation, the YMCA presented a proposal to the AEF command in August 1917 to take over amusement and recreational facilities for American troops at leading French holiday resorts. The army approved the plan, and the YMCA began negotiations with French government officials to obtain access to resort areas.

Interior of the casino now used by the YMCA, Aix-les-Bains, France. YMCA workers are serving refreshments to the soldiers, circa 1918. (Bettmann/Corbis)

The YMCA opened the first leave area in the Savoy area in February 1918 at Aix-les-Bains, Chambéry, and Challes-les-Eaux. American soldiers received a seven-day leave every four months and took special trains to Savoy for their relaxation. When they arrived, they received new uniforms and access to a wide range of entertainment and activities. Secretaries offered theatrical and cinema shows, concerts, vaudeville, dancing, games, and social amusements. Troops dined in fashionable restaurants and cafés, and could be the guests of French families. Red Triangle workers organized bicycle riding, baseball, volleyball, tennis and soccer, sightseeing trips, and steamboat excursions. The YMCA also rented out local hotel and pensions to accommodate 40,000 men at a time.

Recognizing the value of the leave areas, the U.S. Army agreed to pay for the program. The AEF also asked the YMCA to develop another twenty-five centers for 50,000 men across France in eleven additional leave areas. The association program expanded to allow troops to visit Versailles, climb in the Alps, or visit water festivals in the Mediterranean. Soldiers with one-day leaves or weekend passes could take sightseeing tours of Paris or five other cities. Over 1.9 million American soldiers participated in the leave area program in France during the war (Mayo 1920c, 190–192; Young Men's Christian Association National War Work Council 1920, 28–29, 169–176; *The United States Army in the World War* 1992, 159–163, 239–240; Taft, Harris, Kent, and Newlin 1922b, 142–162). For at least one, the experience was memorable:

Now, the enlisted men's Y at Nice was nothing less than the famous Palais de la Jetée, the Jetty Casino, running out beyond the surf about blue water, a huge-roomed house of glass. Leaving the broad sea-front walk to approach the Casino door, one crosses . . . a sort of preliminary bridge. Well, along that bridge ran a dais; over the dais was an awning; on the dais a row of chairs; and in those chairs perpetually sat a row of American doughboys with lordly . . . sublime detachment contemplating sea and distant hills while kneeling "dagoes" polished their boots. . . . Entering, you found yourself in an antechamber, where you could check any encumbrance that you might want to drop.

Then you mounted a few steps to where a broad foyer, expanding before you, revealed four things: on your left an enormous bulletin full of announcements of every kind of show or diversion that you could easily hope to see; ahead, a big, bright breezy room where boys in khaki lounged at ease; on your right, behind a desk marked "Information," a sweet-faced American Y girl in uniform looking straight at you with an inviting smile; and just beside you the woman that you presently were going to think the dearest and kindest and best in all the world, excepting your own mother. . . .

While the canteens ran without stop or stay from early morning until close upon midnight, the shuffleboard floor was always full, sixteen men playing at once. Orchestra music in the music room began at ten o'clock in the morning and again at half after one and at four in the afternoon. This was provided, as a rule, from French sources, and included instrumental soloists. The music played was usually serious in character; and half an hour before its scheduled time every seat in the hall would be taken by enlisted men, with all standing room rapidly filling.

Dancing, with a fine band, began regularly at four in the afternoon, and again in the early evening, to last till midnight, either more or less, as the need might be. No women but those in uniform were admitted. And as their numbers could never equal the demand, a system was instituted by which, at the sound of a whistle blown at regular intervals, the waiting men "cut in" and took each the girl of his choice away from him who had her. Scarcely breaking a step, for time and girls were precious, she would slide into her new partner's arms, and so off again, while the men banked the walls all around, waiting their turn. (Mayo 1920c, 190)

In relation to soldiers, and even officers, in other armies, American enlisted men enjoyed a high rate of pay. The U.S. Army provided each man with food, a billet, and a uniform, leaving soldiers with a relatively high disposable income. As Eddy recalled, there were plenty of vices on which to expend that pay:

Temptations and solicitation in Europe have been in almost exact proportion to the pay that the soldier receives. The harpies flock around the men who have the most money. As our American boys are the best paid, and perhaps the most generous and open-hearted and reckless of all the troops, they have proved an easy mark in Paris and the port cities. As soon as they were paid several months' back salary, some of them took "French leave," went on a spree, and did not come back until they were penniless. The officers, fully alive to the danger, are now doing their utmost to cope with the situation; they are seeking to reduce the cash payments to the men and are endeavoring to persuade them to send more of their money home. Courts martial and strict punishments have been imposed for drunkenness, in the effort to grapple with this evil. (Eddy 1917, 16)

Troops often had no safe and easy way to transmit their pay home. In February 1918, the YMCA offered free banking services to American soldiers to transfer cash to the United States. Before battle, men commonly turned over their money to a Red Triangle worker to send to their families. By the end of the war, YMCA remittances totaled $21.5 million (Young Men's Christian Association National War Work Council 1920, 177–178; Taft, Harris, Kent, and Newlin 1922a, 575–592).

For those who kept their money, the YMCA operated the U.S. Army's post exchange and canteen system in France. Army post exchanges sold goods not provided to soldiers as rations or equipment, and soldiers normally operated the post system. In France, the army lacked the manpower, and the YMCA offered to set up the operation. The association encountered difficulties in transporting goods, as soldiers, arms, and munitions had priority on board merchant ships, but by October 1918 the YMCA operated 1,068 post exchanges in France—a number that would rise to 1,500 by January 1919. To support this vast chain of retail stores, the YMCA operated twenty biscuit factories (producing 10 million packages a month), sixteen chocolate and candy factories (manufacturing 20 million bars a month), and eight jam factories (yielding 2 million tins a month).

The YMCA was supposed to sell post goods at cost; any profits were to be used for the benefit and entertainment of American troops. This policy led to criticism from agencies such as the Knights of Columbus and Salvation Army, which distributed their supplies free of charge. One Red Triangle secretary, however, opined: "We have many calls for tobacco and cigarettes. If we could supply them, it would be a real service, but they should be sold. That which is given free is not valued in proportion to what it cost us" ("A Foyer Secretary on Free Distribution" 1919, 47). Free distribution quickly exhausted available supplies, whereas small fees allowed secretaries to replenish goods to serve soldiers.

Real problems arose, however, when the YMCA set prices that included transportation charges. In May 1919, the U.S. government determined that the army should pay all transportation costs for post exchange goods. As a result, the YMCA made a $500,000 profit, which brought accusations of price gouging and a congressional investigation of the YMCA's business practices. The association responded by pointing out that secretaries freely distributed goods to needy soldiers. Rolling kitchens dispensed hot coffee and chocolate, and secretaries handed out cigarettes and tobacco—a point supported by at least one journalist's description of a "typical" hut kitchen:

> Billy's was a double hut of standard type. Its one half contained a stage and an auditorium for shows, while its parallel twin held scores of small tables where boys might eat and drink, or sit and smoke and chat, or play a game of cards. Billiard tables filled one end of the second part, writing tables the other, a long canteen counter occupied half of one side, and a sufficient number of stoves kept the place really warm. . . .

Billy's canteen contained, of course, the usual supplies of cake, chocolate, tobacco, matches, and all the odds and ends of the post exchange. But Billy's canteen contained, above all things, good and varied homelike food—as much and as varied as he could invent, forage, or by any means provide—dispensed with hearty friendship and kind laughter that were guided with a keen sympathetic eye.

No one ever suspected Billy of a desire to "save a soul" or drive a moral or hand out a tract. Nobody every heard Billy preach—except once or twice when the boys themselves asked for a Sunday service, and Billy had to take the job. Then he did it, and did it well. But nobody ever saw Billy too tired or too busy to see and provide for the last lad's need of body or mind, nobody ever saw him turn a lad away empty for lack of money to pay for his wants. (Mayo 1920a, 151–152)

In total, the association distributed over $2.6 million in free goods, but to allay the storm of criticism, the National War Work Council donated the $500,000 to establish the American Legion (Hergesheimer 1918, 334; "A Shining Mark"1919, 49; "The YMCA Viewed at the Front" 1919, 29–30; "Some Good Words for the YMCA" 1919, 31; "War Department Probe of YMCA 1919, 34; "Workers in Defense of the YMCA" 1919, 32, 38–39, 42; "The YMCA's Mistake" 1919, 36; "The YMCA under Fire" 1919, 88–89; "YMCA Shortcomings as Seen by Our Soldiers" 1919, 178–179; "Refitting the YMCA to War"1918, 36–37; Young Men's Christian Association National War Work Council 1920, 161–166; *The United States Army in the World War* 1992, 70; Taft, Harris, Kent, and Newlin 1922a, 547–574).

Perhaps the most important contribution of the YMCA to the Allied war effort was its entertainment program. To entertain soldiers in the training camps, the YMCA recruited professional entertainers, actors, opera singers, magicians, jugglers, comedians, dancers, and musicians at no cost to the troops. To support the war effort, the association attracted the best dramatic and musical entertainers in the country. The Entertainment Bureau held over 20,000 professional performances in the United States for more than 48 million men during World War I; the number of performances by volunteer soldier entertainers from the ranks could not be estimated (Young Men's Christian Association National War Work Council 1920, 125–131; Taft, Harris, Kent, and Newlin 1922a, 334–342).

Although combat limited secretaries' abilities to conduct educational, spiritual, and physical relief to the fullest extent, the YMCA nonetheless established the largest theatrical enterprise in history by sending 1,470 entertainers to France during the war. Performers worked under whatever conditions they encountered, as one recollected:

> A French piano, at best, is none too fine an instrument; but those which during the war were acquired for use in our army certainly must have been from the backwash of the French Revolution. I have attempted everything from an old-fashioned, wheezy Sunday school melodeon to a concert grand, but the piano I was forced to use on my trail as a jongleur surpassed anything in my previous experience.
>
> One night I was laboring with one which had sixteen missing keys. Turning to my audience, I said, "Boys, I am having an awful time!" With one shout they answered, "We know it!"
>
> On one occasion I was whisked away to an aviation camp tucked out of sight near Challons-sur-Marne where there was no "Y" hut, but the good-natured boys had fixed up their mess tent for the occasion. All went well until I began to sing. To save the piano from dampness they had raised it and the piano stood likewise on stilts. I found it some acrobatic feat to play, sing and keep my balance at the same time. Need I add that both performer and audience lost their equilibrium several times? (Galloway 1920, 95)

The association shipped 23,000 costumes, 18,000 musical instruments, and 450,000 pieces of sheet music to France to support this theatrical undertaking.

It also established four "play factories" in France, which became centers for rehearsals and costume production. Thomas J. McLane organized YMCA theatricals and established circuits for the traveling troupes. Tours started in Paris and went by train to various sectors of the front. The American YMCA also organized the Over There Theater League in April 1918, a group of 454 professional entertainers who performed for Allied troops. This group included actors, opera singers, magicians, jugglers, comedians, dancers, and musicians. Daniel C. McIver, a magician, recalled that

> In the seven days since our landing, August 25th, the Magic Unit has given twenty shows, five of which were under shell fire, some with piano and some without. We have given them with fully equipped stages and also on truck bodies, in airplane hangers, hospitals and stables. Miss Glynn is one of the

best soldiers in the world. She goes everywhere we go and undergoes all the inconveniences without a murmur. The two boys, Hal Pierson and Alfred Armand, are great, and my own work is going very nicely with the boys. We leave today for the front, with full equipment—tin hats, gas masks, knapsacks and blankets. No baggage except the egg bag and music rolls. (Evan and Harding 1921, 132)

Probably the most common form of entertainment offered to doughboys, though, was provided by the YMCA's Cinema Department in France. The YMCA arranged for film crews to visit the hometowns of army units and show the troops pictures "from home," and the Community Motion Picture Bureau sent the latest releases from Hollywood. The Cinema Department shipped over 1,500 miles of film and showed 157,000 motion pictures overseas. Between April 1918 and July 1919 alone, the YMCA set up movie shows at 5,621 locations for audiences totaling some 94 million men. Overall, the Cinema Department estimated that 210 million men viewed association silver screen performances (Evan and Harding 1921; Galloway 1920, 95–96; Von Schrader and Jones 1920, 277–279; Young Men's Christian Association National War Work Council 1920, 125–132; Taft, Harris, Kent, and Newlin 1922a, 619–636).

And the shows did not end even when the war did. More free time for the soldiers, in fact, required an increase in entertainment opportunities for American troops overseas. The YMCA's Overseas Entertainment Bureau continued cinema shows, theatrical performances, and concerts during the armistice period. The Over There Theater League maintained a steady stream of performances while the troops awaited repatriation. The association hired French vaudeville acts to entertain troops, which resulted in 1,236 performances between 1918 and 1919. The YMCA also brought the circus to amuse doughboys in France. To augment performances, the association encouraged soldiers to perform, and the best acts hit the theatrical circuit. During the month of May 1919, the "Y" staged 700 soldier performances. In addition, the YMCA maintained the AEF leave areas in France, and American soldiers continued to enjoy the casinos, music halls, theaters, restaurants, and cafés (Von Schrader and Jones 1920, 339–343; Young Men's Christian Association National War Work Council 1920, 129–132; Taft, Harris, Kent, and Newlin 1922a, 626–636). One entertainer recalled the experience in the following terms:

The visiting truck can do much to break the monotony of dull days. The Dancing Unit, consisting of fifteen young and deliberately pretty girls, with a chaperon described by the military as "herself very far from unattractive," was another successful feature of the Bookwalter Renaissance.

The Dancing Unit, during all the bitter winter weather, each day piling into a big truck with a piano, an Army band, and a hot chocolate apparatus, would move upon some isolated hamlet where American soldiers lay forlorn. Once on the spot, they tried to seek out the best likeness to a dance-hall, which might be anything from an old barn to a ramshackle, cobwebby theater.

Whatever it was, the girls flew to work at once, sweeping, cleaning, decorating. Then they set up their hot chocolate apparatus, turned on the band, and gave a *the dansant* to the enlisted men. After which they messed—with the officers as a rule, not to leave them out entirely—and gave another enlisted men's dance in the evening.

For the girls it meant heavy labor. Living conditions, anywhere outside of Paris, were rougher, dirtier, harder than peace-time travelers can conceive. Short hours of sleep, stiff physical exertion, and the continuous task of working off the accumulated energy of dance-mad doughboys at the rate of perhaps twenty doughboys per "honest-to-goodness American girl" twice daily. No service was more welcomed by the men, and the girls loved it. (Mayo 1920b, 245)

For physical relief, the association provided a wide range of sporting equipment and developed sports leagues to raise morale in camp and keep prisoners in shape. WPA secretaries also encouraged craft programs and held POW expositions that allowed prisoners to sell their work and earn some money. The YMCA provided musical instruments to prisoners to form bands and orchestras, theatrical equipment to produce plays, gramophones and records, and movie projectors to show films as social programs. Prisoners could hone their talents while providing entertainment for the camp inmates.

On the other side of things, American commanders in particular wanted their troops to enjoy sports to stay in shape and release tensions. Because groups of men gathered together were vulnerable to enemy fire, the YMCA found it difficult, but not impossible, to promote athletic events in the war zone. Secretaries brought basketballs, medicine balls, indoor baseball equipment, and quoits up to the front lines so soldiers could play games.

The Y even supported basketball games in the Belleau Wood within reach of German artillery during the American offensive (Young Men's Christian Association National War Work Council 1920, 137–140, 156; Taft, Harris, Kent, and Newlin 1922a, 593–607).The program carried over to the Allies as well. One of the biggest contributions of the YMCA to the French army was the introduction of athletic programming into military training. The association established eight physical education schools in France to train physical directors for the army. As one of the instructors noted at the time,

> It has not taken long for the American soldier to demonstrate to friend and foe alike that he is the fighting man *par excellence*. . . . The French nation has not been slow to recognize the value of our games, both for the training of soldiers and for the development of the physical, mental, and moral qualities so necessary for the rehabilitation of the nation after the war. Already extensive plans have been made and are being put into effect for a comprehensive program of physical training for all the people. Social hygiene occupies a deservedly important place in this program. . . .
>
> There are now about 500 Association physical directors aiding to develop an American sports program for the poilus. Over a thousand Foyers are in operation and the work is being rapidly extended not only in France, but to Saloniki, Corfu, and Morocco. Hundreds of American physical directors are still needed. Large sums of money are needed to buy necessary equipment and to carry on the work. There are boundless opportunities for American money, lives, and ideas to help over here. ("American Sports in France" 1919, 34–35)

The effect of the YMCA program carried on after the war was over. In September 1919 the French army assumed complete control of the *Foyer du Soldat* program and converted the program to a peacetime footing. The French army decided to maintain 300 *foyers* across the country to serve for French troops (Hergesheimer 1918, 334; Roz 1919, 14–17; "The Foyers du Soldat" 1918, 524–525; Potter 1919, 480–481; Von Schrader and Jones 1920; Young Men's Christian Association National War Work Council 1920, 54–57; Taft, Harris, Kent, and Newlin 1922b, 335–358).

The physical program also remained a high priority for American secretaries after the Armistice was signed. General Pershing issued General Order No. 241 (1918) in December 1918 to encourage the development of athletics to keep up morale, develop an esprit de corps, and improve the general fitness of the army. YMCA physical directors took the lead in making troops "fit to go home." Under this general order, the AEF organized army championships in track and field, baseball, football, basketball, tennis, boxing, and wrestling during the Armistice period. Competition was based on single elimination, beginning at the company level. Teams then advanced through battalion, regiment, brigade, and division competition and ended up in AEF championship games. This not only improved physical fitness and morale in the army but also attracted a large number of spectators.

The YMCA also promoted boxing matches as entertainment for the troops. The association featured 400,000 boxing matches, some in the largest venues in Paris, between January and June 1919 and attracted over eight million spectators. These events became so popular that the YMCA booked American, British, and French boxers on tours across France, Italy, and Germany.

Perhaps the most intriguing aspect of YMCA's physical program, though, was the Inter-Allied Games. In October 1918, before the war was even over, YMCA physical director Elwood S. Brown proposed that the army host an Olympiad of athletes from the Allied armies. The program would include mass games, a pageant, and, of course, the athletic competitions. The AEF invited twenty-nine countries to send representatives to the games. The association designed and financed the construction of Pershing Stadium in Joinville; the French donated the land, and the AEF provided the labor. The stadium seated 25,000 spectators and accommodated many sports. The games ran from 22 June to 6 July 1919, and 875,000 spectators paid to see the competitions. According to one contemporary report,

> Thirty thousand spectators rose to their feet on the opening day at the entrance of the military parade headed by the Garde Républicaine Band, and followed by representatives of some of the most famous fighting contingents of the war. Tattered regimental flags, many stained with blood of battles long antedating those of the Great War; national ensigns of all participating nations; uniforms of various sorts—Chasseurs Alpins, Zouaves, Tirailleurs, French, Italian, Serbian, and all the Rest—these, and the presence of thousands of spectators in uniform, were the thrilling reminders of the world-wide character of the long and bitter struggle now brought to a victorious close. The military were followed by 15,000 athletes who lined up in front of the troops marshaled before the reviewing stand. (Taft, Harris, Kent, and Newlin 1922b, 51)

The goal of the Inter-Allied Games was to continue a sense of comradeship between the soldier-athletes created during the long years of warfare (Von Schrader and Jones 1920, 313–317; Young Men's Christian Association National War Work Council 1920, 134–145; *The United States Army in the World War* 1992, 589–591; Taft, Harris, Kent, and Newlin 1922b, 26–54). Eighteen countries sent athletes to the competition, which featured every sport from American baseball to Italian *pelota*. Arab athletes sent by the king of Hedjaz competed in sword matches and camel-fighting. National pride clearly emerged during the games, as one observer recalled:

> France, in spite of her enormous losses of men, made a very remarkable showing. She combed her Army for athletes, held extensive elimination contests, and enlisted the cooperation of her many athletic federations. As a result, she was one of the largest participants in practically every sport. Her fine spirit of cooperation and determination to conquer won her the same admiration in sport that her splendid valor in the field of battle had brought her in the war itself. . . .
>
> Czechoslovakia sent as her soccer team the Prague squad that had been boycotted by the Austrians from 1908 to 1918, and had the great satisfaction of winning the championship in that sport. In fencing, too, the team of this nation gave an excellent account of itself. For the competition in tennis, however, her players had had no practice chiefly because in their country no tennis balls had been available since 1914.
>
> Among all the nations the United States was the least handicapped. Nearly all of her best athletes were in the Army. Comparatively few had been killed. Furthermore, the presence of some 50 athletes from the Army at home was a partial compensation for the absence of many victors in the AEF Championships who could not remain for the Allied Games. These considerations detract nothing from the merits of victorious individuals or teams but they cannot be left wholly out of the reckoning when accounting for the fact that American teams won twelve championships out of a possible twenty-four. (Taft, Harris, Kent, and Newlin 1922b, 50)

Working with soldiers of many nations naturally presented the association with many other challenges as well. When the United States declared war on Germany, for example, the French government immediately requested that YMCA services expand to improve the flagging morale of the French army. In July 1917, the government sought to increase the *Foyer du*

Soldat program. General Henri Pétain and American YMCA officials met in August to establish the Union Franco-Américaine, a formal arrangement between the American YMCA and the French army. Emmanuel Sautter remained in charge of the *Foyer du Soldat* program, but Darius Davis represented the association. The International Committee agreed to expand the number of *foyers* by 100 new facilities. In February 1918, the French ministry of war agreed to provide the YMCA with buildings, tables, benches, light, and heat to establish new *foyers*. The quartermaster general would provide the necessary supplies, and the French army would transport all of the material. In return, the American YMCA would provide secretaries and programming. The only caveat was that the association agreed not to undertake any political or sectarian propaganda among French troops.

The association instituted most of the services available to American doughboys with an emphasis on books, stationery, entertainment (cinema, music, and vaudeville), sports, and canteen service. Recognizing the value of this morale work among French troops, the American YMCA accelerated hut construction. *Foyers* did not differ much from the American hut, according to one description:

> The building is by no means the smallest, but with all its size it is *plein* [full]. . . . The main room was full of soldiers playing games. Not a chair was vacant and men were standing. . . . In the next room there was no noise. Here every table was in use by the *poilus* writing letters home. And in the last room, the reading-room, a still more quiet, homelike atmosphere prevailed. One of the men, looking around at the walls covered with pictures, the fireplace, the plants and flowers in the corners, and the men quietly reading, said: "It's just like home, isn't it?"("The Foyers du Soldat" 1918, 524)

In September 1918 the YMCA opened *Foyer du Soldat* No. 1,000 in Saint Mihiel; the Y opened No. 1,200 in November when the French occupied Metz. By February 1919 the YMCA had established 1,452 *Foyers du Soldat* for the French army during the war. They operated at the front and behind the lines, just as American huts did. One worker recalled the experience:

> Again the dawn broke and with it again the fearful passage of the wounded. Again the battle advanced and again we moved forward. We finally reached Chadun, then a battered target constantly raked with high explosives and gas in great waves of fire. By this time little was left in our sacks. We could still be

useful in liaison work between the French and Americans, still give water and a couple of cigarettes to each wounded man, before we were completely out.

A providential camion arrived from the American Young Men's Christian Association with a full load. We joined the two secretaries established at a cross road, filled our sacks for our men, and all the afternoon passed out to eagerly stretched hands, buns, biscuits, matches, chocolate, tobacco, newspapers, the commonplace things which at home we take or leave with such indifference. The American soldier has not had the long lessons of privation which have fallen to the lot of the French. With all his glorious energy and courage he suffers when without these little comforts.

Up to the battle and back the men passed with long stories, pockets full of souvenirs, and an extraordinary zest for the work of driving the Boche. They were not hardened troops like our Africans, but vigorous, young athletes, carried away with the thought of striking a terrible blow in the good cause. The steady sadness and cold resolution of our old soldiers were foreign to the spirit of these youngsters. And truly to see them playing at this dreadful war like a game, struck me as very new and very strange. They played hard too, not tenderly, not sentimentally. ("American Troops" 1919, 28–29)

The Germans captured or destroyed 130 huts during their spring 1918 offensive, the French transferred 50 huts to the AEF, and the association closed 434 huts as the French army advanced in fall 1918.

The association was active on other fronts as well. After the Italian disaster at the Battle of Caporetto in October 1917, the need for war work in Italy was critical. Shocked by a massive Austro-German offensive, the Italians retreated to the Piave River and regrouped. The Italians had established a welfare system for troops, the *Casa del Soldato* program, with the support of the American YMCA soon after Italy entered the war. But the Caporetto defeat made the Italian government eager to expand war morale services. One secretary described the moment:

There is evidence that the day which we have long been working and praying for is at last coming in Italy, that is, the day when our work can be started for the men at the front. It would take too long to tell the whole story. It is another illustration of the big thing being hidden beneath the little, of the important being masked by the seemingly unimportant. When we began the small work in some of the cities like Rome, Naples, Genoa, Torre Pellice, etc., it was not because we wanted to open our work in these cities, but because we could not begin at the front, where it seemed to us there was the greatest need. Now men who got their training and ideas of our work in those little city Foyers have been mobilized and have gone out to the front to big camps and have secured permissions which we could not get, and have actually started Foyers in at least four different centers. (Davis 1917, 35)

In November 1917 the Italians began negotiations with the American association, and the International Committee sent six secretaries to Italy in January 1918. General Vittorio Zaccone, the Italian chief of staff, negotiated with John S. Nollen, representing the American YMCA, to expand Red Triangle services in February 1918. A formal agreement established the *Opera di Fratellanza Universale Americana YMCA Case del Soldato* (Works of Universal Brotherhood, American YMCA Soldiers' Huts). Under this program, American secretaries avoided all religious teaching but promoted the other features of the fourfold program for Italian troops. In addition, the Americans offered a free canteen service for soldiers, primarily the distribution of chocolate and cigarettes. In return, the Italian government offered free transportation for Y supplies, free franking privileges, fuel, and access to the quartermasters' stores at government rates; it also would requisition buildings at normal rent charges. It was a deal the association welcomed, but not, as one secretary reported, without its own challenges.

> At the other end of the station was the most interesting part of the whole institution, for there the famished soldier could get food and drink. The *Casa [del Soldato]* and dormitory had been in operation some months with complete success, when the major in command at the station came to us with a suggestion. A buffet for the soldiers had been run since the war began, by private individuals on contract. The rooms were dirty, the food hardly passable, the prices exorbitant. It was hard on the soldiers. The concession would expire in about a month. Would we take it over and run the buffet in the same splendid way in which the other Y activities as the Campo di Marte were conducted? The army and railroad authorities would be overjoyed if we would; for they had seen what the Y could do.
>
> It was a tempting proposal. Bur there seemed to be obstacles. Our agreement with the army forbade our selling food to the soldiers in our case. We were not sure that we ought to enter upon a business proposition like this.

Finally, the buffet sold wine, beer, and stronger drinks [which would not be approved by the association].

The first obstacle was quickly removed, for the War Department ruled that the agreement need not stand in the way. General headquarters of the Y at Bologna were willing to have us go into business, if we could guarantee that we would not run the buffet at a loss. Not being business men . . . but a settlement worker and an editor . . . we had faith that we could.

Remained only was the question of wine and things. It was a puzzling question. We were neither of us "drinking men"; we both believed in temperance, in fact in prohibition. But we knew that to induce the Italian to forego his wine with his meals was not within the bounds of human possibility—at least in the time at our disposal! We knew that we could not run that buffet without selling wine. We became convinced, after long and prayerful consideration, that it would be better for the Y to run that buffet, as we knew it could be run, and sell wine there than to leave the business in the hands of those who were doing such a poor job at it, from the point of view of the Italian soldier and his physical and moral relief. So we cast the die in favor of assuming the job and headquarters at Bologna as well as a high representative of the International Committee of the YMCA then in Italy approved our solution. So we went at it. (Howland 1919, 267–268)

The American YMCA opened its first hut at Meolo in April 1918. By November 1918, the association had established 150 *case,* with 50 at the front lines. The Y organized a total of 200 huts in Italy by June 1919, with 75 at the front. To staff these buildings, the association sent almost 100 American secretaries to Italy by the summer of 1918. The number of secretaries peaked at 270 by June 1919, assisted by 500 Italian soldiers in this work. Between February 1918 and November 1919 the American YMCA spent over $3.4 million to support war morale work in Italy (Wannamaker 1923; "The YMCA in Italy" 1919, 324–325; Caviglia 1919, 245; Howland 1919, 245–247, 266–271; Potter 1919, 481–482; Young Men's Christian Association National War Work Council 1920, 63–66; Taft, Harris, Kent, and Newlin 1922b, 369–392). A progress report noted:

In sections where for military reasons it was not possible to erect a Soldiers' House, resort was had to motor cars, furnished by the various army corps, on which were carried about, almost up to the trench lines, letter paper and stationery requisites, so highly prized by those who were able to write to the loved ones at home, and also gramaphones [*sic*] and other means of recreation. Even near the front, moving-picture exhibitions were given, the portable material being set up in some comparatively safe and convenient spot, and every evening from 1000 to 2000 soldiers were able to enjoy the diversion. ("The YMCA in Italy" 1919, 324)

The American YMCA also sent a considerable number of secretaries to support the Russian war effort, especially after the tsar fell in March 1917 and Russia became a republic. In January 1917, General Kuropatkin, impressed with WPA relief work for Central Power POWs, asked that service be extended to troops under his command. To assess the Russian situation and determine how the United States could keep Russia in the war, President Wilson asked Mott to participate in the Root Mission in March 1917.

The mission arrived in Russia three months later. The Russians requested 500 Red Triangle secretaries to improve army morale. Unfortunately, the YMCA found it difficult to recruit secretaries with the necessary foreign language skills to support the operation, but the International Committee did send 125 American secretaries. Including Red Triangle workers conducting WPA operations and secretaries assigned to Allied units, the American YMCA had more than 300 secretaries in Russia by the end of the summer.

After Alexander Kerensky came to power in July, the Russian government embraced the association initiative, and association huts sprang up across the country. Kerensky gave the American association liberal concessions including free transportation of YMCA goods and personnel on Russian railways, customs exemptions on imported supplies, free franking of correspondence, and free access to buildings. As this report demonstrates, the association took up the offer with vigor:

On the 27th of July (by the Russian calendar) there stood in the beautiful grove of trees directly across from the great summer camp for soldiers near Petrovski Park in Moscow a brick house, which had served as a dwelling for the military governor of the Moscow district in times past, but which through the early summer had been closed to all persons. The door handles of brass, the water faucet spouts of nickel, the tables and chairs of cane and wood, all had been removed, and the interior was bare of any furniture or ornamentation. Cobwebs and stale air were primary evidences that life in the brick house had long been absent.

Late in the afternoon of that day the Young Men's Christian Association received their permission to take over the house and grounds for the work among the thousands of soldiers encamped nearby. The next evening at six o'clock a flood of Russians poured in through the doors, each one taking time, however, to glance at the big Red Triangle sign which was posted over the front door. Inside they found prepared for them a writing room with stationery and writing utensils to be given by the attendant to each one who desired; next a reading room for those who wished to see the latest news and illustrated papers and magazines; then a sort of sun parlor with game tables and musical instruments; two rooms for study and school work, and an office and supply room. On the other side of the main lobby was a room which was not yet complete with athletic and sport pictures and equipment; further on two tea rooms, where tea and sugar could be procured for 3 kopeks a glass; and at the rear space for the secretaries, the Russian workers, and for kitchen and supply purposes.

No one will quite be able to tell just how the trick was done in one day; the Russian city newspapers commented on the "American" speed, which had taken a building one day and opened it the next. (Wheeler 1917, 15–16)

The YMCA was soon operating huts in Petrograd, Pskov, Minsk, Kiev, Rostov, Odessa, Tiflis, and Tashkent. The Red Triangle workers instituted a program based on canteen service, cinema performances, and athletic competitions.

After the second revolution came, Red Triangle secretaries worked with Red Army and White Russian troops during the initial confusion of the growing civil war, but tensions quickly emerged between the Protestant welfare organization and the atheistic Bolsheviks. In August 1918 President Wilson issued a proclamation that effectively cut off relations with the Bolsheviks, and the YMCA recalled its secretaries from Soviet territory and Red Army service. By that time, the Bolsheviks had branded the Red Triangle as counterrevolutionary. American YMCA secretaries continued to provide war work relief to White Army forces and general relief work for the Russian people (Heald 1972; Colton 1940, 38–82; Von Schrader and Jones 1920, 318–319; Young Men's Christian Association National War Work Council 1920, 67–69; "For the Men Who Are Rebuilding Europe" 1921; Taft, Harris, Kent, and Newlin 1922b, 419–457).

The American and British associations, on the other end of the spectrum, enjoyed a long and close relationship. The British YMCA developed the same social welfare program for their troops as the Americans. In support of the Allied war effort, American secretaries accompanied British forces in colonial campaigns. When the Ottoman Empire entered the war in November 1914, the British rushed troops to Egypt to protect the Suez Canal, the lifeline of the British Empire. Egypt became the primary base of operations for British military campaigns in the Near East, and the YMCA accompanied the troops. Secretaries set up Y tents "in the shadows of the pyramids" and conducted the fourfold program. The YMCA established a large association hut in the Esbekiah Gardens in Cairo to keep soldiers out of the notorious red light district, as one secretary's report reveals:

> The military authorities turned over . . . the Ezbekiyeh [sic] Gardens, a beautiful public park in the heart of Cairo. The grounds are large enough to accommodate thousands of men. The motto from the start was: "Something doing every night." Concerts, lectures, cinema, wrestling, boxing, fencing, rink hockey, races, writing and reading facilities, hot and cold shower baths, and a well-equipped refreshment bar were provided, in fact everything that a well-organized club would have. The refreshment bar was run by a group of devoted English women who brought into the Garden the home touch. It was not an uncommon sight to see thousands of soldiers seated at once writing home letters, and four to five thousand at a cinema show, wrestling match, or a religious meeting. (Whitehair 1918, 228–229)

Australian and New Zealand troops launched their attack against the Dardenelles from Egypt in 1915, and Red Triangle secretaries set up huts on the beachheads. When British troops ventured into the desert to fight the Senussi in Tripoli or Arabs in the Sudan, YMCA secretaries provided canteen service, entertainment, and recreation, sometimes on the spur of the moment:

> In one of the desert camps [in Egypt] it was near midnight when a lieutenant roused our secretary after a busy day, with the words: "Can you do anything for my men? Provisions are out and we've marched 20 miles since early afternoon." And shortly the 700 dust-covered, weary men whose tongues were well nigh hanging out were served hot cocoa and tea and lime juice and cake. They marched off again at 3 A.M. in new spirits. At 3:30 an-

other officer broke in asking that something be done for his 70 men. In twenty minutes the secretary and his force were serving them. Night or day the work goes on. (Whitehair 1918, 214)

Forty American secretaries worked with the British in Egypt and Palestine during the war. When a second British army resumed the Mesopotamia offensive in February 1917, YMCA secretaries went along to offer support services. Red Triangle workers also set up a center in Baghdad when that city fell in March and continued services as the British reached Mosul in November 1918. The American YMCA also sent secretaries to conduct war morale work with other Allied armies during the war. Because of the American association's deep interest in missionary work in India and the important role of the Indian Expeditionary Force in the Mesopotamia campaign, the International Committee sent an additional thirty-four secretaries to provide services to Indian troops. After the Portuguese declared war on Germany in 1916 and sent a 60,000-man expeditionary force to the western front, they found that language barriers made the Portuguese troops feel isolated. To improve their situation, the American Y sent twenty-three secretaries to provide relief services. This contingent included secretaries from Portugal and Brazil, and they helped bolster Portuguese spirits. After Romania declared war on Austria-Hungary in 1916, the kingdom was overwhelmed by a massive Austro-German invasion. By December 1916 the Romanians controlled only the northern province of Moldavia. When the United States entered the war, the American YMCA sent four secretaries to boost the morale of the Romanian army. Establishing a center in Jassy, the Americans served in the kingdom until the Romanians surrendered in March 1918. The Greek government requested the establishment of a *Foyers du Soldat* program for its troops on the Salonika front, so the American association dispatched ten secretaries beginning in August 1918. By January 1919 the YMCA was operating nine huts in Greece, including two in Athens (Potter 1919, 483; Young Men's Christian Association National War Work Council 1920, 62, 76–77, 114; Taft, Harris, Kent, and Newlin 1922b, 359–361, 381–388).

Perhaps the most interesting welfare effort conducted by the American YMCA in World War I, though, took place in German East Africa. The British, Indian, and South African associations provided most of the secretary manpower in support of the British, South African, Indian, Belgian, Portuguese, and African troops who took part in the four-year campaign against the Germans. (They did not surrender until two weeks after the Armistice was signed on the western front.) The International Committee dispatched seven African-American secretaries to German East Africa to work with native carriers and troops in East Africa. This was the first missionary effort conducted by African Americans from the United States and sparked the imaginations for future African projects. In 1923 African-American associations succeeded in sending Max Yergan, one of the seven wartime secretaries, to work with young men in South Africa on a permanent basis ("What the YMCA Is Doing for Our Soldiers" 1917, 188–189; Potter 1919, 482–483; Webster 1918, 432–433; "With the East African Forces" 1919, 451–454; "The Red Triangle in East Africa" 1918, 1–4; Von Schrader and Jones 1920, 322–328; Young Men's Christian Association National War Work Council 1920, 79–91, 114; Taft, Harris, Kent, and Newlin 1922b, 393–418). The report on their activities ran as follows:

> Five colored men from North America, led by Max Yergan, are rendering magnificent service, characterized officially by the Director of Military Labor as "humane and sympathetic." The Commander-in-Chief cabled the International Committee that he would be "grateful" if additional colored secretaries were sent.
>
> One of them gained a knowledge of the Swahili language in six months, which enabled him to direct the work and to give religious addresses to these needy men in their own tongue. Another has developed night schools and other educational features. The mission schools have been impressed, yielding their trained boys for leadership. Many of these boys have developed capacity which has multiplied the activities and extended the service of the North American leaders. Settlers, missionaries and officials heartily cooperate through the Association, which provide an outlet for their efforts. (Webster 1918, 432)

Another unusual service undertaken by the YMCA during World War I concerned the care and welfare of the Chinese Labor Corps. As a result of military mobilization, an acute labor shortage emerged in France, and the British began to import Chinese labor on a contract basis in 1915. This process accelerated in 1917 when the Chinese government declared war on Germany. The Chinese were unable to send troops to Europe, but the government offered an ample supply of laborers. Within months, over 200,000 Chinese workers were deployed across the western front, assigned to the

British, French, and American armies. These laborers played a critical role in the war effort, digging trenches, building railroads, unloading merchant ships, draining swamps, and working in munitions factories. Serious problems emerged among the Chinese due to language barriers and cultural misunderstandings. Allied officers treated the Chinese as recruits and made few allowances in terms of diet and customs. As a result, Chinese gangs rioted and went on strike, and morale in the labor corps plummeted.

The association, in contrast, had a long history of sending missionaries to China, and Mandarin-speaking secretaries served as intermediaries between the Chinese workers and Allied officers. Armed with an in-depth knowledge of Chinese culture, Red Triangle secretaries addressed the diet problem and explained cultural issues. YMCA secretaries taught illiterate Chinese to read and write in their own language and offered courses in English, French, geography, and history to educated laborers. The association printed a newspaper in Chinese that helped the labor corps members keep abreast of war news and home. To bolster morale, secretaries promoted traditional Chinese theater and festivals. To keep fit, the workers were introduced to soccer, football, volleyball, boxing, and baseball as well as traditional Chinese games such as kite-flying, throwing the stone lock, lifting double stone wheels, and battledore and shuttlecock. One report demonstrated the effect the association representatives could have:

> A great gulf yawned between the 1,400 Chinese, secured to drain and prepare flying fields in an aviation camp in France, and their English-speaking officers. No one in camp could speak the two languages intelligently or act as an intermediary between the two races. Every few days, there was a strike or a riot. . . .
>
> While the situation was at its very worst, there arrived a Mandarin-speaking missionary, one Charles A. Leonard. The Chinese welcomed him as a father and were glad to do anything he suggested. For seven years he had worked in Shantung Province where some of them had known him in their own city, Laichowfu. The Americans also welcomed him, and with a great sigh of relief. Here at last was some one who could bridge the gulf.
>
> Soon after his arrival, there was a great noise in the camp and Leonard was hastily summoned. He found agitated laborers, gesticulating and chattering as they crowded about an American officer, who was vainly trying to quiet them. Pushing his way into the near mob, the Mandarin-speaking missionary motioned for silence, questioning the leaders. Then he turned to the

laborers. "This is not the way we do things in China," said he. "When we have important matters pending, we do not settle them riotously in the middle of the road. We settle them with dignity, and in order, over a cup of tea." "Yes, it is true," they said. "We will wait until we can sit down quietly and decide this over a cup of tea." And so it came to pass that a cup of tea quelled an impending riot in a Chinese labor battalion in France. (Leonard 1919, 375)

The American YMCA sent 131 secretaries to work with the Chinese Labor Corps in France, which included twenty-seven Chinese secretaries, and operated 140 huts. By improving relations between the Chinese laborers and Allied officers, the workers became more productive and played a critical role in preparing the defensive trench systems for the retreating Allied armies during the German spring offensive of 1918 (Leonard 1919, 375, 410–411; Webster 1919, 232–235; Young Men's Christian Association 1919; Young Men's Christian Association National War Work Council 1920, 59–60; Taft, Harris, Kent, and Newlin 1922b, 364–368).

A few months later, the war was over and the two million men of the AEF prepared to go home. The association, however, still had work to do, as one secretary noted at the time:

> The great machine that had been throwing men across the ocean into France now has to be reversed. All the big, nervous effort that had preceded the Armistice had stopped short. The excitement was over. A long, dull pause had ensued. Men had begun to fret and fear about their jobs at home; to ponder at leisure the possible personal cost of their war period. Mail service had been exceedingly defective. For many months, in many cases, home news had been entirely shut off. Meantime in America the influenza had slain its thousands, and every man who failed to hear from family dreaded the possible truth. (Mayo 1920e, 380)

Shipping was in short supply, however, as the British reserved their ships for the repatriation of their troops (British shipping carried almost 50 percent of American troops to Europe) and food shipments for Europe took priority. The AEF estimated that the repatriation of American forces to the United States would take seven months. To maintain American army morale, YMCA secretaries continued their fourfold program for U.S. troops (Young Men's Christian Association National War Work Council 1920, 47). Between August 1918 and July 1919, for instance, the Religious Work Department maintained 721 secretaries (including ninety-seven women) to co-ordinate religious programs in the huts. The YMCA continued to hold services on Sundays after the fighting ended. In addition, secretaries gave away religious literature including Bibles and Bible study courses, Testaments, religious books, and tracts to soldiers. Between October 1918 and June 1919, the Religious Work Department distributed over 11.5 million items to members of the AEF (Von Schrader and Jones 1920, 283–285; Young Men's Christian Association National War Work Council 1920, 183–184; Taft, Harris, Kent, and Newlin 1922a, 607–616).

In preparing soldiers for demobilization and returning to civilian life, the army and the YMCA also recognized that education would play an important role. The AEF simply lacked the resources and expertise to organize an educational system for servicemen after the Armistice. The Y, in comparison, believed that education would prepare men to become better and more productive citizens. In October 1918, the AEF issued General Order No. 192, which standardized educational programs under the YMCA. Under this plan, the YMCA Army Education Commission would establish schools, standardize textbooks, and establish a general educational system for soldiers in France. This program placed a great deal of responsibility on the YMCA, and General Order No. 9, issued in January 1919, modified the original plan. The association no longer established schools but developed courses and materials and recruited education experts.

General Order No. 30, announced in February 1919, gave the association even broader authority; it would organize divisional schools, set up a 25-hour school week (five hours of instruction a day, five days a week), and establish an American university at Beaune. In response to this challenge, the YMCA placed the largest single order for books and supplies, up to that time, for two million men at a cost of $2 million. The association recruited 600 teachers in the United States to teach history, American and European institutions, and technical courses. Secretaries also took a census of U.S. soldiers in France with education experience and identified 40,000 teachers. Courses ranged from basic reading and writing for illiterate troops to university courses for college students. Advanced students also gained the opportunity to study at French and British universities. In January 1919 the YMCA began organizing the AEF University at Beaune, an unfinished hospital camp. The new university consisted of 375 buildings, which included chemistry and botany labs, and a staff of 1,000 educators. In March 1919, the first 500 men matriculated, and by that April, 6,000 students had enrolled. The university offered 240 courses in thirty-six departments in eleven schools. As one report revealed, it was a rather informal arrangement:

> With the exception of teachers of French and of Art, all the staff of this extraordinary school were drawn from the doughboy ranks. And every one of them works without pay, for pure joy of once more using his mind to some purpose. . . . Each one, out of the fullness of real gratitude [is thankful] for offering him "the opportunity to be a man again."
>
> That opportunity came in two shapes. Of these, the first was exemplified in a husky private who came to ask for instruction in engineering. While his own affair was being arranged, he chances to hear other men begging for lessons in trigonometry and calculus. But there is no teacher for them. "Say, I'll teach those chaps, if you like. I can handle 'trig and calculus,'" he breaks in eagerly. And the would-be engineer student, added to "the faculty," soon becomes so enthralled with the pleasure and interest of lending a hand to the many who need him that he quite forgets his personal quest.
>
> The second form of opportunity may be illustrated by the bookkeeping and accounting classes. These were largely composed of men who had held positions as bookkeepers and accountants at home. Yet their experience had been overlaid by a year and a half at war. Their minds had been forcibly turned and held away from former channels. Now, on the eve of homegoing, and with the necessity of fighting for their old livelihood imminent, they were perturbed, bewildered—worrying lest they should find themselves out of the race—unable to handle their old jobs against stay-at-home competition. (Mayo 1920e, 380)

The YMCA reported that 1.4 million American soldiers participated in lectures on general education, business, citizenship, and agriculture across France during the post-Armistice period. Almost 700,000 men were enrolled in army schools (342,000), post schools (130,000), agriculture schools (100,000), divisional schools (55,000), French universities (7,000), the American university at Beaune (6,000), vocational schools (5,800), the farm school at Allerey (2,300), and British universities (2,100). At the request of the YMCA Army Education Commission, the AEF took over the educational program on 15 April 1919. The army commended the association for its efforts and reimbursed the Y with $11.5 million. One additional note must be added. The National War Work Council, recognizing the importance of education and the sacrifices made by American soldiers, appropriated $4 million in 1920 for scholarships for servicemen. These grants paid for the tuition and expenses of education at YMCA schools and colleges across the country. By July 1920 the association had distributed 25,000 scholarships to ex-servicemen. This program became a model for the G.I. Bill, which encouraged soldiers to go to college following World War II (Mayo 1920b, 244–247; 1920e, 379–381; Von Schrader and Jones 1920, 280–283; Young Men's Christian Association National War Work Council 1920, 150–161; *The United States Army in the World War* 1992, 653–654; Taft, Harris, Kent, and Newlin 1922b, 1–25).

When the time came to prepare for embarkation on transports home, the U.S. Army established forwarding camps at Saint Aignan and Le Mans. A housing shortage quickly emerged as the army assigned 250,000 troops to the base. Troops took a medical exam, got deloused, and received new uniforms. Morale was threatened because these men expected to go home immediately after arriving at the base. The YMCA responded by organizing 400 centers in the region around Le Mans with a staff of 580 secretaries (including 268 women). The association set up twenty-seven wooden huts, seventy-one tents, and other facilities including theaters, clubs, and hotels.

Educational programming centered on nine schools in eleven buildings. Fifty-four teachers offered courses in ninety-eight subjects and maintained a diverse lecture series. The American Library Association (ALA) supplied books and the latest American magazines for the camp libraries. The Overseas Entertainment Bureau continued to book performances. In March 1919 alone, the Y sponsored 3,078 performances for a total audience of 3.5 million soldiers. Religious work remained a priority; every hut offered two divine services a week with the support of army chaplains. In April and May 1919, secretaries reported that 2,484 services, with an attendance of almost 475,000 men, and 304 Bible classes were held in association huts. The army stressed the importance of sports to maintain morale, and the YMCA assigned thirty physical directors to the Le Mans region. In March 1919, 525,000 soldiers participated in YMCA games, including fifteen athletic meets. In May 1919, the association supported twenty-nine baseball leagues in Le Mans (Mayo 1920b, 244–247; 1920e, 379–381; Young Men's Christian Association National War Work Council 1920, 47–49; Taft, Harris, Kent, and Newlin 1922b, 163–178).

When troops finally boarded transports home, the YMCA accompanied them. Secretaries gave soldiers friendly send-offs as they left France and England. Red Triangle workers maintained relief services on the ships, and secretaries met the troop ships in the United States. Soldiers then traveled by train to demobilization camps. Red Triangle workers distributed choco-late, gum, cigarettes, postcards, and magazines on these trains. During World War I, association secretaries worked on 10,000 troop trains and served six million men. In terms of YMCA demobilization, doughboys had first priority. The first American secretaries did not leave Europe until May 1919. Their exodus, however, grew significantly in June and July as 4,200 secretaries headed home across the Atlantic. By July 1919 only 150 Ameri-can secretaries remained in France to supervise the salvage of equipment (Young Men's Christian Association National War Work Council 1920, 50–51; Taft, Harris, Kent, and Newlin 1922b, 175–178).

Not all American soldiers were able to go home at the end of hostilities. The nine divisions of the Third Army became the American Army of Occu-pation in Germany by the terms of the Armistice. The YMCA accompanied these soldiers. By April 1919 the association operated 425 full-time centers and eighty-three part-time huts equipped with portable cinemas and visited by rolling canteens. Secretaries developed an entertainment program to maintain the morale of the troops. During the first six months of occupa-tion duty, the YMCA sponsored 7,654 shows (4,935 performances by sol-diers) and supported 214 shows on tour. Motion pictures remained popular; fifty-five centers had movie projectors, and projectors on sixty-three trucks offered a mobile service. The association averaged over 100 movie shows every night.

Secretaries also promoted education. The Y arranged for 1,010 instruc-tors to give classes, and the ALA sent 40,000 new magazines to the dough-boys in Germany. In terms of religious work, the association provided two religious work directors for each division (a total of eighteen) and recruited religious speakers and singers to support divine services.

As in France, the YMCA stressed athletics for the troops in Germany. Sec-retaries organized mass games, basketball, baseball, football, and track and field events. The Army of Occupation conducted its own championship competition in 1919 at the large athletic field near Coblenz, the headquar-ters of the Third Army. The association requisitioned the *Festhalle* in Coblenz, the city's town hall. The building's lobby accommodated 1,500 men, the restaurant held 500 diners, the auditorium seated 2,500, and the facility featured a library stocked with American books, pool tables, bowling alleys, game rooms, and lounges. The building was packed every night.

Given the success of the leave areas in France, the Third Army command asked the YMCA to set up leave areas in Coblenz, Neuwied, Andernach,

Trier, and Neuenahr. The association acquired nineteen hotels and restaurants to accommodate American troops and developed tour guides to identify places of interest. Secretaries offered sightseeing tours of the major German fortress at Ehrenbreitstein and secured seven Rhein excursion steamers with a total capacity of 3,500 seats. Lecturers described the history, geography, and legends of the region as soldiers sailed down the Rhine (Von Schrader and Jones 1920, 291–293; Young Men's Christian Association National War Work Council 1920, 41–46, 129–130, 181–182; Taft, Harris, Kent, and Newlin 1922a, 616–618; 1922b, 157, 200–216).

American YMCA secretaries also played an important role in nation-building in Eastern Europe during the waning months of the national war work effort. Red Triangle workers who had supported the Czechoslovak Legion across Russia accompanied these troops on their voyage back to Czechoslovakia. President Masaryk and the Czech people welcomed the association, and these secretaries laid the foundation for a new Czechoslovak National YMCA movement. By October 1919 the International Committee had assigned forty American secretaries to develop the association program in the new state. The American YMCA was also active in Poland after the war. American secretaries who worked with General Haller's Polish army in France traveled with the troops to Poland after the Armistice. The Polish government appreciated American assistance, and in 1919 the International Committee sent thirty-nine secretaries to support the development of a Polish National YMCA. When the Poles invaded the Ukraine in April 1920, the beginning of the Russo-Polish War, American secretaries provided the fourfold program to Polish troops. When the Red Army counterattacked in June 1920, the American secretaries remained with the retreating Polish army, even when it was almost certain that the Russians would capture Warsaw. Because of their unwavering support, the YMCA became a strong institution in Poland. American secretaries also conducted welfare operations in Estonia, Latvia, Lithuania, Austria, and Hungary, offering services to repatriated prisoners of war and the flood of refugees. These workers helped establish national associations in these lands (Davis 1920a; 1920b; 1921; Young Men's Christian Association National War Work Council 1920, 94–100; Taft, Harris, Kent, and Newlin 1922b, 458–475).

To undertake this monumental war relief program, the YMCA had to develop a system of financing its activities. When the association began WPA operations early in 1915, John Mott turned to a few wealthy individuals for philanthropic contributions. As the scope of the war increased, the YMCA had to develop new sources of income. After the United States entered the war, the association conducted three national financial campaigns, seeking small donations from large numbers of people. The first Y campaign, held from 26 April to 3 May 1917, raised over $5 million; and the second, conducted from 11 to 19 November 1917, resulted in over $53 million. In 1918, the Seven Sisters pooled their resources and organized the United War Work Council. By unanimous decision, the council elected Mott as the director general. The United Campaign, held from 11 to 18 November 1918, raised over $203 million, a record outpouring of American generosity. This total was apportioned pro rata among the Seven Sisters, and the YMCA received a 58.65 percent allocation, or $100.7 million. This financial drive was so successful that it became the model for today's United Way, considered among the most efficient and effective means for funding social programs (Mott 1918a, 277–278; 1918b, 364–365; "How the YMCA Will Spend Its Surplus" 1920, 48; Young Men's Christian Association National War Work Council 1920, 205–206; Taft, Harris, Kent, and Newlin 1922a, 227–247).

Motivation was a critical issue in terms of the scope of social welfare services soldiers received during the Great War. The U.S. Army sought physically fit and intelligent men to serve in the ranks and saw the association's program of athletic competition and education as a means to improve the caliber of American soldiers. The Y also offered a strong morale enhancement program based on entertainment and diversions from vice. American families hoped the YMCA's whole environment overseas would help soldiers avoid straying from traditional values. As former secretary of state William Jennings Bryan wrote,

> I had the chance to learn something of the YMCA's usefulness in times of war as well as during my more than 30 years active membership. During the very brief time that I was myself a soldier, now nearly 19 years ago, one of the things with which I was impressed, as one must be when one is in camp, was the new temptations that surround the young men, many of them away from home for the first time. . . . When these boys go to the front each one goes carrying the hopes of a home, and every mother who gives her boy to the war is anxious that that boy shall come home as good morally as he was when he went away. I believe that it is just as necessary that they should be fed with spiritual nourishment as that their bodies be fed. The government cannot do this, but this organization can. (Bryan 1917, 479)

For the YMCA, the war was an opportunity to serve vulnerable young men, not only to survive the war, but also to come home better men. Through the association's wide range of programs, doughboys would naturally gravitate toward the Red Triangle hut for educational classes, entertainment, sporting competitions, spiritual solace, or just a place to unwind from the demands of military discipline. The association sought members, but it also wished to perform services for young men. As Conrad Hoffman explained to his daughter, "How glad I was able to tell her, yes, God cared for these men; that that was one of the reasons, if not the chief one, why I was there" (Hoffman 1920, 92).

The association also provided an invaluable service to the United States government in helping the Wilson administration meet its international obligations to address the needs of prisoners of war as a neutral power. More importantly, the YMCA offered a wide range of relief operations for American and Allied troops once the United States entered the war. The U.S. Army lacked resources and expertise to provide entertainment to enhance troop morale, to develop an educational system to produce better soldiers and citizens, and to improve the physical fitness of American troops. During the course of the war, the YMCA and its "Sisters" developed a more efficient means of raising financial resources to support their relief efforts through the United War Work Campaign. The association's experience operating the army's post exchange system in France led to a great deal of controversy after the war, but the Y's solution led to the establishment of the American Legion, an organization designed to help ex-servicemen resume their civilian lives. In response to the Great Depression, the federal government began to play a far greater role in mobilizing national resources to address welfare problems. When the United States entered World War II, the Roosevelt administration recognized the value of nationalizing the welfare role played by the Seven Sisters and organized the United Services Organization. After that war, the Truman administration instituted the G.I. Bill, modeled on the YMCA scholarship, to encourage servicemen to enter college after their demobilization. Finally, the United Way emerged as an umbrella organization for a wide range of social welfare agencies and utilizes the financial drives developed by the Seven Sisters during World War I. The YMCA had a revolutionary impact on relief operations during the Great War, not only in the United States but around the world.

—*Kenneth Steuer*

References and Further Reading

"American Sports in France." 1929. *For the Millions of Men Now under Arms* 3, 14 (10 March): 34–35.

"American Troops." 1919. *For the Millions of Men Now under Arms* 3, 14 (10 March): 28–29.

Boyd, Nancy. 1986. *Emissaries: The Overseas Work of the American YWCA, 1895–1970.* New York: Women's Press.

Brown, R. J. 1919. "The Salvation Army in War and Peace." *Independent* 98 (17 May): 252–253.

Bryan, William Jennings. 1917. "Bring My Boy Home Clean." *Association Men* 39 (June): 479.

Carter, Michael D. 1994. "The Crusade for God and Country: The Role of the YMCA in Europe and Russia, 1915–1920." *Fides et Historia* 26: 58–70.

Caviglia, Enrico. 1919. "Italy, America, and the Y." *Independent* 98 (17 May): 245.

Chandler, Susan Kerr. 1995. "That Biting, Stinging Thing Which Ever Shadows Us: African-American Social Workers in France during World War I." *Social Science Review* 69: 498–514.

Chesham, Sally. 1965. *Born to Battle: The Salvation Army in America.* Chicago: Rand McNally.

Colton, Ethan T. 1940. *Forty Years with Russians.* New York: Association.

Davis, Darius A. 1917. "Italy: For Soldiers." *For the Millions of Men Now under Arms* 2, 10 (1 February): 35.

———. 1920a. "Visit to France, Italy, Czecho-Slovakia, and Poland with Dr. John R. Mott (May–June 1920)." *For the Millions of Men Now under Arms* 3, 16.

———. 1920b. "War Work of the Young Men's Christian Association in Poland and Czechoslovakia." *For the Millions of Men Now under Arms* 3, 15.

———. 1921. "The Young Men's Christian Association in Poland." *For the Millions of Men Now under Arms* 3, 19.

Eddy, Sherwood. 1917. *With Our Soldiers in France.* New York: Association.

Egan, Maurice Francis, and John B. Kennedy. 1920. *Knights of Columbus in Peace and War,* vol. 1. New Haven, Conn.: Knights of Columbus.

Evan, James W., and Gardiner L. Harding. 1921. *Entertaining the American Army: The American State and Lyceum in the World War.* New York: Association.

"Extracts from a Letter from a Secretary Who Has Recently Returned to Switzerland from Austria-Hungary." 1915. *For the Millions of Men Now under Arms* 1, 1 (1 March): 15–16.

"For the Men Who Are Rebuilding Europe." 1921. *For the Millions of Men Now under Arms* 3, 17 (28 January).

"A Foyer Secretary on Free Distribution." 1919. *For the Millions of Men Now under Arms* 3, 14 (10 March): 47.

"The Foyers du Soldat." 1918. *Outlook* 118 (3 April): 524–525.

Galloway, Tod B. 1920. "The Trail of a Jongleur: A Fascinating Tale of Wartime Musical Experience." *Etude* (February): 95.

Heald, Edward T. 1972. *Witness to Revolution: Letters from Russia, 1916–1919*. Kent, Ohio: Kent State University Press.

Hergesheimer, Joseph. 1918. "What the YMCA Does with Its Millions." *Current Opinion* 65 (November): 334.

Hoffman, Conrad. 1920. *In the Prison Camps of Germany: A Narrative of "Y" Service among Prisoners of War*. New York: Association.

Hopkins, C. Howard. 1979. *John R. Mott, 1865–1955: 20th-Century Ecumenical Statesman*. Grand Rapids, Mich.: William B. Eerdmans.

"How the YMCA Will Spend Its Surplus." 1920. *Literary Digest* 65 (5 June): 48.

Howland, Harold. 1919. "Putting the Y in Italy." *Independent* 98 (17 May): 245–247, 266–271.

International Committee Monthly Meeting Minutes, 1909–1916. 1916. "Summary of Minutes of Regular Monthly Meetings of the International Committee of the Young Men's Christian Associations." 8 October 1914, 12 November 1914, and 10 December 1914. New York: YMCAs of the USA Archives, University of Minnesota, Minneapolis.

Kauffman, Christopher J. 2001. *Patriotism and Fraternalism in the Knights of Columbus: A History of the Fourth Degree*. New York: Crossroad.

Kennedy, John B. 1919. "Why the Knights of Columbus Made Good." *Outlook* 121 (16 April): 665.

Latourette, Kenneth. 1957. *World Service: A History of the Foreign Work and World Service of the Young Men's Christian Associations of the United States and Canada*. New York: Association.

Leonard, Charles A. 1919. "A Cup of Tea and a Riot: Language Difficulties between the Chinese and the Americans." *Association Men* 44 (January): 375, 410–411.

Lowry, Alfred, Jr. 1917. "Needs of Prisoners in Bavaria." *For the Millions of Men Now under Arms* 2, 11 (1 June): 47–48.

Mayo, Katherine. 1920a. "Billy's Hut." *Outlook* 124 (28 January): 150–152.

———. 1920b. "Bookwalter's Renaissance." *Outlook* 124 (11 February): 244–247.

———. 1920c. "The Colonel's Lady." *Outlook* 124 (4 February): 190–192.

———. 1920d. *"That Damned Y": A Record of Overseas Service*. Boston: Houghton Mifflin.

———.1920e. "The Yankee Schoolmarm." *Outlook* 124 (3 March): 379–381.

McKinley, E. H. 1995. *Marching to Glory: The History of the Salvation Army in the United States, 1880–1992*. Grand Rapids, Mich.: William B. Eerdmans.

Mott, John R. 1918a. "The Largest Voluntary Offering in History." *Association Men* 44 (December): 277–278.

———. 1918b. "Who Wants Millions for U.S. Army War Work." *Current Opinion* 65 (November): 364–365.

New York Times Current History of the European War, vols. 1–3. 1914, 1915 original. Republished 1995, CD-ROM, as *The European War: New York Times Current History.*

O'Neill, Patrick. 1989. "Entertaining the Troops." *Beaver* 69: 59–62.

Perkins, George W. 1917. "The YMCA in War Work: Where Men Can Throw off Military Discipline and Be 'Hail Fellow Well Met' with One Another." *Scientific American* 117 (1 December): 421.

Potter, Frank Hunter. 1919. "War Work of the YMCA: Story of the Association's Services at the Front in Europe and Asia through Four Years." 1919. *New York Times Current History* 9, part 2 (March): 478–483.

"The Red Triangle in East Africa." 1918. *Red Triangle Bulletin* 52 (26 July): 1–4.

"Refitting the YMCA to War." 1918. *Literary Digest* 56 (2 March): 36–37.

Roz, Firmin. 1919. "The 'Y' with the French Army (a French View)." 1919. *Living Age* 300 (4 January): 14–17.

"The Secret Chart, by Junius." 1918. *For the Millions of Men Now under Arms* 2, 13 (10 June): 3–4.

"A Shining Mark." 1919. *Outlook* 121 (8 January): 49.

"Some Good Words for the YMCA." 1919. *Literary Digest* 61 (12 April): 31.

Steuer, Kenneth. 2004. *The American YMCA and Prisoner of War Diplomacy with the Central Powers during the First World War, 1914–1923.* New York: Columbia University Press.

Surface, Frank M., and Raymond L. Bland. 1931. *American Food in the World War and Reconstruction Period: Operations of the Organizations under the Direction of Herbert Hoover, 1914–1924.* Stanford, Calif.: Stanford University Press.

Taft, William Howard, Frederick Harris, Frederic Houston Kent, and William J. Newlin, eds. 1922a. *Service with Fighting Men: An Account of the American Young Men's Christian Associations in the World War,* vol. 1. New York: Association.

———. 1922b. *Service with Fighting Men: An Account of the Work of the Young Men's Christian Associations in the World War,* vol. 2. New York: Association.

The United States Army in the World War, 1917–1919, Volume 16: General Orders, GHQ, AEF. 1992. Washington, D.C.: Center for Military History, United States Army.

Von Schrader, A., and Paul Fortier Jones, eds. 1920. "America's Spontaneous Answer: History of Some of the Organizations that Arise in Time of Need." In *The Armies of Mercy: The Vast Relief Work in All the Nations.* New York: Harper and Brothers.

Wannamaker, Olin D. 1923. *With Italy in Her Final War of Liberation: A Story of the "Y" on the Italian Front.* New York: Fleming H. Revell.

"War Department Probe of YMCA." 1919. *Literary Digest* 61 (10 May): 34.

Webster, C. R. 1918. "Wide Open Africa." *Association Men* 43 (February): 432–433.

Webster, James. 1919. "With the Chinese in France." *Red Triangle* 2 (February): 232–235.

"What the YMCA Is Doing for Our Soldiers." 1917. *Current Opinion* 63 (September): 188–189.

Wheeler, Crawford. 1917. "The Red Triangle at Moscow." *For the Millions of Men Now under Arms* 2, 12 (1 November): 15–16.

Whitehair, Charles W. 1918. *Out There.* New York: D. Appleton.

Wilson, Woodrow. 1917. "A Message from the President." *Association Men* 42 (June): 478.

Wisbey, Herbert A., Jr. 1956. *Soldiers Without Swords: A History of the Salvation Army in the United States.* New York: Macmillan.

"With the East African Forces: A Chapter from the War History of the Red Triangle." 1919. *Red Triangle Bulletin: British YMCA Monthly* 2 (August): 451–454.

"Women's Work in the 'Y.'" 1919. *Literary Digest* 63 (25 October): 35–36.

"Workers in Defense of the YMCA." 1919. *Literary Digest* 60 (4 January): 32, 38–39, 42.

"World's Committee of Young Men's Christian Associations Plenary Meeting of 1920 at Geneva: Report of the Executive for the Period July 1914 to June 1920." 1921. *Sphere* 2, 3: 193–195.

"The YMCA in Italy." 1919. *American Review of Reviews* 60 (September): 324–325.

"YMCA Shortcomings as Seen by Our Soldiers: The Organization's Present Unpopularity Attributed to Many Factors." 1919. *Current Opinion* 66 (March): 178–179.

"The YMCA under Fire." 1919. *Missionary Review of the World* 42 (February): 88–89.

"The YMCA Viewed at the Front." 1919. *Literary Digest* 60 (18 January): 29–30.

"The YMCA's Mistake." 1919. *Literary Digest* 60 (15 March): 36.

Young, Arthur P. 1980. "Aftermath of a Crusade: World War I and the Enlarged Program of the American Library Association." *Library Quarterly* 50: 191–207.

Young Men's Christian Association. 1919. *With the Chinese Labor Corps in France.* Paris: Association.

Young Men's Christian Association National War Work Council. 1920. *Summary of World War Work of the American YMCA: With the Soldiers and Sailors of America at Home, on the Sea, and Overseas.* New York: Association.

PRISONERS OF WAR IN WORLD WAR I

British and Allied Civilian Internees
at Ruhleben Camp, Germany

———————◆———————

THE PRACTICE OF HOLDING CIVILIANS AS HOSTAGES IS AN age-old custom in time of war, although in the relatively "civilized" eighteenth and nineteenth centuries it largely ceased to occur, at least in wars between European nations. At the end of the nineteenth century and the beginning of the twentieth, it is true, the Spanish in Cuba and the British in South Africa both carried out the selective detention of noncombatants in "concentration camps." It was only during World War I, however, that civilian internment became a universal phenomenon, carried out on all sides, albeit often in a haphazard and arbitrary manner (Audoin-Rouzeau and Becker 2000, 87). Indeed, between 1914 and 1918 at least 400,000 civilians were imprisoned as "enemy aliens," not only in Europe but also in Africa, India, Australia, and North and South America (Speed 1990, 141–153; Farcy 1995; Fischer 1989; Luebke 1987; Nagler 2000; Panayi 1993, 53–75; 1991, 70–98; De Roodt 2000). In Great Britain and its colonies, for instance, some 36,000 German and Austrian citizens were being held in internment camps by 1917 (Panayi 1991, 87). In Germany, too, all male British citizens aged seventeen to fifty-five were detained at the

Ruhleben Camp in Spandau, near Berlin. Women, children, and men over fifty-five were exempt from internment but were subject to a variety of restrictions on their movement, including the requirement to carry passports and report regularly to their local police station. In some cases, they did not see their fathers, sons, or husbands again for over four years (Jahr 1999, 297–321).

In total, about 4,000 Britishers were arrested on the morning of 6 November 1914 and taken to Ruhleben under armed escort. The immediate reason given for this measure was the failure of the British government to respond to an ultimatum demanding the release of German citizens held in Britain. In January and February 1915 the internment order was also extended to embrace all male subjects of the British Empire, including Australians, Canadians, and South Africans. Among those taken into German military custody were businessmen, professionals, academics, and sportsmen, as well as a handful of unlucky tourists who had been trapped by the outbreak of war. The largest group, however (about 35 percent of the total), was made up of merchant sailors who had initially been held on ships at Hamburg and were brought from there to Berlin (Stibbe 2005, 8-13).

Apart from the sailors, few of the internees had known each other before the war. Some had lived in Germany all their lives and had sided with Germany at the start of the war, but the majority were decidedly pro-British in outlook. This can also be seen in the organization and cultural life of the camp (Powell and Gribble 1919; Ketchum 1965).

The camp itself was situated on a former race course in the industrial district of Spandau, two miles to the west of Berlin in its pre-1920 boundaries. In German, the word *Ruhleben* means "quiet life," but this was hardly what the internees experienced. They were expected to sleep in the unheated horse stables (described by the German military authorities as barracks), which were extremely overcrowded and had no proper ventilation or electric lighting. Lack of access to hot water for washing and primitive toilet arrangements added to the range of discomforts experienced during the first months of internment. One former inmate, V. V. Cusden, later recalled how

> In the very cold weather, especially when the temperature fell to 24 degrees Centigrade below zero, the walls and ceilings of the lofts would be covered with sheets of ice. Our breath would also congeal into icicles on our blankets. (Cusden n.d., p. 32)

According to Cusden, the food too was "execrable," consisting mainly of German black bread and "thin pea or bean soup, too often . . . not fully cooked, which played havoc with our bowels" (Cusden n.d., 33). After the first few weeks, however, regular Red Cross parcels began to reach the camp from Denmark and Switzerland, which included supplies of fresh food and loaves of bread. The prisoners also hired a part of the race track for gardens to grow their own vegetables, which meant that their average daily diet improved somewhat as time went on. In some ways, indeed, the Ruhlebenites were better off than ordinary German civilians, who were subject to increasing privations as a result of the ever-tightening Allied economic blockade (Cusden n.d., 35–36; Vincent 1985; Davis 2000).

In addition to growing their own food, the prisoners also began to organize themselves to create a more efficient internal administration for the camp and to look after the welfare of its inhabitants. Although Count Schwerin, an elderly retired general, was the nominal commandant, the real responsibility for running the camp was given to his deputy, Baron von Taube (known as "the baron"). One of Taube's first acts was to order the appointment of a "captain" for each "barrack" to act as sole intermediary between the prisoners and the military authorities. The barrack captains in turn formed a "captains' committee," with Joseph Powell, a former cinema owner from Leeds, assigned the job of overall "camp captain." Order within the camp was maintained not by the guards but by an internal police force recruited from among the prisoners themselves. Other prisoners were placed in charge of the internal postal service and medical barracks. Finally, in September 1915 Taube granted a form of "home rule" to the prisoners, withdrawing all guards from the barracks and confining their duties to patrolling the perimeter walls and fences. This situation continued until the end of the war (Ketchum 1965, 101).

Unlike British prisoners of war captured on the battlefield, the inmates of Ruhleben had little or no work forced upon them. Apart from morning roll-calls and mealtimes, most of the day was their own, and boredom became a real problem. A fortnightly magazine, *In Ruhleben Camp,* was formed, as was a "sports control committee," which organized a football (soccer) and cricket league. Soccer was indeed played from the first day to the last, with up to eight league games a day during some seasons (Ketchum 1965, 193).

There was also a Ruhleben Debating Society, a Ruhleben Dramatic Society, and even a Société Dramatique Française du Ruhleben. Theatrical and musical productions were performed regularly on a stage under Grand

A boxing match at Ruhleben Concentration Camp, 1918. (Photograph courtesy of the State Library of South Australia. SLSA:PRG 982/1.8)

Stand 1, often in the presence of the camp commandant and his wife. In April 1916, for instance, the entertainments committee organized a tercentenary Shakespeare festival, including performances of *Twelfth Night* and *Othello* and a program of lectures and Shakespearean music. Other performances included the staging of Gilbert and Sullivan's *The Mikado,* complete with younger men dressed up as Japanese geisha girls (programs for all these events can be found in the Landesarchiv Berlin, Rep. 120, Acc. 1884, B6c., and in the Liddle Collection, Brotherton Library, University of Leeds).

One of the most striking events organized by the Ruhleben Debating Society was the staging of a mock election in July and August 1915 in order to ensure that the "borough of Ruhleben" was properly represented at Westminster (*The Ruhleben Bye-Election* 1915). A total of three candidates stood: Alexander Boss (Conservative), Israel Cohen (Liberal), and Reuben Castang (Votes for Women). A mayor was also appointed to act as returning officer for the borough (*The Ruhleben Bye-Election* 1915, 7). The election campaign lasted for a week, during which the candidates and their supporters made speeches and covered the camp with posters. One of the guards kept a poultry yard, and the Conservative agent caught about six of his ducks and attached the Conservative colors to their necks. The Liberals soon hit back with a poster proclaiming, "Any goose could vote for Boss, vote for Cohen." In the end, however, it was the suffragist candidate Castang who won on the slogan "Vote for us . . . think of your wives and sweethearts and vote for Castang." Needless to say he was not allowed to travel to London to take up his seat.

Education, meanwhile, was in the hands of the Ruhleben Camp School and the Arts and Sciences Union. Courses were set up in languages, science, technical subjects such as woollen and dying trades, navigation for seamen, and commercial subjects in various languages. The camp school also had a handicrafts department with special workshops for book-binding and printing, leatherwork, and silverwork. Reverend Herbert Bury, the Anglican bishop for northern and central Europe, who visited the camp in November 1916, told a correspondent of the London *Daily Telegraph:*

> There is so much studying that I call it the University of Ruhleben. There are many branches of study—music, art, chess, languages, lectures on commerce, navigation, engineering and original research. There is a magnificent laboratory and classes are held in a loft with poor light; it is a marvellous triumph over difficulties. (Sladen 1917, 1; see also Bury 1917)

In spite of the image of solidarity put on for visitors like Bishop Bury, there were also the inevitable tensions between the prisoners, some of which could and did develop into overt manifestations of prejudice and bigotry. Class distinctions of a peculiarly British nature soon came to the fore and were exacerbated by conditions inside the camp. The more money a prisoner received from friends and relatives at home, for instance, the more he could purchase at the camp stores, thus avoiding having to rely solely on the meager rations provided by the German authorities. One or two of the wealthier inmates even paid other prisoners to dress up in white jackets and act as "stewards" for their club meetings, as American ambassador James W. Gerard observed during one of his visits to the camp (Gerard 1917, 125). Later he wrote about his time as the chief representative of British interests in Berlin:

> I found it almost impossible to get British prisoners to perform the ordinary work of cleaning up the camp and so forth . . . and so, with funds furnished

me from the British Government, the camp captain was compelled to pay a
number of poorer prisoners to perform this work. (Gerard 1917, 123)

Some sections of the camp community were subject to more systematic
forms of discrimination. The Jewish prisoners, for instance, who made up
roughly 10 percent of the camp population, were regularly taunted by the
guards with insults such as "Verdammter Judenpack!" and "Judensau!" They
were also regarded with suspicion by some of their fellow British internees,
who made jokes about them being foreign or pro-German, even though
most of the Jews were resolutely patriotic in their outlook. At first the Jewish
prisoners were held in a separate barrack, Barrack 6, which was described by
Israel Cohen as "the oldest and dirtiest stable in the compound" (Cohen
1917, 46). Later this barrack was closed down and its inmates dispersed
among the other barracks, but sporadic "Jew-baiting" continued to feature
in the daily life of the camp, in spite of the fact that the Jews played an important role in the camp community; for instance as tailors, cobblers, and
barbers and also as teachers, musicians, and actors. Cohen himself served as
the chairman of the Ruhleben Debating Society for several months, and he
also featured as the Liberal candidate in the "Ruhleben bye-election," as
noted earlier. Another Jew, F. Charles Adler, was the conductor of the camp
orchestra (Cohen 1917, 208).

While the Jews were at least partially integrated into the life of the camp,
the same cannot be said for the one hundred or so black inmates, mostly
merchant sailors from Senegal and the West Indies. Unfortunately, little is
known about this group of prisoners beyond the fact that they spent most of
their time confined to their own quarters, Barrack 13 (known by the Germans as the *Negerbaracke*), and were not allowed to take part in the usual
camp activities. One internee, G. A. Packe, noted in his diary on 16 November 1915:

Very nearly had a scrap with a party of niggers, on behalf of Lambert, with
whom one of their crowd had had trouble in [the] convalescent barrack. Another item to a/c, for mixing blacks with us Europeans here. To make matters worse the Authorities have deliberately spoilt them, out of spite to us,
and there will probably be a row before the end. (Jahr 1999, 308)

Incidents such as these are also a striking illustration of how important
the belief in the solidarity of the white race still was, even at a time when

one-half of the white race was at war with the other half. Indeed, few of the white prisoners ever got to know anything about the inner life of Barrack 13 and its inhabitants, which may well explain the condescending portraits they later drew. One internee wrote in his memoirs that "the hardships meant less—and the amusements meant more—to them than to most of us" (Gribble 1929, 313). Another declared in a pamphlet written for the Ruhleben Exhibition in London in 1919: "The coloured prisoners . . . suffered much from the cold during the winter months and were seldom seen outside their own barrack except at the compulsory roll-calls which took place daily on the race-course" (*Ruhleben Exhibition* 1919, 27).

A final group who were isolated from the rest of the camp were the "Pro-Germans" (*Deutsch-Engländer*), prisoners who openly supported the German war effort and even tried to stage a celebration to mark the kaiser's birthday on 27 January 1915. This "provocation" led to an incident in which a German imperial flag was cut down by some of the other prisoners in the middle of the night. As a result, the entire camp was placed under barrack arrest for twenty-four hours and all privileges were cancelled for a further week (Ketchum 1965, 88). By April 1915 relations between the pro-German minority and the pro-British majority had become so bad that the German authorities were forced to re-house the pro-Germans in their own barracks (known as the P. G. Barracks). Some of them later applied to be naturalized as Germans and were released after agreeing to volunteer for the German army. Nonetheless, about 600 pro-Germans preferred to stay in Ruhleben rather than do military service. As another former internee put it, "They were anti-British, and yet they were no good whatever to Germany" (Stibbe 1919, 18).

Nearly all the pro-Germans, and a good many of the other internees as well, had wives and families struggling to cope on their own in Germany. As was to be expected, the dependants of internees received no help or support from the German government. In February 1915 a British Emergency Relief Fund was eventually set up to provide financial support to the internees and their dependants via monies sent to the U.S. Embassy in Berlin (Ketchum 1965, 101; Gerard 1917, 123). A series of diplomatic negotiations conducted via American and Dutch mediation also led to the early release of some of the internees, including Israel Cohen and Sir Timothy Eden, the elder brother of future British prime minister Anthony Eden. They in turn were able to raise public awareness of the plight of the remaining internees, and to put pressure on the British government to do all it could to secure further releases, a campaign that met with some suc-cess in the exchange of the remaining "over forty-fives" in January 1918 and the repatriation of a handful of other prisoners in the summer of 1918. By November 1918, however, 2,300 men still were left in the camp (Jahr 1999, 318).

In spite of their isolation, the Ruhlebenites were not entirely unaware of events going on in the wider world. Outgoing and incoming mail was of course subject to strict military censorship, but camp inmates were allowed to buy German newspapers and, by reading between the lines, were able to gain a pretty accurate impression of the course of the war. English newspapers were banned but were nonetheless smuggled in and passed around. One of the prisoners remembered having to pay one mark an hour to read the *Daily Telegraph,* which was usually ten to fourteen days old when it arrived (Stibbe 1919, 23). The most important contact with the outside world, however, re-mained the persistent efforts of relatives and friends to secure the release of their loved ones. "Anyone who has not passed through a similar experience [of internment]," wrote the same prisoner, "will hardly realise what an in-tense relief and comfort it was to know that such enquiries were being made. It helped me to feel less out of the world" (Stibbe 1919, 3).

Some of the more trusted inmates, such as Joseph Powell, were occasion-ally allowed to leave the camp without escort in order to conduct urgent family business. Sometimes, however, the camp authorities played cruel jokes. One officer, for instance, delighted in telling prisoners that they were on the exchange lists, knowing full well that they were not. Another an-swered an inmate's request to be allowed a few days leave to visit his dying fa-ther with the words, "Why don't you wait for a couple of days, then you can attend the funeral?" (Jahr 1999, 313).

Physical violence toward internees was virtually unknown in Ruhleben, however, and conditions gradually improved, at least after the first few months This was a great contrast to the treatment of prisoners of war in other camps in Germany, where soldiers captured on the battlefield and civilians deported from the occupied areas of France, Belgium, and Russia were held (Van Emden 2000; Audoin-Rouzeau and Becker 2000, 85–105).

More difficult to assess, of course, were the psychological effects of long-term imprisonment on the internees. Certainly by 1917 there was evidence of serious mental health problems among some of the inmates, with one or two suffering complete nervous breakdowns and being confined to the psy-chiatric institution at Neu Ruppin near Berlin. A report drawn up for the

Ruhleben Concentration Camp, Wooden Barracks, East End, 1918. (Photograph courtesy of the State Library of South Australia. SLSA:PRG 982/1.7)

British government at the end of 1917 went on to allege fifty cases of "insanity" and fifty cases of "total nervous collapse," although these figures are perhaps suspiciously high (Ketchum 1965, 167–196). Letters and diaries provide more concrete evidence of specific cases but cannot be used to confirm absolute numbers. J. R. Dawson, an internee from Ripon in Yorkshire, later remembered one old sea captain from his barrack who feigned madness in order to be sent home:

> unfortunately it was a delicate business, you know, this playing with your brain in Ruhleben, and he did go mad. He started doing his business in his boots and things like that. Really genuinely off his rocker he was, but he wouldn't have gone off his rocker if he hadn't pretended that he was. (Dawson, interview with Peter Liddle, September 1977, in Liddle Collection, RUH 17)

Others found the distance from their families and the endless uncertainty about the future the hardest things to bear. Edward Morris Falk, for instance, wrote in his postwar memoirs,

To be cut off from one's relatives and friends, to be deprived of freedom of speech and pen, to know that chances in life which will never return are being missed, that one's finances are being ruined and that when the day of release comes at last one will be bankrupt or a pauper; to know that wives and children are doomed to destitution, these are the real hardships of a civilian prisoner of war, compared to which his mere physical hardships are nothing. (Falk 1920, 18)

Significantly, the exchanged prisoner Sir Timothy Eden also chose to emphasise the mental torment of internment when writing an open letter to *The Times* in November 1916, doubtless in order to increase pressure on the government to negotiate for the release of the remaining inmates:

There are no past glories to dream about. No consolation in the remembrance of duty done. The men have nothing to think of save their ruined prospects and the hopelessness of their position. Therefore, I say again that the mental state of these prisoners is most serious. And it is imperative if they are to retain their reason that they be set free at once. (*The Times*, 22 November 1916; see also Eden 1917)

For the younger and fitter internees who never made it on to the exchange lists, the last months of the war were undoubtedly the worst, especially as the political situation inside Germany became increasingly dangerous and chaotic. Indeed, by the summer of 1918 rumors began to circulate that the guards were rummaging through the bins at night looking for usable items left over from the camp kitchens. Some internees now feared that angry crowds of soldiers and civilians would storm the camp compound in search of food and that the British prisoners would all be shot in the process (Swale 1962, 17). In spite of this, the Red Cross food parcels continued to arrive from Denmark and Switzerland in good time, and even in the last weeks of the war there was no evidence of pilfering on the part of the German guards, who acted in a disciplined way to the end. This, it must be said, is truly remarkable under the circumstances.

Finally, after four long years of imprisonment, news of the impending German surrender reached the camp. On 8 November 1918 the guards formed a soldiers' council and hoisted the red flag in the middle of the camp. They also issued a proclamation declaring that Germans and Englishmen were "brothers" and that war was "unnecessary and brutal" (Stibbe 1919, 24–25). Over the next few days the prisoners were allowed to make trips into Berlin, where a republic had been proclaimed after the abdication of the Kaiser. Some of the men took scarce items such as soap and tooth-paste with them and made a handsome profit selling them on the black market. Others spent their first days of freedom sightseeing or getting drunk in bars and cafés. On 22 and 24 November the final 1,500 prisoners, who had requested repatriation to Great Britain, boarded trains for Sassnitz, from where they took a boat first to Copenhagen and then to Hull or Leith. They arrived home a week later and were greeted by cheering crowds and a special message from King George V.

The conditions inside Ruhleben internment camp were unpleasant, but they were never as bad as those experienced by British and Allied prisoners in other camps in Germany. At least as civilians the Ruhlebenites were prop-erly fed and were not required to do forced labor. There were between fifty and sixty deaths, mostly due to old age and chronic ill health, and several cases of insanity, including three suicides and three attempted suicides, but these figures are not very high, especially when set against the grand total of 750,000 POWs from all countries who died of malnutrition and disease while in enemy captivity (Ketchum 1965, 168; Rachamimov 2002, 4). Nonetheless, many of the Ruhlebenites felt that their experience of intern-ment had had a significant impact on their lives, and several of them wrote lengthy accounts of their time in German military custody. Two exhibitions about Ruhleben were held in Britain after the war, one at Westminster Hall in 1919, which was attended by the king, queen, and Princess Mary; and one organized by Humberside Libraries in 1978 to mark the sixtieth an-niversary of the release of the inmates (Humberside Libraries and Ameni-ties 1978). In addition, the Ruhleben Association, made up of former internees and their families, continued to hold annual get-togethers until the 1970s. (The annual dinners of the Ruhleben Association came to an end in 1974, at which time there were still sixty members of the association known to be alive. See Major General R. Llewellyn Brown to W. E. Swale, 28 November 1974, in Liddle Collection, RUH 52, Box 2.)

In 1945 the British returned to Ruhleben, this time as military occupiers. The district of Spandau now formed part of the British sector in the four-power division of Berlin, which lasted until 1990. During the interwar years Ruhleben had again been used as a race course, but no horses ran there after 1939, and in 1958 the site was demolished to make way for a new sewage processing plant (Ketchum 1965, 13 n.2). Today there are no physical traces left of the former internment camp, and the memory of its existence has fallen under the shadow of the far greater horrors of the concentration camps built during the Nazi era. Nonetheless, Ruhleben still holds an important place in our understanding of the experience and treatment of "enemy aliens" in the twentieth century. The fact that successive British governments failed to pay full compensation to civilian internees, and the fact that civilian POWs were rarely mentioned in official accounts of the Great War, needlessly added to their sense of grievance and reinforced the view that they had simply been pawns in a larger game of tit-for-tat played out by the great powers. Or, as one former Ruhlebenite wrote, internment was part of a worrying new trend in international politics, namely "the increasing use of human beings as mere implements of state policy ... and the readiness of millions to acquiesce in it" (Ketchum 1965, xviii).

—*Matthew Stibbe*

References and Further Reading

Audoin-Rouzeau, Stéphane, and Annette Becker. 2000. *14–18, retrouver la guerre.* Paris: Gallimard.

Austin, Summer. 1977. Interview with Peter Liddle. In Liddle Collection, Brotherton Library, University of Leeds, RUH 01.

Bury, Herbert. 1917. *My Visit to Ruhleben.* London: A. R. Mowbray.

Cohen, Israel. 1917. *The Ruhleben Prison Camp. A Record of Nineteen Months' Internment.* London: Methuen & Co.

Cusden, V. V. n.d. "Lingering Rays." Unpublished typescript recollections. Copy in Liddle Collection, Brotherton Library, University of Leeds, RUH 14.

Davis, Belinda J. 2000. *Home Fires Burning. Food, Politics and Everyday Life in World War I Berlin.* Chapel Hill and London: University of North Carolina Press.

Dawson, J. R. Interview with Peter Liddle, September 1977. In Liddle Collection, Brotherton Library, University of Leeds, RUH 17.

De Roodt, Evelyn. 2000. *Oorlogsgasten: Vluchtelingen en krijgsgevangenen in Nederland tijdens de Eerste Wereldoorlog.* Zaltbommel: Europese Bibliothek.

Eden, Timothy. 1917. *The Ruhleben Prisoners: The Case for Their Release.* Pamphlet issued by the Ruhleben Prisoners Release Committee. Copy in Liddle Collection, Brotherton Library, University of Leeds, RUH 18.

Falk, Edward Morris. 1920. "My Experiences in the Great War, 1914–1918." Unpublished typescript recollections. Copy in Liddle Collection, Brotherton Library, University of Leeds, RUH 22.

Farcy, Jean-Claude. 1995. *Les Camps de concentration français de la Première Guerre mondiale, 1914–1920*. Paris: Anthropos.

Fischer, Gerhard. 1989. *Enemy Aliens: Internment and the Home Front Experience in Australia, 1914–1920*. St. Lucia, Queensland: University of Queensland Press.

Gerard, James W. 1917. *My Four Years in Germany*. New York: George H. Doran.

Gribble, Francis. 1929. *Seen in Passing*. London: E. Benn.

Humberside Libraries and Amenities, ed. 1978. *Ruhleben: An Exhibition to Mark the 60th Anniversary of the Release of Local Men from the Ruhleben Internment Camp*. Kingston upon Hull: Humberside.

Jahr, Christoph. 1999. "Zivilisten als Kriegsgefangene: Die Internierung von 'Feindstaaten-Ausländern' in Deutschland während des Ersten Weltkrieges am Beispiel des 'Engländerlagers' Ruhleben." In Rüdiger Overmans, ed., *In der Hand des Feindes: Kriegsgefangenschaft von der Antike bis zum Zweiten Weltkrieg*. Cologne: Böhlau.

Ketchum, John Davidson. 1965. *Ruhleben: A Prison Camp Society*. Toronto: Toronto University Press.

Luebke, Frederick C. 1987. *Germans in Brazil. A Comparative History of Cultural Conflict During World War I*. Baton Rouge: Louisiana University Press.

Nagler, Jörg. 2000. *Nationale Minoritäten im Krieg: "Feindliche Ausländer" und die amerikanische Heimatfront während des Ersten Weltkrieges*. Hamburg: Hamburger Edition.

Panayi, Panikos. 1991. *The Enemy in Our Midst: Germans in Britain during the First World War*. Oxford: Berg.

———. 1993. "An Intolerant Act by an Intolerant Society: The Internment of Germans in Britain during the First World War." In David Cesarani and Tony Kushner, eds., *The Internment of Aliens in Twentieth Century Britain*. London: Frank Cass.

Powell, Joseph, and Francis Gribble. 1919. *The History of Ruhleben: A Record of British Organisation in a Prison Camp in Germany*. London: W. Collins & Sons.

Rachamimov, Alon. 2002. *POWs and the Great War: Captivity on the Eastern Front*. Oxford: Berg.

The Ruhleben Bye-Election. 1915. Copy in Liddle Collection, Brotherton Library, University of Leeds, RUH 20, Box 1.

Sladen, Douglas, ed. 1917. *In Ruhleben: Letters from a Prisoner to His Mother*. London: Hurst & Blackett.

Speed, Richard B., III. 1990. *Prisoners, Diplomats, and the Great War: A Study in the Diplomacy of Captivity*. New York: Greenwood.

Stibbe, Edward. 1919. *Reminiscences of a Civilian Prisoner in Germany, 1914–1918*. Leicester: Privately published pamphlet.

Stibbe, Matthew. 2001. *German Anglophobia and the Great War, 1914–1918*. New York: Cambridge University Press.

———. 2005. "A Question of Retaliation? The Internment of British Civilians in Germany in November 1914." In *Immigrants & Minorities,* 23. London: Routledge.

Swale, William Eric. 1962. "We Band of Brothers: Memoirs of Ruhleben Camp." Unpublished typescript recollections. Copy in Liddle Collection, Brotherton Library, University of Leeds, RUH 52, Box 1.

Van Emden, Richard. 2000. *Prisoners of the Kaiser: The Last POWs of the Great War.* Barnsley, South Yorkshire: Pen and Sword.

Vincent, C. Paul. 1985. *The Politics of Hunger: The Allied Blockade of Germany, 1915–1919.* Athens: Ohio University Press.

MOTHERS, WIVES, WORKERS, AND MORE

The Experience of American Women on the Home Front during World War I

———————◆———————

WITHIN DAYS OF THE OUTBREAK OF WAR IN EUROPE IN AUGUST 1914, an assortment of activist women in New York City, including suffragists, pacifists, society women, and social workers, mobilized to protest the war and to prevent the United States from becoming involved. Borrowing an effective publicity technique from the woman suffrage movement, they organized a major women-only peace parade on 29 August 1914. In early 1915, prominent reformer Jane Addams called for a meeting in Washington, D.C., to discuss the formation of a national women's peace organization. More than 3,000 women attended the meeting to form the new Woman's Peace Party (WPP) and created a platform that included a call for neutral mediation to end the European war, limitations of armaments to prevent future wars, and extending the vote to women. Under Addams's leadership, representatives from the WPP attended the International Congress of Women meeting at The Hague, Netherlands, in April 1915 to denounce the war and to explore possible ways to end it. American women

Members of the Woman's Peace Party arrive for the International Congress of Women, a four-day antiwar protest held at The Hague. Rotterdam, the Netherlands, 28 April 1915. (Corbis)

returned from the conference determined to spread support in the United States for the idea of neutral mediation to bring an end to the war.

Suffrage leader Anna Howard Shaw eloquently articulated the philosophy of the Woman's Peace Party by describing the impact of war on women, and on mothers in particular. "We see two dead," Shaw explained, whenever a soldier was killed in battle, "the man and the life of the woman who gave him birth." Seeing that dead soldier, she asked, "What does a woman know about war? What, what, friends in the face of a crime like that, what does man know about war?" (quoted in Steinson 1982, 44).

The message of peace activists—especially the belief that women, as mothers, were inherently compelled to oppose war—began to reach the public in 1915 with the help of a popular song entitled "I Didn't Raise My Boy to Be a Soldier." Advertised as a "sensational antiwar song hit," and a top-ten item in sheet music sales, the song's first verse laments the loss of soldiers' lives in Europe and mothers' sorrow for those who have gone off to war:

> *Ten million soldiers to the war have gone,*
> *Who may never return again.*
> *Ten million mothers' hearts must break*
> *For the ones who died in vain.*

The chorus assumes a passionate mother's plea:

> *I didn't raise my boy to be a soldier,*
> *I brought him up to be my pride and joy,*
> *Who dares to place a musket on his shoulder,*
> *To shoot some other mother's darling boy?* (Piantadosi and Bryan 1915)

The response to this kind of antiwar sentiment was swift and strong. At a rally for national defense held in Carnegie Hall in February 1916, one woman attacked the women's peace movement, stating: "The woman who brings up her son on the policy that she 'didn't raise her boy to be a soldier' has no right to be defended by some other woman's son" (*New York Times,* 24 February 1916, 2:6). This appeal to mothers' patriotism would be emphasized after the United States entered the war in 1917 and the Wilson administration instituted the first national draft.

Other women committed themselves to relief work for the victims of war, reacting with shock to the horrifying war news from Europe and mobilizing for a variety of voluntary efforts to aid Allied soldiers and refugees. Because the American Red Cross initially focused its efforts not on civilian relief but on aid and supplies to belligerents, a vast array of independent relief organizations proliferated so quickly in 1914 that relief efforts were marked by confusion and duplication of services (Steinson 1982, 165). Many women wanted to volunteer their services, but they often had difficulty finding an effective organization or agency to join.

In an effort to coordinate relief efforts, national women's leaders formed the Woman's Department of the National Civic Federation (WDNCF), which would later develop into the National League for Woman's Service, an umbrella organization for networking, organizing, and assessing needs and services. WDNCF leaders formed, just to name a few, the Surgical Dressings Committee (SDC), the National Patriotic Relief Society, and the National League for Woman's Service. The SDC was headquartered in New York but included subcommittees in several other American cities and was composed of a large volunteer network. Between 1915 and 1917 the SDC shipped more than eighteen million surgical dressings to Europe (Steinson 1982, 169, 171).

Many American women took the well-publicized news of German atrocities in Europe very seriously. They saw especially in Belgium a cautionary tale for the United States. Could the Germans advance across the Atlantic and threaten America? More women took up the cause of "preparedness," an increase in U.S. defensive military strength, as a direct response to the formation of the Woman's Peace Party in January 1915 and the sinking of the *Lusitania* in May 1915. In July of that year, the Woman's Section of the Navy League (WSNL)—the first national women's preparedness organization—was formed. The Navy League had been organized in 1902 to promote the importance of a strong U.S. Navy.

Within one month, the WSNL had attracted 8,000 members who perceived the growing peace movement as a danger and wished to disassociate themselves from outspoken women peace activists. New members pledged to "Think, talk and work for patriotism, Americanism and sufficient national defense to keep the horrors of war far from America's home and shores forever" (Steinson 1982, 177).

Some women specifically attacked the leadership of the Woman's Peace Party. Mary Colvorcoresses, for example, denounced its leaders as "visionaries, emotionalists, [and] impractical idealists who sail about facts in an atmosphere of ethereal fancy" (Steinson 1982, 179). Others sought to counter the argument that a woman's natural role was to promote peace. Margaret Shaw Graham regretted that "many of our thoughtful women are convinced we shall have peace only if we stand before the world unarmed" but insisted that the women she knew "seem to see clearly that our best hope of real peace must come through the power to base our demands for peace upon our ability to maintain peace" by relying on "'the gun behind the door'" that "may never have to be used" (Graham 1916, 892–893).

The women of the WSNL claimed over 25,000 members by the time they held their first conference, on 15 November 1915, in Washington, D.C. The conference marked the establishment of women's service camps, called National Service Schools, which would open in summer 1916 in several states across the country. The camps consisted of two-week sessions for resident and day students following a model set by the (male) civilian training camps set up the previous summer at Plattsburgh, New York. Some suggested that the women at these camps should receive rifle and pistol training, but this idea was rejected in favor of more conventional training in the preparation of surgical dressings, first aid, knitting and sewing, preparation of nutritional diets for the sick, and hygiene. Physical training in the form of military calisthenics, drills, and marching were also compulsory for good physical conditioning, obedience, and discipline, as was attendance at afternoon lectures on the merits of preparedness, often given by well-known speakers.

The first camp, at Chevy Chase, Maryland, featured a speech by the secretary of the navy, Franklin Roosevelt. In addition, army and navy instructors were brought into the camps to teach special classes in cipher study and code work, and wireless telegraphy. There were also plans to teach aviation to some "girls"—as the *New York Times* referred to the trainees—so that they may become "aviation messengers and guides" (*New York Times*, 4 July 1916, 7:7; 11 July 1916, 6:6). Hundreds of young upper-class and upper-middle-class households (participants had to pay for the course and for their uniforms) enrolled in defense training courses in 1916.

In late spring 1917, another National Service School included more advanced courses in map reading, driving and motor repair, and advanced signaling. At a Service School cosponsored by the New York State School of Agriculture, seventy students attended a three-month course on the management of farms and general agriculture (Steinson 1981, 225–239).

Upper-class and upper-middle-class "society women" participated in the preparedness campaign in a variety of other ways. Mrs. Simon McHie of New York City hosted a "preparedness" luncheon in March 1917 in order to interest other prominent New York women in the subject of preparedness. The featured speaker at this meeting informed the women about the benefits of the "aeroplane" for national defense (*New York Times*, 7 Mar 1917, 11:2). Women at other gatherings were told that they could contribute to the preparedness effort by learning to conserve food, by practicing general "thrift and economy in household management," and by learning some basic first aid (*New York Times*, 29 Jan 1916, 10:5).

In Massachusetts, hundreds of women "in comfortable circumstances" prepared to take classes on the preparation of nutritious foods and planned to "turn their country and shore estates" into large gardens (*New York Times*,

19 March 1916, I, 12:8). In Old Orchid, Maine, prominent local suffragists organized the Women's Defense Club to instruct members in the use of firearms "so that if American women are ever called upon to defend their houses, their children and themselves, they will not be helpless as were the Belgian women" (*New York Times,* 17 February 1916, 5:4).

Some New York women organized the Women's American Supply League "to create and develop in the U.S. a militia of patriotic American women, trained and prepared for such service as women can render toward national needs" (*New York Times,* 10 July 1916, 6:2). The league planned to supply necessities both to soldiers and to families of soldiers, and to provide supplies to the Red Cross and other relief agencies for transport to hospitals as needed. Though the league was started in New York, plans were made for branches in other cities across the country as needed, depending on the demand for relief supplies (*New York Times,* 10 July 1916, 6:2).

Finally, seeking to erase the memory of the woman's peace parade in held in 1914, women organized a massive preparedness parade in New York City on 13 May 1916. Other cities followed suit over the next few months. In the New York parade, thousands of women marched in some nineteen different groups, including doctors and nurses, teachers, stenographers, department store clerks, college women, and "independent patriotic women" led by Edith Roosevelt (*New York Times,* 10 May 1916, 9:1; 14 May 1916, I, 1:6).

With the U.S. declaration of war in April 1917, the organized peace movement largely collapsed, and most local branches of the Woman's Peace Party disbanded. Most of those women who had campaigned for peace now worked wholeheartedly in support of the war effort. Many suffragists, who had formerly joined the peace movement in large numbers, now believed that their work for the war effort would prove their patriotism and usefulness, and thus improve their chances of winning the vote in the long run. War work also strengthened the women's claim to full citizenship, as did the U.S. entry into the war to "make the world safe for democracy." The mainstream National American Woman Suffrage Association encouraged its members to support the war effort while leaders pledged to maintain their work for suffrage. A few members of the more militant National Women's Party demanded full equality immediately and picketed the White House during the war.

Overall, however, only small numbers of women continued to protest the war. Emma Goldman was one example. In spring 1917 she helped found the No-Conscription League to promote draft resistance. Within several weeks, she claimed, 8,000 men had pledged not to register, and she reported that "Streams of callers besieged our office from morning till late at night; young men, mostly, seeking advice on whether they should register. . . .There were also distracted mothers, imploring us to save their boys. By the hundreds they came, wrote or telephoned" (Goldman [1931] 1970, 600–601). In June 1917, Goldman's antiwar activities led to her arrest. She was convicted of "conspiracy against the draft" and sentenced to two years in prison (Goldman [1931] 1970, 600–601).

The emotions of those mothers who were terrified of sending their boys into the army were probably the most immediate experience of war for most American women. Officials were concerned that too many mothers would be influenced by the lingering rhetoric of the peace movement's appeal to their "natural" inclination to oppose all wars. The government therefore targeted women, particularly mothers, with patriotic propaganda encouraging them to "do their part" for the war effort and show their patriotism by willingly sacrificing their sons to the army. A U.S. Navy recruiting poster pictured a woman (a mother) shaking hands with Uncle Sam as a young man (her son) looked on. She says, "Here he is, sir," and the caption at the bottom of the poster states "We need him, and you too" (Rawls 1988, 151).

Not only did the U.S. Navy need young men to enlist, but it also needed mothers to encourage their sons to enlist. In another poster, mothers on the home front were targeted for a different purpose. A gray-haired woman (a mother) is pictured with outstretched hands, imploring, "Women! Help America's sons win the war—buy U.S. government bonds" (Rawls 1988, 206). Posters were one of the most effective methods of reaching large numbers of people in these preradio days, with messages and information about the war effort. During wartime, more than twenty million posters, reflecting about 2,500 different designs, were produced to convince the public to sacrifice for the war effort, to elicit patriotism, and to stir hatred of the enemy (Rawls 1988, 11–12).

Not just sons, but husbands, fathers, brothers, uncles, and boyfriends were leaving as well. Emily Newell Blair realized that her husband "wanted to go" serve his country even though he was rejected for military service. He volunteered instead for YMCA duty overseas. Emily Blair agreed that he should go, though in retrospect she wondered if her acquiescence was "wise or foolish" because her husband came back from overseas "a disillusioned man, far more pacifist than I." When her husband left, Blair was more inspired than ever to "do her part" for the war effort, as were so many other women who sent their loved ones off to war. She traveled to Washington to expand her war work in the publicity department of the Woman's Committee of the Council of National Defense. With her husband gone, Blair tried to "put him out of my mind entirely except" when reading his letters and saying her prayers, because the thought of what might be happening to him was too much to bear. She lost herself in her work (Lass 1999, 180–181).

But how would women's war work be organized and coordinated? In 1916, the Wilson administration had created the Council of National Defense to help prepare the nation for possible war. After the United States entered the war in April 1917, the Woman's Committee of the council was created to coordinate nationwide the work that women were doing and would do to help the war effort. A poster appealed to "the spirit of woman power" in urging women to register for a local chapter of the Woman's Committee (Rawls 1988, 56). Anna Howard Shaw, until recently the head of the National American Woman Suffrage Association, was asked to serve as chair of the committee. Shaw was both eager to help the war effort and firm in her insistence that the fight for suffrage should continue even in wartime. In the Woman's Committee she hoped to establish a "civilian army of women to enhance the nation's war efforts" (Linkugel and Solomon 1991, 87).

In order to mobilize the women of the country, the Woman's Committee organized branches in every state. The goals were to establish contacts with private local women's organizations such as the Young Women's Christian Association (YWCA), to establish a network of women, to urge all women to find a way to contribute to the war effort, and to coordinate women's war work in each state. Every state had a chair with whom Anna Howard Shaw maintained close contact. The Woman's Committee established ten separate departments, including home economics, food administration, protection of women in industry, and Americanism in education of children, to organize women's work in a variety of projects.

Some of the work involved the application of technical domestic skills. Women were encouraged, for instance, to learn to dry fruits and vegetables because a shortage of canning containers was anticipated. Women of the state and local branches of the Woman's Committee established lists of potential volunteers, sold Liberty Bonds, raised funds for the Red Cross and other relief agencies, went door-to-door to elicit pledges from women to practice conservation in their homes, and distributed recipe books. Other "work" was less specific. Shaw urged women in late 1917, for example, to practice moderation during the upcoming Christmas holidays. In general, women were urged to practice thrift and to serve as positive role models (Linkugel and Solomon 1991, 82–83).

Shaw emphasized that women must be dedicated and patriotic, stating, "The women have no more right to disobey the command of the government than have the men in the country. The government has a right to conscript us to do any kind of service it needs, if we are able to do it" (Linkugel and Solomon 1991, 84).

She regularly maintained that there was a wide variety of tasks women could learn to do, often citing British women who built a "man-of-war without the assistance of a single man, from beginning to end" (Linkugel and Solomon 1991, 84). The government, she believed, should provide whatever training was necessary to prepare women for whatever jobs would be useful. To that end, the Woman's Committee published pamphlets providing information on war work for women, cooperated with agencies that were developing hospitals in France, and aided with the Liberty Loan drives (Linkugel and Solomon 1991, 89).

Despite all the work that went into organization and implementation of plans, everyone agreed there were problems with the work of the Woman's Committee. Shaw was particularly frustrated at the lack of cooperation between various groups, women's and men's groups, and the competition between relief agencies. For this reason, Shaw began to promote "placing all women's war work under 'military rules' to facilitate cooperation and efficiency," though nothing came of this suggestion (Linkugel and Solomon 1991, 89). Shaw and others were especially upset, for example, that the Woman's Committee and the American Red Cross were often competing with each other for women's volunteer efforts.

The American Red Cross was particularly successful in its recruiting efforts through the use of special appeals to mothers. Perhaps the most well-known Red Cross propaganda poster portrayed "The Greatest Mother in the World"—a Red Cross nurse posed as Mary, mother of Jesus, holding her son, a wounded soldier. National membership jumped from just under half a million before the United States entered the war to more than twenty million.

Domestic Red Cross activities focused on providing necessary supplies to soldiers and European war refugees. American women contributed knitted articles, surgical dressings, and other hospital supplies. The Red Cross of-

The
GREATEST MOTHER
in the WORLD

*A Red Cross poster
recruiting women.
(Library of Congress)*

fered Americans, and especially women, courses in hygiene and home care
of the sick, nutrition, and first aid, and relief for families of soldiers and
refugees (Gavin 1997). Red Cross War Fund Drives raised substantial sums
of money. The Red Cross Home Services Sections provided aid to sick or
disabled veterans and the families of soldiers. The Home Services Section of
the North Carolina chapter of the Red Cross alone assisted over 22,000 families, giving or loaning out almost $30,000 (Henderson 2002).

Women also created Red Cross War Camp Community Services in more
than 600 American communities to provide services and hospitality for soldiers at training camps throughout the United States. The North Carolina
War Camp Community Service Chapter attempted to surround troops "with
the influences of home" in the city of Charlotte near Camp Green, which

had a population of up to 60,000 soldiers. In the fall of 1917, the women of
Charlotte entertained between 3,000 and 4,000 soldiers at their homes for
meals. Other War Camp Community Services included various forms of entertainment for soldiers, such as concerts, movies, dances, and club and
church activities, as well as books and magazines provided from local libraries (Henderson 2002).

When the war broke out in Europe, there were only 107 local Red Cross
chapters in the United States. By the end of the war, there were almost
4,000 chapters. Members of the local chapter of the Red Cross in Indianapolis, Indiana, remembered that during the war they were frequently reminded that "Without the 'army behind the army'—that is without the
support and work of those on the home front—victory could never be won"
(Cecile and Chomel 1920, 92).

Women were praised for "cheerfully" accepting the "drudgery of the Red
Cross workroom," which could include the "deadly monotony of sewing pa-
jama seams week after week, month after month." All sorts of women volunteered, from the stenographer who volunteered on her lunch hour, in the
evenings, and on Saturdays, to the eighty-nine-year-old woman who "took
great delight in knitting for the Red Cross" and who knitted sixty-nine
sweaters and forty-five pairs of socks (Cecile and Chomel 1920, 109, 139).

The establishment of Red Cross offices in U.S. towns and cities gave
women an outlet for the impulses they felt to try to help the war effort in
any way possible. As one volunteer remarked when she made her way to the
newly opened Indianapolis chapter, "My son is in the trenches: Will you
allow me to work here at home for the Red Cross?" (Cecile and Chomel
1920, 91).

Some "society women" were mobilized to volunteer with their automo-
biles for Red Cross errands and as an informal "taxi service" to "carry pas-
sengers on important war business" (*New York Times*, 3 June 1917, IX, 7:5).
Others volunteered to learn to drive Red Cross ambulances for the Red
Cross Motor Corps, organized in March 1917. Women who wanted to join
the motor corps took courses stateside in first aid and general motor repair.
Most hoped for overseas service, and indeed many did eventually drive ambulances in Europe, but many received their first experience driving in the
Washington (D.C.) office of the corps, ferrying patients around the metro-
politan area.

Florence Jaffray Harriman became head of the Washington motor corps
before leaving for Europe in the autumn of 1917. She brought patients to

and from the Walter Reed Army Hospital. On one occasion she was "driving with my girl orderly" with "three very sick soldiers" in the back of the ambulance. The road they were on, leading out of the army camp toward Washington, was newly constructed, and during a thunderstorm their ambulance got stuck in the mud. Because "the rule was that no man, unless in uniform, could accompany us and it was very rare that an officer had time to volunteer to come along," the women needed to find help. So "the girl orderly loped off down the road until she found two kind young men" to give the ambulance a good push. This was not an unusual occurrence, and Harriman noted that her "fleet-footed orderly couldn't always find husky arms to conscript on the lonely country road," so "the girls used to change tires themselves with extraordinary speed when we had a critical case inside" (Harriman 1923, 226–228).

Members of the Washington motor corps worked throughout the war. Usually they were on duty for twenty-four hours at a time, sleeping at a corps' garage in between calls. According to Harriman, their most crucial work came during the influenza epidemic of 1918, when she was in Europe, but the women of the Washington motor corps went bravely "in and out of houses, carrying the stretchers themselves" and took "as many as two thousand patients to the hospitals" (Harriman 1923, 226–228).

When Harriman returned to Washington in 1918, she met with the president to tell him what she had seen in England and France, and then settled back into her myriad activities. She began working again with her colleagues on the suffrage question, mostly lobbying U.S. senators for a "yes" vote on the proposed suffrage amendment, and raising money for the Red Cross by giving speeches. Reflecting on Washington in 1918, Harriman later wrote, "There were committees, good committees and bad committees. Washington fairly swarmed with them" (Harriman 1923, 275–276).

American women did not have to join a specific organization to be able to help the U.S. war effort. They were targeted by government propaganda in a variety of other ways. The U.S. secretary of the treasury created a National Woman's Liberty Loan Committee to educate women about both the "financial advantages" and the "patriotic duty involved in their purchase of Liberty Loan Bonds" (Clark 1918). The ever-present propaganda posters regularly urged women to contribute financially whatever they could. One poster addressed "women of America" and told them, "Joan of Arc Saved France—save your country—Buy war savings stamps."

A government poster encouraging women to participate on the home front. (Library of Congress)

The federal government also created the U.S. Food Administration, headed by Herbert Hoover, during the war. The Food Administration appealed directly to women, as the preparers of meals in the average household, to ensure an adequate supply of food during the war, mostly through voluntary conservation efforts. Hoover famously declared, "Food will win the war," and called upon Americans to pledge their efforts to conserve food by observing "wheatless Mondays," "meatless Tuesdays," and "porkless Saturdays," and by planting "victory gardens." A poster produced by the Food Administration reminded women that they could "Sow the Seeds of Victory" by planting their own vegetables.

Nannie Jeter, the manager of the dining hall at East Carolina Teacher's Training School in Greenville, North Carolina, exemplified the kind of work women were doing all over the country to conserve food. She asked her students to be sure to clean their plates at every meal, determined to keep careful track of all ingredients through careful measurement, and adjusted her recipes to account for shortages of sugar, butter, meat, and white flour.

The students adjusted quickly to meatless breakfasts. The staff and servants at the college were asked to take only what they could eat on their plates. The garbage was inspected each day for waste. Jeter managed to cut down her use of beef by one-quarter. She used her leftovers creatively. She remembered saving "every piece of bread" for use as crumbs on baked dishes or "to roll fish in before baking or frying" and using "every ounce of fat" as "shortening for biscuit, thereby saving many a tub of lard." Those fats she could not use for cooking she saved to make soap. Out of her wartime food management experience, Jeter believed,

> The housewife must learn to plan economical and properly balanced meals which, while properly nourishing her family, do not encourage overeating or waste. . . . This is a war that will be won by the women of the land. . . . The domain of the housewife has been raised from obscurity and hard labor to a position requiring brains to conceive and system to operate. (Jeter 2002)

Even women such as Emily Newell Blair, who had opposed the war before the U.S. entry, were, as Blair later noted about herself, "willing to fight for victory" even though she was "not enthusiastic about the war." She presented speeches on food conservation, Liberty Loans, and the causes of the war. She spurred her audiences on to action by appealing to a common fear—warning them of "Germany's plan to come over and take the United States after she got through with Great Britain and France." She organized meetings in German-American farm communities where she tried to explain that the war was not against the German people, all the while knowing that those German Americans probably had family members still in Germany who were starving (Laas 1999, 179–180).

During the First World War, tens of thousands of women were mobilized for military service or government work. The U.S. civil service warned that the shortage of stenographers in Washington offices was delaying U.S. war preparation. The army needed nurses, typists, stenographers, clerks, laundry workers, and cooks to staff both overseas and stateside hospitals and offices. The majority of American Expeditionary Force (AEF) women volunteers were lower-middle-class women who already worked for wages outside the home. Women who had already had some sort of professional training, especially nurses, were heavily recruited. The U.S. Army Nurse Corps had been created in 1901, but by the time of U.S. entry into the war there were only 400 U.S. Army nurses. By the end of the war, the army counted over 20,000 nurses.

Aside from army nurses, the women who worked for the army were considered civilian employees with no military status. The almost 12,000 women who served in the U.S. Navy during World War I, however, were enlisted into the service with the designation of "yeomen (F)." In March 1917, the U.S. Navy announced its intention to enlist women to perform clerical and support tasks as clerks, stenographers, telephone and telegraph operators, messengers, and other positions as needed stateside in order to free more men for service at sea. Almost 500 women already served in the U.S. Navy Nurse Corps, but those women were neither enlisted nor commissioned (Ebbert and Hall 2002, 1).

Female applicants to the navy varied in age and background. Many were only in their late teens, and others were near middle age. There were no provisions preventing married women or women with children from enlisting, and both were represented. Some applicants had a variety of work experiences that they brought to the navy. Those who had special training from attending a business college or working as telephone operators were especially valuable, but many others had no specialized skills.

Most were motivated to enlist by patriotism and a sincere desire to do something to help the war effort. Many had brothers or husbands already in the service, and a few had already suffered the loss of a family member. Many of the women who served, however, were also motivated by the chance that the U.S. Navy gave them to gain independence, learn new skills, and embark on a great adventure (Ebbert and Hall 2002, 16–18).

Navy recruiters emphasized all these reasons for joining up and relied on the common recruiting technique of the day—the poster—to interest women in the service. Well-known poster artist Howard Chandler Christy was at the naval recruiting station at Los Angeles when a young woman named Bernice Tongate enlisted. He sketched her, and her image became one of the era's most popular and familiar navy recruiting posters.

Tongate herself served on active duty for three years. Navy officials were successful in appealing to potential women recruits such as Tongate, but they often had to overcome the reluctance of parents who could not believe that their *daughter* wanted to join the navy. Some young women were determined to join despite serious parental disapproval, disbelief, and\or fear. One woman recalled that her mother "got quite hysterical and said over and over, 'You can't go—you can't go,'" and another remembered that her mother was "shocked, but my father blew his top" and tried to invalidate her enlistment (Ebbert and Hall 2002, 7, 19).

After enlisting, new women recruits were given orders to report to a new "duty station." Some were stationed close to home and made arrangements to live with family members. Many others, however, left home for the first time only to arrive alone in a large, unknown city. The navy was rarely able to provide housing for the new yeomen, though navy officials did encourage local citizens to open their homes to the new recruits. By and large, though, the women themselves were responsible for finding housing and the means to commute to their new jobs.

In some places, such as Washington, D.C., there was a severe housing shortage (Ebbert and Hall 2002, 21). This, as well as the wartime conditions in Washington, affected not only naval recruits but also the thousands of new female civil service workers and volunteers who poured into Washington to work for organizations such as the Woman's Committee of the Council of National Defense. Emily Newell Blair described Washington as "a nightmare with its awful crowds, the soldiers in uniform, the departmental conflicts, the flu, and the really terrible living conditions" (Laas 1999, 181).

Most of the new female naval recruits went to work immediately in clerical and administrative jobs. They spent their days at the typewriter, filling out (in multiple copies) the orders, requisition forms, invoices, payroll, and other assorted documents that kept the navy running during wartime. Those without clerical skills served as messengers or couriers or in assorted other jobs, such as truck driving, which had previously been considered unsuitable for women. A few women were trained to work in naval intelligence, breaking codes and censoring cables (Ebbert and Hall 2002, 44–48).

Some 2,000 American women contributed to the war effort in an entirely new way, as so-called reconstruction aides, or "re-aides" serving in the U.S. Army Medical Department's reconstruction programs. During World War I, what we now know as physical or occupational therapy was called "reconstruction." American women were recruited into the small number of programs for reconstruction training. At Reed College in Portland, Oregon, women between the ages of twenty-five and forty studied for this new profession. They were expected to have "good personality, good health and physical vigor, and [be] citizens of the U.S. or of one of the countries allied with the U.S." The office of the U.S. surgeon general required that

> Aides must be women . . . able to cooperate generally and capable of demonstrating team play, as it is essential that this new force have a standard and morale of the highest order. On this spirit, more than any other thing, will the physical re-education of soldiers depend. (Gavin 1997, 104)

About 300 reconstruction aides were sent overseas, but the majority worked in U.S. Army hospitals and, after the war was over, when thousands of disabled soldiers came home, in veteran's hospitals.

The war in Europe produced changes at home in the labor force a full two years before the United States entered the war, as women began to move into a variety of nontraditional jobs. About one million women moved into the workforce to alleviate the labor shortage caused by increased wartime production and the draft. Most of the women workers during World War I were not new workers, but women who had already been in the labor force. Now they were able to move into jobs, many of them higher paying jobs, previously closed to them. As Harriet Stanton Blatch observed in 1918, "There is nothing new in our day in a woman's being paid for her work . . . but she has never before been seen in America employed, for instance, as a section hand on a railway" (Blatch 1918, 79–80).

Many of these women, Blatch observed, "certainly have muscles, and are tempted to use them vigorously at three dollars a day" (Blatch 1918, 82). Most were young and unmarried, but a small number of older women—mostly widows or deserted wives, and married women who found that the high prices of wartime made it too hard to make ends meet, or whose husbands were in military service—joined the workforce for the first time. Most, especially the small number who went into heavy industry, realized that their entry into the jobs previously closed to them was temporary, but they took advantage of the chance to show their patriotism during wartime and earn higher wages than had ever been possible for them before.

After the United States entered the war, job announcements for women began to appear regularly in American newspapers. The Pennsylvania Railroad asked its superintendents to report how women could be employed at the railroad in the place of men. The United Cigar Company planned to replace male employees with women. Training schools prepared drafting classes and auto mechanic classes for women. There were calls for dock-workers and increased numbers of saleswomen. The New York Mayor's Commission on National Defense passed a resolution in June 1917 for the addition of "war policewomen." Several months later a woman was appointed deputy sheriff of Ossining, New York (*New York Times,* May–December 1917).

African-American women had fewer opportunities than white women to move into the manufacturing sector. A far greater number of black women remained concentrated in traditional forms of female labor—primarily domestic or agricultural work—during the war years, though more black women *did* find paid work, especially if they moved north. As the number of white women working as domestics dropped—because they left domestic service for better job opportunities—black women in northern cities took their places. Still, some jobs did become available for black women in manufacturing, and most women jumped at the chance to leave domestic service. As one woman recalled after taking a job in a paper box factory, "I'll never work in nobody's kitchen but my own any more" (Greenwald 1980, 22–23).

The tobacco and food-processing industries employed the highest numbers of black women. By 1917, three thousand black women were working in the meatpacking plants of Chicago, but they were offered only the lowest-paying, dirtiest jobs. One woman recalled working in the "fat-washing room" for twenty cents an hour (Brown 2002, 86). Some of the best opportunities for black women were in the garment trades and in the railroad industry. Railroads offered high wages, about twenty dollars a week, and steady employment. Black women worked in railroad offices, mopping floors, washing woodwork, and windows. In the rail yards some women operated electric lift trucks, moving freight, and others distributed linens to Pullman cars (Greenwald 1980, 24–25).

Overall, tens of thousands of women, black and white, were attracted to the railroad industry during wartime. In December 1917, the federal government took control of the railroad industry under the auspices of the new Railroad Administration in order to create an efficient and streamlined national transportation system during the wartime emergency. The federally controlled railroads offered some of the best wages and working conditions during the war, and women actively sought these jobs (Greenwald 1980, 91). Those who already had clerical experience applied to work in railroad offices. The *New York Times* reported in May 1917, "Those who bought tickets in the ferry stations of the Lackawanna Railroad in New Jersey yesterday were surprised to see women on duty in the ticket booths" (*New York Times*, 1 May 1917, 9:1). By October 1918 the number of women in railroad work reached 101,785 (Greenwald 1980, 92–93).

Women were needed in the railroad industry, but this did not mean that they were accepted. Women employees often received little encouragement from their male bosses, and those with aspirations for promotion were frustrated. Women's Service Section inspectors, sent into the factories to report on the adjustments both women and men were making to the presence of women in industry, regularly reported that women were discouraged from applying for better jobs. One female clerk confessed that supervisors generally treated women employees as "either jokes or pets" (Greenwald 1980, 98). Both verbally and physically abusive treatment was reported. Women clerks complained that four men in the auditor's office of the Southern Railroad in Cincinnati tried repeatedly to lift their skirts, pinch their breasts, and touch their necks. Those women who did not complain about the treatment received wage increases. Women, fearful of losing their jobs, rarely initiated formal complaints, and only rarely were male employees reprimanded or terminated for such behavior.

Relations with male coworkers varied from job to job, and from factory to factory. Many men felt as if their "domain" was being "invaded" by women and so treated them with considerable hostility. Some refused to work alongside women. At the Philadelphia Navy Yard men gathered at the entrance to shout insults and obscenities at women who were arriving for their shift. At the Rock Island Arsenal in Illinois, where more than one thousand women operated drill presses, assembled rifles, and worked in the blueprint, drafting, and chemical departments, inspectors from the Ordnance Department and the Woman in Industry Service found so many tensions that they set up segregated facilities for women. Women all worked the same shift, which would start at a different time; and they were given a separate lunchroom and a new locker room in which they changed into their "womanalls," as the bloomer-type overalls worn by women workers were called (Brown 2002, 127–130).

The largest number of women employed in the railroad industry worked as clerks, and the second-largest number worked as cleaners and sweepers in rail yards and roundhouses. Only a small number of women gained access to the skilled labor jobs in the railroad shops, or in any industry for that matter. Most who found employment in the shops worked as helpers, though some became machinists and a handful occupied positions such as electricians, sheet-metal workers, and blacksmiths. Because many male craftsmen perceived the employment of women as a threat, they sought various ways to protect themselves and their crafts from competition by women employees. They were especially fearful that women might try to extend their employment beyond the war years.

Some men, however, welcomed women into their unions as a way of strengthening their position against management. The members of the International Association of Machinists voted in April 1917 to encourage women to join their union in the hope that they would feel solidarity with the men to protect their craft. Women participated in many of the thousands of wartime strikes and other forms of labor agitation when they found that their wages were not high enough to keep up with rising wartime inflation (Greenwald 1980, 119–120).

Women also worked in the munitions industry. Some work, such as the inspection and packaging of shells, required no special training, but women were thought to be particularly suited for some of the tasks of shell assembly. As the *New York Times* noted, "The fitting of the fine screw and the insertion of the tiny springs make the sensitive touch perceptions and delicate handling of a woman's hands really needed" (*New York Times,* 30 December 1917, VII, 6:1).

Harriet Stanton Blatch, inspecting factories with women employees, also noted the "deft fingers" of the female workers. She observed "young women" working "at the lathe" with great "precision and accuracy" (Blatch 1918, 87).

The federal government established watchdog agencies, such as the Women's Branch of the Ordnance Department of the U.S. Army for women workers in munitions plants and the Women's Service Section of the Railroad Administration, to oversee the introduction of women workers into those industries under federal control during the war and to ensure safe working conditions for the women. Problems were reported—the handling of chemicals without protection, industrial poisoning, injury from accidents, accidental explosions, and fatigue and strain—but there were few changes made during the wartime emergency (Brown 2002, 57–58).

Another occupation that opened for the first time to women during the war years was that of streetcar or elevated railway conductor. As with so many women entering new jobs during the war, these women were motivated both by a sense of patriotic duty and by the opportunity to make money. As streetcar conductors and subway guards, women were in very public positions.

Harriet Stanton Blatch noted the "patience and tact" of the woman streetcar conductors since the public was "still a little embarrassed in her presence" (Blatch 1918, 88). By December 1917, the Interborough (New York) Rapid Transit Company counted ninety-two women either already working or in training, and the Brooklyn Rapid Transit Company had more than 100 women already at work. These women received the same training as male employees, had to pass a similar physical exam, were subject to the same age restrictions (21–45 years old), and received the same pay as men (27 cents per hour) (*New York Times,* 30 December 1917, VII, 6:1).

Women filled a variety of other nontraditional jobs for the first time during World War I. They directed traffic on city streets, delivered ice to homes and restaurants, cut hair in barbershops, delivered mail, and operated heavy machinery. Women were employed as elevator operators and, at the Otis Elevator Company in Yonkers, New York, worked on small machine tools in drilling and electrical work. A fire-extinguisher factory employed 275 women workers in 1917. Women with physical strength were recruited into the felt hat industry. Women drove laundry wagons, worked in radium plating, and entered the Sperry Gyroscope Factory (*New York Times,* 30 December 1917, VII, 6:1). At the International Arms and Fuse Company in Bloomfield, New Jersey, women were just being introduced into one of the largest shops in 1917, but it was expected that women would be operating the 1,200 machines in that shop within the month (Blatch 1918, 94).

Women also joined the fledgling airplane industry. In 1914, only fourteen plants employing 214 workers nationwide produced airplanes. By 1918, the airplane industry employed 27,000 people, including 6,000 women. Two thousand of them worked at the Curtiss Aeroplane and Motor Corporation in Buffalo, New York, where they first attended a training school for women before joining their male coworkers in every aspect of manufacturing, from initial woodworking to metal and machinist work to the assembly of wings, rudders, and tails and finally the inspection of every inch of the completed plane (Brown 2002, 142).

Many private companies, under the pressure of the wartime labor shortage, initiated training programs for the women they were now recruiting into their factories. The Recording and Computing Machines Company of Dayton, Ohio, for instance, tallied 5,000 women out of 8,600 total employees during wartime. The women participated in a training program run by one of the company's mechanics, known for his "gentlemanly" manner, and staffed by a number of women employees who had already proven themselves as excellent workers. These female trainers were instructed to serve as role models for the nervous newcomers, most of whom were entering factory work from employment in retail stores, restaurants, or schools. The women received ten days of training after they were separated into two groups: one for work in heavy machinery, and another for lighter work (Greenwald 1980, 47, 55).

The women who moved into these nontraditional jobs were generally praised for their patriotism and for their competence in so many new fields. Most of all, though, they earned respect for their bravery, not only for working in dangerous trades such as munitions but for leaving "[the] established seclusions of their sex [to] endure the curiosity and comment they have to encounter while performing tasks like those of the streetcar conductor and the operator of elevators in tall buildings" (*New York Times,* 21 December 1917, 10:5).

There were indeed problems—relations with male coworkers, housing shortages in industrial areas—but overall the reports on women's labor were optimistic. Many noted the special accommodations that some industries were willing to make for their women workers. Harriet Stanton Blatch noted that many munitions plants were building dormitories "to attract the best type of woman" to their plants because "the haphazard accommodations which men will put up with, won't satisfy women. They demand more, and get more" (Blatch 1918, 99).

Women also moved into agricultural labor, many of them organized into the Woman's Land Army of America, to replace the men who had been called off to war and thus ensure the supply of food for soldiers in Europe. Many colleges and universities organized groups of women to "do farm work, and do it with a will." On many of these farms, women "ploughed with horses, they ploughed with tractors, they sowed the seed, they thinned and weeded the plants, they reaped, they raked, they pitched the hay, [and] they did fencing and milking" (Blatch 1918, 166). Despite some initial worries about the effect of such hard labor on the health and constitution of young women, Harriet Stanton Blatch noted in 1918, "At the end of the season their health wins high approval from the doctors and their work golden opinions from the farmers" (Blatch 1918, 166).

By fall 1918, calls were beginning to go out for more women to join the paid labor force in the factories. This time, so-called wageless, or nonworking women, were targeted. In Bridgeport, Connecticut, on 21 September, six military airplanes dropped leaflets over a crowd of thousands gathered below. The leaflets announced to the crowd that "the Kaiser's airmen" could drop bombs on Bridgeport just as easily as these planes dropped leaflets, and asked: "Why don't you women retaliate? You can fight at the front and live home by enlisting for pleasant easy work in the nearest munitions factory" (Brown 2002, 150). Just at the point at which more women were being recruited into the factories, though, it became clear that the war would soon end with Germany's defeat.

When the Armistice was announced on 18 November 1918, women were laid off from their war jobs in the primary war industries almost immediately. Within days, thousands were released from the Curtiss Aeroplace Corporation, the Remington-Union Metallic Cartridge Company, and large machine shops all over the Northeast. In some of the secondary war industries, such as food processing and railroads, women stayed on to work a bit longer or managed to retain clerical jobs. After all, it would take some time to bring two million American soldiers home from France, and thousands of American workers were sick or dying in fall 1918 from an extraordinary influenza epidemic (Brown 2002, 159).

In 1920 the Nineteenth Amendment to the U.S. Constitution was ratified, giving women the right to vote. Many insist that support for the long-fought-for amendment was partly a response to women's support and work for the war effort. Overall, during the war years tens of thousands of American women joined the armed forces, over one million worked for wages in industries directly related to the war effort, and countless others moved into jobs into secondary industries. Millions of women volunteered their services in a wide variety of organizations such as the Red Cross or the Salvation Army, and millions more did their part by conserving food, buying Liberty Bonds, or stoically sending their husbands and sons off to the war. They had, indeed, sown the seeds of victory.

—*Molly M. Wood*

References and Further Reading

Blatch, Harriet Stanton. 1918. *Mobilizing Woman Power.* New York: The Woman's Press. Accessed online, Library of Congress, Rare Book and Special Collections Division, National American Woman Suffrage Association Collection, http:\\www.memory.loc.gov\ammem\naw\nawsres.html.

Brown, Carrie. 2002. *Rosie's Mom: Forgotten Women Workers of the First World War.* Boston: Northeastern University Press.

Cecile, Marie, and Anselm Chomel. 1920. *A Red Cross Chapter at Work.* Indianapolis: Hollenbeck.

Clark, Ida. 1918. *American Women and the World War.* New York: D. Appleton. Accessed online from digital collection at http:\\www.mtholyoke.edu\acad\-intrel\ww1.htm http:\\www.mtholyoke.edu\acad\intrel\ww1.htm (cited 23 December 2002).

Ebbert, Jean, and Marie-Beth Hall. 2002. *The First, the Few, the Forgotten: Navy and Marine Corps Women in World War I.* Annapolis: Naval Institute Press.

Gavin, Lettie. 1997. *American Women in World War I.* Niwot: University of Colorado Press.

Goldman, Emma. [1931] 1970. *Living My Life.* New York: Alfred A. Knopf. Reprint, New York: Dover.

Graham, Margaret Shaw. 1916. "Another Woman's View of Preparedness." *Outlook* (19 April): 892–893.

Greenwald, Maurine Weiner. 1980. *Women, War, and Work: The Impact of World War I on Women Workers in the United States.* Westport, CT: Greenwood.

Harriman, Florence Jaffray. 1923. *From Pinafores to Politics.* New York: Henry Holt.

Henderson, Archibald. 2002. "North Carolina Women in the War: Electronic Edition." Documenting the American South Collection, University of North Carolina at Chapel Hill, http:\\docsouth.unc.edu\wwi\henderson\henderson.htm (cited 31 December 2002).

Jeter, Nannie. 2002. "What Are We Doing to Conserve Food and Keep down Waste: Electronic Edition." Documenting the American South Collection, University of North Carolina at Chapel Hill, http:\\docsouth.unc.edu\wwi\jeter\jeter.htm (cited 23 December 2002).

Lass, Virginia Jeans, ed. 1999. *Bridging Two Eras: The Autobiography of Emily Newell Blair, 1877–1951.* Columbia: University of Missouri Press.

Linkugel, Wil, and Martha Solomon. 1991. *Anna Howard Shaw: Suffrage Orator and Social Reformer.* New York: Greenwood.

Piantadosi, Al, and Alfred Bryan. 1915. "I Didn't Raise My Boy to Be a Soldier." New York: Leo Feist. In the Star Sheet Music Collection, Lilly Library, Indiana University, Bloomington.

Rawls, Walter. 1988. *Wake Up, America! World War I and the American Poster.* New York: Abbeville.

Steinson, Barbara. 1981. "Sisters and Soldiers: American Women and the National Service Schools, 1916–1917." *The Historian* 43, no 2: 225–239.

———. 1982. *Female Activism in World War I: The American Women's Peace, Suffrage, Preparedness, and Relief Movements, 1914–1919.* New York: Garland.

STRUGGLING NOT
TO FIGHT

The Experience of Radicals and Pacifists during World War I

———————— ◆ ————————

THE HISTORY OF WORLD WAR I IS RIFE WITH THE STORIES OF those who served in the trenches of the western front or on the frozen fields of Russia. Quite often they are stories of disillusionment. Left unnoticed are the stories of those who did not believe in the war from the outset, but nonetheless suffered from it and contributed to it: the pacifists and radicals of the home front. Often denigrated as traitors and cowards, these men and women demonstrated a different kind of bravery. Although many disagreed with those who decided to participate in the war, for instance, they recognized the soldiers' bravery and respected their views. As Fenner Brockway explained,

> I would not for a moment think of leveling the charge of murder against those who engage in war from a high sense of duty. The act must be judged by its motive; and I recognize that many noble men, hating war with all their being, have been impelled to fight from the loftiest principles. They have followed where their consciences have led, and I revere their courage and sacrifice. (Ayles et al. 1916, 8)

Radicals and pacifists during the First World War held a variety of religious, political, and moral beliefs that caused them to withhold their support for the war. Although the majority of religious pacifists based their objections to war on the teachings of Christ, a number of non-Christian denominations also held antiwar views. Some religious organizations were not strictly pacifist but objected to offering allegiance to an earthly authority and to fighting for what they saw as an earthly rather than a spiritual cause (Rae 1970; Kennedy 1989). Many socialist pacifists believed in the international brotherhood of man and therefore objected to killing their fellow men in any circumstances, but the political beliefs of others meant that they would be willing to fight for a cause in which they believed, to create or defend a workers' republic, for example, but refused to participate in the war. Arthur Gardiner, a member of the British Socialist Party, explained, "We were based definitely and soundly on the theory of the class struggle and that the 1914–18 war was merely a fight for foreign markets for which we were not prepared to give our lives" (Pearce 2001, 77).

Political objectors also resisted military conscription because they believed it was the first step toward industrial conscription. Although it was not uncommon for individuals to have both religious and political objections to the war and military service, there were also some men and women who had no religious or political affiliations but still had a strong moral objection either to all war or to this particular war (Allen n.d., 8–13).

The objectives of radicals and pacifists varied. The main concern of some individuals was to have no personal involvement in the war whereas others felt compelled to engage actively in antiwar and pro-peace work. Most opponents of the war were more concerned about achieving peace than with promoting revolution, but a small number of radicals hoped to use the war to bring about social and political change. They argued that

> If the rulers of Germany, France and England decide to involve the people in war, it should be the business of the workers to be prepared for "War" on their own account—not just war against unoffending comrades of other nations, but war for the overthrow of the capitalist system. (*The Worker,* 1 August 1914)

Those who decided to act on their principles, whether radical or pacifist, often incurred penalties. L. S. Florence, an American journalist, gave up her job to devote her time fully to the antiwar movement in the United States

A conscientious objector is publicly humiliated for refusing to join the U.S. Army, 1915. (Hulton Archive/Getty Images)

(Florence 1935, 98). J. H. Hudson, a British socialist, revealed that he and his wife "spent nearly every penny we had saved before the war in supporting Peace Movements" (Ayles et al. 1916, 14). Radicals and pacifists involved in the production and distribution of pacifist or antiwar literature were frequently fined, and some were sentenced to terms of imprisonment. Rosa Hobhouse, a Quaker, was jailed for distributing Christian peace literature considered likely to deter men from joining the army (Hobhouse 1934, 214). Wilfred Wellock, an Independent Methodist lay preacher, was sent to prison for publishing a Christian revolutionary journal intended to promote pacifism (Caedel 1980, 50).

Opposition to the war also led to various forms of discrimination. Because Margaret Ashton had discussed possible terms of peace at a meeting organized by the Independent Labour Party (ILP), she was expelled from three subcommittees of the Education Committee (*The Labour Leader*, 13 January 1916). A female teacher was sacked because "although she did not teach peace in the History lessons, she didn't teach jingo-patriotism either" (White 1917). The professor of mathematics at Cambridge University, moreover, "announced loudly that he wouldn't teach any women at his lectures who were members of . . . any . . . pacifist organization" (Paese 1979). A woman who participated in a tour to promote peace suffered personal injury after being attacked by an angry crowd that also set the peace-tour caravan on fire (Oldfield 1989, 55).

Men of military age who opposed the war often faced additional pressures. In Britain, women presented men who were not in uniform with white feathers, a symbol of cowardice, in an attempt to shame them into volunteering for military service. Some employers threatened, cajoled, and even sacked their employees in an attempt to make them join the army. In some workplaces, opponents of the war were put under pressure to enlist by fellow workmen who threatened to strike unless they gave a commitment to undertake military service. Political objectors who had hoped that a mass demonstration by the working class would prevent the war consequently felt betrayed by the labor movement's almost unanimous patriotism.

Surprisingly, just as socialists met hostility from fellow trade union members, men who objected to war and military service on religious grounds often met with hostility rather than support from their churches. The Payne family were religious pacifists but found that

> The worst pressures came from the religious people. They were the people that made all the noise. They were against us all the time. The minister of the Congregationalist church told us to clear out of the place, he wouldn't have such people in the place. (Payne and Payne 1973)

Disappointment at the support that many churches gave to the war was one of the most negative experiences for religious opponents of the war. John Brocklesby admitted, "I was horrified that the pulpits of Methodist Churches should become recruiting platforms. Now did I begin to have my first serious doubts about a theology that would allow its exponents to invite men to undertake mass murder" (Brocklesby n.d., 14).

Similarly, Will Cormack and his parents were strict Baptists, "but the church's support of war so shocked them that they deserted the church and became members of the Glasgow Study Circle—a body, ethical rather than religious, but specifically pacifist" (Cormack 1972, 1).

Although pacifists and radicals experienced hostility and pressure to enlist even while military service was voluntary, the introduction of conscription altered the situation considerably for many men. Significantly, since the declaration of war, the introduction of conscription and the terms of compulsory military service differed between countries. This meant that nationality was an important factor in determining the ways in which radicals and pacifists experienced World War I. In 1910, for example, defense acts were passed in Australia and New Zealand that required compulsory military training for men and boys above a certain age. New Zealand introduced conscription at the end of 1916, but proposals to conscript men for fighting abroad were defeated in Australia, and full-scale conscription during the war was never adopted. Conscription was never extended to Ireland, but in Britain compulsory military service for single men between the ages of 18 and 41 became law in January 1916. This was soon extended to include married men, and the age limit was eventually raised to fifty. The Selective Draft Act, which made military service compulsory in the United States, became law in May 1917. Although the act applied initially to men between the ages of 21 and 31, the age limit was raised to 45 in 1918. Canada did not adopt its Military Service Act until 1917.

Although France and Belgium were among the states that had no legal provision for men who objected to military service on conscientious grounds, some governments did acknowledge that combatant service would be contrary to the beliefs of a minority of individuals and made provision in their Military Service Acts for the granting of exemption in certain circumstances. In New Zealand, the right to exemption was limited to men who since before the outbreak of war had belonged to a religious body whose tenets and doctrines specifically declared the bearing of arms and the performance of combatant service to be contrary to divine revelation. The equivalent American act also limited exemption to members "of any well-organized religious sect or organization, at present organized and existing, whose creed forbids its members to participate in war in any form" (Hobhouse 1917, 82).

Such specifications meant not only that radical objectors had no legal right to exemption but also that applications for exemption from many religious objectors would be rejected. In comparison, the terms of the British Military Service Act were far more generous. Instead of referring to "conscientious beliefs," the act acknowledged a "conscientious objection" to bearing arms. In theory, therefore, the act entitled objectors to claim exemption on both religious and nonreligious grounds. Unlike the acts of other nations that recognized a conscientious objection to combatant service only, moreover, the British act also allowed absolute exemption in certain circumstances.

Although the British act seemed to offer the chance of exemption to men who would be denied it elsewhere, speaking in front of a tribunal was a new and intimidating experience for many men, and this often prevented them from taking full advantage of the hearing. In Britain, men applying for exemption on any ground, including conscientious objection, had to appear before a tribunal that included a military representative. At the tribunal of A. C. Townsend, for example, the applicant "was very nervous and unable to answer questions lucidly" (*NCF Brighton and District Branch Register of Members' Appearances before Local Tribunals,* Book 1, Entry No.3). H. H. Haynes, a socialist and a Methodist, admitted, "I wasn't very well versed in expressing my views . . . and I'm afraid I didn't make much of a show" (Haynes n.d.).

In Canada, applicants for exemption had to appear before local tribunals that consisted of a county court judge and a layman. In New Zealand and South Africa, magistrates' courts were authorized to make decisions about the legitimacy of applications for exemption. Archibald Baxter, an objector from New Zealand who belonged to no religious denomination, however, noted that "As for exemption, I knew there was no hope for it. The Appeal Boards were farcical as far as objectors were concerned, their members usually ridiculing the objectors who were rash enough to appeal" (Baxter 1968, 10).

Education, experience of lay preaching, and participation in politics or trade union activities could all be beneficial to men applying for exemption, since these provided men with experience of speaking confidently in public and of expressing their views in an articulate manner. In some cases, therefore, radicals as well as pacifists were able to successfully convince the tribunal of the sincerity of their convictions.

Acceptance of sincerity, however, did not always guarantee approval of the requested exemption. Moorehead argued that socialists in particular "were virtually doomed to refusal of exemption of any kind" (Moorehead 1987, 34). Yet when six socialists appeared before the Newton Abbot Tribunal on one day, one of them argued: "It is a commercial war out and out.

My objection to war is that the working classes, as a class, will suffer by it, the same as they have always suffered by it" (*Daily Mercury,* 15 March 1916). Four received exemption from combatant service, and two were granted absolute exemptions, upon condition they continued to support dependent relatives (*Daily Mercury,* 15 March 1916).

It would be equally false to assume that all religious objectors successfully gained exemption under the British act. Four brothers who were members of a "strict" Baptist church, for instance, all had their application for exemption on religious grounds rejected (*Liverpool Echo,* 28 February 1916). When the military representative appealed against the grant of an absolute exemption to Edward Nicholls, a Quaker and the sole support of his seventy-nine-year-old mother, the Appeal Tribunal overturned the earlier decision and awarded him no exemption whatsoever (*NCF Brighton and District Branch Register,* Book 1, Entry No. 35, and Book 2, Entry No. 21).

The support given to the war by the majority of churches was frequently used to undermine applications for exemption on religious grounds. Many religious pacifists, although sincere in their beliefs, were denied exemption because they attended a church where the pastor preached in favor of the war or where many of the young men in the congregation had enlisted voluntarily. An appearance before a tribunal could therefore be a frustrating experience for those who believed that they had a legitimate claim to exemption.

Even when their application was accepted as genuine, the granting of absolute exemption was extremely rare. In the majority of cases, exemption tended to be limited, usually being from combatant service only. Applicants were sometimes allowed exemption from all military service, usually on condition that they engaged in work of national importance. P. C. Wait, for example, belonged to no religious denomination but was entitled to exemption as a result of his occupation as a post office employee. He applied for "Absolute exemption *unconditional* that I remain in my present occupation, which is of national importance. . . . I will endure any penalties which may be imposed upon me. Conditional exemption in respect of my civil employment I cannot assent to" (*NCF Brighton and District Branch Register,* Book 1, Entry No. 18).

Although undertaking work of national importance was an acceptable alternative for many men who objected to military service, for others accepting any form of condition imposed by a tribunal was unacceptable. They usually resented the implication that an applicant was involved in work the tribunal considered to be helping the war effort. Many also feared that undertaking work of national importance meant freeing another man for combatant service. Similarly, although noncombatant service was acceptable to many men, such limited exemption was incompatible with the consciences of others. As Walter Ayles, a Christian and a socialist, explained: "I object to non-combatant service because I cannot assist others to do what to me is morally wrong" (Ayles et al. 1916, 5).

Similarly, Hudson argued, "It seems to me a poor sort of conviction that would lead a man to object to doing the work of killing for himself, yet would permit him to contribute directly the materials or services which enable others to do the killing" (Ayles et al. 1916, 13).

Because many men who objected to military service had no confidence that the tribunal would grant them an acceptable form of exemption even if their application was accepted as genuine, not all of those who were entitled to apply for exemption actually did so. George Thomas, a militant socialist, refused to appear before a tribunal because "Our opposition is not to the decisions of the tribunals but to the existence of the tribunals, in other words, to conscription" (Pearce 2001, 174).

Others raised objections based on the belief that no board had the right to judge the sincerity of a man's beliefs. These viewpoints made many radicals and pacifists reluctant to apply for exemption. Often this changed when colleagues pointed out that militarism and conscription could only be permanently overthrown if there was a change in public opinion. Consequently, many radicals and pacifists decided to apply to the tribunals not because they expected to be granted exemption but in order to gain publicity for their religious or political beliefs. Stanley Rees, an ILP member and an antimilitarist, admitted that he and some friends had an alternative objective in deciding to go before a tribunal. He explained:

> Some of us came to the conclusion that if sufficient of us made an appearance at the same time we would break down the machinery and four or five of us decided that in that case we will go ahead and give ourselves up and that is what we did. (Rees 1971)

One man who appealed for exemption because of his religious beliefs refused to declare from the outset that he had only one leg; he wanted to emphasize that he was, first and foremost, a conscientious objector (CO) (*Liverpool Echo*, 14 January 1916).

A small number of men decided to go on the run rather than be compelled to participate in military service. When a man was to be arrested for failing to report for duty, he was often assisted by a wife or sister who deliberately kept the police at the front door long enough for him to escape over the back fence. Alice and Hettie Wheeldon were famous among those who offered their homes as safe havens to British radicals before assisting in smuggling them to Ireland and the United States (Rowbotham 1986, 1; Pearce 2001, 172, 280, 281). Many French Canadians ran off to camps in the immense north woods in order to avoid conscription (Useem 1973, vii). One man even went on the run after the Armistice was declared but before he was freed from the terms of the Military Service Act. Accompanied by his wife and daughter, he moved from place to place, spending time with relatives or in lodgings and relying on his wife to support the family financially (Peet n.d.). Ernest Hunter, a member of the ILP, also avoided conscription by going on the run. Although the authorities sought him for two years, Hunter continued to play an active part in the work of the No-Conscription Fellowship (NCF) until he was caught just two weeks before the war ended (Kennedy 1981, 149).

The experience of arrest varied. A New Zealand man whose beliefs did not legally entitle him to exemption recalled:

> I was handed over to the military authorities. A guard of four men with bayonets fixed took me to the St. Kilda Battery. We marched down the middle of the principal street, arousing plenty of interest and comment in the passersby. The future held many worse experiences in store for me, worse from every point of view, but nothing ever cut me again like that first, deliberately inflicted, public humiliation. (Baxter 1968, 14)

Brocklesby's arrest, however, was quite different. As he recounted it,

> On the Saturday morning the most gentlemanly police officer I have ever met, P. C. Kaye, called for me. He suggested that I should walk to the railway station while he followed some distance behind, so that it would not appear I was under arrest. He was full of such considerate ideas to save me from any unpleasant feelings. (Brocklesby n.d., 31)

Similarly, Will Cormack recalled:

The officer who accepted me from the escort and signed their papers was a pleasant young man. He then said that if I gave him my word of honour to return by 9 p.m. to the camp, I could go into Edinburgh and enjoy my last few hours of freedom, which I readily promised to do. (Cormack 1972, 10)

Once officially under military control, pacifists and radicals had to decide whether to accept military authority. A number of those conscripted into the regular army abandoned resistance and obeyed military orders, as did a percentage of those involved in noncombatant service under military control. Some groups and individuals were prepared to accept noncombatant duties, although with certain reservations. Members of the Christadelphians, for example, were prepared to work on munitions. The majority of men involved in noncombatant work, however, were opposed to dealing with munitions in any form, including its transportation. A group of Seventh-Day Adventists accepted noncombatant duties but refused to work on their Sabbath. The situation became violent as a result:

> These men rushed at us and knocked us down in turn with their fists . . . this treatment was repeated. We still refused to work and the attack was renewed with sticks. In several instances we were kicked brutally whilst on the ground. . . . A corporal drew his revolver, placing the barrel to my forehead, threatening to shoot me if I again objected. (*The Tribunal,* 4 April 1918)

For refusing to obey military orders, these men were eventually charged and sentenced to imprisonment with hard labor (Rae 1970, 193).

A number of radicals and pacifists refused to compromise with militarism in any way, despite the consequences. George Frederick Dutch, a Quaker, refused to wear a military uniform. The authorities attempted to force him to give in; his tent was

> taken right up on top of the cliff overlooking the sea. That was in November, and it was pretty cold, misty weather. . . . Just to make things worse they rolled the tent walls up so that the wind came right into the tent. . . . I think it must have been ten days and nights in just my singlet and pants and socks . . . before I'd been there many hours I was frozen right through with exposure. (Goodall 1997, 15)

Dutch nonetheless refused to the end to don the uniform. In several other cases men were physically and even brutally forced to obey orders, though (Boulton 1967, 154–155). When Ernest England, a Quaker, was taken ill during his first night in prison, his repeated requests for a chamber pot were refused. England eventually had to make use of the floor. The next morning the warder took him by the scruff of his neck and buried his face in his excrement, after which England was ill and unable to work for many weeks (Boulton 1967, 254). Extreme forms of cruelty were rare, however, and harsh treatment of COs was not always tolerated or accepted. Many of the worst cases of brutality led to punishment and even dismissal for the perpetrators.

Refusal to obey orders nevertheless often led to the punishment of radicals and pacifists by legitimate means. As a memorandum from Adjutant General Macready in May 1916 stated,

> It cannot be too clearly understood that once a man is handed over by the decision of a tribunal to the military authorities as a soldier, it is not for the military authorities to consider the reasons such a man may have for refusing to do his work. It is the clear duty of every Commanding Officer to do his best with the legitimate means at his disposal to make every man who is handed over to him into an efficient soldier. (Copy in Liddle Collection, CO 102)

As another commandant explained when imposing a sentence of field punishment: "I have no special instructions about COs and I shall treat you as ordinary soldiers" (Peet n.d., 42).

Punishment endured by COs, therefore, was more commonly the result of the application of an already existing harsh code of discipline rather than of deliberate acts of persecution for their beliefs. Field punishment, for example, involved being tied to a wooden framework with arms outstretched for varying lengths of time. Ordinary soldiers found guilty of misdemeanors suffered this as well as pacifists and radicals. Because objectors consistently resisted military coercion, however, this meant that unlike ordinary soldiers, they had the misfortune of having to endure repeated sentences of field punishment.

The decision to treat men as soldiers rather than as conscientious objectors also meant that there were men who had no intention of fighting but were still sent into the war zone. One man who continued to resist military service was placed alone in an area that was heavily shelled. Before the various attempts to make him give in and fight were done, he was physically and mentally exhausted (Baxter 1968, 10).

The ultimate punishment for disobeying military orders while deemed to be on active service was the death penalty. Even this threat failed to turn some radicals and pacifists into soldiers. Harry Stanton, a British Quaker, was sent to France as an unwilling member of the Non-Combatant Corps (NCC). He believed that the threat of the death sentence was very real. As he explained,

> We were told that some people were determined that we should be made an example of but of course, all sort of talk was going on then. You didn't quite know what to believe. I wasn't too frightened about being put to death. After all, it was happening to a great many people in the war who hadn't got the faith that I had got. (Stanton 1976)

A total of thirty-four British men who continued to resist military authority while in France were sentenced to death. In every case, however, the sentence was commuted to ten years' penal servitude.

Among the other legitimate punishments for refusal to obey military orders was a term of imprisonment in military custody. It was not an easy option. General Childs eagerly referred visitors to *The Rules for Military Detention Barracks and Military Prisons,* "Lest they be misled into believing that the infliction of statutory punishment required by the rule is a species of cruelty designed to break the spirit of COs" (Kennedy 1981, 144).

It did, however, often have that effect. Joseph Walden spent time in military detention following a court-martial, and "the confinement, and the deprivation of food so told upon him that he felt as if his brain were giving way, and at last he obeyed the military orders" (Gloucestershire Tribunals, in Liddle Collection, CO 102). Radicals and pacifists deemed to be soldiers were escorted back to their army units after serving their sentence. If they again refused orders, they received another court-martial and another term of imprisonment.

Some who maintained their resistance used their incarceration as an opportunity to preach to the soldiers. K. Otley, for example, declared, "I feel the time I have spent amongst the soldiers has not been in vain, as I have preached the Gospel of Brotherhood and Internationalism, from the workers' point of view, to them whenever possible" (Boulton 1967, 147).

J. P. M. Millar also took advantage of his enforced stay in the guardroom "to give some elementary lessons on socialism and war" to the soldiers present (Millar 1935, 240).

Political dissenters were not the only ones who attempted to convert the soldiers. The military authorities, however, were as eager to prevent the conversion of soldiers to religious pacifism as they were to prevent the spread of radicalism, and they therefore punished all those who attempted it. Millar, for example, was removed to a separate cell to prevent him communicating with other soldiers (Millar 1935, 240). American draftees who held a variety of religious beliefs were "segregated, sometimes for a year in army camps and subjected to harassments. For disobedience to an order not to speak to soldiers one group had been deprived of food for a week" (Bainton n.d.).

The experiences of radicals and pacifists in the military were not, however, always so negative. After being physically mistreated for refusing to obey an order, Archibald Baxter revealed that the other men in his tent "insisted on making my bed for me, and often, I know, would put their own blankets and overcoats under me to make it a little easier for me" (Baxter 1968, 114).

There are also examples of officers who treated objectors to military service kindly. Sergeant Ringer-Hewitt, for one, was unrepentant after being punished for showing leniency to a CO (Vellacott 1980, 111). He later wrote letters and notes expressing his sympathy and concern for the health of another CO under his command (Vellacott 1980, 275). Understandably, such acts of kindness and concern, whether from officers or soldiers, were highly appreciated by the men who received them.

Many pacifists and radicals were never mistreated, even when continually resisting military authority. The commanding officer of the NCC at Farnborough, for example, was sympathetic toward COs. He tried to give them duties that they could conscientiously accept. He offered Millar, a socialist, repeated opportunities to undertake work of a nonmilitary nature, including asking him to weed the paths around the huts. Millar, however, was not prepared to compromise with militarism in any way. He continued to refuse all military orders until there was no alternative but to court-martial him (Millar 1935, 236).

Many men who refused to accept military orders had to serve terms of imprisonment in civilian prisons. In Britain, the majority of COs were sentenced to the 3rd Division with hard labor. For the first fourteen days of their sentence, no mattress was allowed. The first twenty-eight days were spent in solitary confinement, seeing no one except the warder and perhaps a chaplain. They were not allowed to write or receive letters or a visit for two months (Hobhouse 1917, 44–45). Even after that initial period had passed, conditions in prison were far from ideal. A New Zealand objector described the bedding in his cell:

> No sheets, no pillowcase; only blankets, hard and brittle with age and much baking, and foul-smelling beyond belief. The pillow was a greasy, filthy bit of ticking, filled with some sort of hard pellets of what appeared to be metal of some sort. . . . The blankets were too old and hard to have much warmth in them. They were baked to destroy germs and lice, but the knowledge that the dirt and the odor were hygienic did not help me much that first night. (Baxter 1968, 27)

Harold Bing recalled similar hardships in his prison life:

> The cell was about 6 feet by 13 feet with one small window above one's head so that you couldn't see out of it except by standing on your stool—for which of course you might be punished if you were found doing it. In the door there was a little spyhole with a cover on the outside so that the warder could come along and open the spyhole and spy on you at any time . . . so that you had the sense of being watched the whole time—which gave you a very uncomfortable feeling at first until in time you grew indifferent to it. . . . There was also a small table and stool, the chamber pot, the can for water and a metal bowl in which to wash, a little shelf on which one kept one's knife, spoon and fork, a pot of salt and any photographs which one was allowed to have in. One was normally permitted not to have more than two or three photographs and they must be of members of one's family. (Goodall 1997, 28–29)

Prisoners spent a great deal of time alone in their cells, and this made boredom a real problem. It was not only religious pacifists who welcomed a visit from a chaplain or the opportunity to attend services while in prison, since it gave them a rare opportunity to exercise their voices and the chance to have the company of a fellow human being.

Some chaplains were even sympathetic and supportive. Their visits or sermons were often seen as a real help to the men. Brocklesby, a religious pacifist, received regular visits from a Methodist minister named Wardell. Though not a pacifist himself, Wardell tried hard to see both sides. "It is very difficult to understand how conscience drives men in exactly opposite directions. Both my boys joined the army as a matter of conscience, and one has paid with his life" (Brocklesby n.d., 33). His remaining son was later killed as well, yet Wardell was not bitter. Brocklesby asserted that "Never (I must emphasize this) did he by word, look or gesture, express any condemnation of my attitude" (Brocklesby n.d., 33).

Not all religious ministers treated COs with understanding or kindness. Evans was a Roman Catholic who lost faith in Catholicism after two priests came to visit him in his cell and tried to persuade him against the stand he was taking (Evans 1973). Other men simply stopped attending prison services because of the nature of the sermons. The Church of England chaplain at Winchester Prison, for example,

> took much pride in his patriotism. His sermons expounded the righteousness of war and the baseness of the German people. When the passage "Forgive your enemies" occurred in the reading for the day, he said that it was indeed right to forgive our enemies, but in this case we had to kill them first! (Stanton n.d., 168)

One popular way for prisoners to occupy themselves while alone in a cell was to read a copy of the Bible. Initially the only book allowed to prisoners, it was available in every cell. Like the sermons, of course, the Bible was more acceptable to some objectors than others. Millar explained, "As Christians were blowing each other to pieces . . . and quoting the book in support of the process, the Bible did not attract me" (Millar 1935, 241).

Eventually prisoners were allowed to have other books in their cells, and reading became an important occupation that helped keep the men sane. Rees, a socialist, was sentenced to two years' solitary confinement but, as he recalled,

> I had made my mind up that I wasn't going to feel the strain. I had a rich and varied background. I had been interested in poetry and things like that and I could keep myself going and I happened to get from the prison library a Shakespeare. (Rees 1971)

Some men memorized whole passages from the books that they read, both as a way of passing the time and as a means of exercising their mental faculties.

Still, all types of COs found it difficult to obey the strict prison rules. Newspapers and small pieces of charcoal were smuggled into prison, and inmates sometimes used their ingenuity to make newspapers of their own. The rule of silence in particular was often broken. The Payne brothers, for example, admitted that another prisoner "taught us how to use deaf and dumb language . . . and he got caught by the warder and they put him on bread and water for three days" (Payne and Payne 1973).

Another method of communication was to knock on the pipes between the cells. A group of COs in Walton Prison in Liverpool, England, staged a full-scale rebellion against the silence rule. The rebellion ended when the ringleader was transferred to another prison, where he spent three months on bread and water and eight months in solitary confinement (Moorehead 1987, 46).

It was not unusual that a prisoner's health suffered as a result of ordinary prison life. Harry Wheatcroft was hospitalized due to undernourishment while in prison (Wheatcroft 1976). At another prison, two COs collapsed in the chapel for lack of sustenance; the weight loss of a further twelve to fifteen COs was reported as being "specially serious" (*Scraps of Paper: An Examination of Government Pledges with Regard to Conscientious Objectors* n.d.). One man, according to his brother, had a breakdown in prison because of "close confinement and the worry, and not being able to write and receive any letters from his wife and child and parents" (Hobhouse 1917, 66). In Britain alone, ten COs died while in prison, and sixty-one others were considered to have died as a result of the rigors of prison treatment (Hobhouse 1934, 243).

Conditions for some imprisoned COs eventually improved as some of the rules were relaxed, though this did not happen everywhere. The silence rule was eased in England but not in Scotland, for example, and in some prisons objectors were allowed newspapers and some of their own books. In addition, a number of seriously ill prisoners were released.

Even before that, however, it was not unusual for prison warders to bend or break the rules to make the experiences of COs a little easier. In one prison many of the warders were members of the ILP and allowed socialist objectors to see the socialist newspapers every week (Wheatcroft 1976). There were also warders who allowed objectors to talk without punishment

A crowd of conscientious objectors to military service during World War I at a special prison camp. United Kingdom, ca. 1915. (Hulton-Deutsch Collection/Corbis)

or who would warn them if another warder was approaching (Payne and Payne 1973; Brocklesby n.d., 39). Sybil White, whose husband was imprisoned a short train journey away, recalled that

> Each day I pushed the . . . pram onto the verandah to make my enquiries and hand in letters and periodicals. The response was an invitation to occupy one of the private cells! Thus Andrew and I and our child had privacy and the enjoyment of whatever refreshments I had brought. (Wells n.d., 45)

In Britain, another option to prison was made available when Home Office camps were set up to provide COs with the opportunity to leave prison in order to undertake work of national importance under civilian control. The Home Office scheme was offered to both pacifists and radicals. The response varied, because some objectors believed that acceptance of the scheme meant compromising with the Military Service Act whereas others viewed the scheme as an acceptable alternative to military service or, at least, as a better alternative than prison. This led one absolutist to argue that "our friends are really our enemies. . . . If COs had refused the Scheme the Government would have given in weeks ago. They would not have had enough prisons to put us in" (Kennedy 1981, 162).

A number of radicals accepted the scheme with the intention of being deliberately uncooperative. Mark Hayler revealed on the way to one camp that a number of anarchists admitted that they fully intended to escape or create havoc. Once at the camp, they argued and fought with the camp warders and staged work slowdowns (Moorehead 1987, 62). They were sent back to prison as a result.

Other objectors were prepared to accept the scheme but decided to use the opportunity of freedom from prison not to escape, but to pay a short, unauthorized visit home. The first task of one Mr. Cheyne, a civilian appointed to supervise one of the camps, was to accompany men between prison and the camp. He recalled,

> I gave the governor a receipt for these 50 men . . . then we got to Liverpool Street Station . . . and I'd lost 4 of them on the way across . . . and at times other men disappeared but in every case they returned either compulsorily or voluntarily in a matter of a few days. (Cheyne 1971)

Other problems with the scheme occurred as well. Cheyne also noted that

> I had to go to the army clothing depot . . . and get supplies of shirts, pants and undervests. . . . That caused a row straight away because they were army issue and these fellows weren't going to have anything to do with the army. (Cheyne 1971)

Evans, who was concerned about workers' rights, complained for a totally different reason. As he explained,

> We found out that they were paying the contractors the Trade Union level of wages and so I went and interviewed the foreman in charge and asked if this

was so. He said it was and I told him we weren't working any more. (Evans 1973)

Walter Manthorpe, a Quaker, accepted the Home Office scheme but added:

> My stay there was not very long as the man in charge . . . asked me to send on
> to him what I considered was not my duty which was that he should be given
> the secret attitudes and intentions of the COs who were working there. Be-
> cause of my refusal I was then sent back to Dartmoor. (Manthorpe n.d.)

Some camps were based in former prisons where the cells were used as sleeping quarters but the doors were left unlocked. In contrast, at the Red Roses camp,

> The C.O.s live in a wooden hut built on props. The roof is of zinc. The front
> door leads immediately into the common room where one dines, writes,
> reads, plays and takes part in the social activities that sometimes occur here.
> The room is 18 ft. square and is all the accommodation for the aforemen-
> tioned purposes that is supplied for about 32 men. The sleeping arrange-
> ments are as follows: There are eight cubicles, each 9 1/2 ft. by 7 1/2 ft.
> Each contains four wooden hammocks or bunks arranged two on each side
> of the cubicle, one above the other barely three ft. apart. Each cubicle is in-
> conveniently stocked with four men's luggage, and the condition of the
> men's clothes after a long day's work on the potato field and a long walk over
> muddy roads can better be imagined than described. There is also a bath
> and bathroom, but heating arrangements are inadequate and the water sup-
> ply has to be carried by an already overworked staff of orderlies from a dis-
> tance of over a quarter of a mile. (*The Tribunal*, 5 December 1918)

In addition, the sanitary facilities at the camp were poor (*The Tribunal*, 5 December 1918).

A number of men died while employed at Home Office camps. Ernest England was put on shovel work in the snow, after which he contracted influenza and died (Boulton 1967, 255). Although most deaths were from natural causes, they were also probably avoidable. Because the majority of men had been in prison before accepting the scheme, many were often in a weakened condition as a result of a poor diet and, in some cases, physical abuse. Most were not used to either outdoor or manual work. Concessions to men of vulnerable health were refused, however, and the level of medical support available to men on the scheme tended to be inadequate.

Nonetheless, conditions could be considerably easier than in prison. The silence rule did not apply, and printed programs still exist that reveal the wide variety of entertainment available at the camps, including fancy dress balls, orchestral performances, and dramatic recitals, as well as educational opportunities. Another bonus was that COs who had refused to accept pay while officially in the military were paid while on the Home Office scheme. (Home Office men were paid 8d, or 8 pennies, which was two-thirds of the minimum wage of a private, thus demonstrating that financial loss continued to be a consequence of refusing to accept military service; Rae 1970, 171.) This was particularly important for married men, who had been relying on charity or income from their wives in order to support their families. As a result of a tribunal decision, a number of radicals and pacifists continued to work for the civil service or private employers. A Treasury circular from 10 February 1917, however, argued that COs

> exempted by Tribunals and allowed to remain on their civil duties should receive only their former actual rate of remuneration, without increment, or the rate which would be paid to a temporary substitute performing the duty, whichever was less, and their service should not count for pension or increment. (War Office Paper, WC 298; copy in Liddle Collection, CO 102)

Objectors were also free to leave the camps, though they earned penalties if not back by a specified time. Many COs took advantage of this to have greater contact with family members. When Frederick Peet accepted work at a camp in South Wales, his wife and daughter took lodgings on a nearby farm so that they could see each other regularly (Peet n.d.). More frequently, family members took short holidays close by and were able to go for picnics and walks together. Restrictions on the receiving and sending of letters were also more relaxed than in prison, which meant that communication between Home Office men and their relatives improved even when actual visits were not practical.

Freedom to leave the camps also meant that objectors came into contact with locals. Brocklesby said of the people who lived near his camp,

The Scots of Aberdeenshire were some of the pleasantest people I have ever met. I remember no word of denigration from the local inhabitants. . . . It was the highlight of the week to tramp six miles to the Meeting House in Aberdeen where the good Friends . . . always welcomed us with substantial refreshments. (Brocklesby n.d., 29–30)

Sometimes objectors were only allowed exemption from military service if they accepted work that was more than a certain distance away from their home. Quakers notably always offered a warm welcome to objectors, whether or not they had religious beliefs. In other areas, however, the Home Office men experienced a mixed response and even violent hostility. One of the Payne brothers related one incident where

In Wakefield a chap simply put his fist up and smashed me straight in the face. Things were getting very bitter in Wakefield at that time. We used to be welcomed into a Quaker house . . . and a lot of people in Wakefield knew of this and they went up to smash up this house. (Payne and Payne 1973)

Similarly, a CO at another camp was thrown off his bicycle and stabbed in the neck with a steel picker (Millar 1935, 253).

The desire to ensure that objectors were experiencing some form of penalty was also demonstrated by the success of B. N. Langdon-Davies's offer to accept work as a baker. Langdon-Davies knew and had records "of a schoolmaster being forced to become a market gardener and a market gardener a school master in the interests of national efficiency" (Langdon-Davies 1935, 193). He was therefore not surprised that, upon his offer being accepted, one of the committee members explained, "We think you are so unsuited to the job that it is of national importance that you should do it" (Langdon-Davies 1935, 193).

Other objectors received work of national importance after serving a prison sentence. Leonard and Roland Payne, religious pacifists, were released to do work for their father. This was greatly resented by the local community. The local newspaper reported,

There were riotous scenes at Lutterworth last week owing to the presence of two young Conscientious Objectors, the sons of Mr. J. G. Payne, basket maker, Church Street. Public feeling was aroused, and considerable damage was done to Mr. Payne's property. (Newspaper cutting in Payne and Payne 1973)

Millar also spent time in prison before being offered and accepting work of national importance. Although employees at a market garden threatened to strike rather than work with him, in general he was treated "more or less as a normal human being" (Millar 1935, 265, 257). He noted in particular the kindness of one woman who gave him a present of a little money as he left to take up work elsewhere (Millar 1935, 259).

Many pacifists volunteered for medical or relief work, or accepted such work as an alternative to enforced combatant service. Others, however, argued that "If we restore to health a wounded soldier, we are faced by the grave responsibility of making him fit to go out and inflict death again" (*The Labour Leader*, 17 February 1916).

For those who did accept medical or relief work, it was often a rewarding and enjoyable experience. When Roland Bainton, an American Quaker, was shipped to France, he traveled "first class, because as members of the Red Cross we were all officers, conscientious objectors trying to combine service with protest" (Bainton n.d.). Charlie Dingle, a religious pacifist, joined the Friends Ambulance Unit (FAU) and went to France in 1917. He said of his work on an ambulance train, "In many ways it was the happiest time of my life. They were a very nice lot of fellows and we all had various what you might call the spiritual side of life in common and they were very friendly and I was very happy" (Dingle 1977).

David Garnett was involved in work for the relief of war victims, building homes for the French about ten miles away from the war. He recalled that "The generosity of these people was amazing; before we had been there a month, they were giving us most of our food" (Garnett 1935, 136–137).

Medical and relief work could, however, also involve hardship and even danger. At Garnett's post, "The thud of guns was often continuous all through the day and a heavy bombardment sometimes woke us up with rattling window-panes during the night" (Garnett 1935, 136–137).

Olaf Stapledon was working for the FAU in France during the bitterly cold winter of 1916–1917. As he remembered it, "I used to sleep out in a 'tourer' that I was driving at this time. A suitcase formed part of my bed. In the suitcase was a bottle of ink. It froze under me. Everything froze, the wine, the bread, our boots" (Stapledon 1935, 367).

Stapledon did a lot of work transporting the wounded to hospitals and spent some time in an area where "occasional shelling afforded the required sense of danger" (Stapledon 1935, 367). He sometimes had to drive down a particularly bad stretch of road that was "constantly shelled. Shells were landing all around. One was near enough to stuff the car sideways" (Stapledon 1935, 367). Rather than avoiding danger, some pacifists welcomed it, for it gave them the opportunity to prove that their objection to military service was genuinely based on their conscientious beliefs and not on cowardice.

Clearly, many factors affected the ways in which radicals and pacifists experienced World War I. The attitude of family members was also important, since family could be a source of support for objectors or a further source of pressure. Stanley Rees's father and mother were socialists and were happy to support him in his antimilitarist stand (Rees 1971). Sybil White was asked by a prison governor to use her influence to persuade her husband to accept work of national importance, but she refused, pointing out that her husband had to make his own decisions (Wells 1989, 46).

In contrast, Raymond Postgate, who was also a socialist, received a letter from his father that stated:

> The pursuit of peace to the damage of one's own country is nothing short of treason. Pacifism with you, as with many of your contemporaries, appears to be conjoined with an attitude to the state and present society which, to speak frankly, is that of advocates of robbery and revolution. (Postgate 1917)

Similarly, one of the Payne brothers remembered of the man in the next room, "They used to regularly bring his wife to see him and his wife used to plead with him to give in[,] but the fellow stuck to his guns and wouldn't obey his wife even" (Payne and Payne 1973).

Charlie Dingle was turned out of the family home because of his views (Dingle 1977). His mother had to appeal for help to enable Charlie to join the FAU since, as she explained: "My husband has completely cast the lad off because [Charlie] is unable to fight, so it is quite impossible to get any financial assistance from him" (Dingle 1916).

As Harold Bing explained about the offer of the Home Office scheme to men in prison, "For some men . . . with family responsibilities or whose wives were unsympathetic, it was always a terrific pressure on them to get out. . . . It was in some cases a necessity to save a marriage" (Goodall 1997, 42).

Married or not, family willing or not, radicals and pacifists who had been incarcerated, put in camps, or otherwise detained by the government were not immediately free to return to their lives after the signing of the

Armistice in November 1918. Demobilization from the army or release from prison, the Home Office scheme, or work "of national importance" often did not occur for many months. Many pacifists who had volunteered for relief work believed, moreover, that there was still a great deal of work for them to do and so chose to stay many miles from home in order to continue.

Once released from their obligations under the Military Service Acts, some men had little difficulty in returning to their previous forms of employment, whereas others discovered that it was difficult for COs to find work. Donald Fraser, a religious pacifist, was unable to return to university to finish his degree because a professor would not allow COs to continue their studies (Shears 1977). Although some objectors were welcomed home by their family and friends, Fraser was disinherited by the whole of his mother's family (Shears 1977). Raymond Postgate and his sister were also disinherited because of their socialist and pacifist beliefs (Cole 1977). Although not always enforced effectively, in Britain, COs were further disenfranchised for a period of five years.

The psychological effects of time spent as an objector continued to affect some men after they had returned home. Harold Blake noted that "my rest was broken and disturbed—frequently destroyed—by horrible and nerve-wracking dreams" (Goodall 1997, 62). Millar confessed to still having nightmares about being back in solitary confinement seventeen years after the war was over (Millar 1935, 243). As with the veterans who fought, the trauma of the First World War did not necessarily end for those who objected to the fighting with the signing of the Armistice.

—Anne-Marie Pennington

References and Further Reading

Allen, C. n.d. "The Faith of the NCF." In *The No-Conscription Fellowship: A Souvenir of Its Work during the Years 1914–1919*. London: NCF.

Ayles, W., et al. 1916. *Why I Am a Conscientious Objector: Being Answers to the Tribunal Catechism*. London: NCF.

Bainton, R. H. n.d. Typescript recollections. In Liddle Collection, University of Leeds, CO 003.

Baxter, A. 1968. *We Will Not Cease: The Autobiography of a Conscientious Objector*. Christchurch: Caxton. Copy in Liddle Collection, University of Leeds, CO 005.

Boulton, David. 1967. *Objection Overruled.* London: MacGibbon and Kee.

Brocklesby, J. H. n.d. "Escape from Paganism." Typescript recollections. Copy in Liddle Collection, University of Leeds, CO 011.

Ceadel, M. 1980. *Pacifism in Britain, 1914–1945: The Defining of a Faith.* Oxford: Clarendon.

Cheyne, Mr. 1971. Interview (September). In Liddle Collection, University of Leeds, CO 018.

Cole, M. 1977. Interview, September. In Liddle Collection, University of Leeds, DF 035.

Cormack, W. S. 1972. Typescript recollections. In Liddle Collection, University of Leeds, CO 022.

Dingle, A. 1916. Letter to the Secretary of the FAU. In Liddle Collection, University of Leeds, CO 024.

Dingle, C. F. 1977. Interview, September. In Liddle Collection, University of Leeds, CO 024.

Evans, A. W. 1973. Interview, May. In Liddle Collection, University of Leeds, CO 030.

Florence, L. S. 1935. "The Ford Peace Ship and After." In J. Bell, ed., *We Did Not Fight 1914–1918: Experiences of War Resisters.* London: Cobden-Sanderson.

Garnett, D. 1935. "War Victims Relief." In J. Bell, ed., *We Did Not Fight 1914–1918: Experiences of War Resisters.* London: Cobden-Sanderson.

Goodall, F. 1997. *A Question of Conscience: Conscientious Objection in the Two World Wars.* Stroud, UK: Sutton.

Haynes, H. H. n.d. Interview. In Liddle Collection, University of Leeds, CO 045.

Hobhouse, Mrs. Henry. 1917. *"I Appeal Unto Caesar": The Case of the Conscientious Objector.* London: Allen and Unwin.

Hobhouse, S., ed. 1934. *Margaret Hobhouse and Her Family.* Rochester: Stanhope.

Kennedy, Thomas C. 1981. *The Hound of Conscience: A History of the No-Conscription Fellowship, 1914–1919.* Fayetteville: University of Arkansas Press.

———. 1989. "'They in the Lord Who Firmly Trust': A Friend at War with the Great War." *Quaker History* 78: 87–102.

Langdon-Davies, B. N. 1935. "Alternative Service." In J. Bell, ed., *We Did Not Fight 1914–1918: Experiences of War Resisters.* London: Cobden-Sanderson.

Manthorpe, W. n.d. Typescript recollections. In Liddle Collection, University of Leeds, CO 060.

Memorandum from Adjutant General Macready, 16 May 1916. Copy in Liddle Collection, University of Leeds, CO 102.

Millar, J. P. M. 1935. "A Socialist in War Time." In J. Bell, ed., *We Did Not Fight 1914–1918: Experiences of War Resisters.* London: Cobden-Sanderson.

Moorehead, Caroline. 1987. *Troublesome People: Enemies of War, 1916–1986.* London: Hamilton.

NCF Brighton and District Branch Register of Members' Appearances before Local Tribunals. Books 1 and 2. In Liddle Collection, University of Leeds, CO 102.

Oldfield, S. 1989. *Women against the Iron Fist: Alternatives to Militarism, 1900–1989.* Oxford: Blackwell.

Payne, L. J., and R. J. Payne. 1973. Interview, February. In Liddle Collection, University of Leeds, CO 070.

Pearce, C. 2001. *Comrades in Conscience: The Story of an English Community's Opposition to the Great War.* London: Francis Boutle.

Pease, H. 1979. Interview, June. In Liddle Collection, University of Leeds, CO 071.

Peet, F. n.d. Typescript recollections. In Liddle Collection, University of Leeds, CO 072.

Peet, H. W. n.d. "The Men Sentenced to Death." In *The No-Conscription Fellowship: A Souvenir of Its Work during the Years 1914–1919.* London: NCF.

Postgate, J. P. 1917. Letter to Son, 4 November. In Liddle Collection, University of Leeds, CO 075.

Rae, John. 1970. *Conscience and Politics: The British Government and the Conscientious Objector to Military Service, 1916–1919.* London: Oxford University Press.

Rees, S. 1971. Interview, October. In Liddle Collection, University of Leeds, CO 077.

Rowbotham, Sheila. 1986. *Friends of Alice Wheeldon.* London: Pluto.

Scraps of Paper: An Examination of Government Pledges with Regard to Conscientious Objectors and the Present Position of 1,137 Men in Prison. n.d. London: NCF.

Shears, E. 1977. Interview, April. In Liddle Collection, University of Leeds, CO 034.

Stanton, H. n.d. *Will You March Too?* Copy in Liddle Collection, University of Leeds, CO 092.

———. 1976. Interview, July. In Liddle Collection, University of Leeds, CO 092.

Stapledon, O. 1935. "Experiences in the Friends' Ambulance Unit." In J. Bell, ed., *We Did Not Fight 1914–1918: Experiences of War Resisters.* London: Cobden-Sanderson.

Useem, M. 1973. *Conscription, Protest, and Social Conflict: The Life and Death of a Draft Resistance Movement.* New York: John Wiley and Sons.

Vellacott, J. 1980. *Bertrand Russell and the Pacifists in the First World War.* Brighton: Harvester.

Wells P. M., ed., 1989. *"Quick, Thy Tablets, Memory!" Sybil W. White, Lifelong Quaker, Pacifist and Internationalist—Her Reminiscences.* Nottingham: privately published. Copy in Liddle Collection, University of Leeds, CO 099.

Wheatcroft, H. 1976. Questionnaire. In Liddle Collection, University of Leeds, CO 098.

White, S. 1917. Diary. In Liddle Collection, University of Leeds, CO 099.

Wilcock, E. 1987. "The Revd. John Harris: Issues in Anglo-Jewish Pacifism, 1914–1918." *Jewish Historical Studies* 30: 163–174.

TIMELINE

---◆---

1914

28 June   Archduke Franz Ferdinand and Archduchess Sophie of Austria-Hungary are assassinated in Sarajevo, Bosnia, by Gavrilo Princip.

23 July   The Austro-Hungarian ambassador to Serbia delivers the ultimatum of his government to the Serbs.

28 July   Austria-Hungary declares war against Serbia.

1 August   Germany declares war against Russia.

3 August   Germany declares war against France.

4 August   Germany declares war against Belgium; Great Britain declares war against Germany.

5 August   Austria-Hungary declares war against Russia; Montenegro declares war against Austria-Hungary.

6 August   Serbia declares war against Germany. French forces capture two German outposts in the Cameroons.

10 August   France declares war against Austria-Hungary.

12 August   German forces shell Liege, Belgium. Russia launches its invasion of East Prussia with General Pavel Rennkampf commanding the First Army.

16 August   Liege surrenders.

23 August   Japan declares war against Germany. German forces execute 612 Belgian civilians in the town of Diment.

25 August   German forces capture Namur, Mulhouse, and Sedan. The Belgian city of Louvain is burned by the Germans "in reprisal" for civilians firing on German soldiers.

26 August   The Battle of Tannenberg begins.

27 August   The Battle of Heligoland Bight marks the first naval action of the war.

30 August   A single German plane bombs Paris with leaflets and ordnance. The three bombs dropped by the pilot kill two people.

31 August   The Battle of Tannenberg draws to a close. German forces surround the Russian Second Army, capturing over 100,000 prisoners. General Alexander Samsonov, the Russian commander, commits suicide.

1 September   Saint Petersburg, Russia, is rechristened Petrograd to avoid any allusions to things German.

2 September   Twenty-four thousand Japanese troops land on the Shantung Peninsula of China, threatening the German colonial possession at Tsingtao. In Europe, the French government relocates to Bordeaux in the face of the rapid German advance.

3 September   Russian troops occupy Lemberg (L'viv).

5 September   The Battle of Masurian Lakes begins on the eastern front; on the western front, French forces make a desperate stand on the Marne River, opening the First Battle of the Marne.

11 September   French forces halt the Germans on the Marne and send them into retreat, saving France.

13 September   The Battle of Masurian Lakes, another stunning victory for the Germans, comes to an end. It is largely without meaning for Germany in light of the defeat on the Marne.

26 September   German troops lay siege to Antwerp.

27 September   The Ottoman Empire declares the Bosphorus closed to Allied shipping at the behest of General Otto Liman von Sanders, the head of the German Military Mission to Constantinople.

9 October   Antwerp surrenders to the Germans.

16 October   The first contingent of the New Zealand Expeditionary Force—8,574 men—sails for France.

17 October   The first contingent of the Australian Expeditionary Force—20,226 men—sails for France.

20 October   German forces launch an offensive along the entire front in Flanders, in the Netherlands, with the German Fourth Army facing the British Expeditionary Force (BEF) near Ypres.

25 October   The Dutch dikes are opened to stop the German offensive in Flanders at the command of French general Ferdinand Foch.

1 November   General Paul von Hindenburg assumes command of the German eastern front.

4 November   British troops attack the town of Tanga in German East Africa.

7 November	Tsingtao surrenders to the Japanese.
15 November	The First Battle of Ypres comes to an end with massive losses on all sides. The Germans suffer 130,000 casualties, and the British and French lose 58,000 to 60,000 men each. The lines of trenches on the western front will remain relatively stable from this point until April 1918.
18 November	The French government returns to Paris.
1 December	Austro-Hungarian forces capture Belgrade.
15 December	The Austro-Hungarian troops are forced to evacuate Belgrade.
25 December	An unofficial truce holds along the front in Flanders. German and British troops exchange songs and gifts.

1915

4 January	Russian troops defeat the Ottomans at Sarikamish. The Turkish forces suffer 78,000 casualties in a force of only 90,000.
18 January	Two German zeppelins raid England.
29 January	The first large naval confrontation of the war takes place in the North Sea. The Battle of Dogger Banks has little impact, however.
31 January	The Germans unveil a new weapon in the battle against the Russians at Bolimow: chlorine gas. Low temperatures render the gas ineffective.
4 February	Germany announces a submarine blockade of Great Britain.
19 February	The Allies begin the campaign to open the Dardanelles, sending a naval squadron of eighteen battleships that includes two "mini-Dreadnoughts" and the *Queen Elizabeth*, a super-Dreadnought.
1 March	Great Britain announces a naval blockade against Germany.
10 March	The British Expeditionary Force launches an offensive at Neuve Chapelle.
18 March	The Russian commander-in-chief, the Grand Duke Nicholas, decrees that Russian operations will concentrate on the southern portion of the front, against the Austro-Hungarian forces. Against the Germans in the north, Russian troops have met only defeat.
21 March	Three German zeppelins bomb Paris.
22 March	The Austrian fortress of Przmysl falls to the Russians, yielding over 120,000 prisoners of war.
1 April	The first aerial "dogfight" takes place on the western front as French pilot Lieutenant Roland Garros shoots down a German foe.

8 April	Ottoman forces begin a systematic campaign of extermination against the Armenian population of the empire.
22 April	The Germans open the Second Battle of Ypres with a massive gas attack against French colonial troops. The gas is more effective this time, but the Germans fail to follow up effectively.
25 April	The Allied attack on Gallipoli begins.
26 April	Italy agrees to join the Allied side in the war, signing the Treaty of London. Secret clauses guarantee the Italians, who began the war as members of the Triple Alliance, territorial gains in South Tyrol, Dalmatia, and Istria.
7 May	The *Lusitania* is torpedoed and sunk by a German submarine. More than 1,000 passengers lose their lives, including 128 American citizens.
11 May	Russian forces begin a full-scale retreat before the Austro-Hungarian "Black-Gold offensive" along the southern portions of the eastern front. The withdrawal will end three months later, more than 250 miles to the east.
23 May	Italy declares war against Austria-Hungary; contrary to the provisions of the Treaty of London, Germany is not included in the declaration.
25 May	The Second Battle of Ypres comes to a close. Once again, losses on all sides are staggering.
27 May	Italy attacks Austria-Hungary along the Isonzo River front, opening the first of a dozen campaigns there.
3 June	The fortress at Przmysl is recaptured by troops of the Central Powers.
4 June	ANZAC (Australian and New Zealand Army Corps) forces establish a beachhead wide enough to bring trench warfare to the Gallipoli Peninsula.
5 June	The German government adopts restrictions on submarine warfare, hoping to avoid the entry of neutral countries in the conflict.
22 June	The Central Powers retake Lemberg (L'viv).
5 July	The First Isonzo campaign comes to a close. Italian casualties total 13,411. Their opponents lose 8,800 men.
9 July	German Southwest Africa surrenders to British forces.
18 July	The Second Isonzo campaign opens.
20 August	Italy declares war against the Ottoman Empire.
26 August	German and Austro-Hungarian troops capture the cities of Brest-Litovsk and Bialystok in Russian Poland.

5 September   Tsar Nicholas II assumes command of all Russian forces. To perform his duties, he will relocate to army headquarters at Mogilev, leaving the tsarina and Rasputin essentially a free hand in the administration of the capital.

6 September   Bulgaria, reputed to be the "Prussia of the Balkans," joins the Central Powers in exchange for a promise of Macedonian and Ottoman territory. The Bulgarian army numbers 517,000 men, with an additional 300,000 in reserve.

18 September   German forces capture Vilnius.

25 September   The Central Powers' eastern offensive comes to a close, just as France launches an offensive on the Champagne front in the west.

9 October   Austro-Hungarian forces, augmented by a German division, retake Belgrade.

30 November   A fierce storm drowns some 200 Allied soldiers still pinned down on the beaches at Gallipoli.

8 December   The evacuation of the Allied beachheads at Sulva Bay and ANZAC Cove begins. Carried out with extreme caution and craft, the withdrawal is accomplished without the death of a single Allied soldier.

1916

10 January   The British evacuation of Cape Helles marks the end of the Dardanelles campaign. To counter the release of pressure on the Ottoman forces, the Russians launch an offensive at Koprukoy.

17 January   Montenegro surrenders to the Central Powers.

21 February   German forces open a campaign against the French network of fortifications at Verdun. Labeled "Justice" by the German commanders, the offensive employs 1,220 pieces of artillery on a front of just eight miles.

26 February   After Douaumont, one of the outer forts around Verdun, is taken by the Germans, General Phillipe Petain assumes command of the French front. Among his first messages is the now-famous byword: "They shall not pass."

18 March   The Russians launch a premature offensive against the Germans around Lake Narotch in an attempt to relieve the pressure on Verdun. An unseasonal thaw renders the battlefield first a swamp and then a glacier. The Russians gain no ground.

16 April   Seven U.S. pilots, known as the "Layfayette Escadrille," officially become part of the French air force stationed in Luxeuil.

24 April   Irish nationalists, supported by the German fleet, stage a rising in Dublin. Using increasingly brutal tactics, the British quell the rebellion by 29 April; the rebel leaders are summarily executed.

29 April   British forces besieged in the town of Kut in Mesopotamia since 7 December 1915, surrender to the Ottomans. Most of the Allied soldiers will be marched across the open desert to Baghdad and imprisoned.

15 May   Austria-Hungary launches an offensive against Italy in the Trentino instead of on the Isonzo, and manages to break through the Italian lines within a week.

31 May   The Battle of Jutland begins. The only significant contest between the British Grand Fleet and the German High Seas Fleet is one of the most confusing naval battles in history. The Germans sink three British battlecruisers, three cruisers, and eight destroyers and claim victory. After the Battle of Jutland, however, the German fleet never ventures into open waters again.

4 June   To relieve Austrian pressure on Italy and the continuing German campaign against Verdun, the Russians open a new offensive in the east. Though designed to press the Germans in the north, it is General Alexei Brusilov, commander of the southwestern front, who sees the greatest success. Within a few weeks, the offensive that will take his name recovers most of the territory lost in Galicia during 1915.

22 June   The Germans introduce a new form of chemical warfare, using phosgene gas against the French at Verdun.

1 July   The Allied offensive on the Somme River opens.

19 July   The Allies begin a second offensive in Flanders. Within two weeks, each side suffers more than 160,000 casualties.

4 August   Inspired by the success of the Brusilov offensive, Romania agrees to join the Allies in the war. This turns out to be a great addition—for the Central Powers.

17 August   Bulgarian, German, and Austro-Hungarian troops attack Romania.

15 September   Eighteen tanks participate in the battles on the Somme. Forty-nine were intended to take part in the offensive, but most of the new weapons broke down or got lost.

10 October   The Brusilov offensive collapses under its own weight. Though the Russians gain huge amounts of territory, it costs them more than 1.4 million casualties.

24 October   Douaumont returns to French hands.

5 November   Kaiser Wilhelm II of Germany and Kaiser Franz Josef of Austria-Hungary issue a decree—the "Two Emperors" Manifesto—

declaring Poland a semi-independent kingdom under Hapsburg protection.

19 November The Battle of the Somme ends. Each side suffers more than 600,000 casualties.

21 November Franz Josef dies in Vienna. He is succeeded by his grand nephew, Karl I.

7 December The Central Powers occupy Bucharest. They are denied the use of Romania's oil resources, however, through the actions of a British agent, who managed to set the oil fields aflame.

12 December German chancellor Theobald von Bethman-Hollweg attempts to initiate peace talks. He is denounced by the Allies in public statements on 30 December.

22 December The Germans finally call off the campaign against Verdun, having suffered 337,000 casualties. In the longest battle in history, the French sustain 377,231 casualties but defeat the German strategy of attrition.

30 December Rasputin is murdered in Petrograd.

1917

9 January Germany returns to unrestricted submarine warfare, though this is not announced until 31 January.

16 January German foreign minister Arthur Zimmerman sends a message to the German minister to Mexico proposing a possible alliance with that country should the United States enter the war.

1 March The Zimmerman Telegram is revealed to the American public.

14 March The Petrograd Soviet, a revolutionary governmental body that has proclaimed itself in charge of Russia during a period of riots and disorder, issues its first order. Order No. 1 nullifies the existing chain of command in the army and calls on the soldiers of Russia to obey only the soviet. Surprisingly, many do.

16 March Tsar Nicholas II abdicates in favor of his brother Michael during a stopover in the city of Pskov. A provisional government is declared in Petrograd. The tsar was on his way back to the capital to quell the disturbances there when government and military officials convinced him it was useless. Three hundred years of rule by the Romanov dynasty come to an end the next day when Michael renounces the throne.

7 April The United States declares war against Germany.

16 April Vladimir Ilych Lenin arrives in Petrograd, courtesy of the German government.

30 April	Brought to desperation by the German submarine blockade, the British navy adopts the convoy system. More than 830,000 tons of shipping had been lost in April alone.
3 June	Over 35,000 French troops protest their orders to return to the front. It is the largest of many mutinies in the French army that spring. Most, however, had been kept secret to this point.
18 June	The Russians launch a new offensive to recapture Lemberg (L'viv). The Italians take the offensive in the Trentino.
20 June	The troops of the Russian Seventh and Eleventh Armies mutiny, ending the offensive before it can really begin. The Eighth Army, under General Lavr Kornilov, holds out until 2 July before succumbing to disorder.
6 July	T. E. Lawrence and a band of Howeitat tribesmen capture the Arab city of Aqaba after a two-month march across the desert.
19 July	The German *Reichstag* passes a "Peace Resolution" by a vote of 212–120.
20 July	The draft is initiated in the United States.
31 July	The Third Battle of Ypres, called simply "Passchendaele" by some, begins. It will be one of the most costly and tragic battles of the war.
14 August	China declares war against Austria-Hungary and Germany. This is essentially a ploy to claim the colonial possessions of these powers in Asia and the Pacific.
5 September	German forces capture Riga.
12 September	An attempted coup led by General Kornilov fails. His troops are halted less than sixty miles from the capital by railway workers who wrecked the line and then convinced the soldiers to join them in supporting the Bolsheviks.
16 September	A battalion of Russian troops serving in France is surrounded by another battalion of Russian troops serving in France and captured. Troops loyal to the provisional government of Russia defeat those loyal to the Bolsheviks.
31 October	British foreign secretary Arthur J. Balfour issues his famous declaration in favor of establishing a Jewish national homeland in Palestine.
7 November	Led by Leon Trotsky, the Bolsheviks stage a successful coup in Petrograd, seizing control of the government there almost unopposed.
22 November	The new Bolshevik government proposes an immediate end to the war and publishes the secret prewar agreements of the Allies, complete with promises of territorial gain.
6 December	Romania sues for an armistice.

11 December   British forces led by General Edmund Allenby enter Jerusalem.

15 December   Germany and Russia agree to an armistice.

1918

8 January   U.S. president Woodrow Wilson announces his "Fourteen Points" in a hurriedly convened joint session of Congress.

19 January   The Bolsheviks dissolve the Constituent Assembly in Russia and proceed to rule by decree.

28 January   Led by the ultra–left-wing Spartacus League, workers stage a general strike for peace in Berlin.

3 March   Russia and Germany sign the Treaty of Brest-Litovsk. The agreement cedes large amounts of territory to Germany or to German-dominated governments, but gets Russia out of the war.

11 March   The first cases of what will become a worldwide influenza epidemic are noted at a U.S. Army base in Kansas.

14 March   German troops occupy Odessa.

21 March   Germany launches an offensive on the Somme.

14 April   General Foch is named as Allied commander-in-chief.

7 May   Romania signs a peace treaty granting Germany control over two ports, a ninety-year lease on the Romanian oil fields, and guaranteeing deliveries of food at low fixed prices. Like the Treaty of Brest-Litovsk, the Peace of Bucharest becomes a symbol of German aspirations and brutality.

6 June   The American Expeditionary Force (AEF) sees its first significant action in the Battle of Bellau Woods. The U.S. Marine Brigade of the Second Division suffers 1,087 casualties.

16 June   Austria-Hungary launches an offensive against Italy along the Piave River.

16 July   Tsar Nicholas and his family are murdered by the Bolsheviks at Yekaterinburg.

3 August   A division of Japanese troops lands in Vladivostok.

10 August   A division of American troops lands in Vladivostok. At the same time, the U.S. First Army is officially formed in France and tasked with attacking the Saint Mihel salient.

20 September   Australian cavalry forces capture Jenin, giving the Allies control over the plain south of Nazareth.

1 October   The Australian cavalry enter Damascus.

3 October   Prince Max of Baden, the new German chancellor, sends President Wilson a note accepting the Fourteen Points as the basis

for peace negotiations. The Austro-Hungarian government echoes the sentiment on 7 October.

13 October   Allenby's forces occupy Tripoli.

18 October   Thomas Masryk issues a Czech Declaration of Independence intended to gain Allied sympathy for the cause of Czech nationalism.

29 October   Sailors in the German fleet mutiny against the order to head to sea for what they presume will be a suicide mission.

9 November   Prince Max announces the abdication of Kaiser Wilhem II. He then convinces the kaiser that it is useless to remain in power, and Wilhelm flees to the Netherlands. Romania declares war against Germany once again.

11 November   The Armistice is signed in a railway car outside of Paris. Karl I abdicates the thrones of Austria and Hungary.

BIBLIOGRAPHY

Adams, R. J. Q., ed. *The Great War, 1914–1918: Essays on the Military, Political, and Social History of the First World War*. College: Texas A&M University Press, 1990.

Barnett, Correlli. *The Swordbearers: Supreme Command in the First World War*. Bloomington: Indiana University Press, 1964.

Barrie, Alexander. *War Underground: The Tunnellers of the Great War*. London: Tom Donovan Publishers, 1988.

Becker, Jean Jacques. *The Great War and the French People*. New York: Berg, 1985.

Beckett, Ian, and Keith Simpson. *A Nation in Arms: A Social Study of the British Army in the First World War*. Manchester: Manchester University Press, 1985.

Bourne, J. M. *Britain and the Great War*. London: Edward Arnold, 1989.

Bristow, Nancy K. *Making Men Moral: Social Engineering during the Great War*. New York: New York University Press, 1996.

Brook-Shepherd, Gordon. *November 1918*. Boston: Little, Brown & Co., 1981.

Cecil, Hugh, and Peter Liddle, eds. *Facing Armageddon: The First World War Experienced*. London: Cooper, 1996.

Coffman, Edward. *The War to End All Wars: The American Military Experience*. New York: Oxford University Press, 1968.

Condell, Diana, and Jean Liddiard, eds. *Working for Victory? Images of Women in the First World War, 1914–1918*. London: Routledge and Kegan Paul, 1987.

Conner, Valerie Jean. *The National War Labor Board: Stability, Social Justice, and the Voluntary State in World War I*. Chapel Hill: University of North Carolina Press, 1983.

Constantine, Stephen, Maurice W. Kirby, and Mary B. Rose, eds. *The First World War in British History*. New York: St. Martin's Press, 1995.

Craig, Grace Morris. *But This Is Our War*. Toronto: University of Toronto Press, 1981.

Culleton, Claire A. *Working Class Culture, Women and Britain, 1914–1921*. New York: St. Martin's Press, 2000.

Dakers, Caroline. *The Countryside at War, 1914–1918*. London: Constable, 1987.

Evans, Raymond. *Loyalty and Disloyalty: Social Conflict on the Queensland Homefront, 1914–1918*. Sydney: Allen & Unwin, 1987.

Feldman, Gerald D. *Army, Industry and Labor in Germany, 1914–1918*. Princeton: Princeton University Press, 1966.

Field, Frank. *British and French Writers of the First World War: Comparative Studies in Cultural History*. Cambridge: Cambridge University Press, 1991.

Fridenson, Patrick, ed. *The French Home Front, 1914–1918*. Oxford: Oxford University Press, 1977.

Fuller, J. G. *Troop Morale and Popular Culture in the British and Dominion Armies, 1914–1918*. Oxford: Clarendon Press, 1990.

Grayling, Christopher. *A Land Fit for Heroes: British Life after the Great War*. London: Buchan & Enright, 1987.

Gwyn, Sandra. *Tapestry of War: A Private View of Canadians in the Great War*. Toronto: HarperCollins Publishers, 1992.

Haber, L. F. *The Poisonous Cloud: Chemical Warfare in the First World War*. Oxford: Oxford University Press, 1986.

Harris, J. P. *Men, Ideas, and Tanks*. Manchester, U.K.: Manchester University Press, 1995.

Healy, Maureen. *Vienna and the Fall of the Habsburg Empire: Total War and Everyday Life in World War I*. Cambridge: Cambridge University Press, 2004.

Horn, Daniel. *The German Naval Mutinies of World War I*. New Brunswick, N.J.: Rutgers University Press, 1969.

Horne, John N. *Labour at War: France and Britain, 1914–1918*. Oxford: Clarendon Press, 1991.

———. *State, Society and Mobilization in Europe during the First World War*. Cambridge: Cambridge University Press, 1997.

Hurwitz, Samuel J. *State Intervention in Great Britain: A Study of Economic Control and Social Response, 1914–1919*. New York: Columbia University Press, 1949.

Hynes, Samuel Lynn. *A War Imagined: The First World War and English Culture*. New York: Atheneum, 1991.

Keene, Jennifer D. *Doughboys, the Great War, and the Remaking of America*. Baltimore: Johns Hopkins University Press, 2001.

Kennedy, David M. *Over Here: The First World War and American Society*. Oxford: Oxford University Press, 1982.

Kirschbaum, Erik. *The Eradication of German Culture in the United States, 1917–1918*. Stuttgart: H. D. Heinz, 1986.

Liddle, Peter H. *Home Fires and Foreign Fields: British Social and Military Experience in the First World War*. London: Brassey's Defence Publishers, 1985.

———. *The Soldiers' War, 1914–1918*. London: Blandford, 1988.

Liddell-Hart, Basil H. *The Real War, 1914–1918*. Boston: Little, Brown & Co., 1930.

Lih, Lars. *Bread and Authority in Russia, 1914–1921*. Berkeley: University of California Press, 1990.

Liulevicius, Vejas G. *War Land on the Eastern Front: Culture, National Identity and German Occupation in World War I*. Cambridge: Cambridge University Press, 2000.

Macdonald, Lyn. *Somme*. London: M. Joseph, 1983.

———. *They Called It Passchendale: The Story of the Third Battle of Ypres and the Men Who Fought It*. New York: Atheneum, 1989.

Mackaman, Douglas, and Michael Mays, eds. *World War I and the Cultures of Modernity.* Jackson: University Press of Mississippi, 2000.

MacKenzie, Jeanne. *The Children of the Souls: A Tragedy of the First World War.* London: Chatto & Windus, 1986.

Marwick, Arthur. *The Deluge: British Society and the First World War.* New York: Norton, 1970.

———. *Women at War, 1914–1918.* London: Fontana Paperbacks, 1977.

McClymer, John F. *War and Welfare: Social Engineering in America, 1890–1925.* Westport, CT: Greenwood Press, 1980.

Mitchell, David J. *Women on the Warpath: The Story of the Women of the First World War.* London: Cape, 1966.

Mitrany, David. *The Land & the Peasant in Rumania: The War and Agrarian Reform.* New York: Greenwood Press, 1968.

Piper, John F. *The Social Policy of the Federal Council of the Churches of Christ in America during World War I.* Durham, NC: Duke University Press, 1965.

Raynsford, William. *Silent Casualties: Veterans' Families in the Aftermath of the Great War.* Madoc, Ontario: Merribrae, 1986.

Read, Daphne, ed. *The Great War and Canadian Society: An Oral History.* Toronto: New Hogtown Press, 1978.

Robb, George. *British Culture and the First World War.* Basingstoke, U.K.: Palgrave, 2002.

Robson, Stuart. *The First World War.* New York: Longman, 1998.

Rosenwald, Aviel, and Richard Stites, eds. *European Culture in the Great War: The Arts, Entertainment and Propaganda, 1914–1918.* Cambridge: Cambridge University Press, 1999.

Rozenblitz, Marsha L. *Reconstructing a National Identity: The Jews of Habsburg Austria during World War I.* Oxford: Oxford University Press, 2001.

Ruck, Calvin. *The Black Battalion, 1916–1920: Canada's Best-kept Military Secret.* Halifax: Nimbus, 1987.

Saunders, Nicholas J. *Trench Art: Materialities and Memories of War.* New York: Berg, 2003.

Schmitt, Bernadotte, and Harold Vedeler. *The World in the Crucible, 1914–1919.* New York: HarperCollins, 1984.

Simkins, Peter. *Kitchener's Army: The Raising of the New Armies, 1914–1916.* Manchester, U.K.: Manchester University Press, 1988.

Slosson, Preston W. *The Great Crusade and After, 1914–1928.* Chicago: Quadrangle-Books, 1971.

Stallings, L. *The Doughboys: The Story of the AEF, 1917–1918.* New York: HarperCollins, 1963.

Stibbe, Matthew. *German Anglophobia and the Great War, 1914–1918.* Cambridge: Cambridge University Press, 2001.

Sweeny, Regina M. *Singing Our Way to Victory: French Cultural Politics and Music during the Great War.* Middletown, CT: Wesleyan University Press, 2001.

Thayer, John. *Italy and the Great War: Politics and Culture, 1870–1915.* Madison: University of Wisconsin Press, 1964.

Thompson, John Herd. *The Harvests of War: The Prairie West, 1914–1918.* Toronto: McClelland and Stewart, 1978.

Travers, Tim. *How the War Was Won.* London: Routledge, 1992.

Van Wienan, Mark W. *Partisans and Poets: The Political Work of American Poetry in the Great War.* Cambridge: Cambridge University Press, 1997.

Verhey, Jeffrey. *The Spirit of 1914: Militarism, Myth, and Mobilization in Germany.* Cambridge: Cambridge University Press, 2000.

Waites, Bernard. *A Class Society at War, England 1914–1918.* New York: Berg, 1987.

Wall, Richard, and Jay Winter, eds. *The Upheaval of War: Family, Work, and Welfare in Europe, 1914–1918.* Cambridge: Cambridge University Press, 1988.

Watkins, Gordon S. *Labor Problems and Labor Administration in the United States during the World War.* 1920. Reprint, New York: Johnson Reprint Corporation, 1970.

Watson, Janet S. *Fighting Different Wars: Experience, Memory, and the First World War in Britain.* Cambridge: Cambridge University Press, 2004.

Watt, Richard. *Dare Call It Treason.* Reprint, New York: Dorset, 2001. New York: Simon & Schuster, 1963.

Weintraub, Stanley. *A Stillness Heard Round the World: The End of the Great War, November 1918.* New York: Allen & Unwin, 1985.

Williams, John. *Home Fronts: Britain, France, and Germany, 1914–1918.* London: Constable, 1972.

Wilson, Trevor. *The Myriad Faces of War: Britain and the Great War, 1914–1918.* Cambridge: Cambridge University Press, 1986.

Winter, J. M. *The Great War and the British People.* London: Palgrave Macmillan, 1985.

———. *The Experience of World War I.* Oxford: Oxford University Press, 1989.

———. *Sites of Memory, Sites of Mourning: The Great War in European Cultural History.* Cambridge: Cambridge University Press, 1995.

———. *Capital Cities at War: Paris, London, Berlin, 1914–1918.* Cambridge: Cambridge University Press, 1997.

Wynn, Niel A. *From Progressivism to Prosperity: World War I and American Society.* New York: Holmes & Meier, 1986.

Zeman, Z. A. B. *The Breakup of the Habsburg Empire, 1914–1918.* London: Octagon Books, 1961.

LIST OF
CONTRIBUTORS

MAARTJE ABBENHUIS
University of Auckland
"In a Stupid Cap and a
Grey Jacket": Soldiers'
Experiences of
World War I in the
Neutral Netherlands

ALAN ALLPORT
University of Pennsylvania
"Like Climbing into
the Witch's Oven":
The Experience of Tank Combat
in World War I

DANIEL GORMAN
Trent University
The War on the Periphery:
The Experience of Soldiers
Fighting in European Colonies,
1914–1918

KATHERINE BURGER JOHNSON
University of Louisville
"It's Only the Ones Who
Might Live Who Count":
Allied Medical Personnel
in World War I

SHAUN M. JONES
Virginia Military Institute
"A Miserable and Impoverished
Existence in Lousy Scratch Holes":
The Experience of Trench Warfare
during World War I

DAVID OLIVIER
Wilfrid Laurier University, Brantford
Life in a Tin Can:
The Experience of
Submarine Personnel
during World War I

ANNE-MARIE PENNINGTON
Liverpool Hope University College
Struggling Not to Fight:
The Experience of Radicals
and Pacifists during World War I

KIRSTY ROBERTSON
McGill University
Victims of a Greenish Cloud:
The Experience of a Gas Attack
during World War I

"A Miserable and Impoverished
Existence in Lousy Scratch Holes":
The Experience of Trench Warfare
during World War I

DAVID J. SILBEY
Alvernia College
"Over the Dirty Waters":
The Experience of
British Indians in World War I

KENNETH STEUER
Indiana University
"Service for Soldiers":
The Experience of
American Social Welfare
Agencies in World War I

MATTHEW STIBBE
Sheffield Hallam University
Prisoners of War in
World War I:
British and Allied
Civilian Internees at
Ruhleben Camp, Germany

BOB WINTERMUTE
Army Heritage Center Foundation
The African-American Experience
in World War I

MOLLY WOOD
Wittenberg University
Mothers, Wives, Workers,
and More: The Experience of
American Women on the
Home Front during World War I

INDEX

Abbenuis, Maartje, 73, 337

Addams, Jane, 273

Addy, J. L., 140

AEF. *See* American Expeditionary Force

Africa

Dodoma-Iriniga line, 63

hospital tents, 165

landscape and climate, 55–56

tsetse line, 63

See also Colonial soldiers; East Africa

African Americans, 1–28

air service, 22

Buffalo Soldiers (of American frontier), 20

Bulletin No. 35 and, 7–8

confined to Camp Funston, 7–8

consigned to U.S. duty, 14–15, 20

courts-martial for, 9, 19

exclusion from the military, 4

French warned against, 11–13

labor battalions, 14–15, 20

medals/honors won by, 22, 23, 25

MPs kept unarmed, 9

NAACP and, 5

as officers, 5–7, 15–16

post-war return to United States, 27–28

race riot in Houston, 9–10

racism at home, 4–10

racism in the military, 6–14, 27–28

relief work in Africa, 244

Selective Service Act and, 4–5

service in France, 11–13, 15–27

specific divisions and regiments

24th Infantry, 9, 14

25th Infantry, 14

59th Infantry, 26

73rd Infantry, 26

92nd Infantry, 7–8, 15, 16–17, 19–20, 27

93rd Infantry, 15, 20–22, 26, 27

157th Infantry, 26

367th Infantry, 17, 17 (photo)

368th Infantry, 15–16, 17–19

369th Infantry, 6, 21, 21 (photo), 22–26, 24 (photo), 27

370th Infantry, 21, 26

371st Infantry, 21, 26–27

372nd Infantry, 21, 26

the Buffalos, 17 (photo)

Harlem Hellfighters, 23, 27

Les Perdrix (The Partridges), 26

Ninth Cavalry Regiment, 14

The Red Hand, 26

Schwarze Teufel (Black Devils), 26

Tenth Cavalry Regiment, 14, 20

stereotypes of, 10–11

women, war work of, 4, 290

Airplanes, use in Africa, 57–58

Aisne River, 92
ALA. *See* American Library Association
Allied internees at Ruhleben Camp,
    Germany, 259–272
Allied medical personnel, 161–203
    ambulance services, 167–168,
        283–284, 318–319
    American Military Hospital at Neuilly,
        165 (photo), 166, 168, 179, 190
    American Red Cross (ARC), 163–166
    diseases and insects, 177–186
    experiences at the front, 188–192
    female physicians, 192–194
    front line work, 191–192, 194
    medical observers, 167, 177
    nurses, 162–163, 175–176, 190–191,
        193–194
    preparedness at start of war, 162–163
    recruitment of doctors and nurses,
        170
    transport of medical personnel, 170
    Voluntary Aid Detachments (VADs),
        193–194
    volunteers at start of war, 162–166
    See also Medical care
Allison, Jim, 142
Allport, Alan, 127, 337
Ambrine treatment for burns, 182
Ambulance (French military hospital),
    166
Ambulance services, 167–168, 283–284,
    318–319
American Ambulance Field Service, 167
American Committee for Training in
    Suitable Trades the Maimed
    Soldiers of France, 206
American Expeditionary Force (AEF)
    African-American soldiers in, 11, 14,
        15, 25–26
    doctors in, 167
    educational programs under the
        YMCA, 247
    relief work and, 215–216, 222
    tank warfare forces, 144–147, 145
        (photo)
    women in, 286–288

American Fund for French Wounded,
    206
American Library Association (ALA),
    208, 249
American Military Hospital (Neuilly,
    France), 165 (photo), 166, 168,
    179, 190
American Red Cross (ARC), 163–166,
    193, 214, 215
    Red Cross Home Services Sections,
        282
    Red Cross War Camp Community
        Services, 282–283
    Red Cross War Fund Drives, 282
    women on the home front and, 275,
        281–283
American Red Triangle, 209, 210–211,
    217–219, 241
American Relief Administration (ARA),
    208
American social welfare agencies,
    205–257
    American Library Association (ALA),
        208, 249
    American Red Triangle, 209,
        210–211, 217–219, 241
    American Relief Administration
        (ARA), 208
    banking services for soldiers, 227–228
    Chinese labor camp work, 244–246
    early war work, 206–208, 207 (photo)
    entertainment programs, 229–233
    financing of, 251–252
    food relief programs, 206–208
    huts (Soldiers' Homes), 216–224, 220
        (photo), 235–240
    Inter-Allied Games, 234–235
    Knights of Columbus, 208, 209, 215,
        228
    leave areas for U.S. soldiers, 224–227,
        225 (photo)
    morale and, 205–206, 235, 243,
        252–253
    National War Work Council, 215,
        248–249
    post-war education programs,
        247–250

Principle of Reciprocity, 210, 217
profits and, 228–229
religious roots of, 208–209
repatriation/demobilization work,
  246–251
Salvation Army, 208, 209, 215, 228
"Seven Sisters," 208, 222, 252, 253
sports and physical program, 232–235
United Services Organization (USO),
  206, 253
United War Work Campaign, 252, 253
U.S. neutrality policy and, 209–210,
  214, 216
War Camp Community Service, 208
War Prisoner Aid (WIP), 210–215
YMCA (Young Men's Christian
  Association), 205–206, 208–253
YMHA (Young Men's Hebrew
  Association), 208, 215
YWCA (Young Women's Christian
  Association), 208
American Volunteer Motor-Ambulance
  Corps, 167, 168
American Women's Hospital (AWH),
  192–193
Amiens, Battle of, 135
Andrew, A. Piatt, 167, 168
Anesthesiology, 188, 195
Anglo-American Volunteer Motor-
  Ambulance Corps, 167
Antisemitism, 264
Antiseptics, 187
Antiwar protests. *See* Pacifists and
  radicals
Antwerp, 79–81
ARA (American Relief Administration),
  208
ARC. *See* American Red Cross
Armistice
  American Army of Occupation in
    Germany, 250
  medical relief work after, 194
  social relief work after, 214–215,
    250–251
  U.S. women laid off from war jobs,
    295
Army Nurse Corps, 4

Arras, Battle of, 132–133
Ashe, Elizabeth, 190
Ashton, Margaret, 299–300
Askaris, 55, 57–58, 68
Asquith, Herbert, 47
Audoin-Rouzeau, Stephane, 98–100,
  101–102, 108–109
Austria-Hungary, *Soldatenheimen*
  (Soldiers' Homes), 216–217
Austro-Prussian War (1866), 92
AWH (American Women's Hospital),
  192–193
Ayles, Walter, 304

Bahadur, Risalder-Major Kalander
  Khan, 43
Bainton, Roland, 318
Bakari bin Salimu, 64
Baker, George R., 178, 189
Ballou, Charles C., 7–8, 15
Baluchis, 34, 57
Barbed wire fences, 94–95
Barclay, Harold, 189
Bardin, Lieutenant, 27
Base hospitals, 168–170, 189–192
Basra, 43
Bath, Tod, 116
Battle of Amiens, 135
Battle of Arras, 132–133
Battle of Cambrai, 133–135, 141
Battle of Caporetto, 237
Battle of Loos, 121, 122
Battle of Menin Road, Belgium, 171
  (photo)
Battle of Neuve Chapelle, 30, 35, 41
Battle of the Somme, 100–101, 127–128,
  131, 137
Battle of Verdun, 103, 168
Battles of Ypres, 116–118, 133, 141–142
Baxter, Archibald, 302, 309
BEF. *See* British Expeditionary Force
Belgium
  Commission for the Relief of
    Belgium, 206
  refugees in the Netherlands, 79–81,
    80 (photo)
  Ypres, gas attacks at, 116–118

Bigelow, Glenna, 162–163
Binarville, 18–20
Bing, Harold, 310, 319
Bist, Umed Sing, 35
Bitray, France, 169
Black, Elizabeth, 174–175, 191, 193–194
Blacks
    interned at Ruhleben Camp,
        Germany, 264–265
    See also African Americans
Blair, Emily Newell, 279–280, 288
Blake, Harold, 320
Blatch, Harriet Stanton, 289, 292, 293,
    294
Bolimov, Russia, 116
Bosboom, Nicolas, 83
Boylston, Helen, 179, 190
BRC (British Red Cross), 167, 168
Brighton Pavilion, 38 (photo), 39
British Emergency Relief Fund, 265
British Expeditionary Force (BEF)
    General Hospital No. 9, 169
    Indian troops in, 30, 32–33, 33
        (photo)
British Indians, 29–50
    Baluchis, 34, 57
    caste and class among, 31, 45, 67
    casualties among, 34, 35, 46
    cavalry, 30 (photo)
    concern for women at home, 48–49
    desire to remain in England, 39–40
    disillusionment with the war, 46–48
    Dogras, 31
    food and, 37–39, 65–66
    French women and, 35–36
    Gurhkas, 31
    Indian Army, 30 (photo), 31, 59–60
    Indian Expeditionary Force, 61
        (photo), 243
    Indian Voluntary Aid Contingent, 29,
        38
    izzat (honor) and, 45–46
    life in England, 38–41
    life in France, 35–38
    martial races, 31, 67–68
    medals/honors won by, 46
    mutinies among, 42–44, 65

national identity and, 54–55
    as officers, 41
    Punjabis, 34
    Rajputs, 67–68
    relationship of British soldiers to, 31
    religion and, 37–38, 45, 65–66
    reputation as soldiers, 33–34
    return to India, 49–50
    self-inflicted wounds and, 34–35
    sepoys, 31–32, 42
    service in Africa, 59–60, 62 (photo)
    service in France, 30–31, 32–33, 33
        (photo)
    service in the Middle East, 30–31,
        42–44, 60–62
    Sikhs, 31, 34, 35, 45, 46
    sports and, 66
    treatment of wounded soldiers,
        38–39, 40–41, 42
    See also Colonial soldiers
British Military Service Act, 301–302, 314
British Red Cross (BRC), 167, 168
British Socialist Party, 298
British YMCA, 242
Brocklesby, John, 300–301, 305, 311,
    316–317
Brockway, Fenner, 297
Brown, Elwood S., 234
Brown, Fred R., 18
Brown, Horace, 122
Brown, John Horace, 107
Bryan, William Jennings, 252
Buchanan, Angus, 68
Bullard, Eugene Jacque, 22
Bullard, Robert L., 19–20
Bully beef, 110
Burell, Herbert, 91
Burns, 182
Burr, Elsie, 166
Burrell, Private, 104
Bury, Herbert, 263
Buswell, Leslie, 172

Cachy-Fouilloy road, 143
Call, Donald, 146
Cambrai, Battle of, 133–135, 151
Camel Transport Corps, 62 (photo), 63

Camp Funston, Kansas, 7–8
Camp Hancock, Georgia, 6
Camp Pike, Arkansas, 6
Camp Taylor, Kentucky, 6
Camp Wadsworth, South Carolina, 6
Canadian Expeditionary Force, 45
Caporetto, Battle of, 237
Carrel, Alexis, 187
Carrel-Dakin wound cleaning method, 177, 187
Carrier pigeons, 139
Carriers (in Africa), 62–64
Casa del Soldato (Soldiers' Home), 217, 237–239
Cavalry, 116
Censorship, 32
Chamberlain, Austen, 35
Champagne offensive, 23
Charteris, Brigadier General, 34
Chemical warfare, 183
Cheney, Dorothy, 194
Chevy Chase, Maryland, 277
Cheyne, Mr., 314
Childs, General, 308
Chilembwe, John, 69–70
Chinese labor camps, 244–246
Chlorine gas, 116–119
Chloroform, 188
Christadelphians, 306
Christy, Howard Chandler, 287
Church, James Robb, 194
Churchill, Winston, on World War I, viii
Cinema program of the YMCA, 231
Civilian internment. *See* Ruhleben Camp, Germany
Clapham, H. S., 125
Cloete, Stuart, 103–104
Cohen, Israel, 265
Colby, Francis Thompson, 168
Colonial soldiers, 51–57
    African landscape and climate, 55–56
    airplane use, 57–58
    carrier battalions, 62–64
    convoy system, 63
    corporal punishment and, 56
    cultural problems, 64–66
    discipline and, 56, 58–59
    dislocation due to war, 64–65
    food and, 65–66
    forced marches, 55–56
    German askaris, 55, 57–58
    King's African Rifles (KAR), 56–57
    language problems, 59–60
    leisure time, 66
    names/nicknames of, 64
    nationalist sentiments/movements, 69–70
    recruitment/conscription of, 53–54
    relationship of Europeans to, 67, 68–69
    resources/supplies for, 55–57
    reticence about the war, 52–53
    roles of, 55
    sports and, 66
    tactics and, 57–58
    war fronts in Africa, 52
    women and, 66–67
    YMCA relief work and, 242–244
    See also British Indians
Colvorcoresses, Mary, 276
Commission for the Relief of Belgium, 206
Concentration camps, 259
Conscription. *See* Draft
Contrexeville, France, 169
Convoy system, in Africa, 63
Coppard, George, 94
Cormack, Will, 305–306
Council of National Defense, Woman's Committee of, 280–281, 288
Coyle, Edward, 163
Crile, George, 188
The Crisis, 2–3, 5–6, 9–10, 11, 15
Croix de Guerre, 22, 23, 25
Crowder, Enoch H., 5, 10–11
Cugny, France, 174
Cusden, V. V., 260–261
Cushing, Harvey, 179
Czechoslovakia
    Inter-Allied Games and, 235
    nation-building after the war, 251

Dakin, Henry, 177, 187
Dakin solution, 187

Daniels, Burt, 116
Das, Pokhar, 37
Davis, Darius A., 216, 222, 236
Dawson, J. R., 267
De Wolfe, Elsie, 192
Depew, Mrs. C. Mitchell, 163
Des Moines, Iowa, 6, 15
Deventer, Major General, 60
Dinga, Abudu, 69
Dingle, Charlie, 318, 319
Diseases, 177–186
Distinguished Service Cross, 23
Dodoma-Iriniga line, 63
Draft, 275
    exemptions, 301–304
    Military Service Act (British),
        301–302, 314
    No-Conscription Fellowship (NCF),
        305
    No-Conscription League, 279
    resistance, 279, 298–300
    Selective Service Act (U.S.), 4–5, 301
DuBois, W. E. B., 2–3, 6
Dutch, George Frederick, 306–307

East Africa, 58–60
    25th Royal Fusiliers, 68
    King's African Rifles in, 56–57
    tsetse line, 63
    West African troops in, 58
    YMCA work in, 243–244
Eddy, Sherwood, 219–220, 222–224, 227
Eden, Anthony, 265
Eden, Timothy, 265, 268
Eisenhower, Dwight D., 144, 147
Elles, Hugh, 130
England. See Great Britain
England, Ernest, 307
Entertainment program of the YMCA,
    229–233
European colonies. See Colonial soldiers
Evans, A. W., 311, 314–315
Exemptions to military service, 301–304

Falk, Edward Morris, 267–268
FAU (Friends Ambulance Unit),
    318–319

Fitzsimmons, W. T., 192
Flers, tank warfare at, 132
Flesquieres Ridge, 141
Florence, L. S., 298–299
Flu pandemic, 185
Food
    British Indian soldiers and, 37, 38, 39
    conservation/education programs
        (U.S.), 282 (photo), 285–286
    Hindus and, 37–39, 65–66
    Muslims and, 37–39, 65–66
    relief programs, 206–208
Forced marches, 55–56
Fort Columbus, New Mexico, 9
Fort Des Moines, Iowa, 6, 15
Foyer du Soldat programs, 215, 233,
    235–237, 243
France
    Foyer du Soldat program, 215, 233,
        235–237
    French Flying Corps, 22
    French Red Cross, 167
    Inter-Allied Games and, 235
    medical preparedness at start of war,
        162, 164–165, 177
    Neuilly, American Military Hospital
        at, 165 (photo), 166
    Service de Santé, 177
    Union-Franco-Américaine, 236
Franco-Prussian War (1870), 92
Fraser, Donald, 120, 320
French Flying Corps, African-American
    soldiers in, 22
French, John, 32
French Red Cross, 167
Friends Ambulance Unit (FAU),
    318–319
Fuller, J. F. C., 133–134
Fusell, Paul, 92, 93–94

G. I. Bill, 249, 253
Gallipoli, 43, 52, 110–111
Gallishaw, John, 108
Gandhi, Mohandas K., 29–30, 38, 49
Gangrene, 180
    gas gangrene, 178–179
Gardiner, Arthur, 298

Garnett, David, 318
Gas attacks, 115–126
    Allied use of, 110–120, 183–185
    chlorine gas, 116–119
    defenses against, 119
    familiarity/humor in, 122–123
    gas masks, 117 (photo), 120, 122, 124
        (photo), 183
    gas masks for horses, 123–124, 124
        (photo)
    gas transport, 120–121
    mustard gas, 119
    phosgene gas, 120 (photo)
    tactics and, 116
    treatment of personnel, 183–185
    at Ypres, 116–189, 117 (photo)
Gas gangrene, 178–179
General Hospital No. 9, 169
Gerard, James W., 210, 263–264
German askaris, 55, 57–58
Germany
    allied medical units in, 194
    campaigns in Africa, 55
    German trenches, 92–93
    medical preparedness at start of war,
        162
    Soldatenheimen (Soldiers' Homes),
        216–217
Gibbs, Phillip, 97–98, 102, 105
Ginchy-Delville, 127–128
Gold Palm, 25
Goldman, Emma, 278–279
Gorman, Daniel, 51, 337
Graham, Margaret Shaw, 276
Gray, Billy, 103, 122
Great Britain
    Brighton Pavilion, 38 (photo), 39
    British Red Cross (BRC), 167, 168
    British YMCA, 242
    civilian internees at Ruhleben Camp,
        Germany, 259–272
    Eagle Hut, 220, 220 (photo)
    King George, 39
    London Street Patrol, 221–222
    medical preparedness at start of war,
        162
    Royal Naval Hospital, 165

    Scottish Women's Hospital (SWH),
        193
    Women's Hospital Corps (WHC), 193
    See also British entries; British Indians
Gregory, Alice, 193
Gregory, Henry, 104
Gregory, Herman, 93
Gurhkas, 31

Haber, Fritz, 110
The Hague, Netherlands, 273–274
Haig, Douglas, 34
    on cavalry in WW I, 116
    tank warfare and, 131, 132
Haller, General, 251
Hankey, Maurice, 129
Hard tack, 110
Harjes, H. Herman, 167
Harjes Formation, 167
Harlem Hellfighters, 23, 27
Harriman, Florence Jaffrey, 283–284
Harris, Harvey L., 144–145, 146
Harte, Archibald C., 209–210, 214
Harvard University surgical unit,
        166–167, 179
Harvey, Harold, 97
Hayler, Mark, 314
Haynes, H. H., 302
Hays, Ian, 94
Head injuries, 179
Health care. *See* Medical care
Heath, A. G., 110
Hibbard, Carlisle V., 209–210
Hickey, D. E., 130
Hill 188, 26–27
Hindenburg Line, 133, 134 (photo),
        142
    Hill 188 on, 26–27
Hindus, food issues for, 37–39, 65–66
Hobhouse, Rosa, 299
Hoffman, Conrad, 211–212, 214, 253
Home front. *See* Pacifists and radicals;
        Women on the home front (U.S.)
Hoover, Herbert, 206–208, 285
Hospitals. *See* Allied medical personnel;
        Medical care
Houston, Texas, race riot in, 9–10

Howard, Gordon, 101, 107
Howell, William B., 188
Huard, Frances, 163
Hudson, J. H., 299
Hughes, G. W. W., 123
Hunter, Ernest, 305
Huxley, Elspeth, 69
Hysterical Disorders of Warfare (Yealland, 1918), 181

ILP. *See* Independent Labour Party
Independent Labour Party (ILP), 299–300, 304, 305, 312
India
    caste and racial identity, 31, 45, 67
    Indian Army, 30 (photo), 31, 59–60
    Indian Expeditionary Force, 61 (photo), 243
    Indian Expeditionary Group B, 59
    Indian National Congress, 49
    Indian Voluntary Aid Contingent, 29, 38
    nationalist independence movement, 39, 50
Indians, British. *See* British Indians
Industrial Revolution, welfare organizations as response to, 208
Infections, 177–179
Ingils, Elsie, 193
Insects, 186
Inter-Allied Games, 234–235
International Congress of Women (The Hague, Netherlands), 273–274
Internment camps. *See* Ruhleben Camp, Germany
Italy
    Casa del Soldato (Soldiers' Home), 217, 237–239
    Inter-Allied Games and, 235
Izzat (honor), 45–46

Jeter, Nannie, 285–286
Jewish prisoners in Ruhleben Camp, Germany, 264
Johns Hopkins medical unit, 195
Johnson, Henry, 23–26, 24 (photo)

Johnson, Katherine Burger, 161, 337
Jones, Shaun M., 91, 337

Kaombe, Vmande, 54
KAR (King's African Rifles), 56–57
Kerensky, Alexander, 240
Kestell-Cornish, Second Lieutenant, 119
Khan, Alam Sher, 46
Khan, Ghufran, 37
Khan, Ghulam Hasain, 48
Khan, Jemandar Abdul, 66
Khan, Kasim Ali, 47
Khan, Mahomed Mazafar, 45
Khan, Mahomed Usuf, 45–46
Khan, Muhammad Ali, 34
Khan, Nasab Ali, 48
Khan, Risalder Mir Jafar, 44
Kikuyu, 64
King's African Rifles (KAR), 56–57
Kipling, Rudyard, 70–71
Kitchener, Horatio, 47–48, 135
Kivandi, Mbwika, 66–67
Knights of Columbus, 208, 209, 215, 228
Ku Klux Klan, 28
Kuropatkin, General Alexei, 240
Kut, 60–61, 65–66

Lafayette Escadrille, African-American soldiers in, 22
Lal, Ghirdari, 47–48
Landships. *See* Tank combat
Landstorm (Netherlands reserves), 83–84
Langdon-Davies, B. N., 317
Lawrence, Walter, 40
Lee, A. E., 141–142
Lee-Enfield rifles, 65
Legion d'Honneur, 22
LeMaitre, R., 186–187
Lettow-Vorbeck, Paul von, 55, 58
Liberty Bonds, 280
Lice, 104, 186
Lloyd George, David, 47, 131
London Street Patrol, 221–222

Loos, Battle of, 121, 122
Lusitania, sinking of, 276

Machine guns
  in tanks, 128, 135
  in trench warfare, 100
MacLaren, George, 116
Macready, Adjutant General, 307
Mahomed, Mahsud, 48
Mal, Sowar Jivan, 42
Malawi, nationalist sentiments in, 69–70
Malingerers, 182
Manthorpe, Walter, 315
Marne, Miracle on the, 92
Mars Center, 176
Martial races, 31, 67–68
Masaryk, Thomas, President of
      Czechoslovakia, 251
Maxillofacial surgery, 179, 195
McIver, Daniel C., 230–231
McKinney, James P., 26–27
McLane, Thomas J., 230
Medical care, 161–203
  abdominal wounds, 180
  advances during the war, 177–182,
      195–196
  ambulance (French military
      hospital), 166
  ambulance services, 167–168
  American Military Hospital (Neuilly,
      France), 165 (photo), 166, 168,
      179, 190
  anesthesiology, 188, 195
  antiseptics, 187
  base hospitals, 168–170, 175–176,
      189–192
  bullet removal with magnets, 187
  burns, 182
  Carrel-Dakin wound cleaning
      method, 177
  convalescent hospitals and camps,
      176
  debridement, 186–187
  dental surgery, 179–180
  diagnosis tags, 174
  disease prevention, 186

  dressing stations, 171–172, 171
      (photo)
  evacuation hospitals, 174–175
  facial injuries, 179
  female physicians, 192–194
  field hospitals, 172–174
  flu pandemic, 185
  gas gangrene, 178–179
  gas poisoning, 183–185
  General Hospital No. 9, 169
  head injuries, 179
  hospital centers, 176
  hospital trains, 175
  infections, 177–179, 187
  insects, parasites, and vermin, 185
  malingerers, 182
  Mars Center, 176
  maxillofacial surgery, 179, 195
  Mobile Hospital No. 5, 169
  mobile hospitals, 169, 176–177
  mobile laboratories, 188
  occupational therapy, 188
  preparedness at start of war, 162–163
  reconstruction, 188
  recruitment of doctors and nurses,
      170
  rehabilitation, 188, 195
  Service de Santé, 177
  shell shock, 181–182
  survival rates, 172
  tetanus, 182
  treatment in the trenches, 171–172,
      173 (photo)
  treatment of wounded colonial
      soldiers, 38–39, 40–41, 42
  trench fever, 181
  trench foot, 180–181, 182
  triage, 173, 195
  venereal disease, 185–186
  wound mortality rate, 162
  wound treatment, 177, 186–187, 195
  X-rays, 177, 195
  See also Allied medical personnel
Mesopotamia, 42, 43, 60–62, 65
Meuse-Argonne offensive, 17, 20, 26–27
  medical treatment during, 169
  tanks used in, 144

Mexican border war of 1916–1917, 214
Middle East
    British Indian troops in, 30–31,
        42–44
    colonial troops in, 52
Military Service Act (British), 301–302,
    314
Millar, J. P. M., 318
Mobile hospitals, 169, 176–177
Molkte, Helmuth von, 82–83
Moorehead, Caroline, 302
Morale, 205–206, 235, 243, 252–253
Morgan-Harjes Section, 167
Mortimore, H. W., 127, 131
Moton, R. R., 3–4
Mott, John R., 209, 214, 215, 240, 251,
    252
Movie program of the YMCA, 231
Mud, 105–107, 106 (photo), 142
Mudros, 52 (photo)
Muslims
    fighting other Muslims, 42
    food issues for, 37–39, 65–66
    Ramadan and, 37
Mustard gas, 119

NAACP, 5
National American Woman Suffrage
    Association, 278
National Association for the
    Advancement of Colored People
    (NAACP), 5
National League for Women's Service,
    275–276
National Patriotic Relief Society, 276
National Service Schools/Camps,
    276–277
National War Work Council, 215,
    248–249
National Woman's Liberty Loan
    Committee, 284
Nationalism (of colonial troops), 39, 50,
    69–70
NCC (Non-Combatant Corps), 308, 309
Needham, Mary, 163
Nehru, Jawaharlal, 49
Nelson, Alice Dunbar, 4

the Netherlands, 73–90
    AWOL soldiers in, 82–83
    barbed wire fences, 94–95
    Belgian refugees in, 79–81, 80
        (photo)
    border accessibility in, 76–79
    border patrols, 84–85
    conscription in, 74–75, 83
    demobilization in, 83–84
    electric fence along Belgian border,
        77–78, 77 (photo)
    The Hague (International Congress
        of Women), 273–274
    Harskamp, 86–87
    internment camps in, 78, 79
    Landstorm (reserves) in, 83–84
    military training in, 75
    mobilization in, 73–75, 81–84
    morale in, 82, 83–84
    neutrality of the border, 78, 79–81
    revolution in, 86–87
    smuggling and, 84–85
    spies and, 76–78
    war deprivations, 85–86
    war protests, 86
    Wilhelmina, Queen of, 74, 87
Neuilly, France, American Military
    Hospital at, 165 (photo), 166, 168,
    179, 190
Neurasthenia (shell shock), 98–99,
    181–182
Neuve Chapelle, 30, 35, 41
Nguyo, Mulei, 68
Nicholls, Edward, 303
Nitrous oxide, 188
No-Conscription Fellowship (NCF),
    305
No-Conscription League, 279
No-man's-land, 95, 99
Nollen, John S., 238
Non-Combatant Corps (NCC), 308,
    309
Northwestern University medical team,
    189
Norton, Richard, 167, 168
Nurses, 162–163, 166, 175–176,
    190–191, 193–194

Occupational therapy, 188
Olivier, David, 149, 337
Osodo, Raphael Simigini, 54
Otley, K., 308–309
Ottomans, 42–44, 242

Pacifists and radicals, 297–322
   antiwar protests by American women,
      273–275, 278–279, 298–299
   arrest of, 305–306
   attitude of family members, 319–320
   death sentence for, 308
   demobilization and, 319–320
   disappointment with church
      activities/stance, 300–301, 311
   discrimination against, 299–300
   exemptions to military service,
      301–304
   experiences in prison, 310–313
   failure to report for duty, 305
   Home Office prison camps, 313–317,
      313 (photo)
   kind treatment in the military, 309
   Non-Combatant Corps (NCC), 308,
      309
   non-combatant service, 303, 304, 306
   objectives of, 298
   penalties for, 298, 298–300, 299
      (photo)
   preaching to convert other soldiers,
      308–309
   pressured to join military, 300
   psychological effects of CO status,
      320
   punishment for refusal to obey
      orders, 306–310
   religious pacifists, 298, 301–304
   social pacifists, 298, 301–303
   tribunals for exemptions, 302–304
   white feathers, 300
   Woman's Peace Party (WPP), 267,
      273–274, 274 (photo), 278
   work of national importance
      assigned, 317–319
Palazzo, Albert, 115
Parasites, 186
Passchendaele, 133

Paternalism, 68–69
Patton, George S., 144, 147
Payne, Leonard and Roland, 317
Payne, Mrs. Harry, 163
Payne, Mrs. J. G., 317
Peet, Frederick, 316
Pennington, Anne-Marie, 320, 338
Les Perdrix (The Partridges), 26
Pershing, John J.
   on African American officers, 16, 20
   on athletics program, 233–234
   Pershing Stadium, 234
   on the U.S. Medical Corps, 162
Pétain, Henri, 236
Phosgene gas, 120 (photo)
Pitt, Bernard, 99–100
Plattsburgh, New York, 277
Plautnauer, J. B., 121
Poisonous gas. *See* Gas attacks
Poland, YMCA in, 251
Postgate, Raymond, 319, 320
Powell, Joseph, 261, 266
POWs. *See* Prisoners of war
Prasad, Durga, 44
Principle of Reciprocity, 210, 217
Prison camps
   for civilian internees (Ruhleben,
      Germany), 259–272
   for pacifists and war resisters,
      313–317
Prisoners of war (POWs)
   American relief organizations and,
      209–214
   at Ruhleben Camp, Germany,
      259–272
   in Russia, 210–215
   in Turkey, 61–62
   War Prisoner Aid (WPA) operations,
      210–215
   See also detailed listings under Ruhleben
      Camp

Quakers, 299, 306–307, 308, 315, 317

Race riot in Houston, Texas, 9–10
Racism. *See under* African-Americans
Radicals. *See* Pacifists and radicals

Rahman, Havildar Abdul, 46–47
Railroad industry, 290–292
Rajputs, 67–68
Rats, 1–6, 104, 123
Reciprocity, Principle of, 210, 217
Red Cross. *See* American Red Cross;
    British Red Cross; French Red
    Cross
Red Strangers, 69
Rees, Stanley, 304, 311, 319
Rehabilitation, 188, 195
Religion
    and American social welfare agencies,
        208–209
    of British Indian troops, 37–39, 65–66
    and pacifism, 298–308, 311, 317–320
Ringer-Hewitt, Sergeant, 309
Ritter, P. H., 74
Roberts, Harold, 146–147
Roberts, Needham, 23–26, 24 (photo)
Robertson, Kirsty, 91, 115, 338
Roosevelt, Franklin, 277
Root Mission, 240
Royal Fusiliers, 25th, 68
Royal Naval Hospital, 165
Royal Tank Corps, 133–135
Rufiji River, 56, 57
Ruhleben Camp, Germany, 259–272,
        267 (photo)
    after German surrender, 268–269
    barrack captains, 261
    boredom in, 261
    class distinctions among prisoners,
        263–264
    discrimination in, 264–265
    early release from, 266–267
    education in, 263
    exchange of prisoners, 266–267
    food in, 261
    German leaders of, 261
    Jewish prisoners in, 264
    lack of physical violence in, 266
    living conditions in, 260–261, 269
    news in, 266
    number of deaths in, 269
    post-war fate of camp, 269–270

post-war repatriation of internees,
        269–270
    Pro-Germans in, 265
    psychological effects of imprisonment
        in, 266–268
    Ruhleben Association annual
        dinners, 269
    Ruhleben Debating Society, 261–263
    Ruhleben Dramatic Society, 261–262
    social/cultural activities in, 261–263
    sports in, 261, 262 (photo)
Runners (in trench warfare), 96
Russia
    Bolimov, use of gas in, 116
    medical preparedness at start of war,
        162, 165
    prison camps in, 210–215
    relief work in, 217, 240–241
    war events, 92
Russo-Polish War, 251
Rutkow, Ira M., 195

Saint Mihiel, 26, 144, 236
Saint Omer, 32
Salvation Army, 208, 209, 215, 228
Sanfort, Barthe de, 182
Sautter, Emmanuel, 216, 236
Schwarze Teufel (Black Devils), 26
Schwerin, Count, 261
Scott, Emmett J., 3
Scottish Women's Hospital (SWH), 193
SDC (Surgical Dressings Committee),
        275–276
Seasickness, 152
Selective Service Act (U.S.), 4–5, 301
Self-inflicted wounds, 34–35
Sepoys, 31–32
Serbia, medical conditions at start of
        war, 163–165
Serbian Relief Committee of America,
        206, 207 (photo)
Services for soldiers. *See* American social
        welfare agencies
"Seven Sisters" (relief organizations),
        208, 222, 252, 253
Seventh-Day Adventists, 306
Shaiba, 43

Shand, David, 105, 118
Shaw, Anna Howard, 274, 280
Shellshock, 98–99, 181–182
Shrapnel, 177
Sikhs, 31, 34, 35, 45, 46
Silbey, David J., 29, 338
Sinclair, Ian, 116–118
Singh, Bigya, 46
Singh, Bisham, 49
Singh, Chattar, 35
Singh, Ganda, 44–45
Singh, Gunga, 43
Singh, Hazur, 47
Singh, Hoshiar, 45
Singh, Jagindar, 39
Singh, Man, 46
Singh, Natha, 39
Singh, Prayg, 48–49
Singh, Sham, 45
Singh, Waryam, 45
Sjambok, 58
Sloane, William, 215
Smuts, Jan, 57
Snijders, C. J., 87
Social welfare agencies. *See* American
     social welfare agencies
Socialists, 298, 301–303
Soldatenheimen (Soldiers' Homes),
     216–217
Somme, Battle of the, 100–101,
     127–128, 131, 137
Spandau, Germany (Ruhleben Camp),
     260, 269–270
Spanish-American War (1898), 2, 19,
     214
Spanish Flu, 185
Spartanburg, South Carolina, 6–7
SS *Mendi*, 64
Stanton, Harry, 308
Stapledon, Olaf, 318–319
Stasnley, H. M., 63
Stern, Albert, 132
Steuer, Kenneth, 205, 338
Stibbe, Matthew, 259, 338
Submarines, 149–159
     bilge water in, 153
     chlorine gas production and, 153

cleanliness of crew, 152
closeness of death, 158
condensation in, 153
crew, 156 (photo)
drinking/cooking water, 152
ice and, 153
K class, 154–155
lack of privacy on, 150–151
life on, 150–154, 151 (photo),
     158–159
officer-crew relationships, 150
running on surface, 149–150
seasickness and, 152
stress relief by crew, 157–158
superstitions of crew, 154
toilets in, 152
U-boats, 155–157, 158
Suffragists, 273–274, 278, 280, 284, 295
Surgical Dressings Committee (SDC),
     275–276
Sweeney, W. Allison, 1, 13
Swinton, E. D., 129–130

Tank combat, 127–148
     American tank forces, 144–147, 145
          (photo)
     armor-piercing weapons, 140–141
     artillery and, 141–142
     casualty rates for, 145
     communications during, 139
     crew for, 136 (photo), 137
     exhaust fumes, 140
     experience of, 137–143
     German tanks, 143
     hazards for tanks, 138–143
     initial use in battles, 131–135
     inventor of the tank, 129
     limitations of, 135, 141–143
     machine guns in, 128, 135
     medals and honors for, 146–147
     models of tanks, 135–137
     mud and, 142
     names for tanks, 129–130, 136–137
     noise of, 139
     prototype tanks, 129
     psychological effect of, 128
     range of tanks, 142

Tank combat (continued)
  recruitment for, 130
  Royal Tank Corps, 133–135
  secrecy surrounding, 131–132
  tank-versus-tank battles, 143–144
  temperature and dust and, 139–140
  training for, 130–131
  visibility inside tanks, 138
Taube, Baron von, 261
Teahan, John Patrick, 99, 119
Tengatenga (carriers), 62–64
Tetanus, 182
Thomas, George, 304
Timeline of World War I, 323–332
Toland, Edward, 167–168
Tongate, Bernice, 287–288
Townsend, A. C., 302
Townshend, Major General Charles,
  43–44, 65–66
Trench fever, 181
Trench foot, 106–107, 180–181, 182
Trench warfare, 91–113
  Allied trenches, 93–94
  battles between trenches, 100–104
  camaraderie in, 107–109
  communications and, 96
  creeping barrage, 99
  defenses against gas, 119
  drum fire, 98–99
  food and, 109–110
  German trenches, 92–93, 95 (photo)
  machine guns and, 100
  morale during, 107–110
  mud in, 105–107, 106 (photo)
  national styles in, 94–95
  night patrols, 96–97
  no-man's land, 95, 99
  over-the-top, 100 (photo)
  rodents and insects and, 104
  saps (small trenches), 95
  shell shock, 98–99
  "stand to" orders, 97
  total length of trenches, 92
  trench foot, 106–107, 180–181, 182
Triage, 173, 195
Troelstra, P. J., 87

Tsetse (nickname of German officer in
  Africa), 58–59
Tsetse line, 63
Turkey
  British Indian troops in, 42–44, 60–62
  colonial troops in, 52
Tuskegee Institute, 3–4
Typhoid, 186

U-boats, 155–157, 158
  See also Submarines
Union-Franco-Américaine, 236
United Services Organization (USO),
  206, 253
United States
  civilian internees at Ruhleben Camp,
    Germany, 259–272
  entry into the war (1917), 275, 278
  medical preparedness at start of war,
    162–163
  national draft, 275
  neutrality policy, 209–210, 214, 216
  Union-Franco-Américaine, 236
United States Constitution, Nineteenth
  Amendment, 295
United States Food Administration, 282
  (photo), 285
United War Work Campaign, 252, 253
United Way, 253
USO (United Services Organization),
  206, 253

VADs (Voluntary Aid Detachments),
  193–194
van Winkle, Mina C., 282 (photo)
Vanderbilt, Anne Harriman, 167
Venereal disease, 185–186
Verdun, Battle of, 103, 168
Verwey, Albert, 78–79
Victoria Cross, 46
Villers Cotterets, France, 193
Voluntary Aid Detachments (VADs),
  193–194

Wait, P. C., 303
Walden, Joseph, 308
War Camp Community Service, 208

War Children's Christmas Fund, 206

War Prisoner Aid (WPA), 210–215, 240

Washington, Booker T., 3

Watson, W. H. L., 130–131

WDNCF. *See* Woman's Department of National Civic Federation

Welfare agencies. *See* American social welfare agencies

Wellock, Wilfred, 299

Western Reserve University medical unit, 166

WHC (Women's Hospital Corps), 193

Wheatcroft, Harry, 312

Wheeldon, Alice and Hettie, 305

White feathers, 300

White, Sybil, 313, 319

Whitney, Gertrude Vanderbilt, 163

Wilhelm II, Kaiser of Germany, 87

Wilhelmina, Queen of the Netherlands, 74, 87

Willcocks, General, 32

Wilson, Woodrow, 208, 209, 214, 240

Wintermute, Bob, 1, 338

Woman's Army General Hospital Unit, 192

Woman's Committee of the Council of National Defense, 280–281, 288

Woman's Department of National Civic Federation (WDNCF), 275–276

Woman's Land Army of America, 294

Woman's Peace Party (WPP), 267, 273–274, 274 (photo), 278

Women on the home front (U.S.), 273–296

  American Red Cross work, 275, 281–283

  antiwar protests by, 273–275, 278–279, 298–299

  defense groups/militia, 278

  firearms use, instruction in, 278

  food conservation/education, 282 (photo), 285–286

  layoffs due to end of war, 295

  Liberty Loan Bonds program, 284

  military service/government work, 286–288

  motor corps, 283–284

  National League for Woman's Service, 275–276

  patriotic propaganda for, 275, 279, 284

  patriotism and, 276–278, 281

  preparedness organizations, 276–278

  reconstruction aides, 288–289

  relations with male coworkers, 291, 294

  relief work for war victims, 275–276

  right to vote, 295

  suffragists, 273–274, 278, 280, 284

  war work by, 281, 285–295

  watchdog agencies for working women, 292

  Woman's Committee of the Council of National Defense, 280–281, 288

  Woman's Department of National Civic Federation (WDNCF), 275–276

  Woman's Land Army of America, 294

  Woman's Peace Party (WPP), 273–274, 274 (photo), 276, 278

  Women's Section of the Navy League (WSNL), 276

  women's service camps, 276–277

Women physicians, 192–194

Women's Defence Club, 278

Women's Hospital Corps (WHC), 193

Women's Section of the Navy League (WSNL), 276

Wood, Leonard, 93

Wood, Molly, 273, 338

World War I

  as defensive war, 116

  overview of actions on the western front, 92

  timeline of, 323–332

  See also Armistice

World's Alliance of YMCAs, 208–209, 214, 216

Worms, 186

Wounds. *See* Medical care

WPA. *See* War Prisoner Aid

WPP. *See* Woman's Peace Party

Wright, Patrick, 130
WSNL. *See* Women's Section of the Navy
  League

X-rays, 177, 195

Yealland, Lewis R., 181
Yergan, Max, 244
YMCA (Young Men's Christian
    Association), 208–253
  banking services for soldiers, 227–228
  British YMCA, 242
  Casa del Soldato (Soldiers' Home),
    217, 237–239
  Chinese labor camp work, 244–246
  embarkation point services, 218–219
  entertainment program, 229–233
  financing of, 251–252
  Foyer du Soldat programs, 215, 233,
    235–237, 243
  huts for soldiers, 217–218, 220
    (photo), 222–224
  Inter-Allied Games, 234–235
  International Committee, 215–216,
    244
  leave areas for U.S. soldiers, 224–227,
    225 (photo)
  morale and, 205–206, 235, 243,
    252–253
  nation-building activities after the
    war, 251
  National War Work Council, 215

post-war education programs,
    247–250
  profits and, 228–229
  relief work in Russia, 217, 240–241
  Religious Work Department, 247
  repatriation/demobilization work,
    246–251
  services after U.S. entry into the war,
    235–246
  Soldatenheimen (Soldiers' Homes),
    216–217
  sports and physical program, 232–235
  War Prisoner Aid operations,
    210–215
  welcome services, 219–221
  World's Alliance of YMCAs, 208–209,
    214, 216
YMHA (Young Men's Hebrew
    Association), 208, 215
Young, Francis Brett, 56, 57, 68
Young Men's Christian Association. *See*
  YMCA
Young Men's Hebrew Association
    (YMHA), 208, 215
Young Women's Christian Association
    (YWCA), 208, 280
Ypres
  gas attacks in, 116–118
  tank use at, 133, 141–142
YWCA (Young Women's Christian
    Association), 208, 280

Zaccone, Vittorio, 238

ABOUT THE EDITOR

———————◆———————

TIMOTHY DOWLING, PH.D., is assistant professor of history at the Virginia Military Institute in Lexington, Virginia. His published works include ABC-CLIO's *Personal Perspectives: World War II.*